AF521778

SÈVRES THEN AND NOW

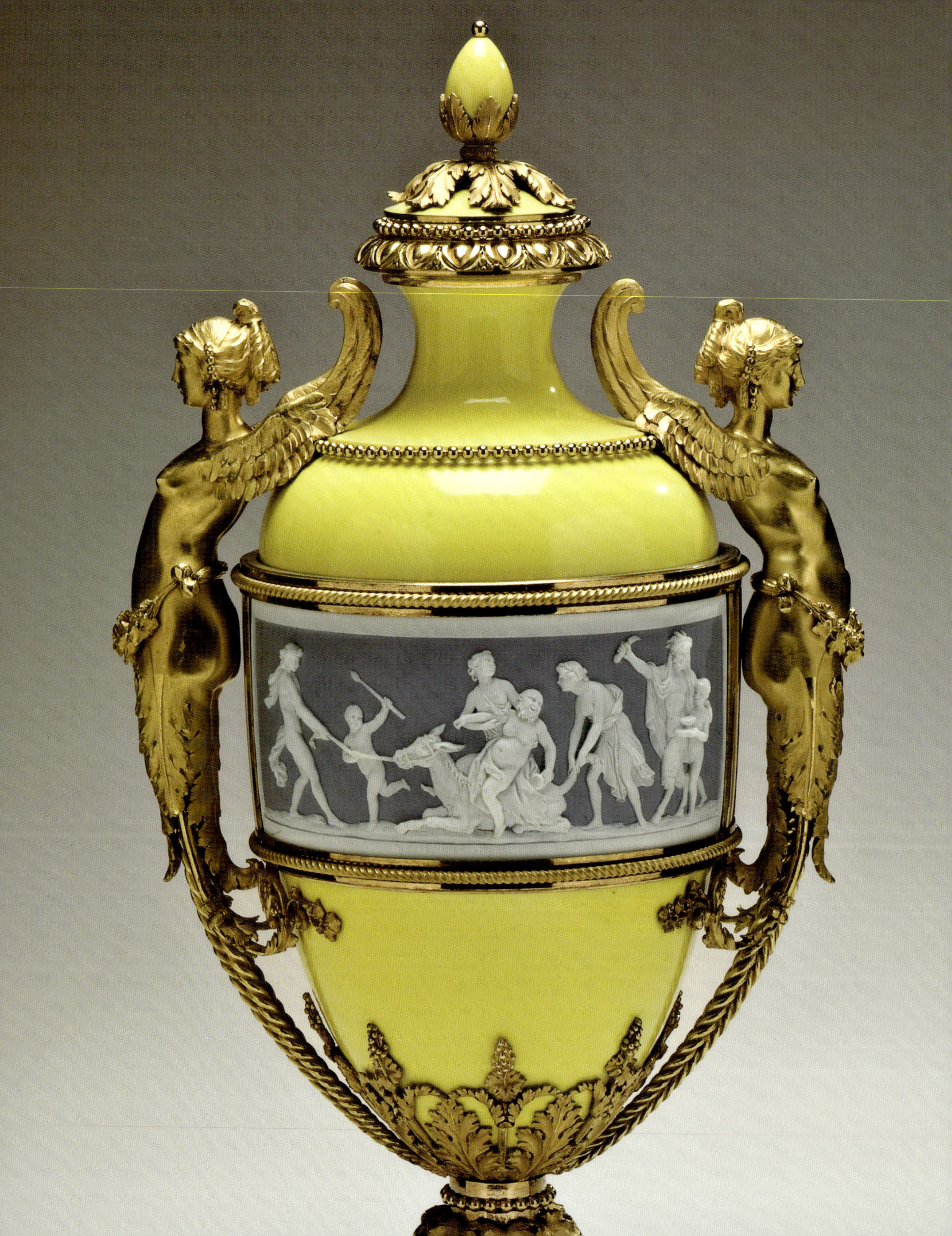

SÈVRES THEN AND NOW

Tradition and Innovation in Porcelain, 1750–2000

Liana Paredes

HILLWOOD MUSEUM AND GARDENS FOUNDATION, WASHINGTON, D.C.
in association with
D GILES LIMITED, LONDON

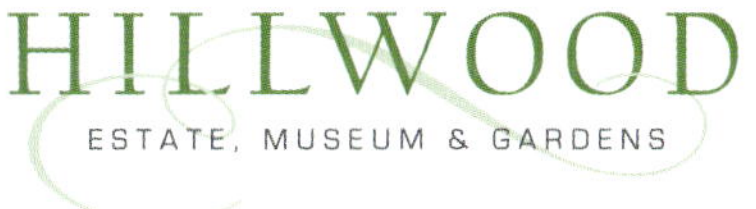

First published in 2009 by GILES
An imprint of D Giles Limited
4 Crescent Stables, 139 Upper Richmond Road
London SW15 2TN, UK
www.gilesltd.com

Library of Congress Cataloging-in-Publication Data

Paredes, Liana, 1961-
Sèvres then and now : tradition and innovation in porcelain, 1750-2000 / Liana Paredes.
p. cm.
Published to accompany an exhibition at Hillwood Museum and Gardens.
Includes bibliographical references and index.
Summary: "Surveys the Sèvres Porcelain Manufactory of France, including its history and a variety of ceramic works, from the factory's inception in Vincennes in the 1740s through to the twenty-first century"--Provided by publisher.
ISBN 978-1-904832-63-8 (hardcover : alk. paper) -- ISBN 978-1-931485-08-1 (softcover : alk. paper) 1. Sèvres porcelain. 2. Manufacture nationale de Sèvres--History. I. Hillwood Museum and Gardens. II. Title. III. Title: Tradition and innovation in porcelain, 1750-2000.
NK4390.P37 2009
738.20944'364--dc22
2009025710

ISBN (hardcover): 978-1-904832-63-8
ISBN (softcover): 978-1-931485-08-1

For Hillwood Museum and Gardens Foundation:
Director, Hillwood Estate, Museum & Gardens: Frederick J. Fisher
Senior Curator of Western European Art, Hillwood Estate, Museum & Gardens: Liana Paredes

For D Giles Limited:
Copy-edited and proof-read by Sarah Kane
Designed by Helen Swansbourne, London
Produced by GILES, an imprint of D Giles Limited, London
Printed and bound in Hong Kong

All measurements are in inches and centimeters;
height precedes width precedes depth.

Front cover: Tureen and platter, Vincennes, 1754 and *Diane* plate, decoration designed by Serge Poliakoff, 1969–72
Back cover: Black chinoiserie bottle cooler, 1791
Frontispiece: Yellow vase (*vase "bas relief"*) for the comte d'Artois, ca. 1786

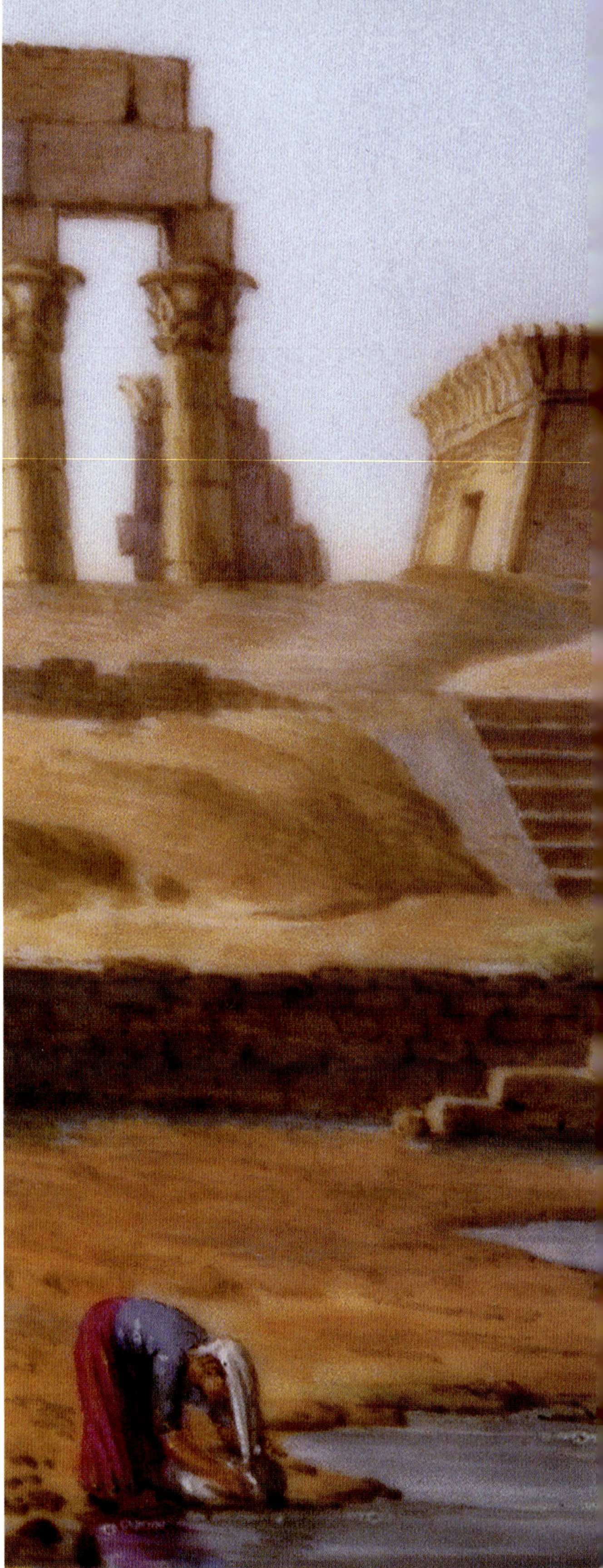

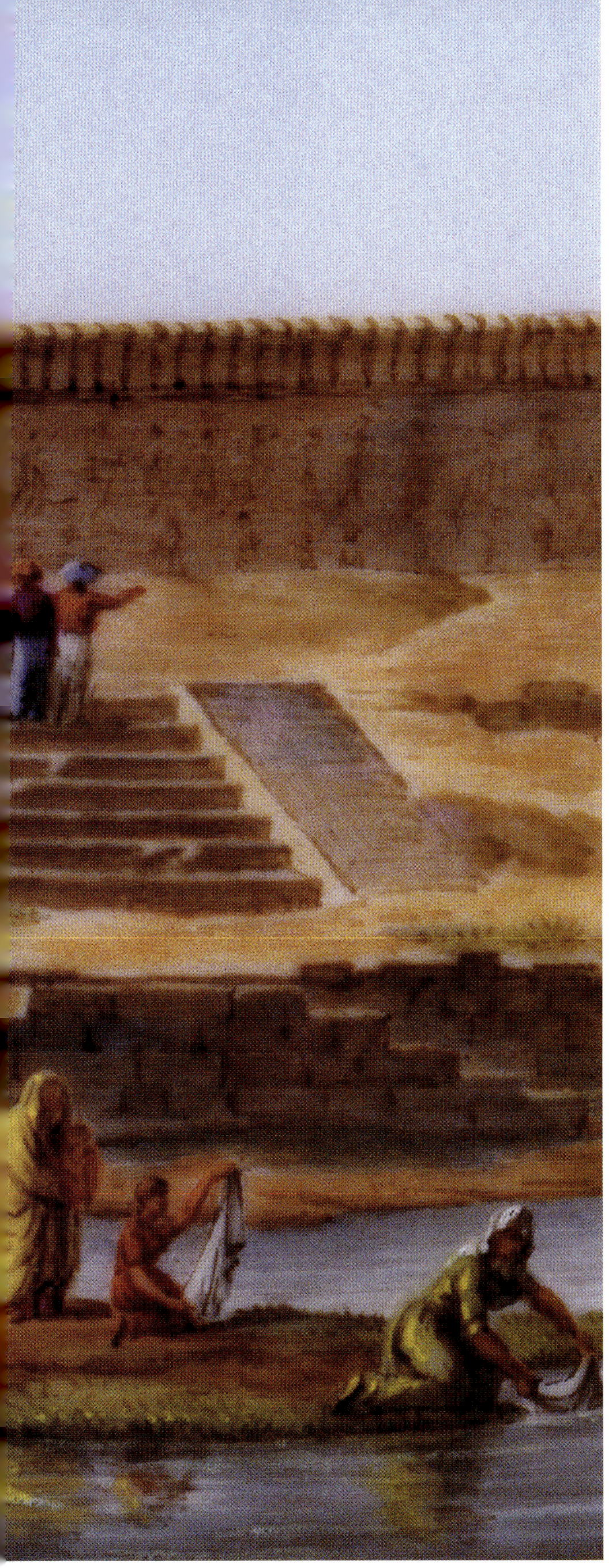

Contents

Ambassade de France
aux Etats-Unis

L'Ambassadeur

n° 2102

November 10, 2008

Dear Mr. Fisher:

Founded in 1740 during a century that established the nobility and elegance of domestic life, the Manufacture Nationale de Sèvres is the affirmation of a vision: maintaining an unparalleled savoir-faire and esthetic rigor, perpetuating the integrity of a style from generation to generation. Each and every artist who worked there – including such luminaries as François Boucher, Albert Carrier-Belleuse, Jean Arp and Alexander Calder – placed the Manufacture's longstanding traditions in the service of his own era.

It is this melding of the tried-and-true with the avant-garde that we so admire in "**Sevres Then and Now: Tradition and Innovation in Porcelain 1750-2000**." I would like to express my gratitude to the Hillwood Museum- a symbol of the ideal enlightenment cherished by both of our countries – as well as the generous lenders and curators who made this magnificent project possible.

I am certain that visitors to the Hillwood Museum will be enthralled by this dream of transparency, and will appreciate this vision of refinement forged by the never-to-be-tamed fires of creativity.

Sincerely yours,

P. V

Pierre Vimont

Mr. Frederick J. Fisher
Executive Director
Hillwood Estate, Museum and Gardens
4155 Linnean Ave, NW
Washington, DC 20008

Foreword

During the first half of the twentieth century, French decorative arts were considered by the American elite to be the epitome of fine craftsmanship, and the collecting of these pieces evidence of exceptional taste and sophistication. With this in mind, Marjorie Merriweather Post, under the guidance of art dealer Sir Joseph Duveen, began in the 1920s to assemble a magnificent collection of French furniture and decorative art. By turning her attention toward the collecting of Sèvres, she further established herself as a cultivated and discerning collector.

Today, Hillwood, the museum founded by Marjorie Merriweather Post, has become home to one of the most important Sèvres collections in America. With an emphasis on the manufactory's early production in the eighteenth century, including magnificent vases and celebrated services purchased both for display and entertaining, this focused assemblage reflects the founder's taste for finely crafted pieces, aristocratic French interiors, and porcelain's place in them as a complement to elegantly decorated spaces.

The conventional interpretation of Sèvres, as primarily a product of an aristocratic eighteenth-century France, will be challenged and expanded with the exhibition *Sèvres Then and Now: Tradition and Innovation in Porcelain, 1750–2000*, and this accompanying publication. The exhibition seeks to offer new insights into Sèvres, examining for the first time in America the full range of the preeminent factory's work. With artistic and historic links to significant pieces from Hillwood's collection as a foundation, the exhibition brings together international loans of works, many never seen before by American audiences, from all periods of the factory's two and a half centuries of production to demonstrate its continued pursuit of originality and innovation.

Liana Paredes, Senior Curator of Western European art at Hillwood, contributes outstanding new research about Sèvres as well as an exceptional point of view about its longevity and its modernization. Her deep knowledge of European porcelains and astute premise for the exhibition has brought about a show that juxtaposes for the first time the most magnificent examples from all periods of Sèvres production.

Sèvres Then and Now has been generously supported by gifts from the Richard C. von Hess Foundation, the Florence Gould Foundation, the Marjorie Merriweather Post Foundation, the National Endowment for the Arts, and International Humanities. Like so many initiatives at Hillwood, this exhibition would not have been possible without the strong support of the trustees of the Hillwood Museum and Gardens Foundation. Their guidance has been critical in the development of the exhibition.

Of course, no complete examination of Sèvres would be possible were it not for the discernment and prescience of Hillwood founder Marjorie Merriweather Post. Surely, were she still collecting today, its lasting significance as revealed in *Sèvres Then and Now* would not be lost on her.

FREDERICK J. FISHER
Executive Director
Hillwood Estate, Museum & Gardens

Acknowledgments

Many institutions, foundations, and individuals are to be thanked for their help and support with this book and exhibition.

First and foremost, I would like to convey my deepest appreciation to the many people at Hillwood Museum Estate & Gardens who have contributed with exceptional commitment and enthusiasm to this exhibition and publication: Frederick Fisher, Executive Director, Angie Dodson, Associate Director and Director of Interpretation and her staff, and Joan Wetmore, Director of Development and her staff. A very special thanks goes to the collaborative effort of all departments and especially to the Collections Division: Scott Brouard, Director of Exhibitions and his staff (Manuel Rouco and Manuel Diaz, Conservation Technicians), and Ruthann Uithol, Assistant Director for Collections and Collections Manager and her staff (Heather Corey, Visual Resources manager, Stephanie Thornton, Assistant Registrar and Kristen Regina, Chief Art Librarian and her assistant Pat Lynagh who took care of my endless research requests while writing this book). Thanks also to Anne Odom, Curator Emeritus for reading over the manuscript. A most deserved note of gratitude goes to Gina Raimond, curatorial assistant on this project who worked above and beyond the call of duty. Kudos to Edward Owen, whose genial eye has produced splendid images of Hillwood's objects.

Hillwood and I extend a very special thank you to the lenders, upon whose generosity this exhibition rests: at the Musée National de Céramique, Sèvres: Antoinette Hallé, Director, and Marie-Chantal de Tricornot, Head of the International Loan Programs; at the Manufacture Nationale de Sèvres: M. David Caméo, Director, Tamara Préaud, Director of Archives and Collections, and Ombeline d'Arche, Director of Outreach and Marketing; at the Mobilier National: M. Bernard Schotter, General Administrator; at the Metropolitan Museum of Art: Philippe de Montebello, former Director, Dr. Thomas P. Campbell, Director, and Jeffrey H. Munger, Curator, Department of European Sculpture and Decorative Arts; at the Wadsworth Atheneum Museum of Art: Ms. Susan Lubowsky Talbott, Director, and Linda H. Roth, Chief Curator; at the Walters Art Museum: Dr. Gary Vikan, Director, William Johnston, Curator, and Danielle Hall Bennett, Assistant Registrar for Loans and Exhibitions; at the Smithsonian Institution National Museum of American History: Dr. Brent D. Glass, Director, and Bonnie Lilienfeld, Deputy Chair and Curator, Division of Home and Community Life; at the Cleveland Museum of Art: Mr. Timothy Rub, Director, and Stephen Harrison, Curator of Decorative Arts and Design; and to the following individuals: Mr. Dan Mingledorff and Mr. Richard A. Mitchell, Dr. William W. McGuire and Nadine M. McGuire, Dr. Bruce Wilson, Mr. and Mrs. Fred A. Krehbiel, Mr. Richard Baron Cohen, Dr. and Mrs. Richard C. Crisler, Jr., Mme. Mathilde Bretillot, and other private lenders.

I would like also to acknowledge the many colleagues and prominent scholars who have been extraordinarily forthcoming in their answers to inquiries and my research on Sèvres for this project: the late Tracey Albainy, the beloved late Judy C. Arend, Donna Corbin, Sheila Tabakoff, Antoine d'Albis, John Whitehead, Michele Beiny, Jodie Wilkie, Letitia Roberts, Madeleine Deschamps, David Peters, Adrian Sassoon, Edgar Harden, Giles Ellwood, Philippe Sacerdoce, Mattia Bonetti, Bertrand Rondot, Cyrille Froissart, Hervé de la Verrie, Martin Bonham-Carter, Bernard Dragesco, Didier Cramoisan, and Ivan Day.

Much recognition goes also to Richard Molinaroli and his team at MFM Design, Inc., for designing this exhibition at Hillwood, and to the publisher of this volume in London, D Giles Limited, including Dan Giles, Managing Director, Sarah McLaughlin, Project Manager, Sarah Kane, Editor, and Helen Swansbourne, Designer. I am grateful to my family for their patience and support while working on this project and to my wonderful hosts during my several trips to Paris for this project, Ambassador José María Ullrich and Michele le Menestrel. I would also like to acknowledge the gracious support this project had received from the Ambassador of France to the United States, M. Pierre Vimont and the Cultural Attaché and Director of La Maison Française, Roland Celette.

Clearly this exhibition and catalog would have been impossible without the help and support of the board of trustees of the Hillwood Museum and Gardens Foundation and the generous funding received from the Richard C. von Hess Foundation, the Florence Gould Foundation, the Marjorie Merriweather Post Foundation, the National Endowment for the Arts, and International Humanities.

LIANA PAREDES
Senior Curator of Western European Art
Hillwood Estate, Museum & Gardens

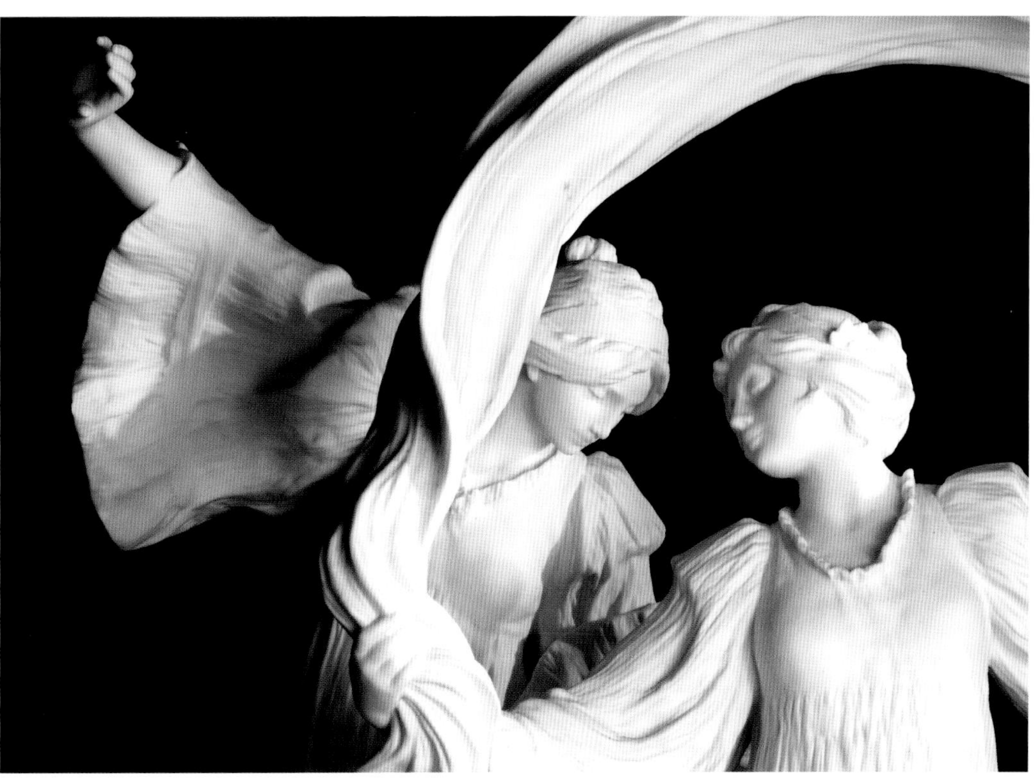

Detail of fig. 73, figures from the *Jeu de l'Écharpe* centerpiece, 1900

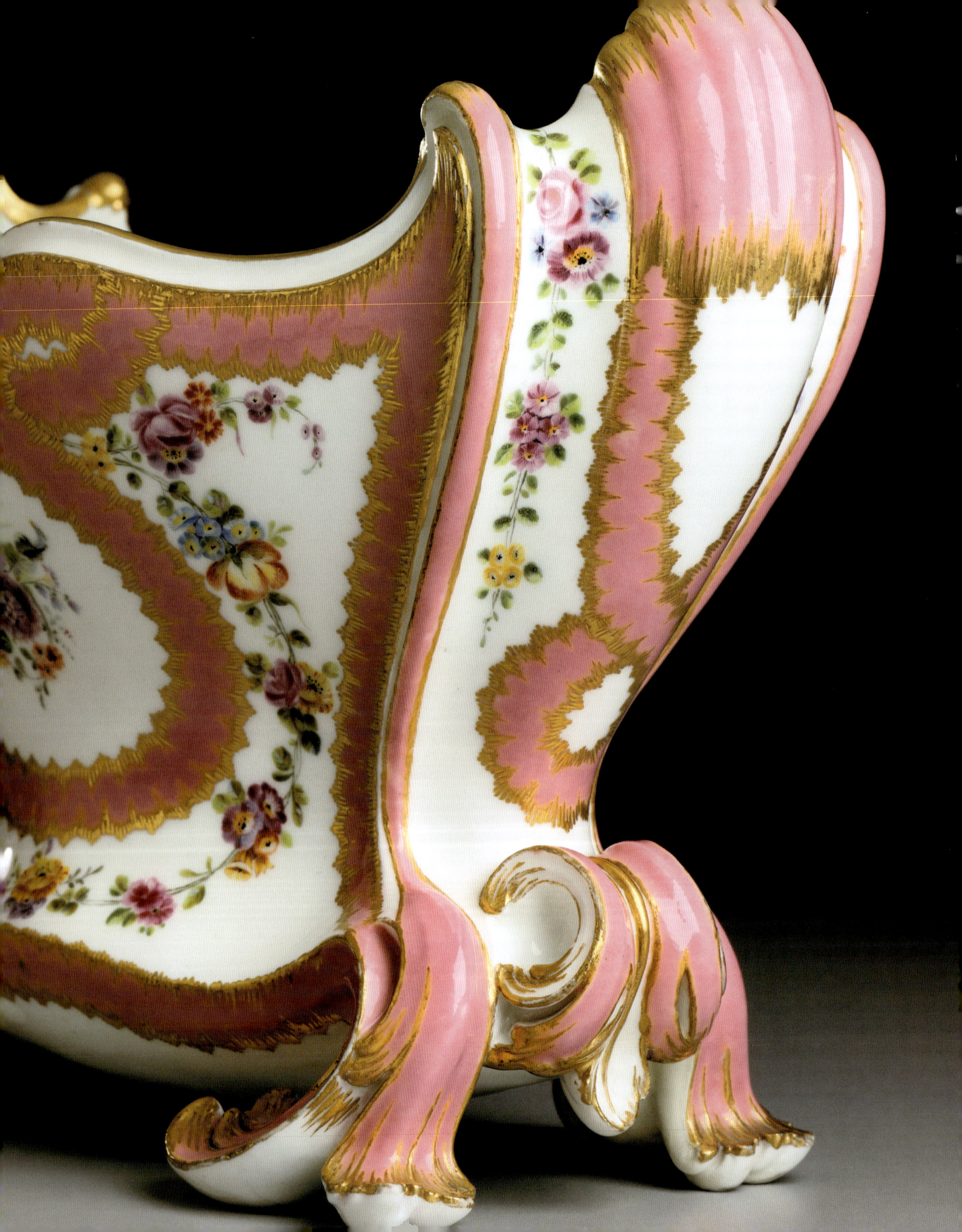

Introduction

"The heavy and the trivial should be avoided; we should produce the light, sensitive, new and varied." These visionary words, proffered by Hendrick van Hulst in 1751[1] in the very early days of the factory's existence, denote a clear desire from the beginning to set Vincennes/Sèvres apart from all other European porcelain factories.

Two and a half centuries later, George Touzenis, director of the manufactory, shared the same vision about Sèvres' unique inventiveness when he said that Sèvres had always manifested an "insolent scorn for repetition."[2]

Both quotations are eloquent proof that the initial striving for originality and inventiveness that drove the factory in its formative stages still drives it today.

The sustained creativity and unparalleled invention of Sèvres seems to have been a defining common denominator that unites the factory's productions from its inception to the present day. This vision, enduring over two and a half centuries, has endowed Sèvres designs with an inherent artistry that transcends utility and transforms the most ordinary vessels of everyday life into works of art.

To achieve a harmonic symbiosis of form and decoration is a daunting task, not without risk or the potential for failure. During each century of its long life, the Sèvres manufactory has faced critical moments of crisis. The path to survival in a sea of political and artistic change has been neither easy nor straightforward.

Unlike many of the early European porcelain factories that sprouted in the eighteenth century under royal or princely patronage, Vincennes/Sèvres was born as a private enterprise. The initial factory at Vincennes, then later at Sèvres, began as a private venture thanks to the ambitions of a government official, not of a king. It was not until 1759 that the factory was taken over by King Louis XV who, in order to save it from financial trouble, decided to buy all shares in the company and make it a royal enterprise.

The Vincennes/Sèvres venture faced challenges from the very outset by coming into direct competition with Meissen and with a soft paste much harder to work and fire than the hard paste of its competitors in Saxony. The Sèvres factory managed to overcome this adverse circumstance by playing up and perfecting the best qualities of soft-paste porcelain, namely a pleasant whiteness and fine translucent glaze that was able to absorb vibrant colors beautifully.

Around 1774, when Louis XVI became king, Sèvres again faced a period of creative and financial crisis due in part to changes in administration and competition from other Parisian factories. Under the auspices of other members of the royal family, competitors sought to undermine Sèvres privileges in the use of figural decoration, gold, and, more importantly, the new kaolin discovered in the Limoges area. Kaolin, the indispensable material necessary to produce true porcelain, opened up wonderful opportunities and dreams

OPPOSITE
Detail of fig. 7, flower vase (*cuvette "Mahon"*), 1757

for many to embark on the production of true hard-paste porcelain in France.

The biggest blow to the survival of the factory came only a few years later, when at the time of the French Revolution, the National Convention was faced with the dilemma of either closing the factory or keeping it running. Viewed as one of the "glories of France," the Sèvres manufactory was preserved.

In the early 1800s, Sèvres director Alexandre Brongniart's decision to sell blank/undecorated pieces had unprecedented repercussions. Unscrupulous people proceeded to decorate a staggering number of these blanks in imitation of Sèvres and thereby affected the public perception of what a Sèvres piece really looks like.These numerous fakes have created a general sense that blue and pink reigned supreme and that sentimental and Watteau-esque gallant scenes and portrait of kings and their royal families were central to the Sèvres style. Doubtless, this tainted the "good taste" of the factory in the public eye.

Half a century later, in the 1850s, Sèvres faced constant accusations of being an obsolete enterprise. These attacks led to a reorganization of production and a newfound drive to be a model for the ceramic industry at large. One hundred years later, in the 1950s, when the expressive qualities of clay, spontaneous brushwork, and utility came to be primary concerns for the modern potter, Sèvres remained quite oblivious to these trends. To some, the factory seemed rather stuck in the past.

The 1960s inaugurated something of a renaissance. Recognized artists were commissioned to design for Sèvres: a brave attempt to bring the factory up to date with current artistic trends. Jean Arp and Alexander Calder among others embodied the concepts of painting and sculpture in porcelain, making their pieces inseparable from high art.

The weight of history and tradition for contemporary artists can be invigorating but also daunting. Ettore Sottsass spoke about his initial intimidation at the prospect of working in the shadow of the kings, queens, and mistresses that had formed part of the factory's life in the past. He found that "penetrating a white and silent world," as he referred to the workshops filled with dust and clay, and joining the expert workers in the factory as they ventured to produce new works was, ultimately, greatly rewarding.

As for the groundbreaking innovations of Sèvres ceramics, it is easier to appreciate them in today's creations, when familiar concepts of contemporary art are transposed into porcelain. In fact, transcending and giving free rein to the material as so many of the twentieth-century collaborators have done is part of the course of contemporary ceramics. It may be more difficult, however, to appreciate the daringness of some of Sèvres' early creations, but these were as revolutionary as their modern counterparts. If one begins to get acquainted with Rococo design, one can appreciate the precarious equilibrium that characterized most designs of that period: an added curve or another applied ornament could transform a piece from being graceful and balanced to toppling and "over the top." The *cuvette "Mahon"* in fig. 7 is exemplary because it charmingly flaunts its curvy shapes and loopy decoration without becoming vulgar or "overdone."

By the early 1800s, porcelain had lost its aura, mystery, and exclusivity with the knowledge and secrets of its manufacturing broadcast to virtually every country in Europe. The critical innovations of Sèvres in the nineteenth century thus had to move beyond manufacturing techniques. Innovations revolved around contributions to the technical aspects of

OPPOSITE
Detail of fig. 48, plate from the *Service des Liliacées*, 1821

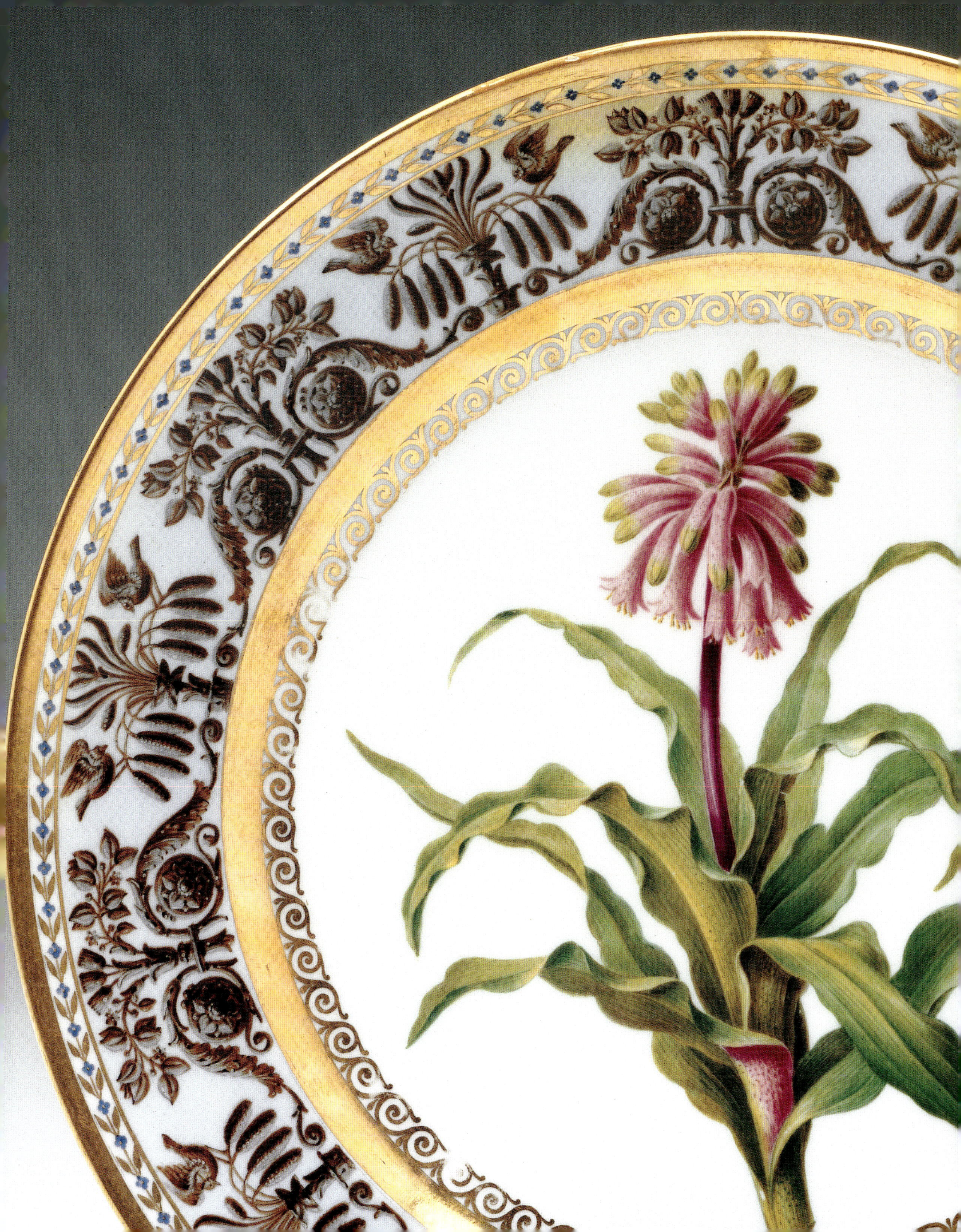

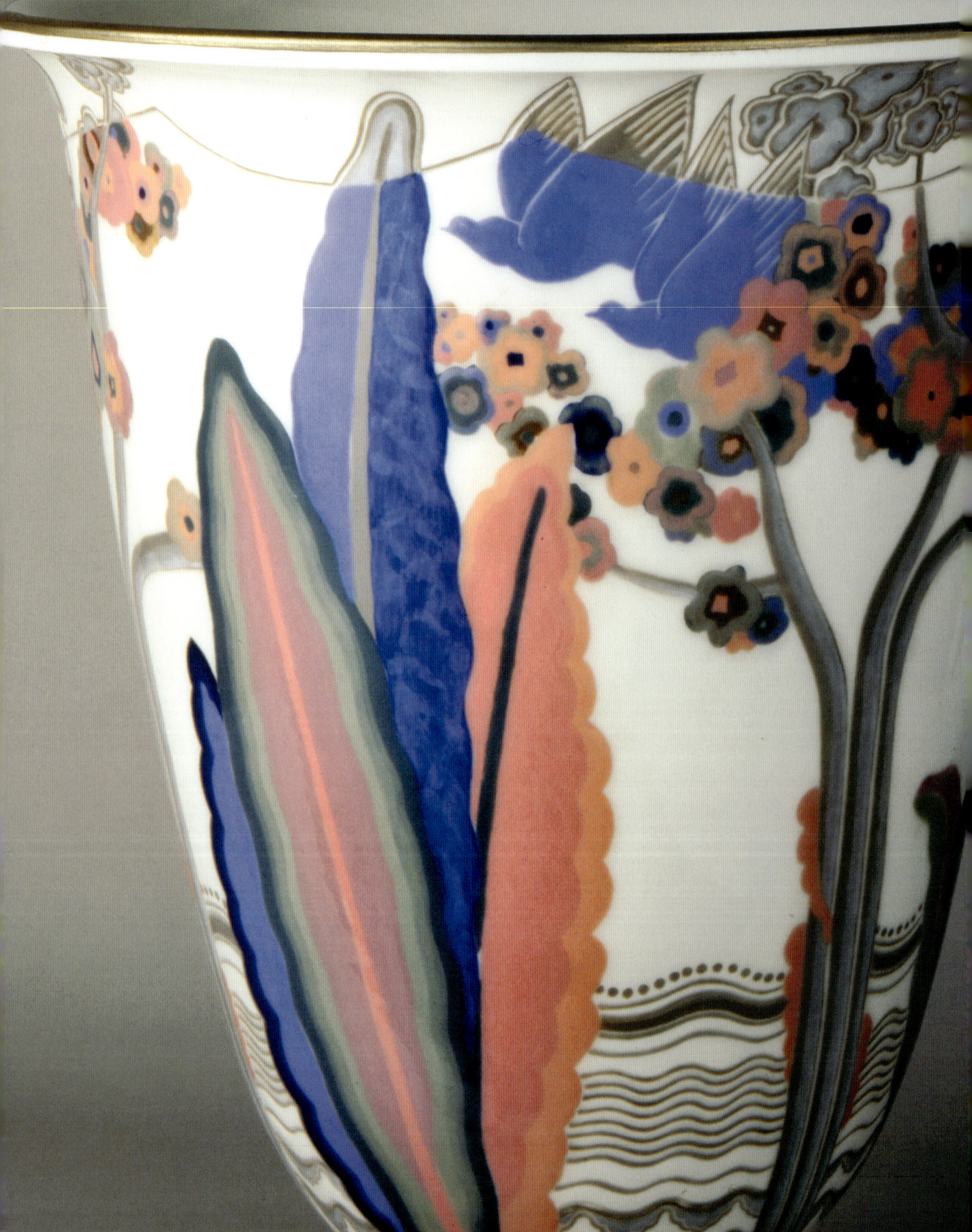

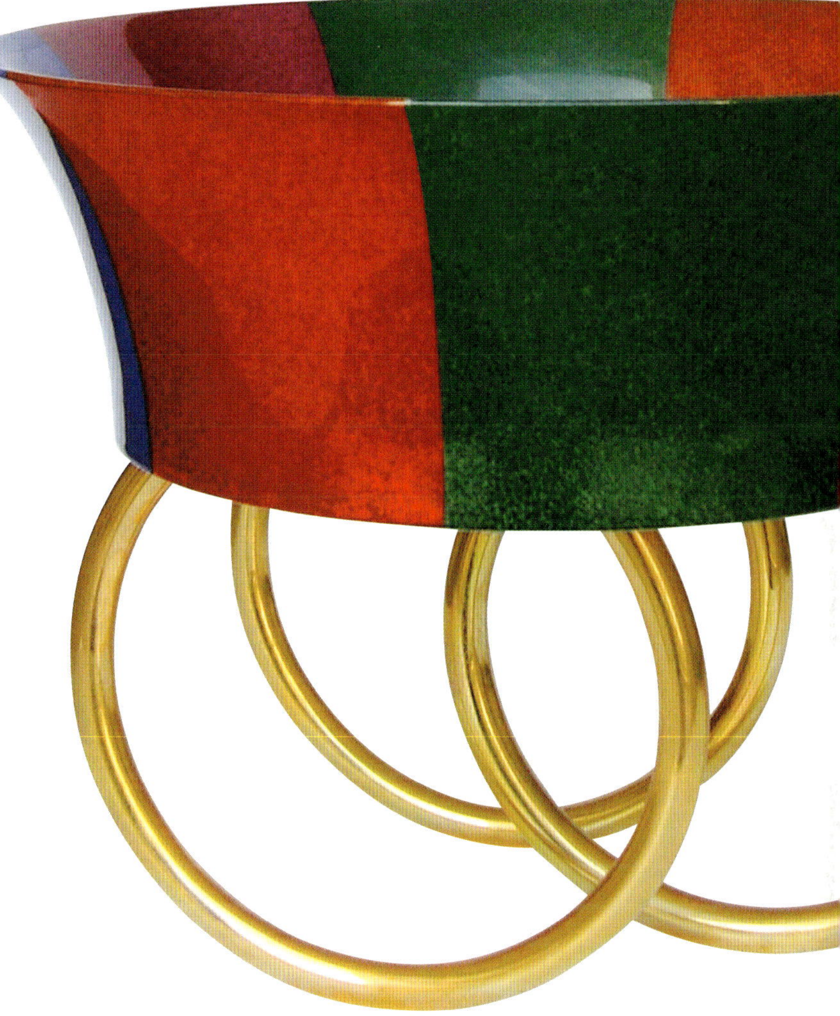

ceramic production and their sharing of knowledge with the outside world. The precise painting characteristic of so many of the nineteenth-century pieces retains a certain lyricism. Rather than constituting a prosaic and slavish interpretation of the world around, certain details on the scenes and ornamentation lend these pieces a highly decorative and artistic quality, elevating them above mere documents of the ability of the painters to emulate reality and fine art.

In terms of the market and audience for Sèvres, the shameless aristocratic character of the eighteenth-century productions set the tone for a factory that has been consistently oblivious to general public taste and disdainful of mass market trends. This position, which can be perceived as not without a certain dose of arrogance, is also transgressive in its boldness, and arguably it is precisely this defiant attitude towards established forms and decorations that has pushed the boundaries of creativity in the factory.

In view of these ups and downs in the course of its history, the survival of the factory through the turmoil of French history is nothing short of miraculous. Kings, emperors, and presidents of the French Republic have come and gone, yet the French have striven to maintain the royal, then imperial, and now national manufactory of porcelain afloat.

Is it not, perhaps, Sèvres' determination to translate into ceramic the art and spirit of the times, its sustained creativity and excellent technique, and its desire to operate outside the industrial and commercial molds, that have assured its uniqueness and its survival to date?

Detail of fig. 104, *coupe "Excelsior"* by Mathilde Bretillot, 1996–7

NOTES

1. In a letter to the director Jacques-René Boileau dated September 21, 1751 (Georges Touzenis, *Créations diverses à Sevres depuis 1765*, Paris, 2002, p. 8).
2. Ibid, p. 8.

OPPOSITE
Detail of fig. 79, vase designed by Émile-Jacques Ruhlmann, 1926–7

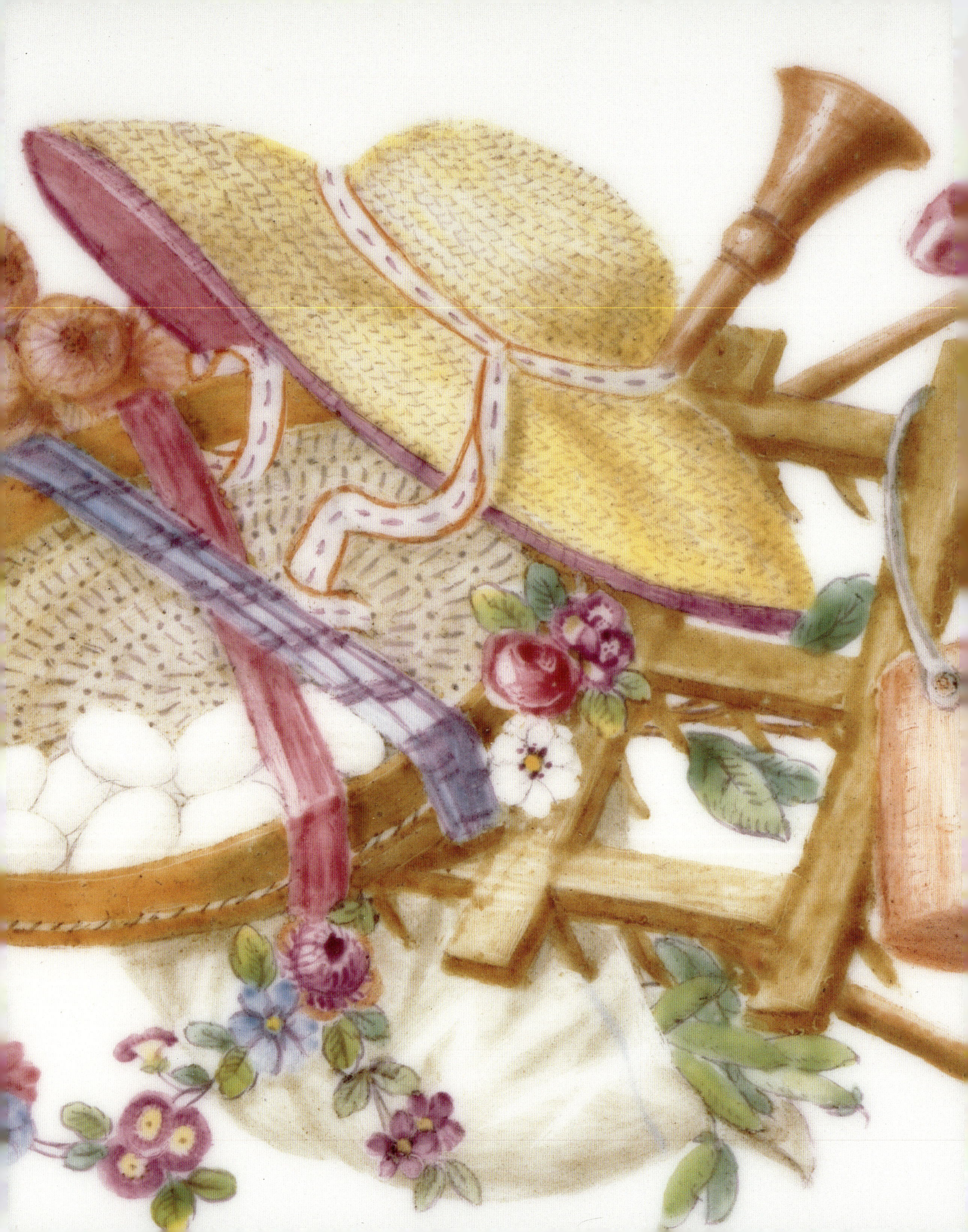

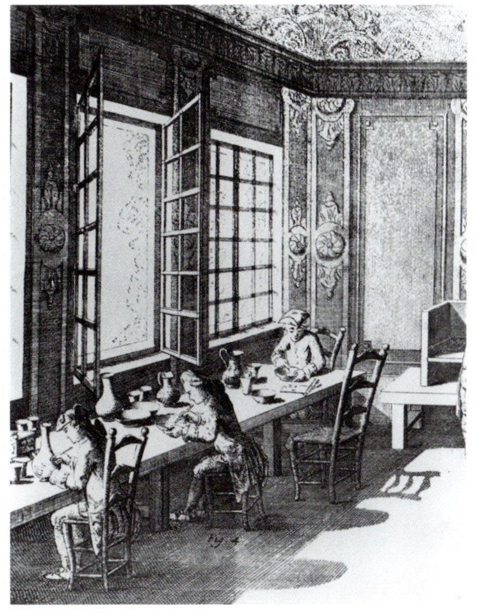

CHAPTER ONE

The Eighteenth Century

In the eighteenth century, the production of porcelain as it had been made in China since the seventh or eighth century was the subject of fierce competition among many European countries. The commercial endeavors of the East India Companies in the seventeenth century led to an enormous influx of oriental porcelain into Europe, which triggered a "Chinamania" fad and a surge of European interest in discovering the secret recipe for porcelain.

Manufacturing porcelain in large quantities on French soil was not just a matter of whimsy. Administrators knew too well the great economic advantages to be derived from a native production. French-produced porcelain would cut down on the massive import of Chinese ceramic wares. It would also curtail the increasingly expanding market of Meissen, the factory that had produced true porcelain since 1709 under the patronage of Augustus the Strong, Elector of Saxony and King of Poland (reg. 1694–1733).

ABOVE

Fig. 1: Plate from Diderot's *Encyclopédie, ou Dictionnaire raisonné des sciences, des arts et des métiers* illustrating a porcelain painter's workshop

OPPOSITE

Detail of fig. 17, pastoral trophy painting on platter

With this goal in mind, the French state counselor, financial superintendent and director of the French East India Trade Company, Jean-Henri-Louis Orry de Fulvy (1703–1751), established his own porcelain works at the château de Vincennes. The catalyst seems to have been the arrival in 1740 of two runaway workers from Chantilly, the brothers Gilles and Robert Dubois, who claimed they had the secret formula for producing true hard-paste porcelain. Orry de Fulvy, excited about the prospect of becoming the first to manufacture such coveted material in France, gave them lodging at the château de Vincennes and supplied them with all the resources they needed to prove their point.

The incompetence of the brothers and the falsity of their claim became apparent after their first fruitless experiments. Aware of their difficult position, they called on a friend from Chantilly, Louis-François Gravant, who had some experience working in faience. In a relatively short period, Gravant developed a paste, a glaze, colors, and firing procedures. His exciting formula was different from the true hard-paste ceramic body produced in China and at Meissen and would be known as "soft-paste" porcelain.

Gravant's fruitful results led to the creation in 1745 of a company in the name of Charles Adam (who was in fact Orry de Fulvy's *valet de chambre*), which was granted the exclusive license to manufacture "porcelain in the manner of Saxony, that is, painted and gilt with human figures," and

Fig. 2 (cat. 1): Porcelain flowers, Vincennes, ca. 1750

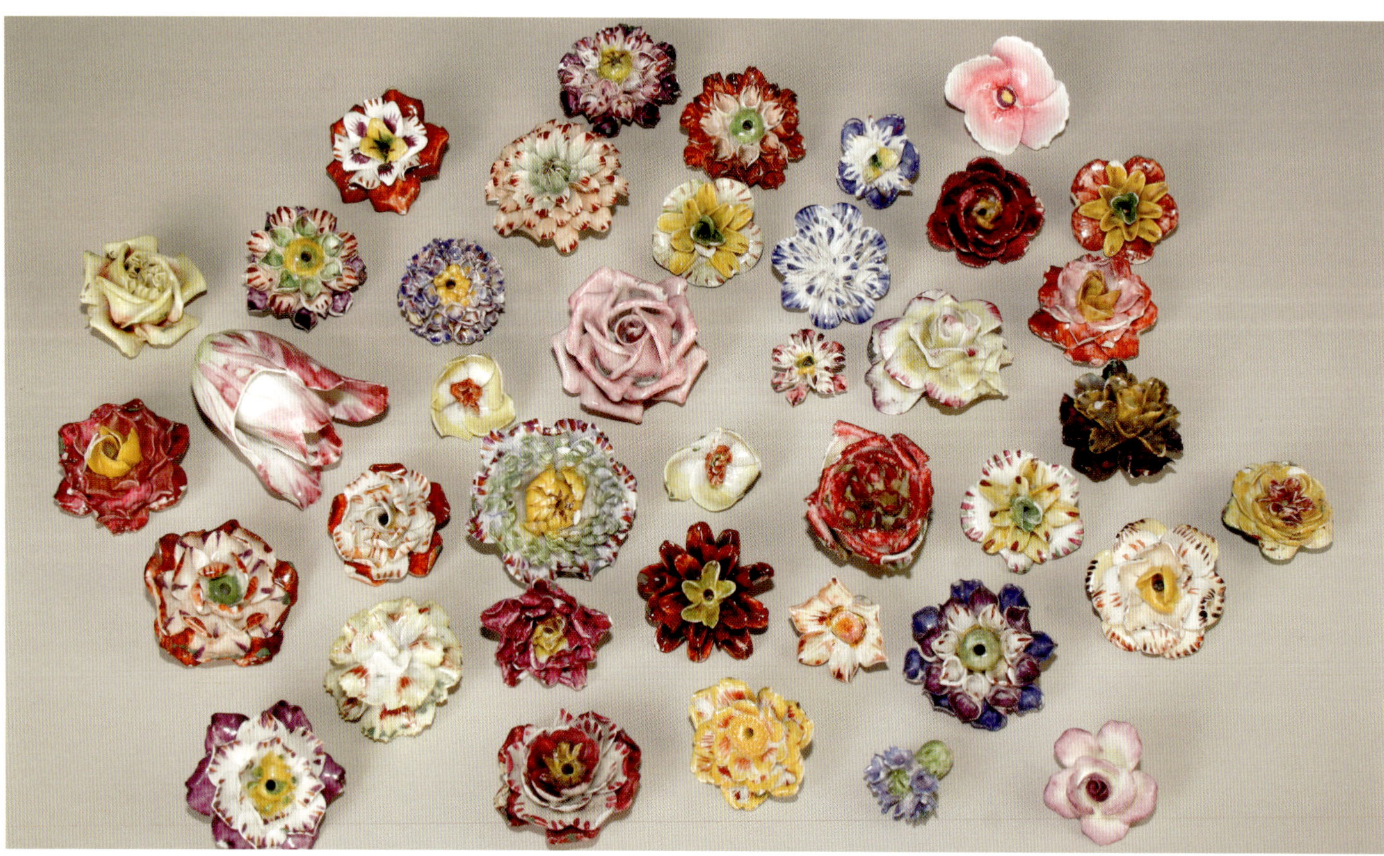

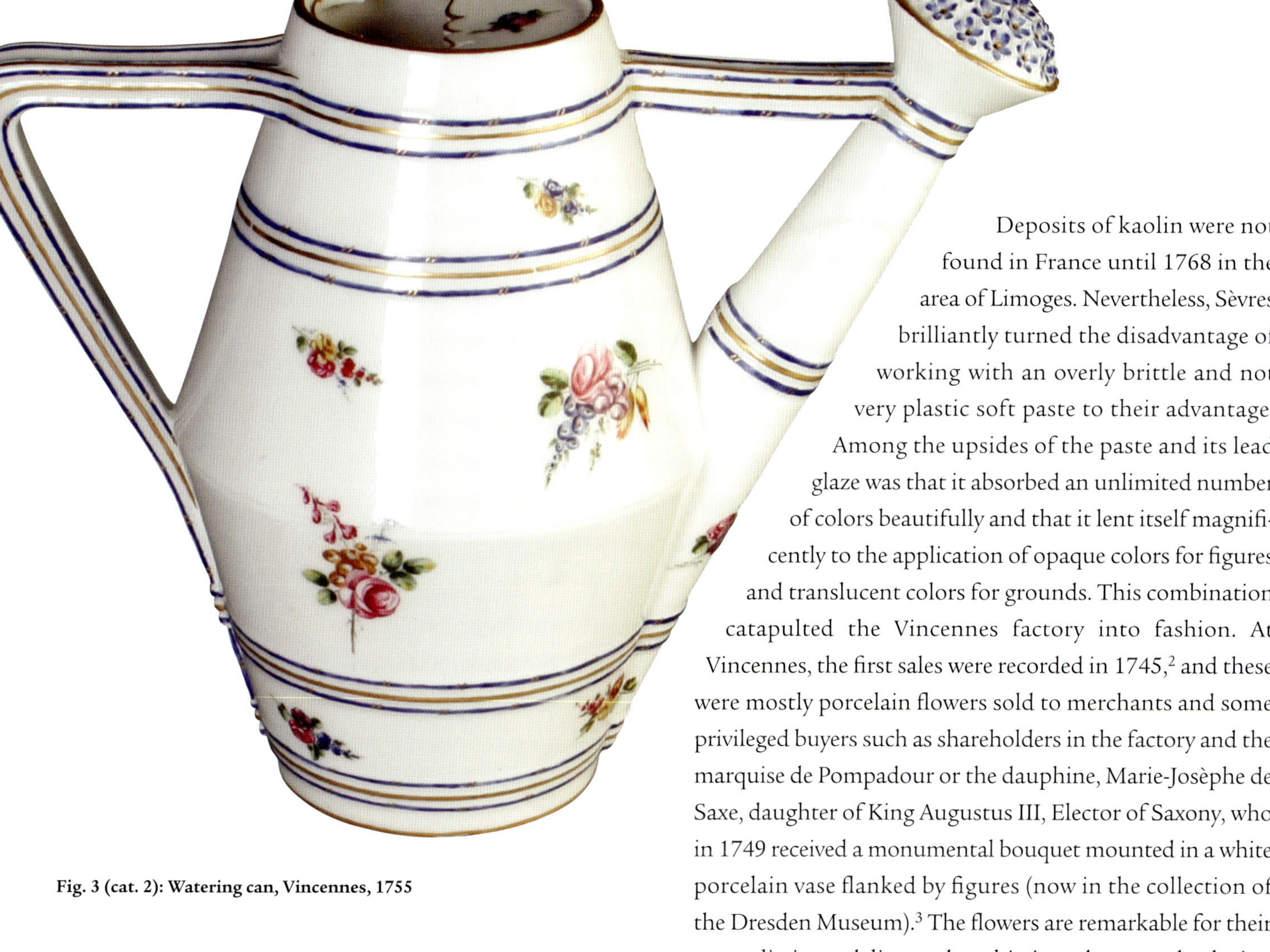

Fig. 3 (cat. 2): Watering can, Vincennes, 1755

Deposits of kaolin were not found in France until 1768 in the area of Limoges. Nevertheless, Sèvres brilliantly turned the disadvantage of working with an overly brittle and not very plastic soft paste to their advantage. Among the upsides of the paste and its lead glaze was that it absorbed an unlimited number of colors beautifully and that it lent itself magnificently to the application of opaque colors for figures and translucent colors for grounds. This combination catapulted the Vincennes factory into fashion. At Vincennes, the first sales were recorded in 1745,[2] and these were mostly porcelain flowers sold to merchants and some privileged buyers such as shareholders in the factory and the marquise de Pompadour or the dauphine, Marie-Josèphe de Saxe, daughter of King Augustus III, Elector of Saxony, who in 1749 received a monumental bouquet mounted in a white porcelain vase flanked by figures (now in the collection of the Dresden Museum).[3] The flowers are remarkable for their naturalistic modeling and sophisticated nuanced coloring at such early stages of the factory's production (fig. 2).

to compete with "all the other works and manufactories of porcelain white or painted in the Japanese manner."[1] The decree also restricted the movements of workers to discourage them from revealing the secret of porcelain.

In Europe, the race to produce a glassy, impermeable, translucent, white ceramic body developed in two ways. The distinction is a purely technical one, expressed by the terms hard paste and soft paste. The Meissen factory, under the patronage of Augustus the Strong, was the first in Europe to make true (hard-paste) porcelain, like that produced in China, in 1709. Its formula successfully combined kaolin—the white clay indispensable to making hard-paste porcelain—with quartz feldspath. The mixture was fired at high temperatures (1250–1350 degrees centigrade), which resulted in a fusion of materials to form an impermeable, glassy ceramic body.

At this time, gardening and enjoying the simple pleasures of nature became a fashionable aristocratic pastime. Baroque formal gardens were out; naturalistic floral sprays like the ones depicted on the watering can in fig. 3 reflect the tastes of a clientele who enjoyed a more relaxed lifestyle and a renewed interest in the natural world. The watering can is a rare form, which was only produced for a short period in the early years of the factory.

The legendary mistress of Louis XV, Jeanne-Antoinette Poisson, marquise de Pompadour (1721–1764), showed an initial interest in the porcelain enterprise at the death of Orry de Fulvy, of whom she was not particularly fond.[4] His death presented an opportunity for change, and change as she saw it meant developing a more French-looking production, while abandoning the models of Meissen and the Far East. Around 1752 she teamed up with the new appointee, controller general of finances Jean-Baptiste de Machault d'Arnouville (1701-1794), to convince the king to invest in the enterprise and to make it a royal manufactory. In 1753 the company was recapitalized and the king subscribed for a quarter of its shares. At that same time, the king authorized the factory to use the royal monogram—two intertwined Ls—as its mark.[5] During the year the king became a shareholder, there was a marked evolution in the factory's style: monochrome decorations first appeared and color grounds were first used. These innovations endowed Vincennes/Sèvres with a very distinctive style that would soon become its hallmark.

Madame de Pompadour was also partially responsible for the factory's move in 1756 from Vincennes to Sèvres, a location closer to Versailles. It was obvious that she hoped to engage the king at a time when she needed to reinforce her relationship even further, and Sèvres gave her an opportunity. The marquise was passionate about porcelain. As the inventory drawn up on her death shows, over 3,000 porcelain objects were disseminated around her various residences. Around 2,500 were Sèvres and all were contemporary.[6] She was at the forefront of collectors who, rather than amassing groups of old ceramics, were collecting works of their own time. The elephant vases in fig. 9 are illustrative of her distinguished taste.

In 1759, after several years of subsidizing the enterprise, King Louis XV bought the factory outright and transformed it from a private profit-making business into a state-financed royal enterprise. The factory never went back into private hands and from that date forward it has been state-owned.

Sèvres played a key role in the breakaway of Western ceramics from their Eastern counterparts. Curtailing the importation of Chinese ceramics was of economic importance. Casting away the flat, somewhat abstract Chinese figures suspended in space was a step towards the stylistic affirmation that European ceramics should relate to a Western artistic sensibility. This aesthetic was directly connected to the search for perspective, narrative, and a naturalistic idiom that had been central to the European manner of representation since the Renaissance. To transpose these ideals into porcelain, ceramists needed more than the five-color transparent palette that the Chinese had developed to date. The new enamel colors ranged from opaque to semi-opaque to translucent, allowing for shades achieved by layering them from thin to thick. In order to achieve opaqueness in color, the porcelain workers followed the technique of enamel workers on metal by adding a flux to the pigment which would fix the color on the porcelain and make it opaque when fired.[7] With this palette, artists could engage in painting landscapes, portraits, and miniatures on porcelain in line with Western European painting. This approach is well illustrated by the Vincennes water ewer and basin (fig. 4), which is more ambitiously decorated than other early examples of this kind. Amphitrite, Greek goddess of the sea, is depicted enthroned on a sea shell on the ewer surrounded with Rococo garden elements. The dominating purplish-pink color was one of several red and crimson colors supplied to the factory by painter Pierre-Antoine-Henry Taunay (1728–after 1781) in the early 1740s and which were used quite profusely in polychrome painting and monochrome (*en camaïeu*) scenes. The influence of Meissen is apparent in the color palette and the predominant white ground with scattered naturalistic floral sprays.

In the 1720s, the porcelain manufactory at Meissen was the first in Europe to formulate a new palette and free itself from the oriental influence. By 1735, painter Johann Gregorius Höroldt (1696–1775) had successfully formulated nearly sixty new colors for use on Meissen wares. Saxony was indisputably the European leader in the world of ceramics by the time the venture at Vincennes/Sèvres began. It is therefore not surprising that when the royal privilege was

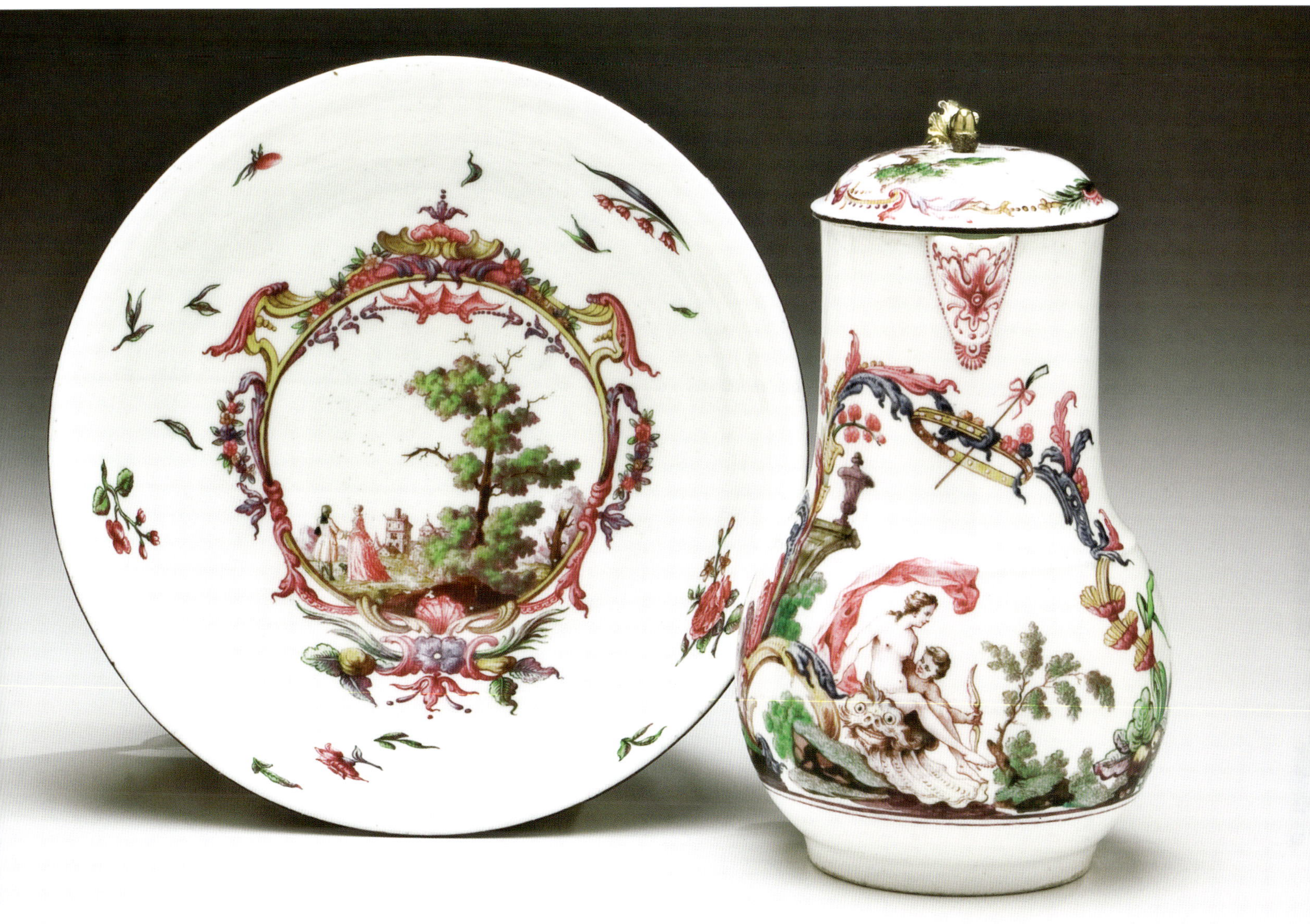

Fig. 4 (cat. 4): Ewer and bowl, Vincennes, ca. 1747

bestowed upon Sèvres in 1745 relating to the use of gold and figural decoration, it specified it to be in the Saxon manner or style. This royal privilege was granted in exclusivity and thus did away with any possible competitors.

Orry de Fulvy's aim must have been to develop as many colors as Meissen and for that he spared no expense. He recruited enamel workers such as Jean-Adam Mathieu and Louis Liot, and he paid exorbitant amounts of money to Taunay, who had inherited from his father formulas from a series of gold-based carmine, red, and violet colors. But technical prowess alone was not enough to raise Sèvres to new heights in the field of artistic porcelain production. The talent at Sèvres pushed the boundaries of utilitarian porcelains into the realm of high art. The integrity of the object, where form and decoration fuse into a homogeneous ensemble, with the decoration in total symbiosis with the shape, was the highest achievement at Sèvres (fig. 5).

After the king became a shareholder in 1751, new talent was brought in to work under the enterprise's new director Jacques-René Boileau (d. 1772). The gifted team comprised Jean Hellot as technical director (in charge of the paste), Hendrick van Hulst as artistic director, Jean-Jacques Bachelier as director of the painting workshops, and Jean-Claude Duplessis as chief modeler. Duplessis was a stellar

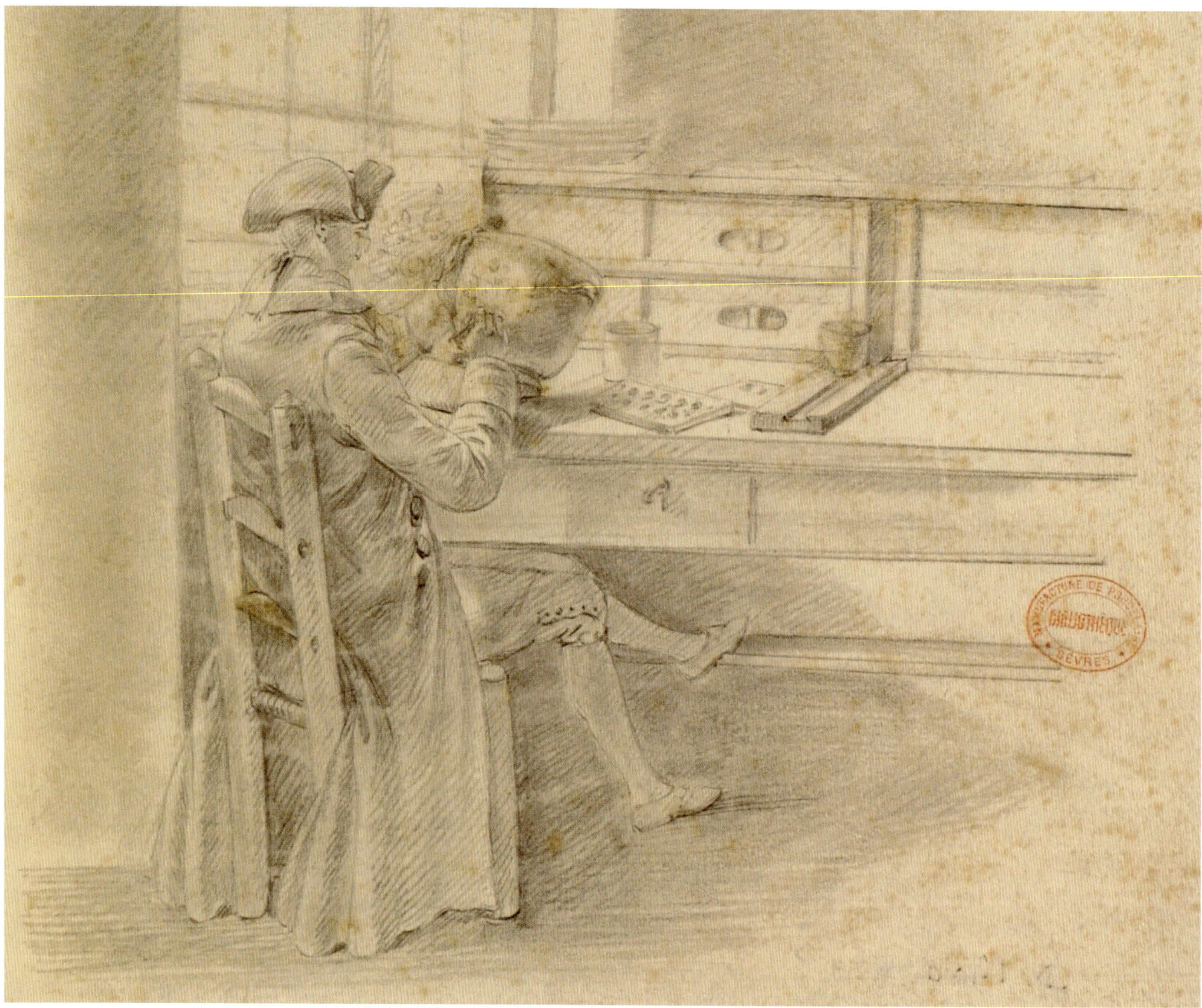

Fig. 5: Drawing of a Sèvres factory painter, late eighteenth century

designer who understood porcelain and created designs with the character of the material in mind, thereby freeing the factory from models based on metalwork or sculpture.

The arrival of Jean-Claude Duplessis *père* (ca. 1695–1774) at Vincennes energized the production enormously. Originally from Turin, he was a designer and goldsmith who had worked with the greatest ornamentalists of the Rococo period—Juste-Aurèle Meissonier, Gilles-Marie Oppenord, and Nicolas Pineau. Recent scholarship has determined that Duplessis arrived in Paris from Turin around 1735 under the patronage of Victor-Amédée de Savoie, prince de Carignan and lieutenant general of the French army.[8] Although Duplessis never received a workmaster title such as goldsmith, he was able to circumvent the deficiency by seeking royal patronage that would allow him to work on the margins of the guild system. Thanks to the comte d'Argenson, from 1749 to 1755 Duplessis secured lodgings at the Louvre, where privileged artisans kept their workshops and were not subject to guild restrictions. The factory records show that Duplessis began to work at Vincennes in 1748. For the first three years he worked on contract and supplied highly sculptural models, so well designed that most survived changing fashions and kept on being reused and adapted to newer styles.

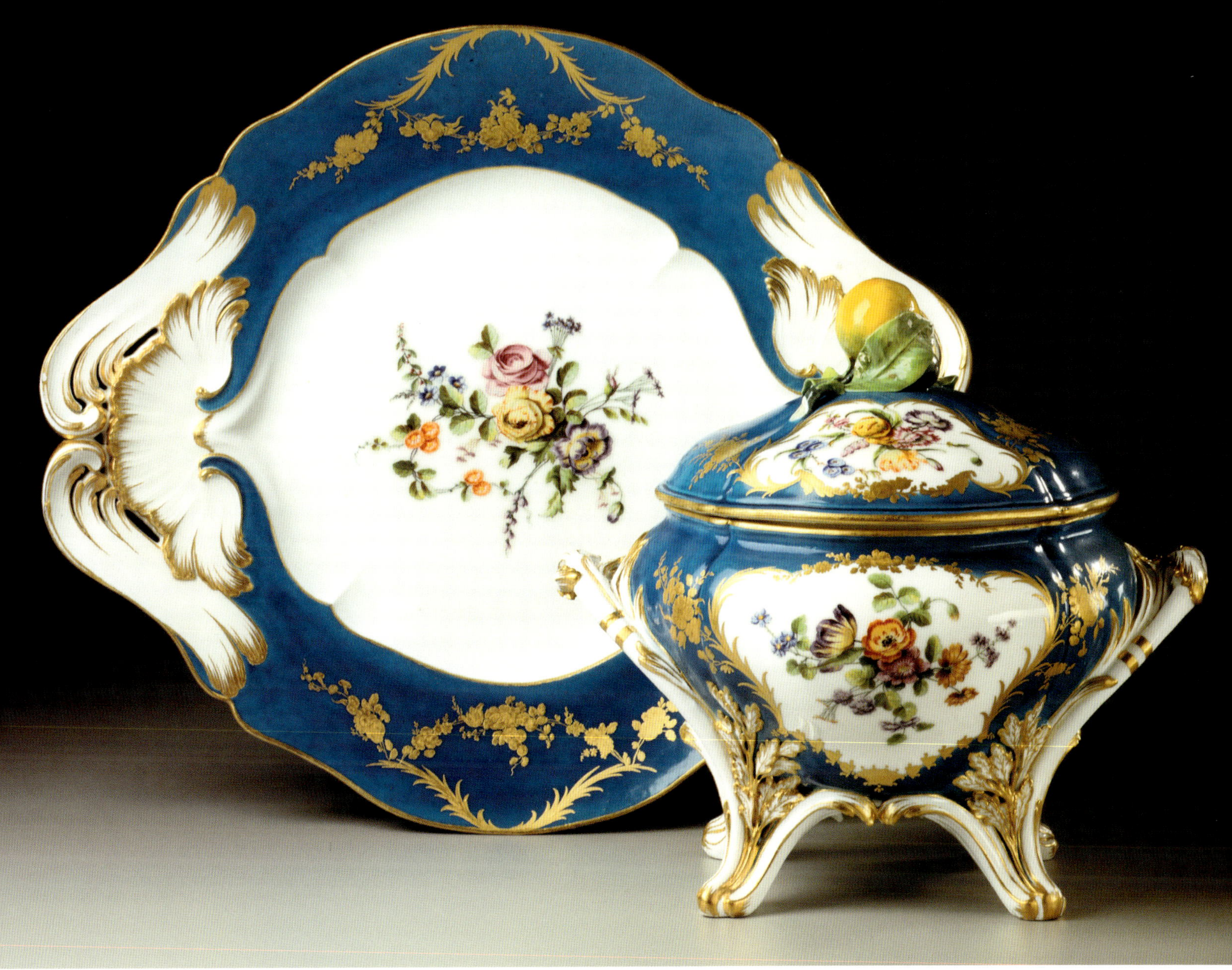

Fig. 6 (cat. 3): Tureen and platter, Vincennes, 1754

The turquoise blue tureen and platter (*pot à oille "du roi" et son plateau*) is illustrative of the wonderfully sculptural shapes that Duplessis created for Sèvres (fig. 6). Its affinity with contemporary metalwork is inescapable. The two pieces are also an eloquent example of the characteristic style developed by the Vincennes/Sèvres factory in the early years. The luscious and deep blue turquoise color was commercially introduced in 1753. Created by the factory's chief chemist, Jean Hellot (d. 1766), the color was called *bleu céleste* ("heavenly blue") or *bleu du roi* ("the king's blue"), as it was the color of the first entire dinner service made at Vincennes and delivered to King Louis XV in the course of 1753–5. This first service, presented with great fanfare on Christmas Eve of 1753 at Versailles, was afterwards dispatched to Paris to be exhibited at *marchand-mercier* Lazare Duvaux's establishment with the intention of impressing courtiers and distressing the King of Saxony.[9] Tureens like these were customarily the most expensive component of a dinner service. Often they were sold separately, as is possibly the case of Hillwood's *pot à oille*, identified to be the one that Lazare Duvaux sold to the comte d'Egmont (1727–1801).[10] The word *oille* is derived from the Spanish *olla*, a type of stew made with several kinds of meats and vegetables. This dish is one of a number of Spanish traditions that were introduced

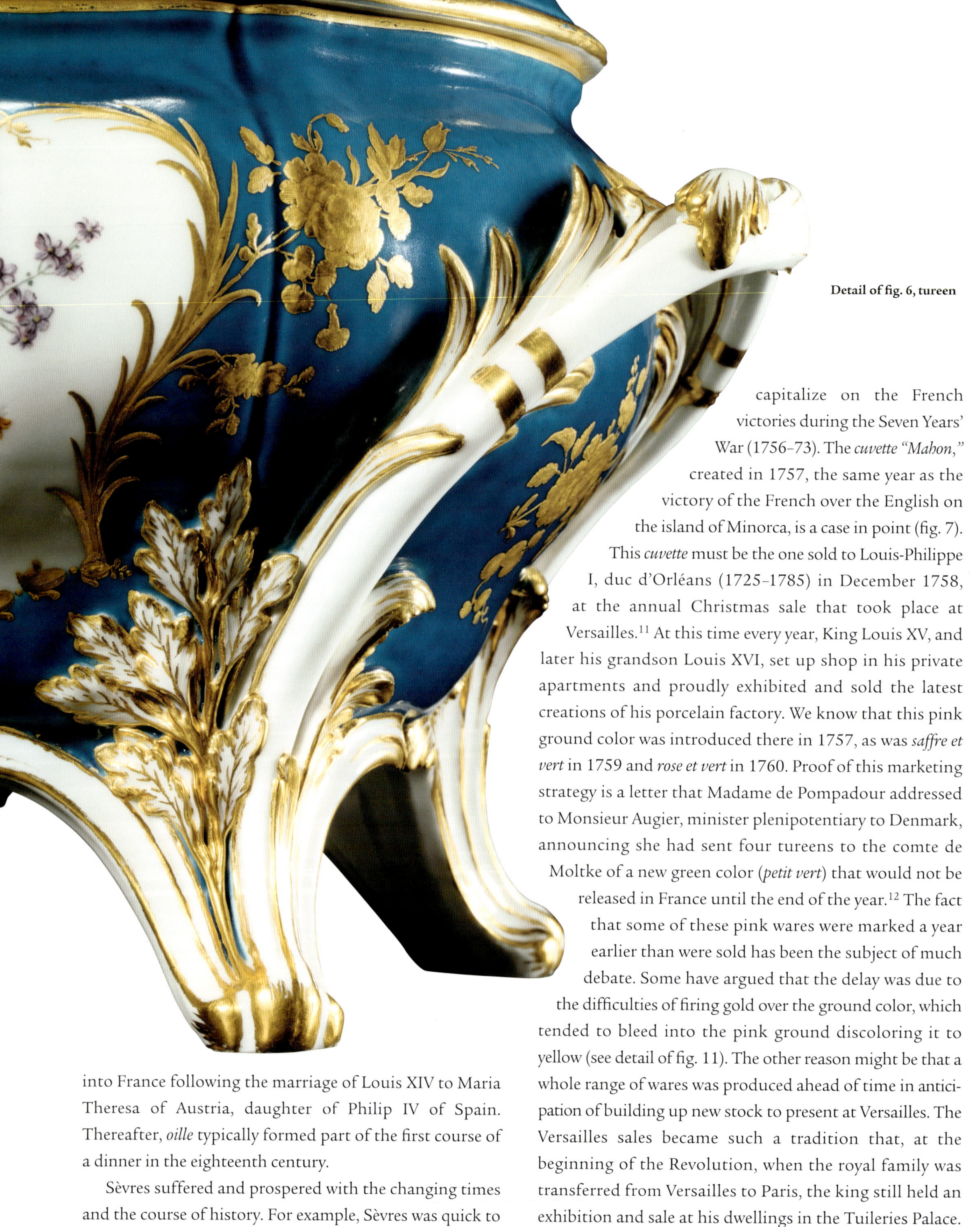

Detail of fig. 6, tureen

into France following the marriage of Louis XIV to Maria Theresa of Austria, daughter of Philip IV of Spain. Thereafter, *oille* typically formed part of the first course of a dinner in the eighteenth century.

Sèvres suffered and prospered with the changing times and the course of history. For example, Sèvres was quick to capitalize on the French victories during the Seven Years' War (1756–73). The *cuvette "Mahon,"* created in 1757, the same year as the victory of the French over the English on the island of Minorca, is a case in point (fig. 7). This *cuvette* must be the one sold to Louis-Philippe I, duc d'Orléans (1725–1785) in December 1758, at the annual Christmas sale that took place at Versailles.[11] At this time every year, King Louis XV, and later his grandson Louis XVI, set up shop in his private apartments and proudly exhibited and sold the latest creations of his porcelain factory. We know that this pink ground color was introduced there in 1757, as was *saffre et vert* in 1759 and *rose et vert* in 1760. Proof of this marketing strategy is a letter that Madame de Pompadour addressed to Monsieur Augier, minister plenipotentiary to Denmark, announcing she had sent four tureens to the comte de Moltke of a new green color (*petit vert*) that would not be released in France until the end of the year.[12] The fact that some of these pink wares were marked a year earlier than were sold has been the subject of much debate. Some have argued that the delay was due to the difficulties of firing gold over the ground color, which tended to bleed into the pink ground discoloring it to yellow (see detail of fig. 11). The other reason might be that a whole range of wares was produced ahead of time in anticipation of building up new stock to present at Versailles. The Versailles sales became such a tradition that, at the beginning of the Revolution, when the royal family was transferred from Versailles to Paris, the king still held an exhibition and sale at his dwellings in the Tuileries Palace.

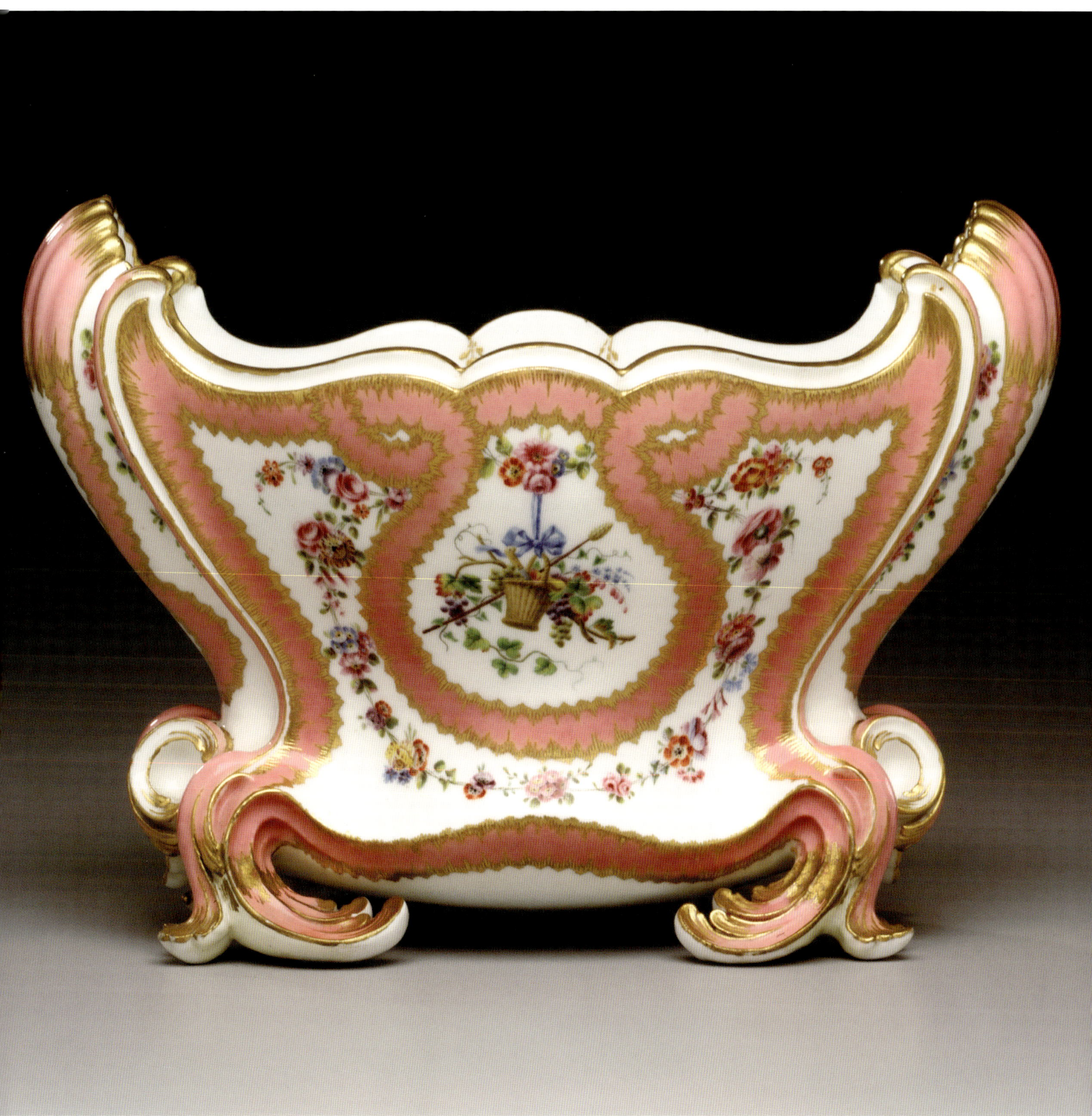

Fig. 7 (cat. 5): Flower vase (*cuvette "Mahon"*), 1757

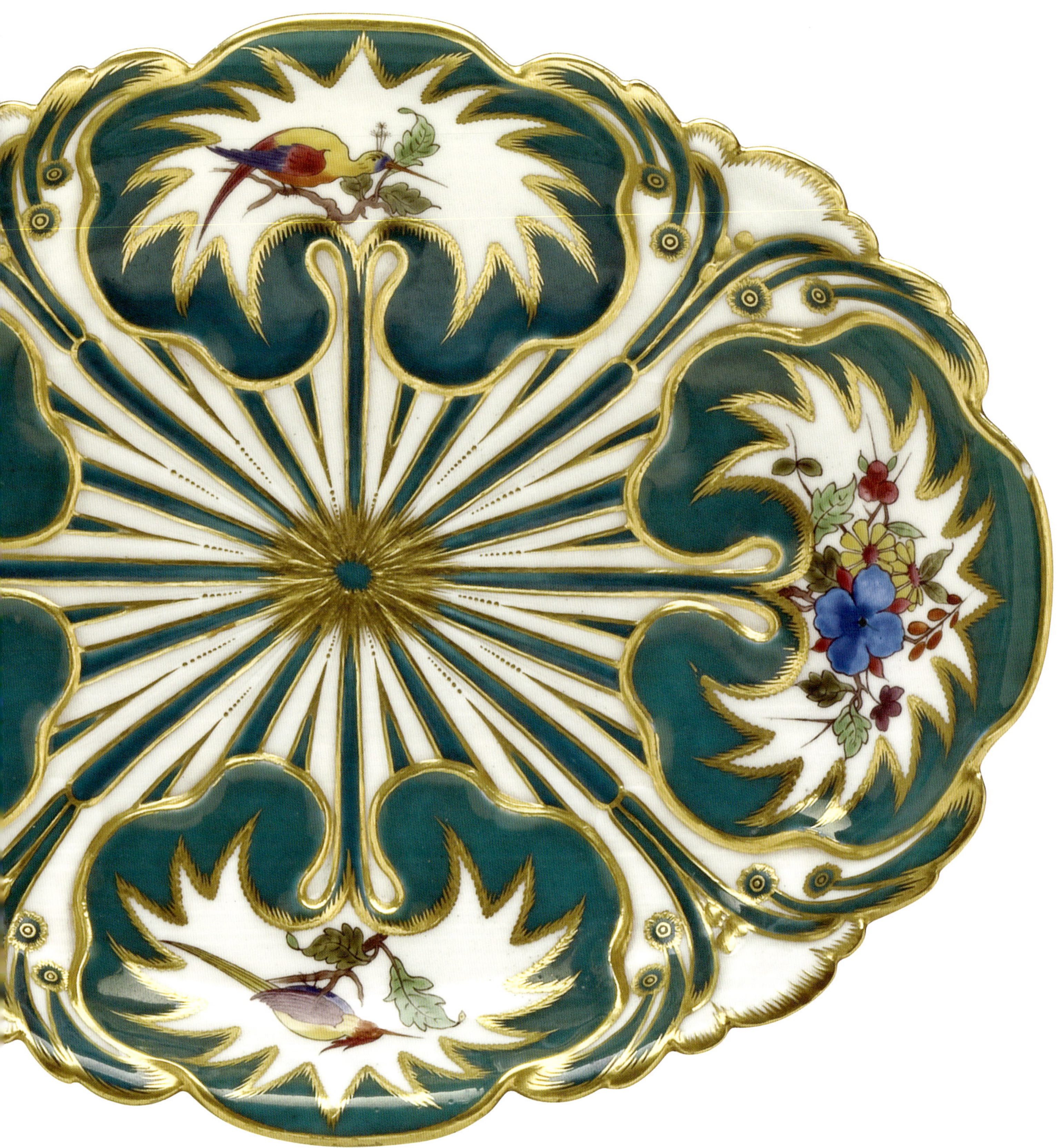

Detail of fig. 8, waterleaf bowl

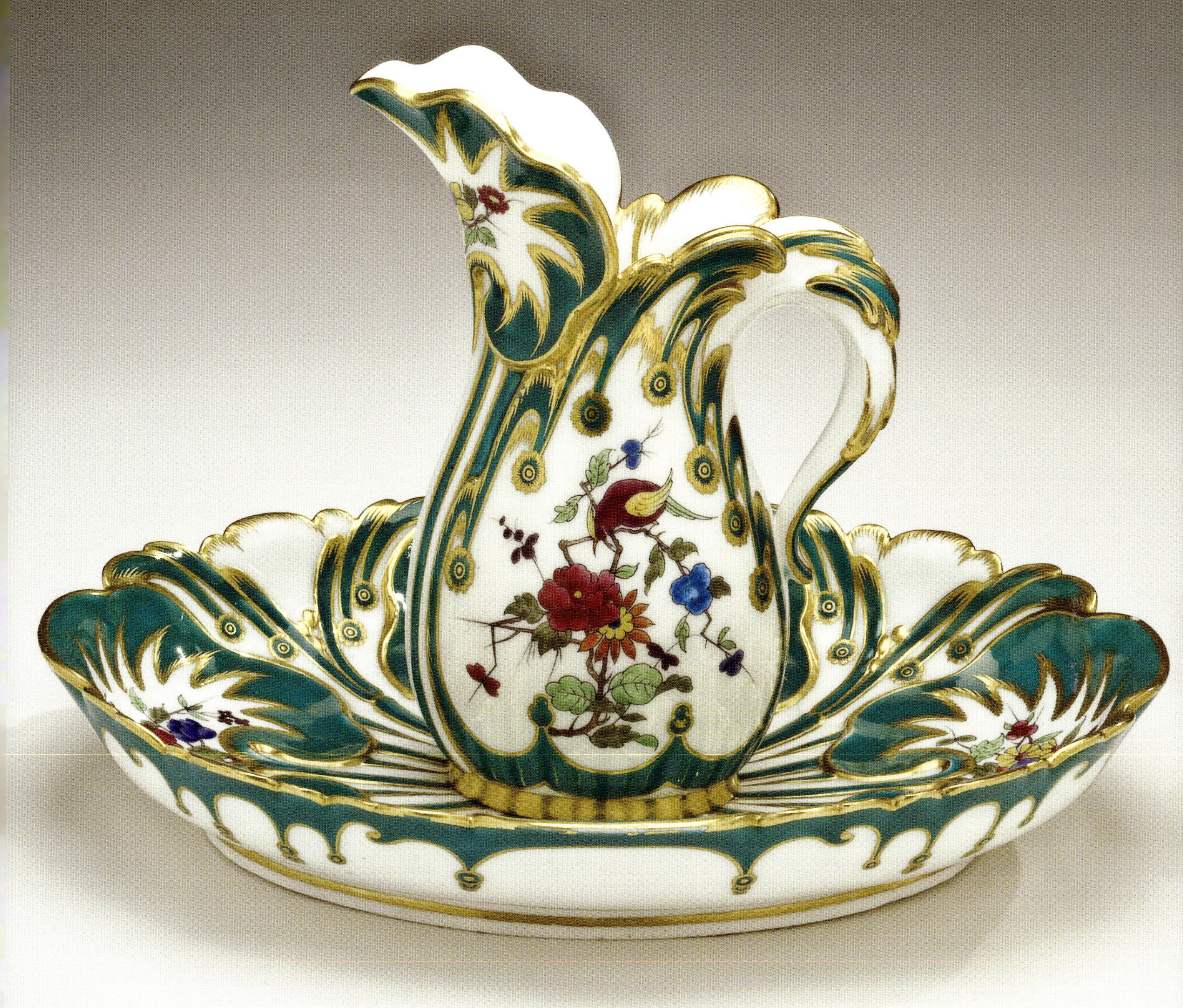

Fig. 8 (cat. 6): Waterleaf ewer and bowl, 1759–60

The green waterleaf ewer and basin is almost certainly another product of Duplessis' creative genius—in this case, the combination of graphic rendering of splashes of water with a relief decoration of water-lily pads to adorn the dynamic undulating shapes of the jug and basin (fig. 8).[13] These pieces present another distinctive characteristic, for they are among a small group of objects produced between 1759 and 1763 and decorated with flat, strong-colored flowers in the Kakiemon style. Only a few of these dainty, yet utilitarian, sets survive.[14] The present example, formerly in Welbeck Abbey, seat of the dukes of Portland, was only identified recently. The painting is almost certainly by the hand of Charles-Nicolas Dodin (1734–1803), one of the finest painters in the factory who specialized in figural painting and was regularly entrusted to decorate pieces for the most important clients, including Louis XV, his mistresses Madame de Pompadour and Madame du Barry, and Louis XVI and his two brothers, to name a few.[15]

OVERLEAF
Fig. 9 (cat. 9): Pair of candelabra vases with elephant heads, 1760

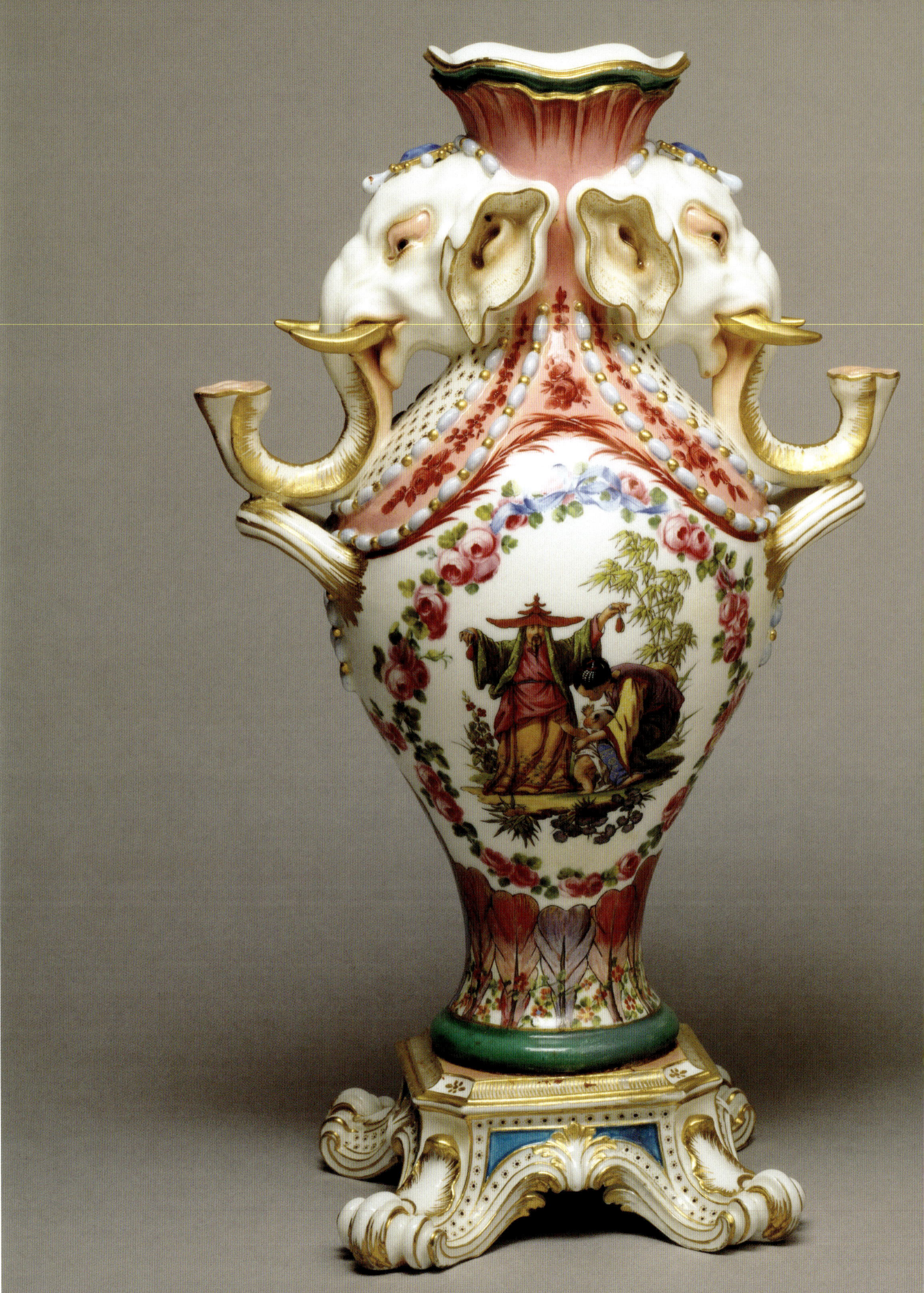

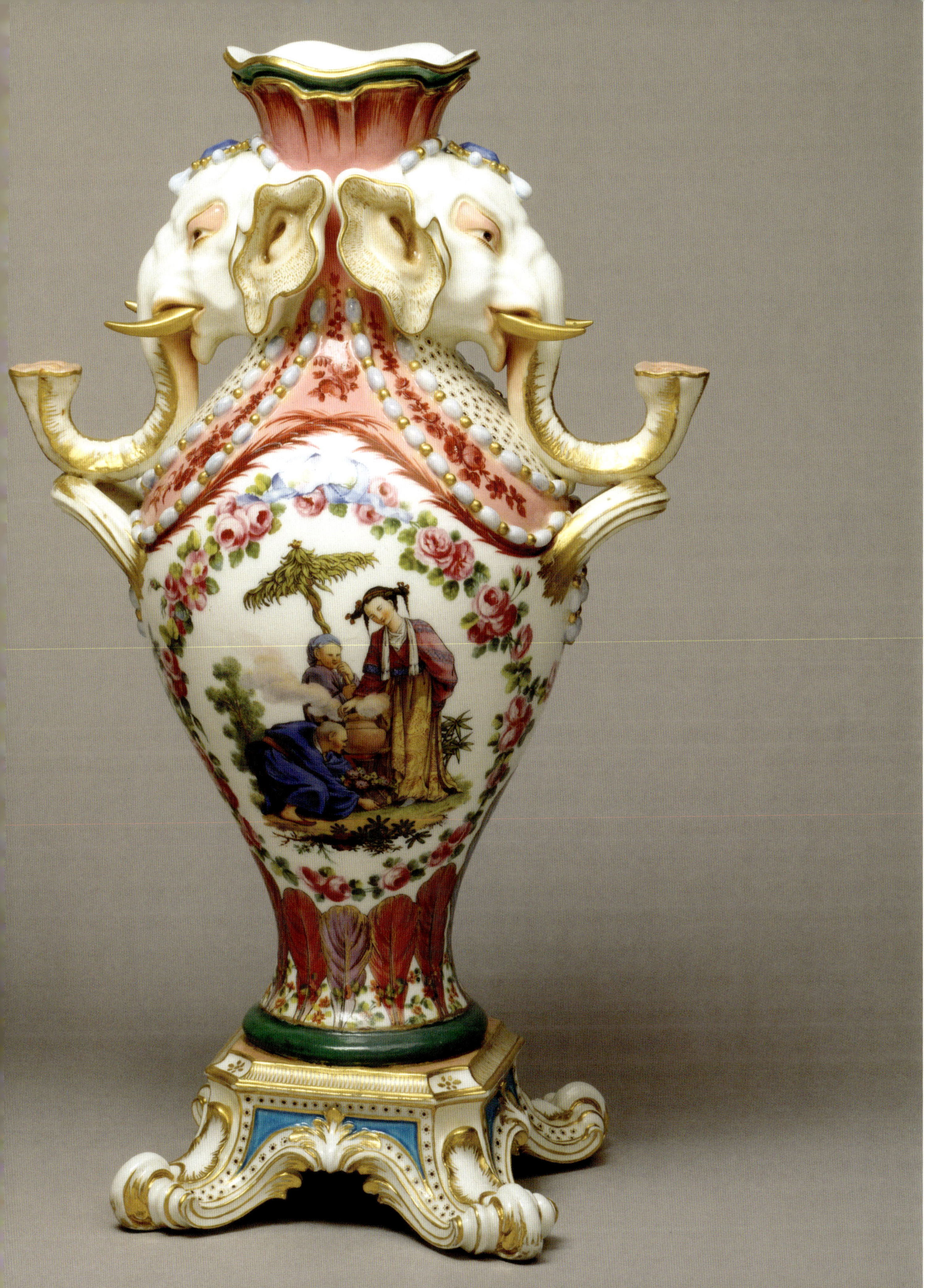

The *vases à têtes d'éléphants* exemplify the daringness of Sèvres designs from the early years and provide another example of the flat, oriental style of decoration (fig. 9). Produced around 1760, these vases formed part of a five-piece garniture—the only known examples of Sèvres of this date to display three different ground colors. Both vases are painted in a distinctive *famille rose*-type palette with Chinese-influenced scenes, or chinoiseries. The scenes consist of allegorical representations of "Hearing" and "Smell" by Charles-Nicolas Dodin. Dodin copied engravings by Gabriel Huquier after paintings by François Boucher (1703–1770) and rendered them in a flat manner and in a palette evoking the enamel colors of Canton. This pair of vases may be the vases "a têtes d'elephants roses et verds chinois" that the marquise de Pompadour acquired in 1762.[16] They are very much in the taste of the marquise, who loved the most extravagant forms and elaborate novel decorations. She had a predilection for chinoiseries and ordered two fancy garnitures decorated by Dodin. Owning a pair of vases like these in the eighteenth century would have denoted sophisticated tastes and deep pockets.[17] They are a good example of how sensibilities change, and how some objects deemed elegant and graceful at one time could be viewed as "ridiculous and slightly vulgar" in another time. Such were the words with which renowned British art historian, Sir Kenneth Clark, described one such pair of vases in a televised broadcast on "What is good taste" in 1958.[18]

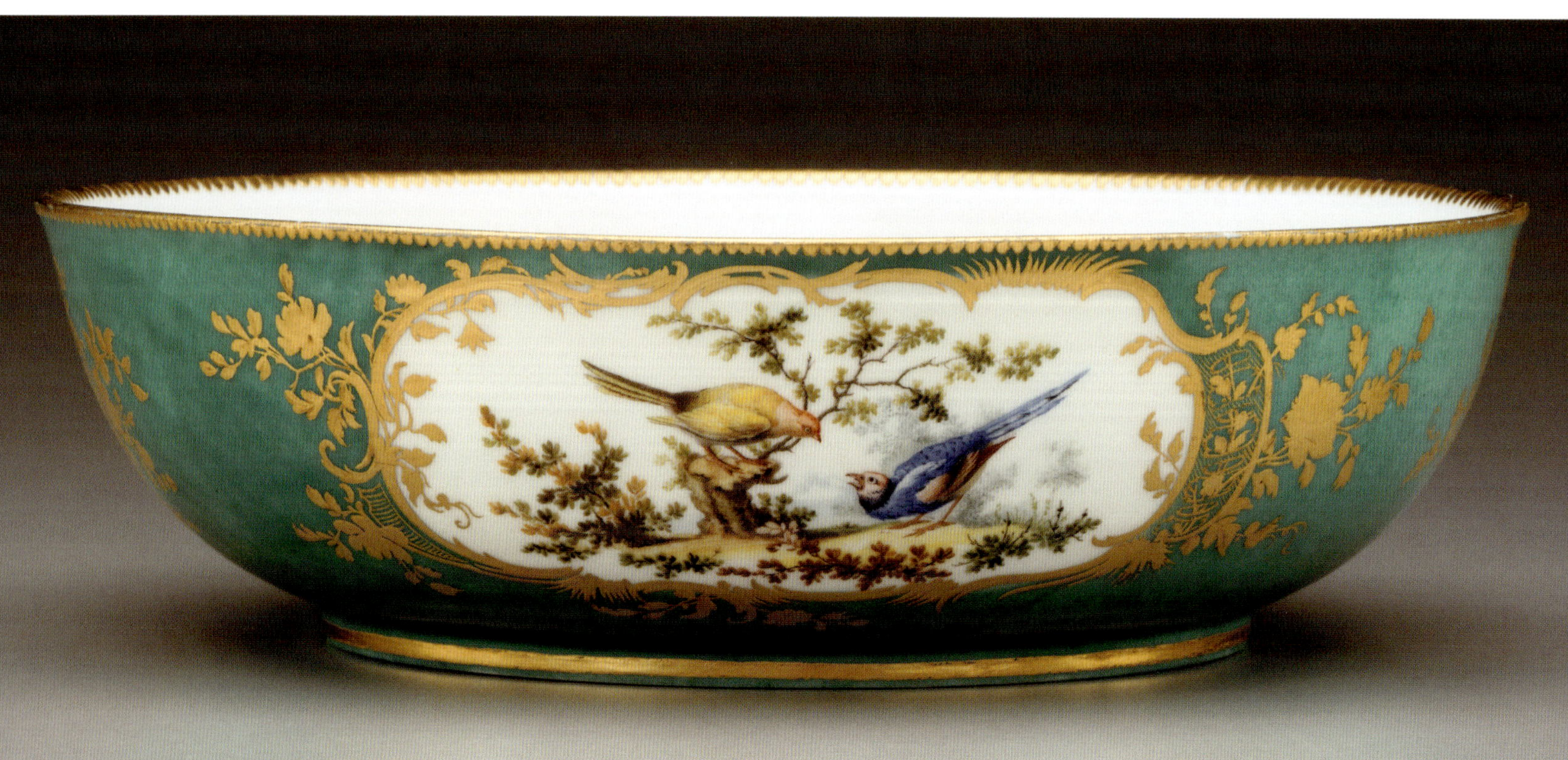

Fig. 10 (cat. 8): Green fruit bowl from the service for the King of Denmark, 1756–7

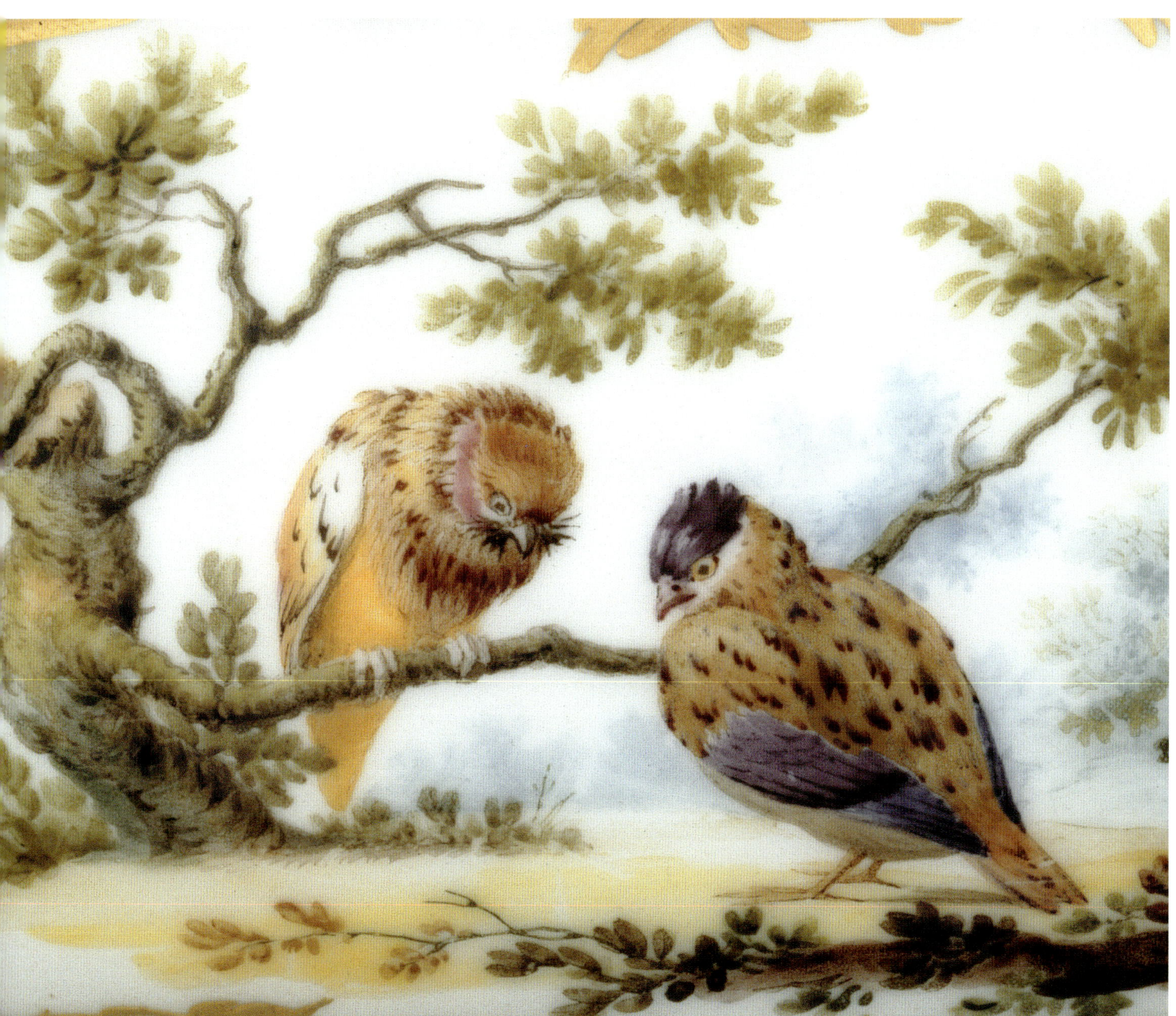

Detail of fig. 10, painting of birds

Novelties from Sèvres soon proved to be an eloquent way of illustrating the largesse of French kings, who would give French luxury products as diplomatic gifts. The first beneficiary of a complete Sèvres dinner service was King Frederick V of Denmark (reg. 1746–65), who in 1758 received a green ground service decorated with figures, flowers, and birds. The hue of this green color was one of the novelties of that year and thus deemed appropriate for a royal gift of such proportion.[19] The service was a thank-you present to the Danish king for a great stallion he had sent Louis XV the year before.[20] The bowls (*jattes*) from this service were intended for the display of fruits and/or flowers during the dessert course (fig. 10). Lazare Duvaux, employed as intermediary to supply this impressive service, provided a set of mirror plates as supports for these bowls.[21] The intricacy of the gilded cartouche frames and the careful depiction of birds on each reserve would have been lost without the reflection of these areas that the mirrors afforded the diners.

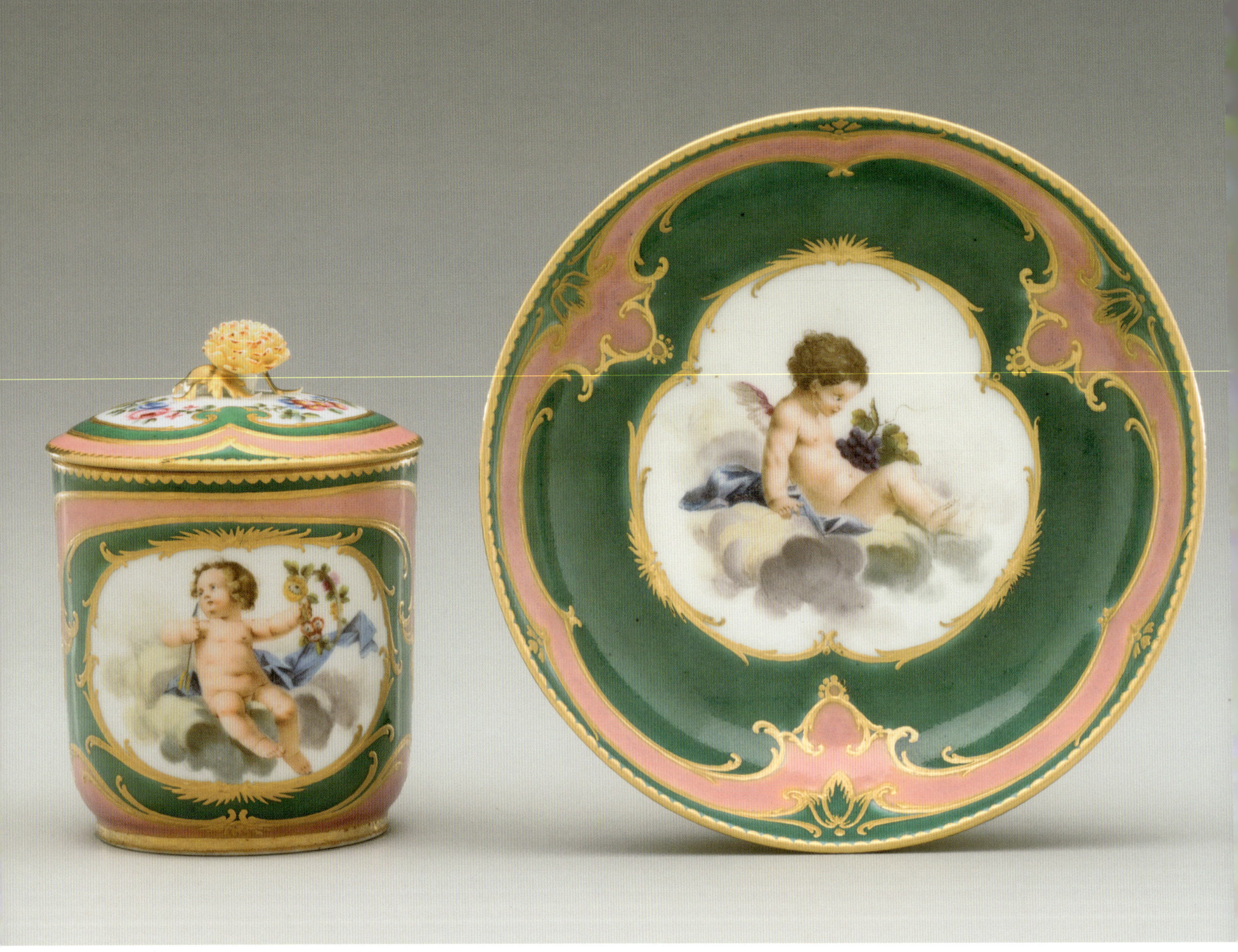

Fig. 11 (cat. 10): Pink and green cup and saucer with cherub painting, 1759–60

By 1758 the factory had begun to produce wares combining green (*vert*) and dark blue (*bleu lapis*) grounds. From 1759 to 1761 several pieces combining green with pink (*rose*) were created, like this cup and saucer (fig. 11). The short-term production of some of these decorations gives us a sense of how quickly fashions changed and how fast Sèvres had to come up with new shapes and styles to maintain itself at the cutting edge of design and fashion. The covered cup (*gobelet couvert*) was meant for tea and normally would have been part of a *déjeuner*, or tea set. Cupids and chubby children like the one on this cup are virtually synonymous with the painter François Boucher. Although difficult to identify with a particular source, they most likely were part of a core group of drawings and prints of children and cupids that the master supplied to the factory in the early years and which served as inspiration for many decorations and biscuit sculptures.[22] Madame de Pompadour had a fondness for the subject of cherubs and children dressed in costume and engaged in grown-up tasks, and thus they appear frequently on Sèvres and other fine and decorative pieces. She often organized soirées where children disguised as characters from the Commedia dell'Arte sang and danced, and she commissioned numerous pictorial works representing children from artists Carle Van Loo, Jean-Baptiste Greuze, François-Hubert Drouais, and François Boucher. Madame de Pompadour was one of Boucher's most fervent patrons and may have had some influence in getting him to work for Sèvres.

Soft paste and its glaze worked wonderfully with alkaline colors and gilding, but they were not so good for sculpture. Glazed and painted sculpture had been produced at Vincennes since the late 1740s, but the final product could not match the quality of similar Meissen wares. The sculpture in soft paste was clumsy, with the details blurred by the viscous, pooling glaze. In 1749 the Sèvres art director Jean-Jacques Bachelier (1724–1806) proposed transforming this shortcoming into a virtue by simply issuing finished statues in their biscuit state, that is, fired but not glazed. The surface of the unglazed porcelain was polished with a sandstone abrasive to produce a soft, matte appearance, much like the natural beauty of white marble sculpture. The biscuit group of the three Graces carrying Cupid was designed by François Boucher and translated into a three-dimensional model by factory sculptor Louis-Simon Boizot (1743–1809) around 1769 (fig. 12). The group was then included in the table decorations to accompany the exceptional service made for Catherine II of Russia (reg. 1762–96) in 1778–9. The Bather in fig. 13 is based on a model by Rococo period sculptor Étienne-Maurice Falconet (1716–91) and exemplifies the type of classical figures produced in the 1770s.

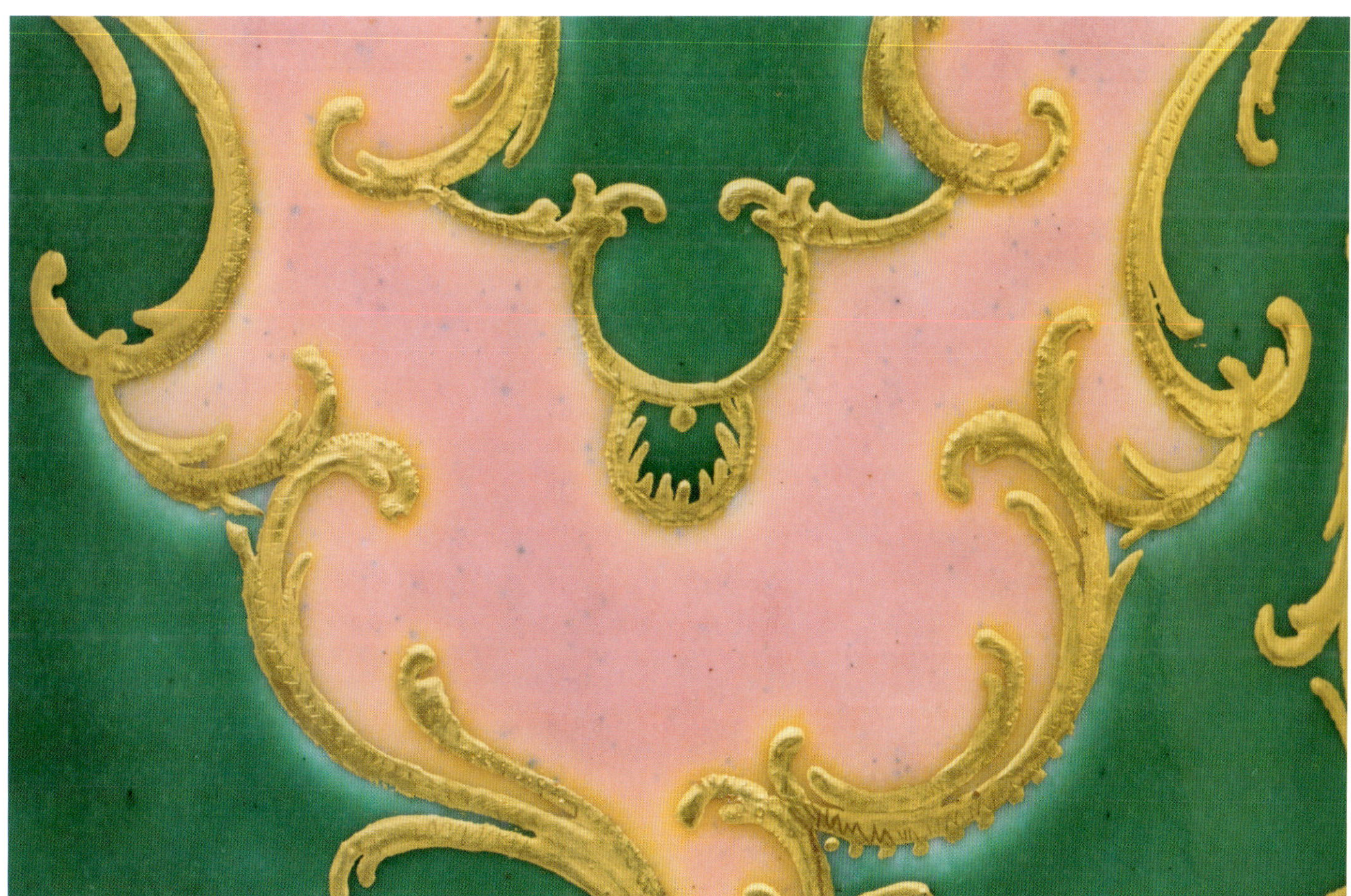

Detail of fig. 11, pink and green ground colors

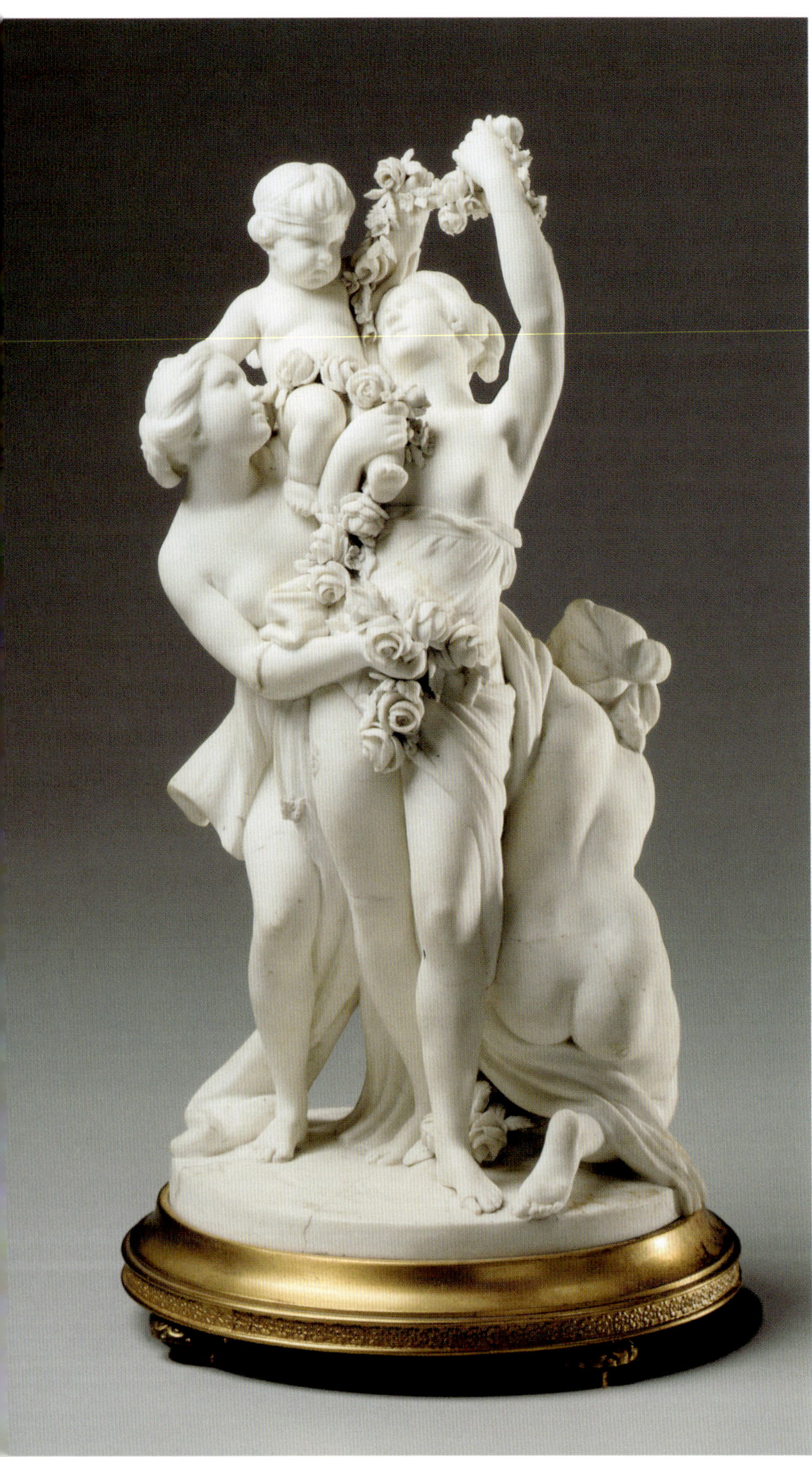

Fig. 12: "Three Graces Carrying Cupid" biscuit group, ca. 1769

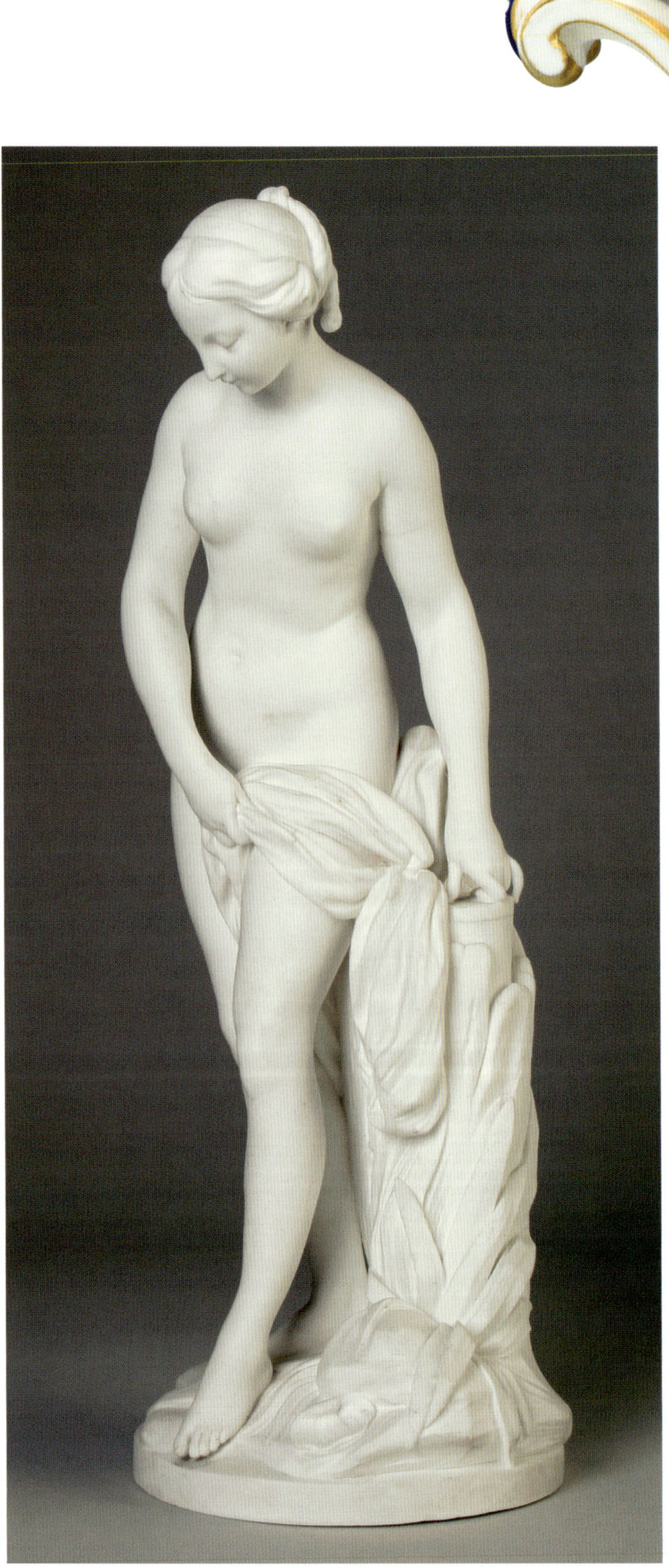

Fig. 13 (cat. 84): Biscuit figure of a bather, ca. 1770

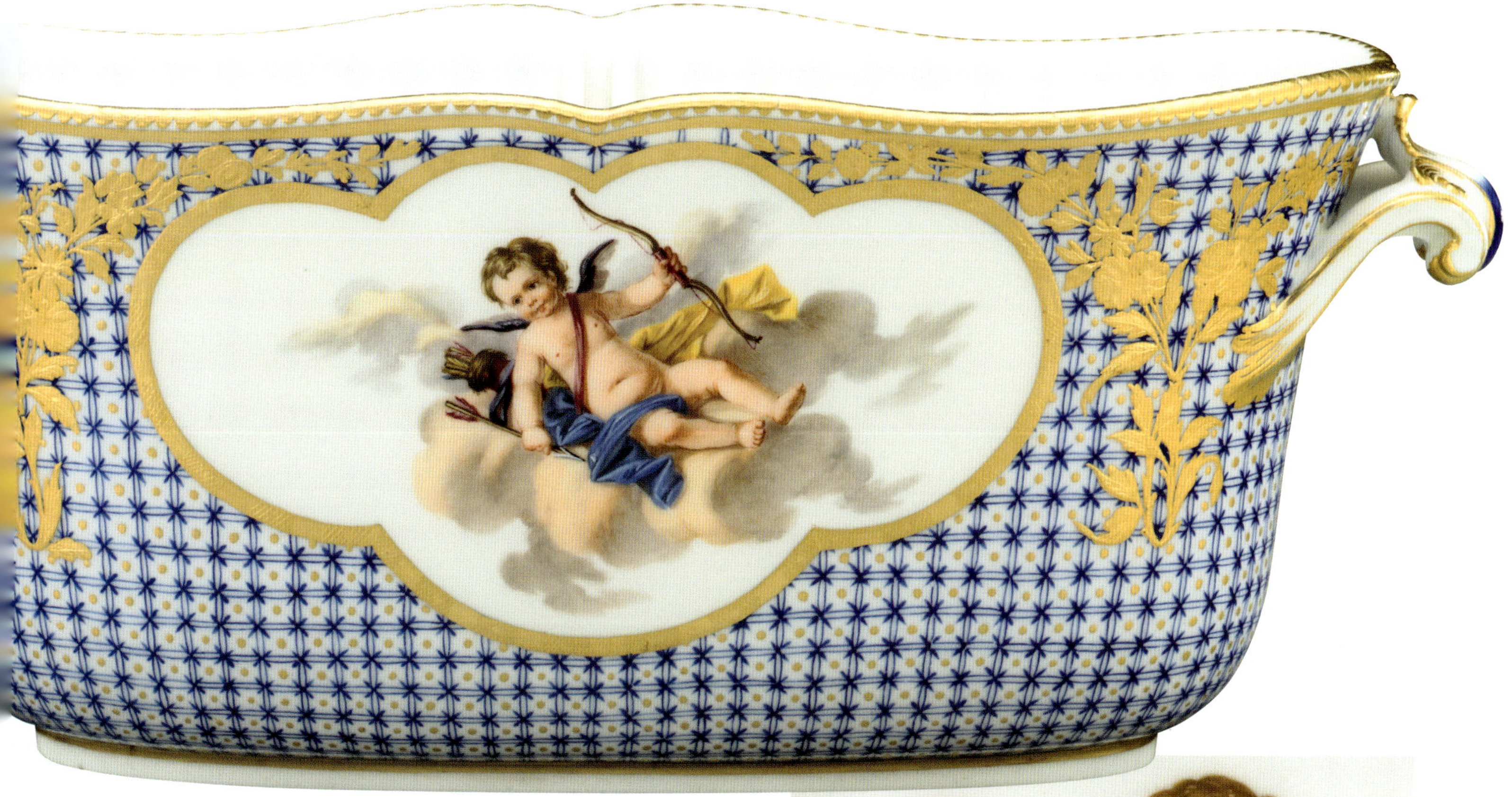

Fig. 14 (cat. 7): Bottle cooler from a service for Louis XV, ca. 1768

Although figural decoration was not as prevalent as fakes have led us to believe, King Louis XV ordered a service decorated with cherubs and trophies to boast his factory's exclusive privilege. This oval liquor cooler sports a lavish Chantilly-like trellis pattern ground (*mosaïque*) in blue and gold, with shaped reserves containing polychrome putti and trophies separated by looped, gilt flower garlands (fig. 14). The cooler forms part of a set of wares sold by the *marchand-mercier* Madame Lair in the course of 1768–9. These pieces seem to complement a group of plates sold to the king in 1759. The emblematic images of love may allude to the forging of the relationship between King Louis XV and Madame du Barry, who would become the king's official mistress in 1769.[23] The small service is perhaps the most private of services ever delivered to the king.[24] Some years later, in 1791, Louis XVI purchased a supplement to this service during the time the royal family was imprisoned at the Tuileries Palace.[25] The popularity of this subject at this time cannot be underestimated. The use of children to enact adult activities and stand as personifications of virtues, arts, or other values not necessarily inherent to childhood was a way of making light of some otherwise serious subjects, like love in this case. In the course of the year December 1767 to December 1768, the king ordered several ceramic figures of this subject, some likely for table decorations, and others perhaps as Christmas gifts.[26]

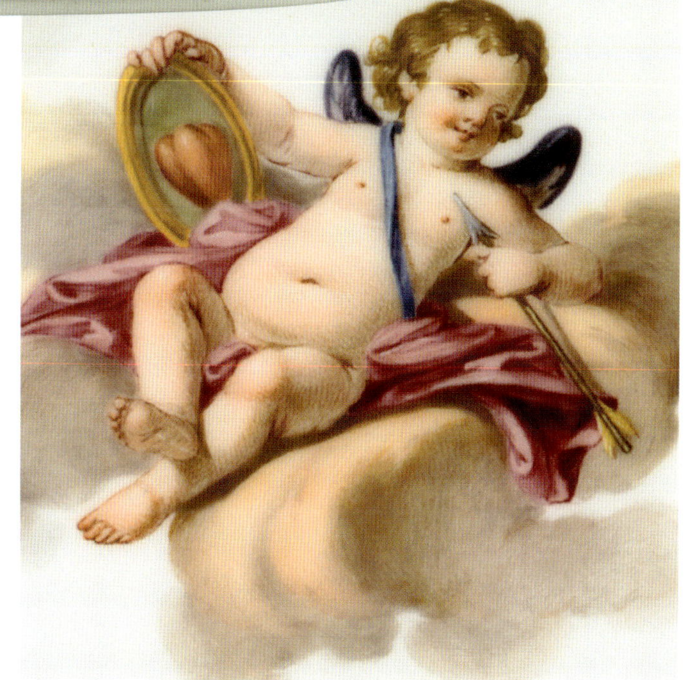

Detail of fig. 14 (reverse), cherub painting

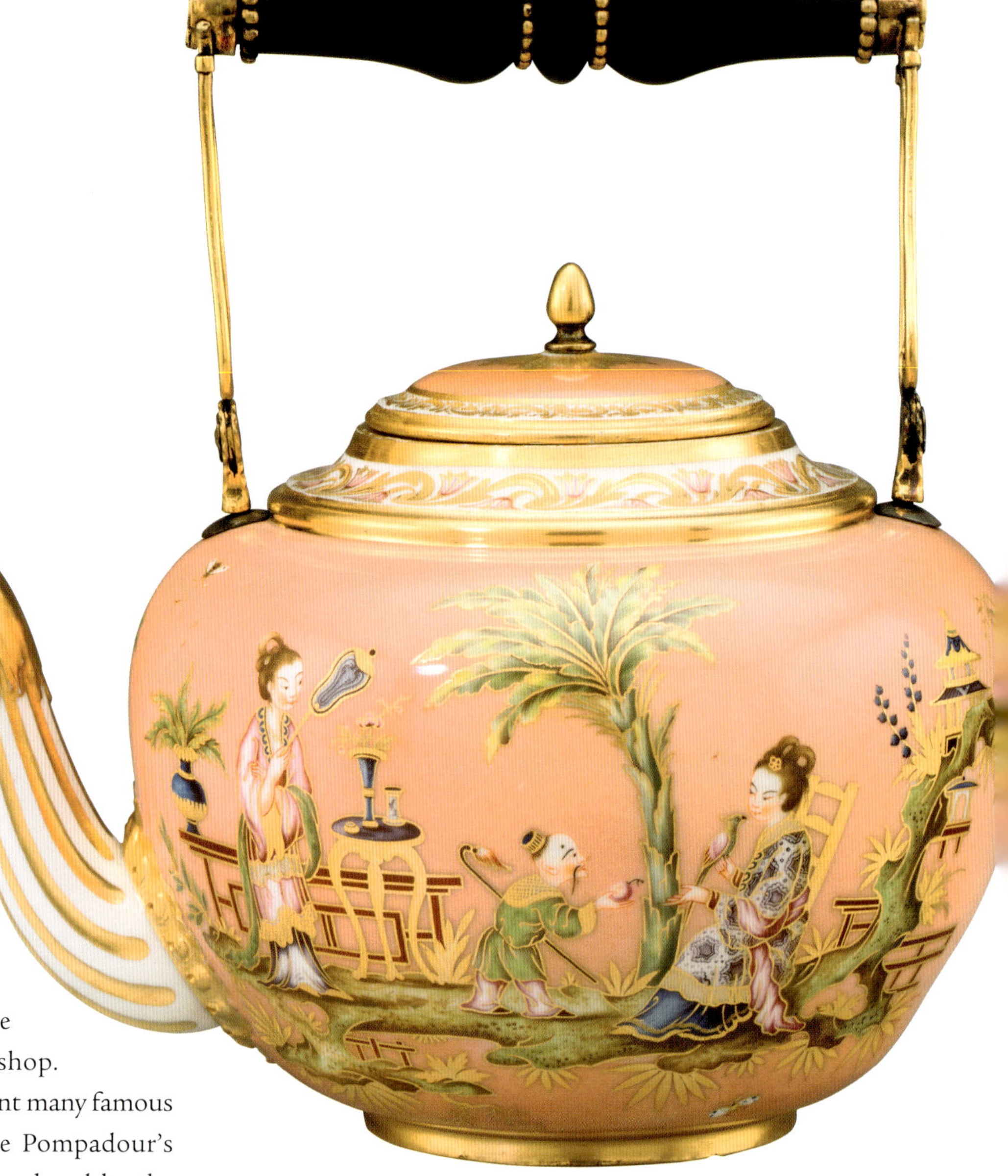

Fig. 15 (cat. 11): Tea kettle with chinoiserie painting, ca. 1778

The mid-1770s were difficult years for the factory. The proclamation of Louis XV's grandson as King Louis XVI (reg. 1774–92) in 1774 coincided with a period of transition and slight decline. After the departure of Étienne-Maurice Falconet as head of the sculpture workshop in 1765, the long-time director of painting, Jean-Jacques Bachelier, became involved with modeling and making forms. In 1773, at a time when a revamping of the repertoire of shapes was very much needed, Louis-Simon Boizot became the new director of the sculpture workshop. Boizot was gifted and would go on to invent many famous designs. In that same year, Madame de Pompadour's brother, the marquis de Marigny, was replaced by the comte d'Angiviller (1730–1810) as *superintendent des bâtiments* and, in such capacity, as administrator of Sèvres and other royal factories. On the heels of the discovery of kaolin in France, Sèvres felt the pressure and competition of other Parisian outposts that were striving to put out a simple, less expensive, yet attractive array of porcelains in the market. These small factories constantly questioned and circumvented the exclusive privilege Sèvres held in the use of gold and figural decoration. Many of them successfully sought the patronage of other members of the royal family as a manner of protecting their production against the all-powerful Sèvres manufactory.

The introduction of hard-paste porcelain in the early 1770s brought about the greatest change in the factory's organization since its establishment. A whole series of workshops were created, new kilns were built, and a completely new range of colors was developed. The excitement brought about by the production of hard paste made possible pieces like this tea kettle, or *bouillotte*, which was unthinkable in soft paste (fig. 15). The new hard paste, which could withstand very hot temperatures and perhaps even direct contact with a flame, made porcelain tea kettles possible. How were the contents heated? According to contemporary accounts these may have been accompanied by a small heating device from which they often became separated.[27] The inventory of the Nissim de Camondo residence (now a

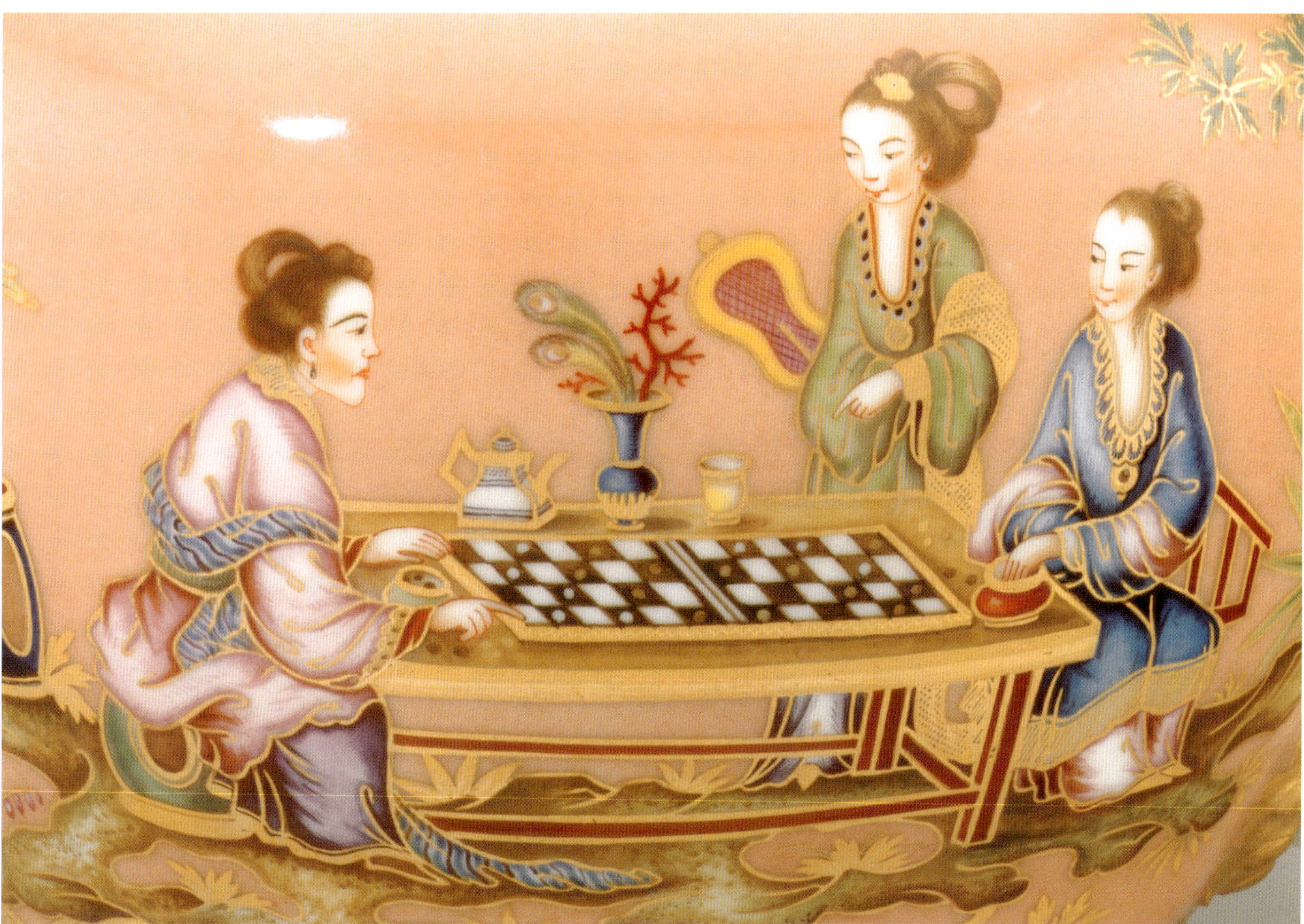

Detail of fig. 15 (reverse), chinese ladies playing checkers

museum) in Paris mentions a Meissen example with its heater.[28] *Bouillottes* were not common in the eighteenth century and are rare in porcelain. The relatively few examples produced at Sèvres were all expensively decorated. *Bouillottes* were produced in the course of roughly a decade, from 1774 to 1783. Of the ten known examples, four are decorated with chinoiserie figures, including this one.[29] The Sèvres records reveal that this tea kettle was one of three sold in the course of 1778–9. Madame Adélaïde of France (1749–1803), daughter of King Louis XV, purchased one in 1778 for 360 livres, and the king and queen each purchased one in 1779, at 312 and 288 livres, respectively.[30] The registers of painters (over time) also mentioned two decorated in November 1778—one in "brune" (light brown, perhaps the example now at the Musée National de Céramique at Sèvres), and the other one in "couleur de Bellevue,"[31] which alludes almost certainly to the present example. Thus this piece must have been the one bought by Madame Adélaïde. Madame Adélaïde lived with her unmarried sisters at Bellevue, the château previously owned by Madame de Pompadour, which they bought after inheriting a great sum from their mother in 1768. Later, when tensions between Marie Antoinette and Madame Adélaïde were high, King Louis XVI ordered his aunt to retire to Bellevue. Adélaïde was an important collector who may even have followed Madame de Pompadour's example in her support of the decorative arts, particularly with commissions for Bellevue.[32] The Chinese subject befitted the decorations commissioned by Madame de Pompadour for the château which included a Chinese boudoir and two *paysages chinois* for the drawing room. Despite its elaborate decoration, this teapot nevertheless was not intended for show but for personal use in an important household, where the private rooms were distinct from the public quarters, and where one could retire to enjoy a more private existence.

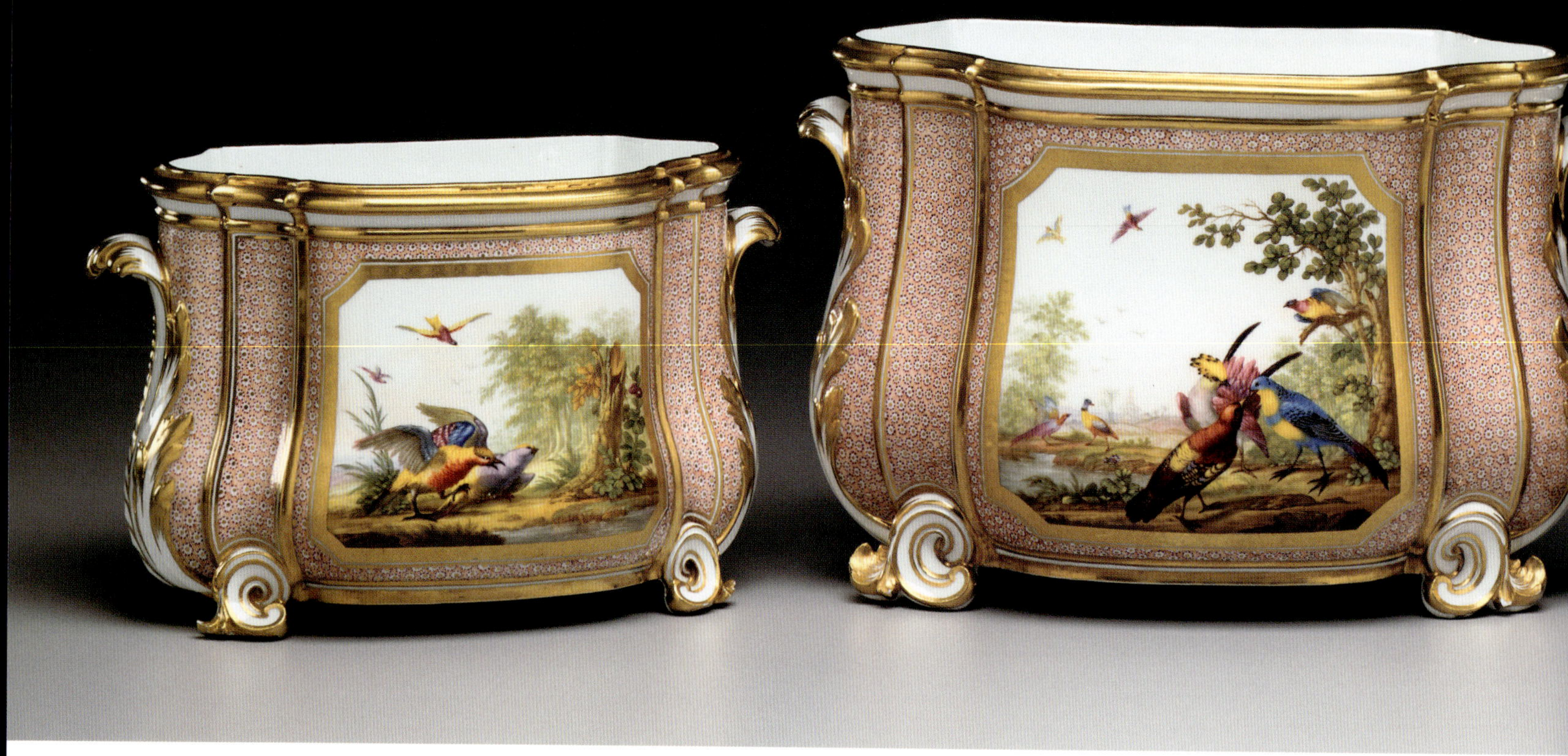

ABOVE: **Fig. 16 (cat. 19): Garniture of three vases (*cuvettes "Courteille"*), 1782**

BELOW: **Detail of fig. 16, side**

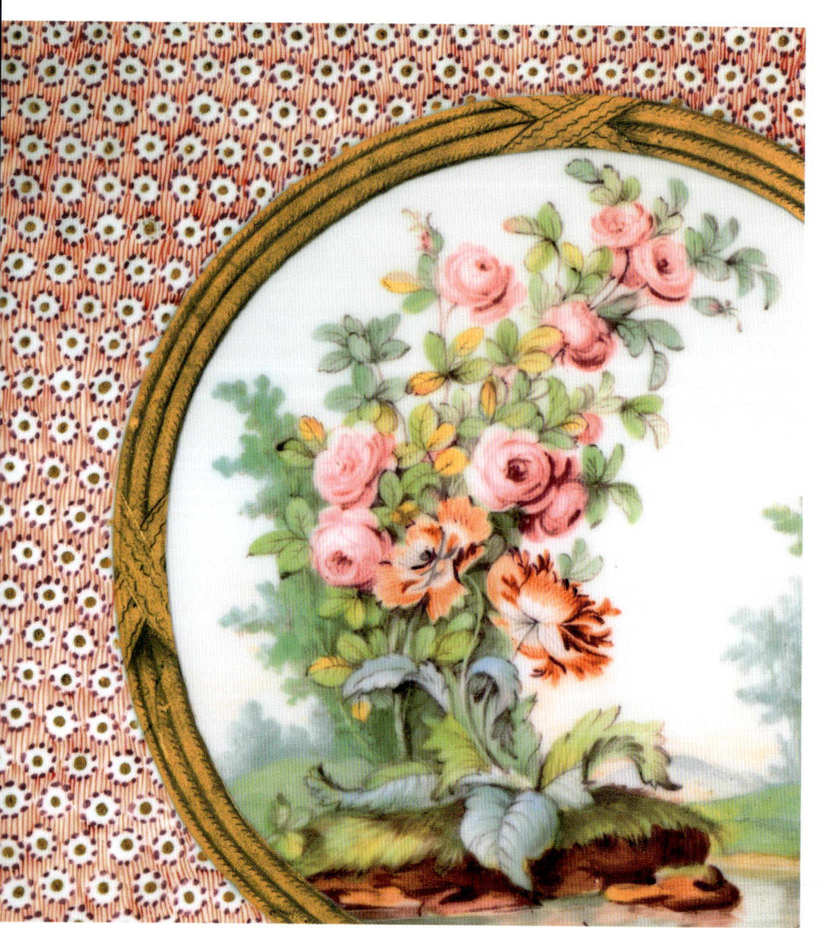

The *cuvettes "Courteille,"* also of hard-paste porcelain, were designed to contain flowers (fig. 16). The detailed bird paintings on the fronts by Philippe Castel (active 1772–97) and the flowers on the back, perhaps suggest that they were meant to be placed on a mantelpiece or before a mirror. The backgrounds, composed of a painted field of thin, soft red stripes—high-firing colors developed for the new hard-paste kilns—is interrupted by an *oeil-de-perdrix* pattern consisting of dotted red circles centered by a gold dot. These were painted by Geneviève Taillandier (active 1774–98), wife of the Sèvres painter Vincent Taillandier, for whom this pattern was named. This patterned ground in the same tonalities can also be found on a pair of vases acquired by Louis XVI at the annual Sèvres exhibition at Versailles in 1780, and which are now on view at the king's private apartments at Versailles.[33] The shape of the garniture is named after the marquis de Courteille, secretary of finances under King Louis XV and one of Sèvres' first administrators (1751–67). Although the first set of these vases was presented to its namesake in 1751, this form (like others at Sèvres) was used until the end of the eighteenth century and adapted to the prevailing neo-classical style by means of the painted decoration.

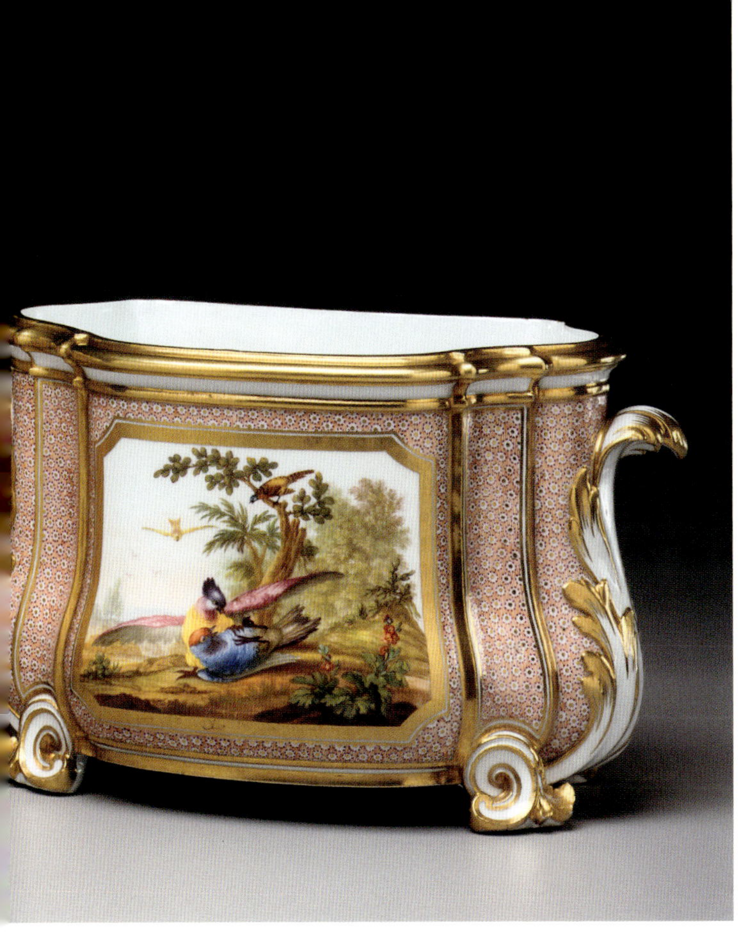

The international prestige of Sèvres, promoted by the court via diplomatic gifts, extended rapidly beyond France's borders. Princes, ambassadors, and aristocrats from Europe and beyond returned to their homelands laden with Sèvres. Hillwood's pair of white and gold tureens and platters decorated with flowers and pastoral trophies are good examples of the kind of pieces earmarked for diplomatic presentation (figs. 17, 18). Other tureens closely related to this

Detail of fig. 16, bird painting on largest vase

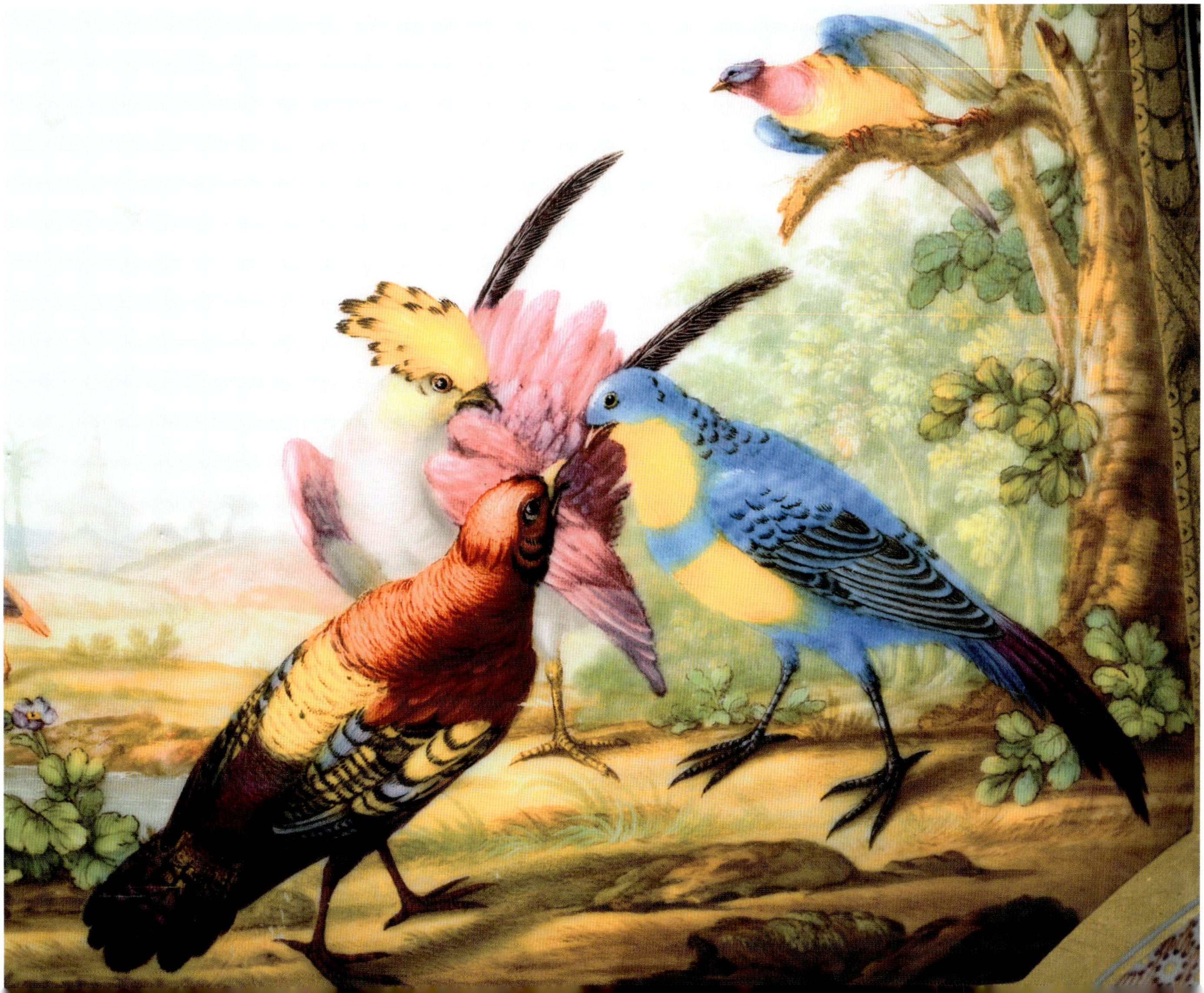

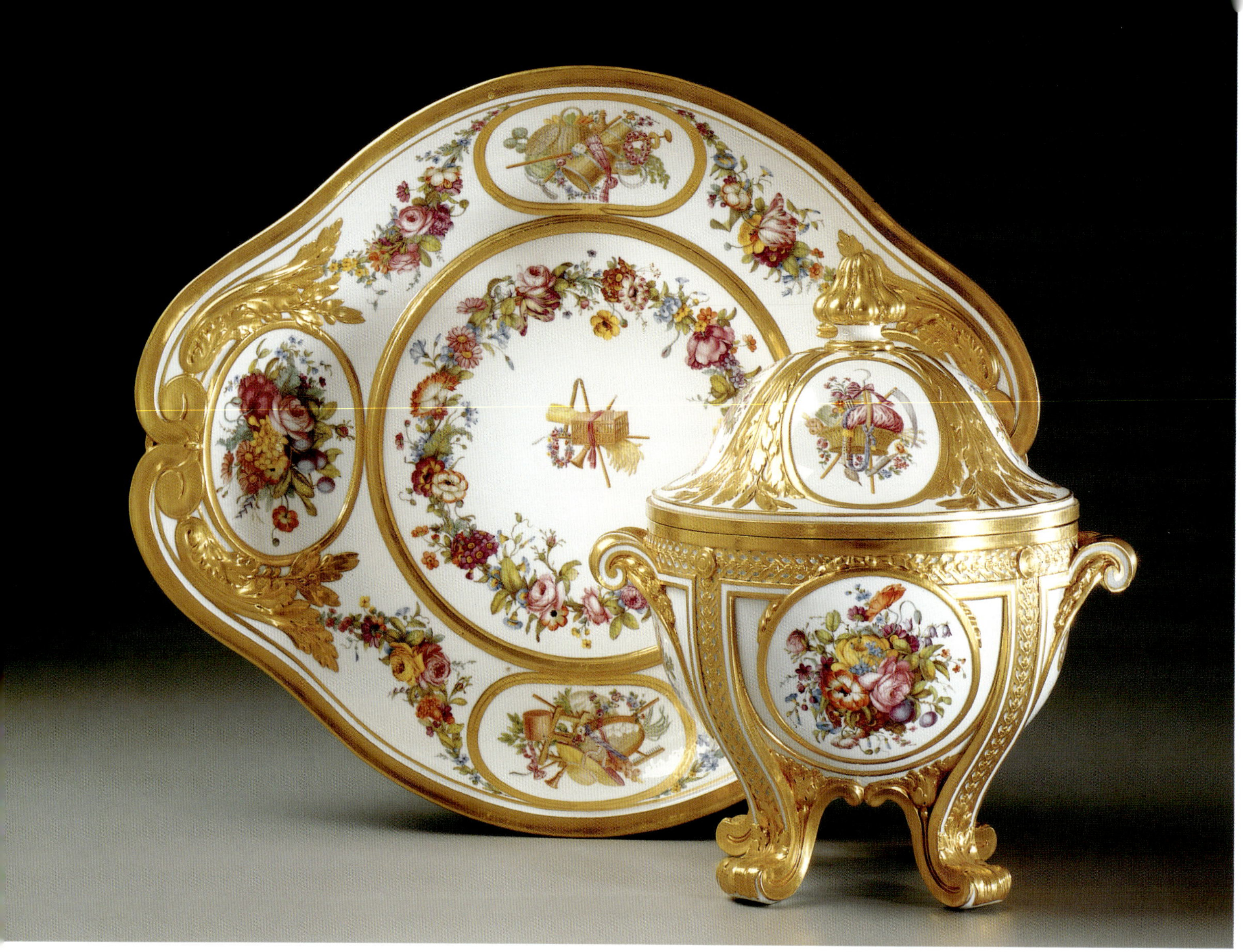

Fig. 17 (cat. 20): Tureen and platter (one set of a pair), ca. 1783

pair were produced as single items and given as important diplomatic gifts. In 1777 two oval tureens (*terrines*) and two soup tureens were given to Joseph II, Regent of the Holy Roman Empire, who traveled to Paris under the clandestine name of Count Falkenstein. This pair has feet and handles decorated with sprigs of wheat in relief in gold. Weeks later, according to Sèvres records, Louis XVI bought four tureens of similar design.[34] In 1784 two tureens almost identical to the Falkenstein tureens were presented to Gustav III of Sweden (one of them now being at the Metropolitan Museum of Art in New York). These tureens differ somewhat in that they are decorated with gold leaves in relief rather than with wheat sprigs. Furthermore, although it has not been identified in the Sèvres sale records, a plaster cast, named "pot à oglio à olives," exists in the factory archives.[35] The detailed floral decoration and clusters of triumphs are first rate, as can be observed in the magnified detail of fig. 17.

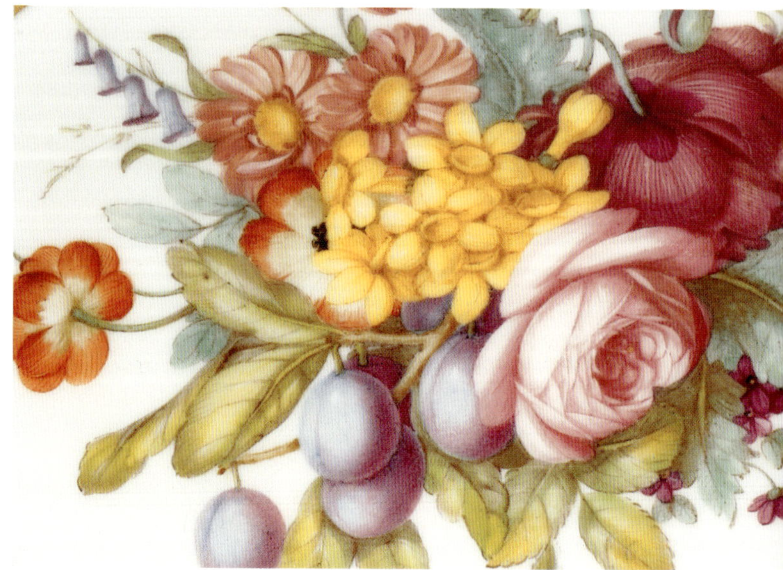

Detail of fig. 17, floral painting on platter

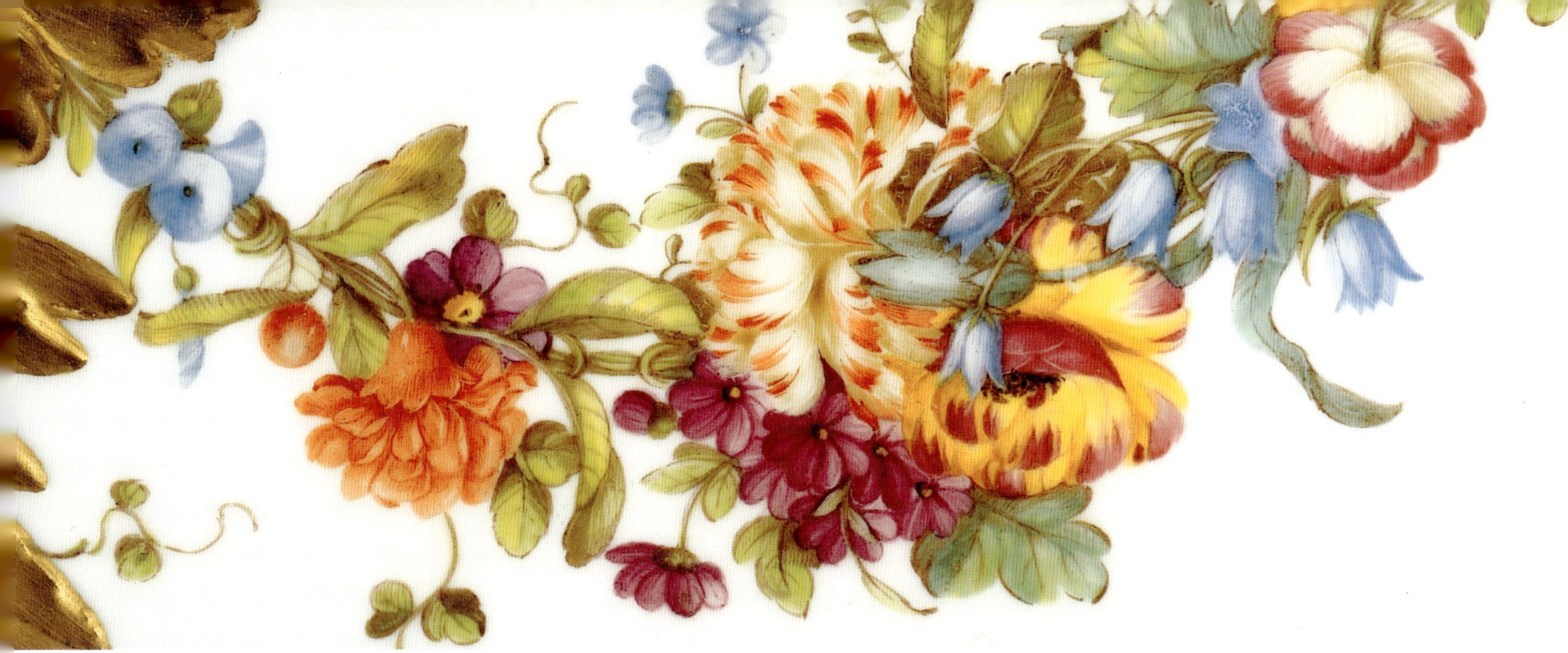

Detail of fig. 18, floral painting on platter

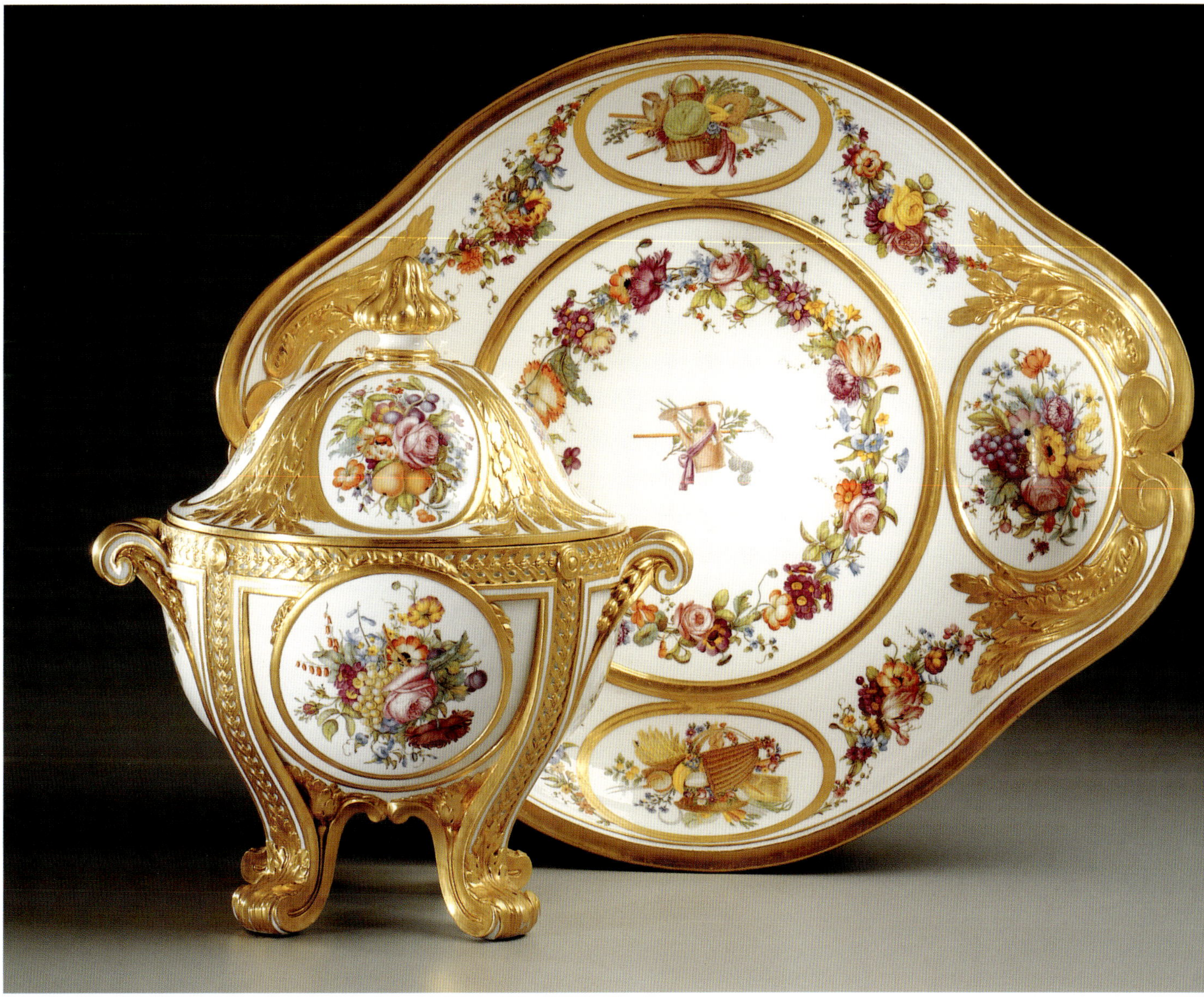

Fig. 18: Tureen and platter (second set of a pair), ca. 1783

FRANKLIN

On several occasions, Sèvres produced pieces to highlight historical events. To honor the signing of the treaties of Amity, Commerce, and Alliance between France and the United States in 1778, several cups and saucers were issued in 1779 featuring the portrait of Benjamin Franklin (1706–1790), the American envoy to Versailles during the American War of Independence (fig. 19). An instrumental figure in securing France's recognition of the American Revolutionary War, Franklin became popularly regarded as an apostle of liberty and his likeness appeared in all kinds of media. Mobbed wherever he went in Paris, Franklin wrote to his daughter in June 1779 that all these likenesses "have made your father's face as well known as the moon.... From the number of dolls now made of him he may be truly said to be *i-doll-ized* in this country."[36] The creative Sèvres modeler Jean-Claude Duplessis can be credited with the invention of the *gobelet "litron."* The simplest, yet most eternal of all Sèvres designs, the *gobelet litron* comprises a simple cylinder cup where the ornament has been reduced to the handle.

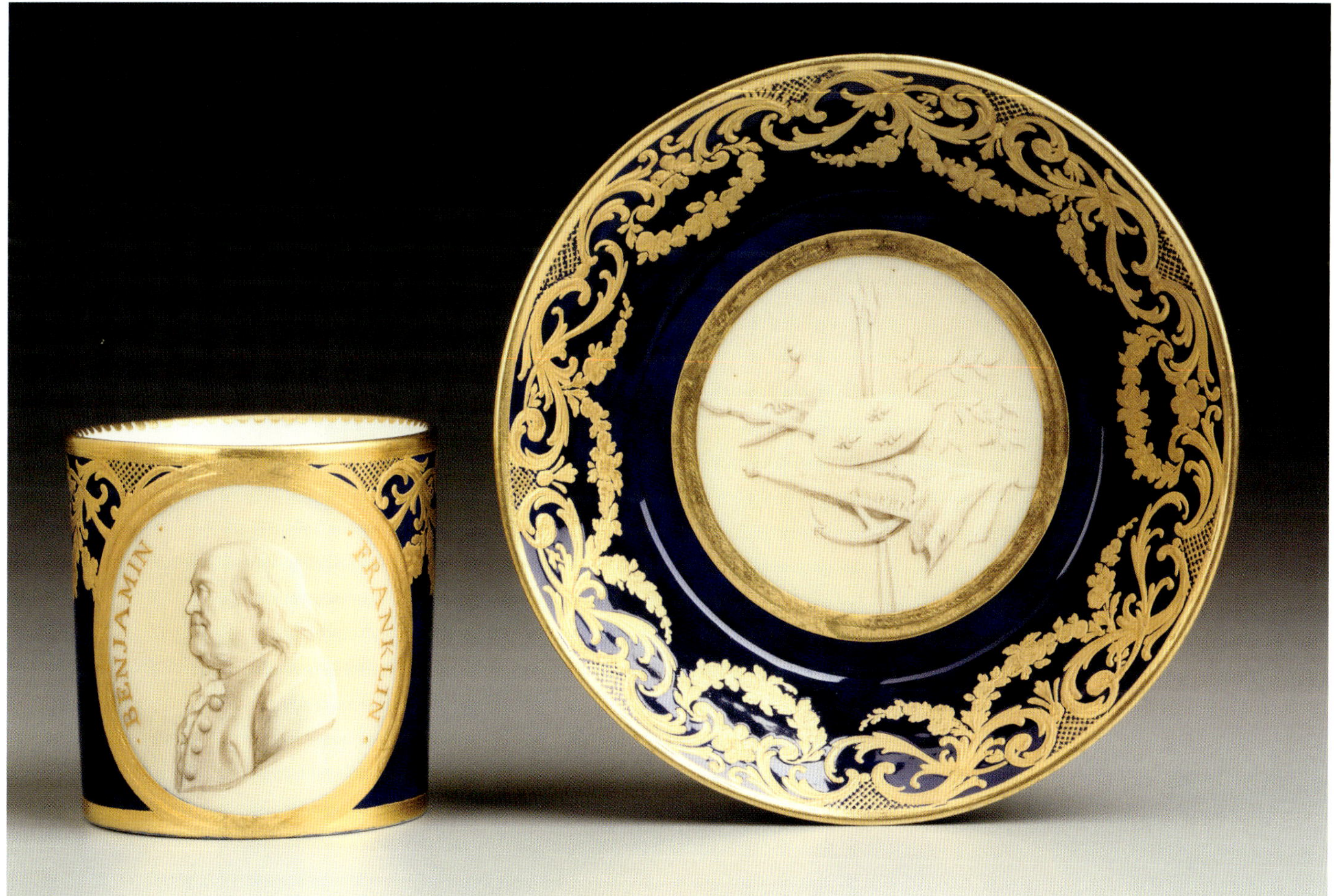

Fig. 19 (cat. 16): Commemorative cup and saucer with portrait of Benjamin Franklin, ca. 1779

OPPOSITE: **Detail of fig. 19, gilding on cup**

Despite the abundance of portraits appearing on fake Sèvres pieces, portraiture was not that common in the eighteenth century. The cup and saucer with the portrait of noted financier Nicolas de Beaujon (1718–1786) is a good example of the complexity involved in rendering light and depth with enamel colors (fig. 20). The bust-length portrait of Beaujon is surrounded by an elaborate frame in imitation of giltwood against a *bleu nouveau* ground. Echoing contemporary fashions in interior decoration and the prevailing fondness for contrasts of shiny and matte surfaces in gilt bronzes, goldwork, and gilt furniture, the artist at Sèvres achieved similar effects by contrasting burnished and unburnished areas of gilding. Nicolas de Beaujon was an immensely rich banker. In 1774 he acquired from the king

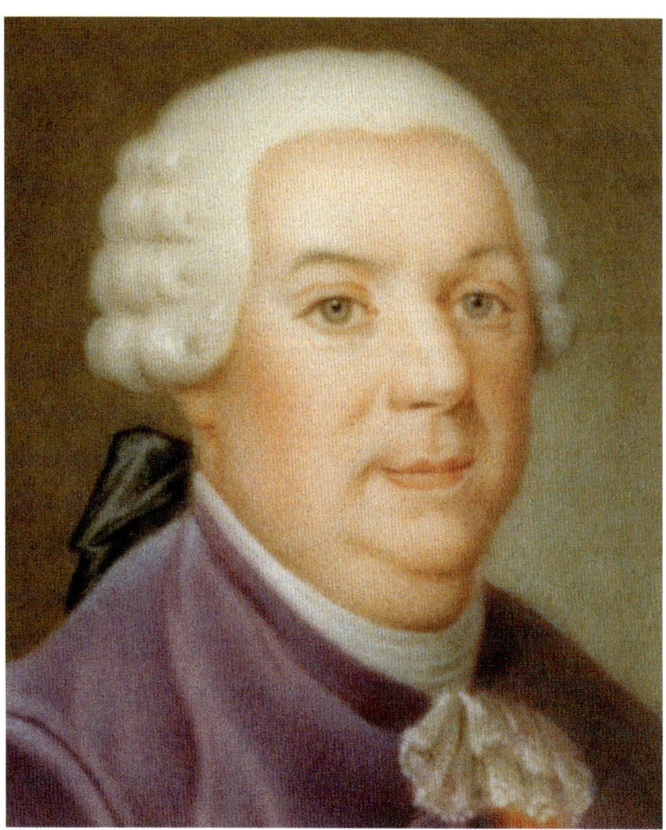

Detail of fig. 20, portrait painting

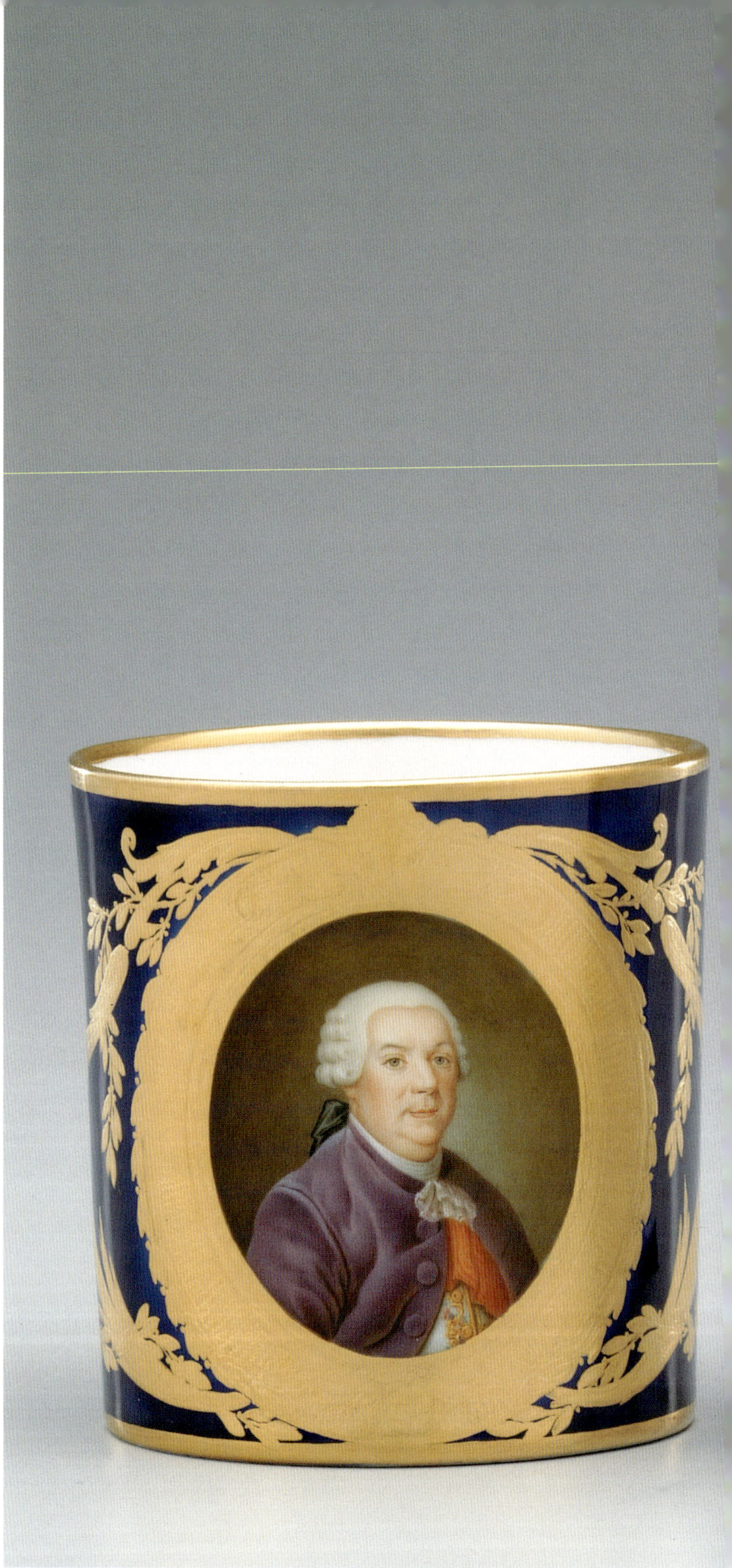

Fig. 20 (cat. 17): Cup and saucer with portrait and cipher of Nicolas de Beaujon, 1782

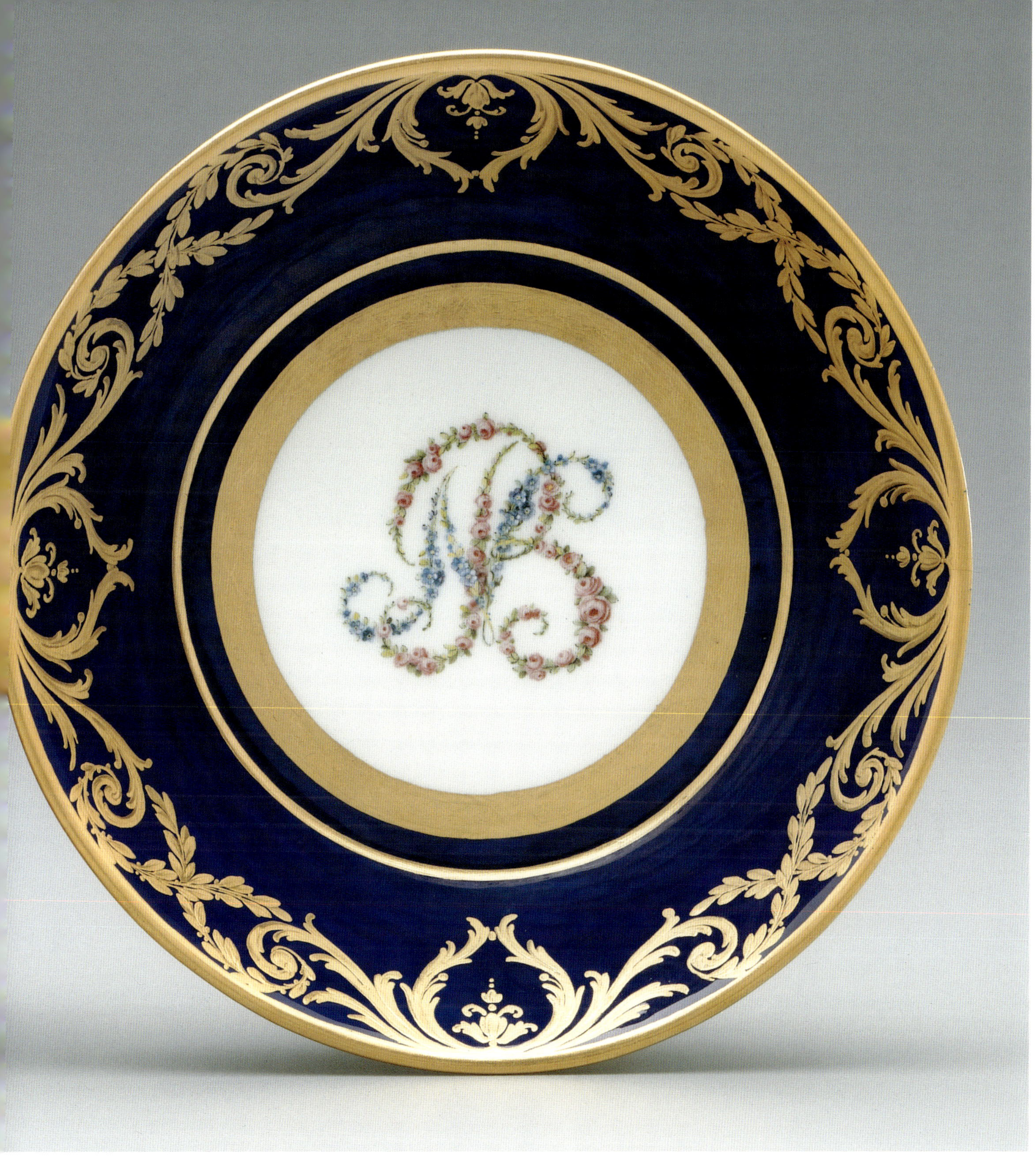

a prestigious residence in the Faubourg-Saint-Honoré. Built for the comte d'Evreux in 1718, it later became the Parisian residence of Madame de Pompadour and, in 1873, the Elysée Palace, residence of the president of the French Republic. Like many notable financiers, Beaujon was a client of Sèvres.[37] The floral initials *NB* on the saucer relate to a particular fashion of the time and reflect the interior decoration of Beaujon's residence. Beaujon employed the visionary architect Étienne-Louis Boullée (1728–1799) to design his home and the furniture within, including a furniture set comprising a commode and two cupboards painted with flowers intertwined with ribboned garlands.[38]

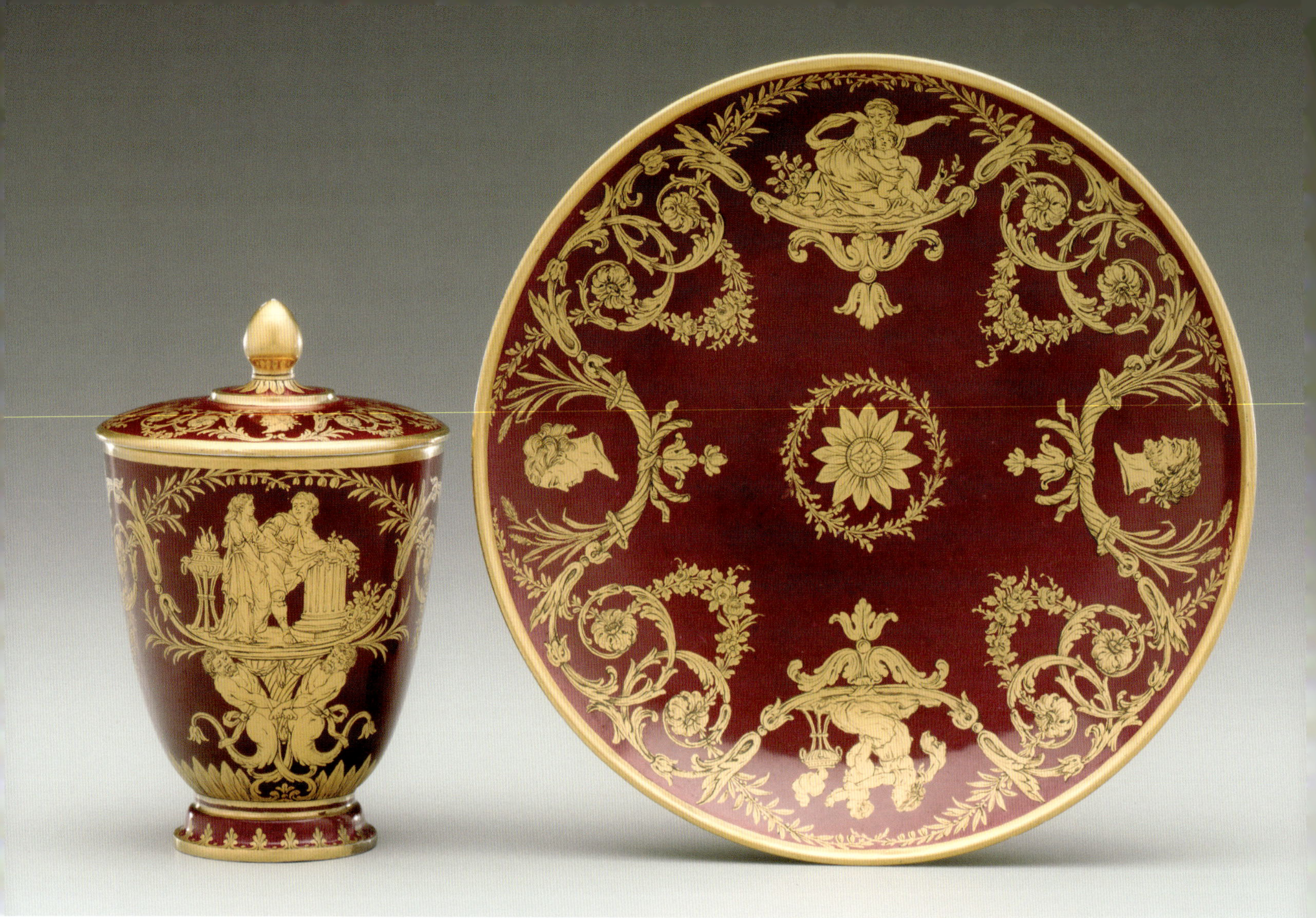

ABOVE: **Fig. 21 (cat. 18): Covered cup and saucer with gold figures in the "Etruscan" style, 1784**

BELOW: **Detail of fig. 21, "Etruscan" style figures on cup**

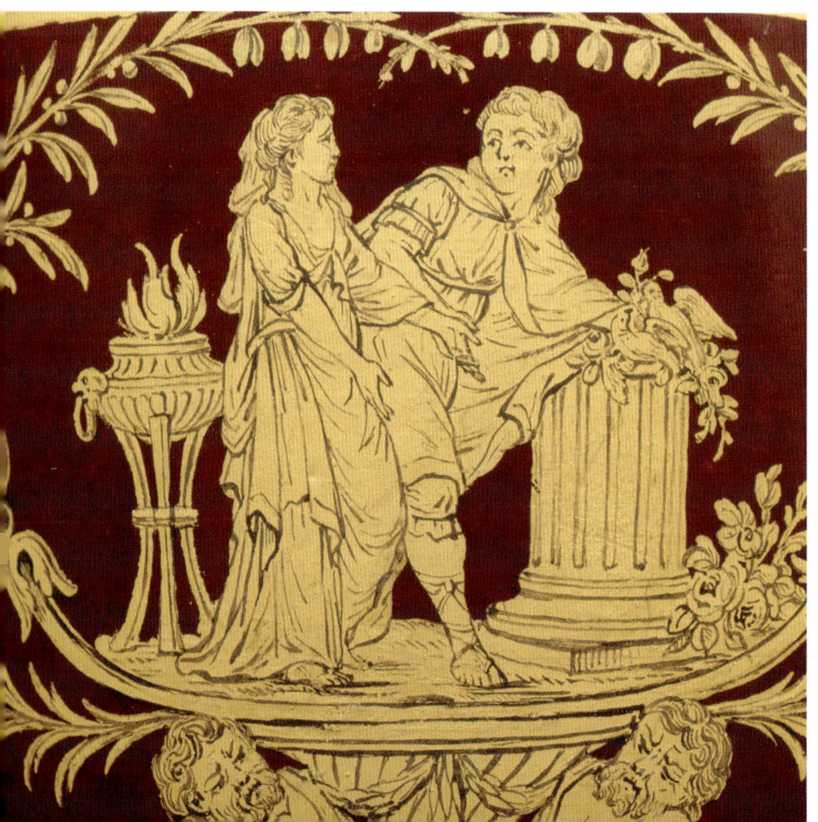

The decade of the 1780s was distinguished by its decidedly neoclassical style and its reliance on archeological pieces as sources. In the early 1780s, a particular type of neoclassical decoration emerged at Sèvres. Called "Etruscan," a vague allusion to the ancient pre-Roman civilization in Italy and Corsica, the style was characterized by matte-gold figures delineated with black enamel lines and silhouetted against a solid color ground. This complex manner of decoration embellishes the surface of the deep claret ground on this *gobelet de la toilette* (fig. 21). The arabesque and floral friezes with profiled heads are reminiscent of the work of Henri Salembier (1753–1820), a Parisian ornamental designer and engraver. The mythological scenes are executed after designs and engravings by the famous French artist Philippe-Louis Parizeau (1740–1801).[39] This type of decoration was used for the first time in the dressing table set presented in 1782 by Marie Antoinette to Maria Fedorovna (1759–1828),

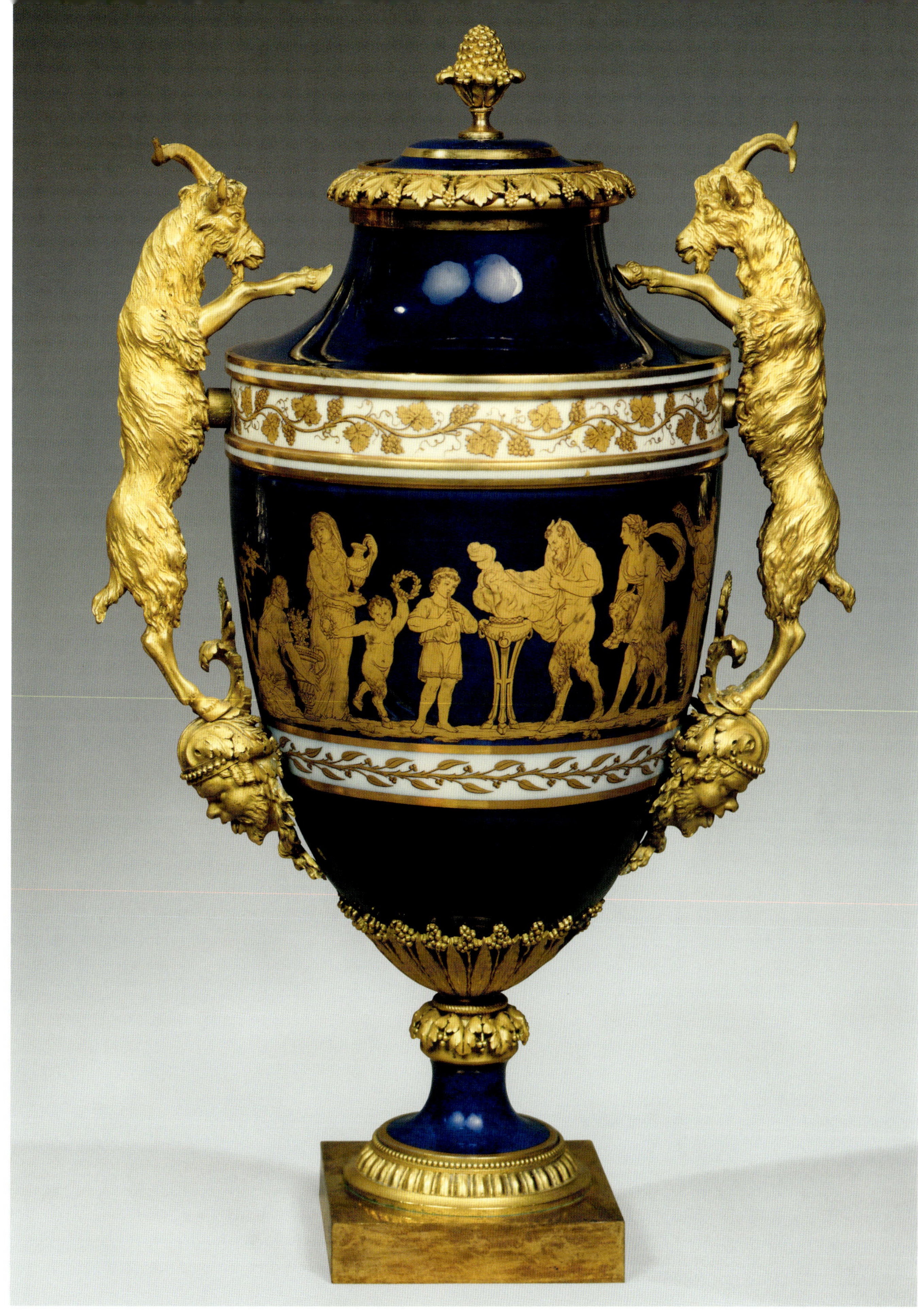

Fig. 22 (cat. 12): Covered vase (*vase "Boizot"*) with gilt bronze mounts of rampant rams, ca. 1784

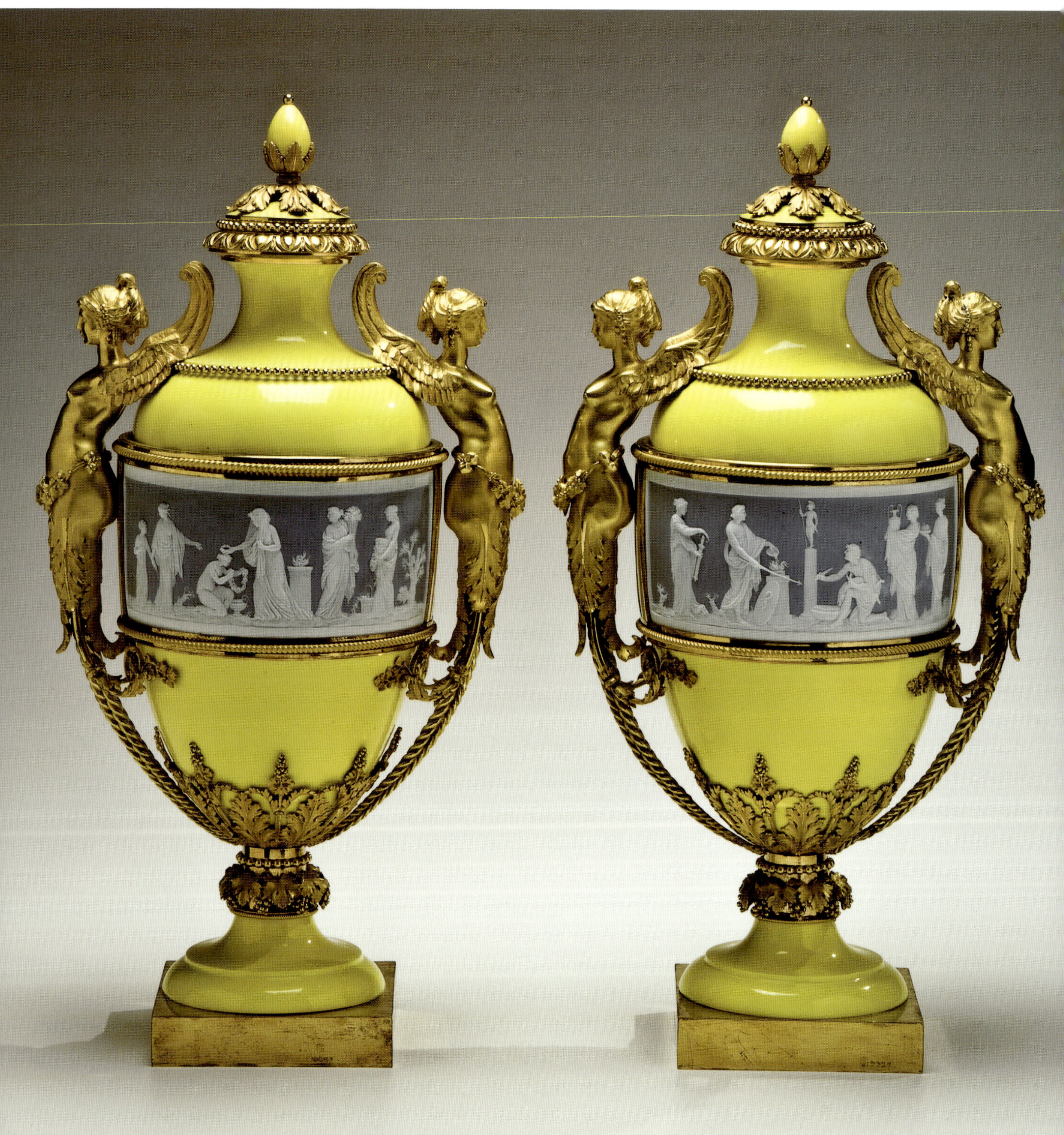

Fig. 23 (cat. 13): Pair of yellow vases (*vases "bas relief"*) for the comte d'Artois, ca. 1786

wife of Grand Duke Paul and future Tsarina of Russia, during their visit to Paris.[40] Pieces like these existed in a world of close and privileged circles. The ladies' process of dressing and primping, called the *toilette*, was a formal affair in well-to-do homes. It was customary for the lady of the house to receive selected visitors during the lengthy *toilette*, at which time she would have some tea or coffee or perhaps some broth—which, if she was lucky and discerning enough, would be served in a piece as impressive as this splendid example.

During the 1780s, the comte d'Angiviller kept the factory under tight supervision. Bachelier remained in charge of artistic matters and continued to devise models in his elaborate style. Boizot was more in tune with changing tastes and created many shapes in a pure neoclassical style. Although the *vase "Boizot"* (ca. 1784) is named after the head sculptor of the factory, its design owes more to master bronze caster Pierre-Philippe Thomire (1751–1843) than to anyone else (fig. 22). At the death of Jean-Claude Duplessis *fils* (ca. 1730–1783), who had been in charge of supplying bronze mounts, Boizot called upon Thomire to replace him. This collaboration yielded some spectacular sculptural pieces where the bronze work is not just an accessory but an integral part of the overall design. The monumental rampant rams, chiseled to the last detail by the brilliant gilt bronze maker, are as central to the design as is its ceramic body and its decoration. Another pair of vases of the same design, dated ca. 1782–4 and decorated with arabesques in polychrome colors, were delivered to King Louis XVI at Versailles and are now part of the British Royal Collection.[41]

The spectacular yellow ground vases with blue and white low-relief biscuit panels also display mounts which can be attributed to Thomire (fig. 23). Everything about these vases is special—from the exquisitely cast and chased bronze winged female term handles to the strikingly bright yellow color and the rare blue and white biscuit plaques in the style of Wedgwood. The vases were most likely the pair sold to Charles-Philippe (1757–1836), comte d'Artois, brother of Louis XVI, who would later become King Charles X (reg. 1824–30).[42] D'Artois was a *bon vivant* and a passionate collector. Like his dear companion in leisure pursuits, his sister-in-law Marie Antoinette, he relished collecting luxurious works of art of superb quality that reflected his eclectic taste, which ranged from classicism to the exotic with an interest in Turkey and Ottoman culture in particular. After the Revolution, the vases were removed from the residence of the comte d'Artois, the Palais du Temple, to the Luxembourg Palace. They reappeared a few years later inventoried with Empress Joséphine's furnishing at the Tuileries. They are both stamped with *TH* and a fleur-de-lis, an inventory mark for the Tuileries Palace during the reign of Louis XVIII (reg. 1814–24).

Despite the fact that few egg-shaped vases are mentioned in the Sèvres records, a few examples now reside in private collections. The egg-shaped vases in fig. 24 have several applied elements of decoration embellishing the plain oviform shape, including gilt floral swags terminating in female masks and angular handles. The ground color is *bleu foncé*. The most notable element is an oval medallion on each front enclosing a biscuit portrait of King Louis XVI and Marie Antoinette. The one of the king is framed with cockerels and birds on scrollwork, while the one of the queen is supported by cornucopias and scrolls—emblems alluding to the couple's royal stature. These vases correspond to pieces recorded in the archives as "vase oeuf garni." The medals are most likely the creation of Louis-Simon Boizot after official medals of the royal couple. The pair of vases relate to an earlier vase, "à medallion du roi," with a green ground and a biscuit medallion of Louis XV on its front at

OVERLEAF: **Fig. 24 (cat. 15): Pair of egg-shaped vases with biscuit medallions of King Louis XVI and Queen Marie Antoinette, ca. 1774**

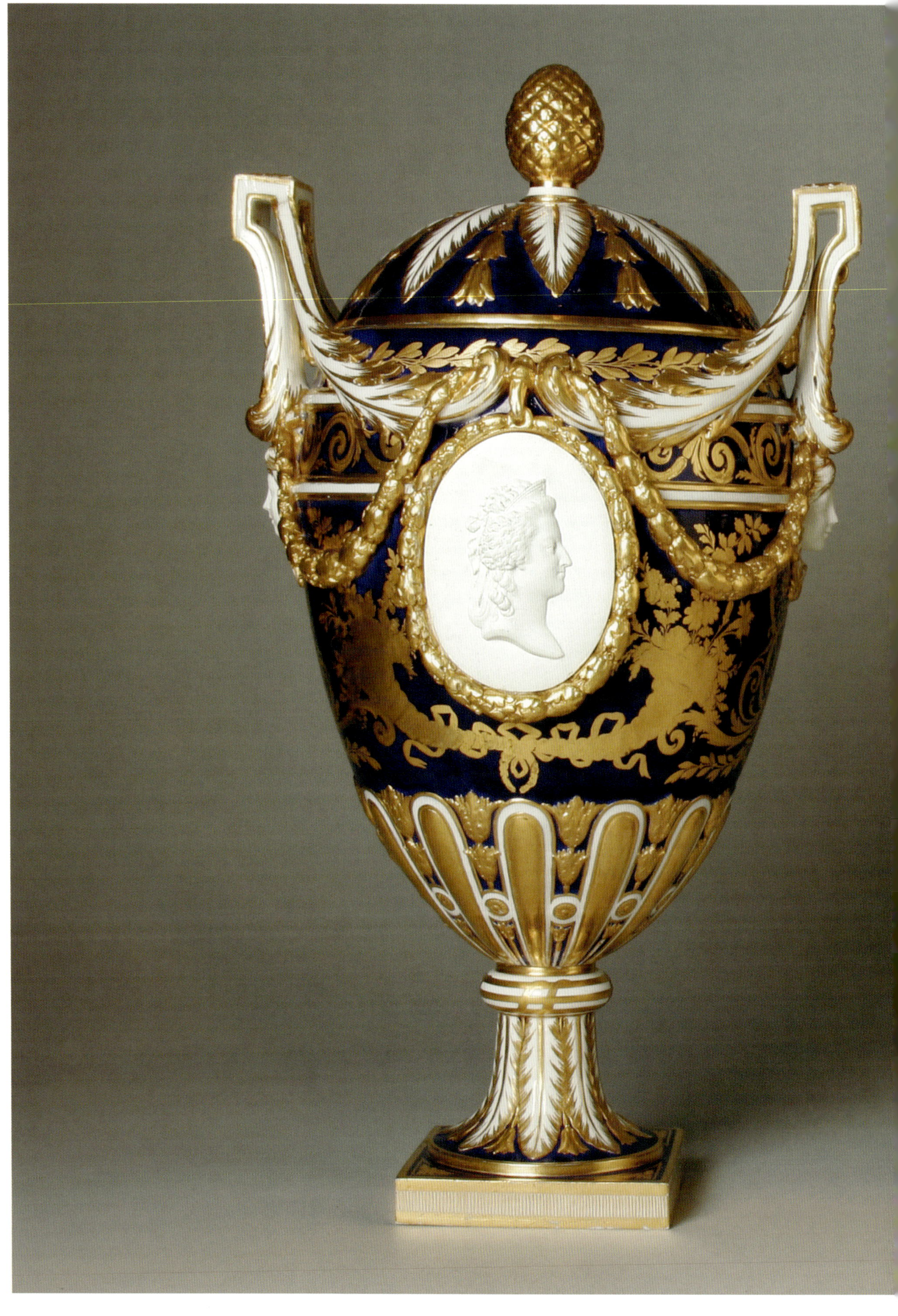

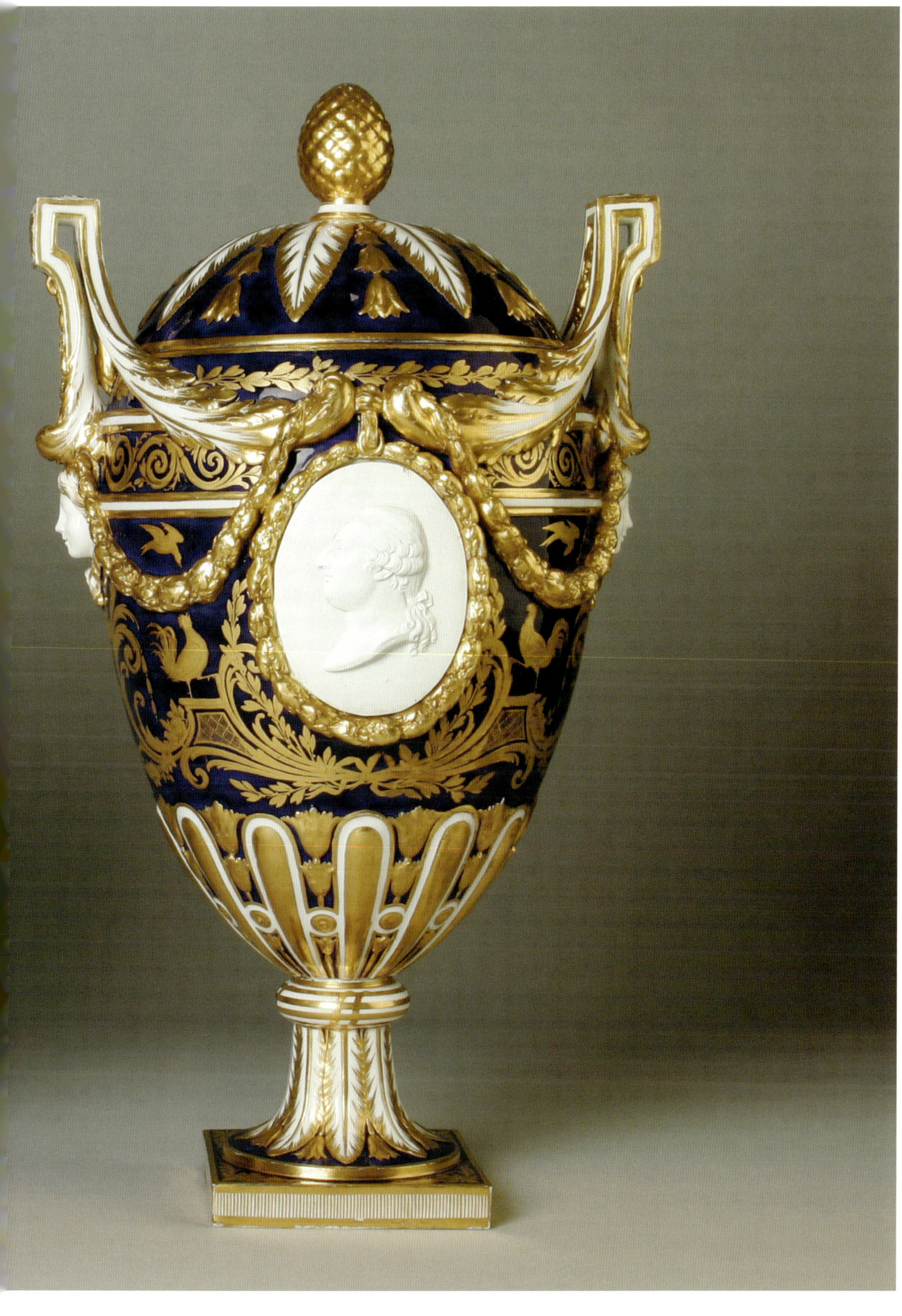

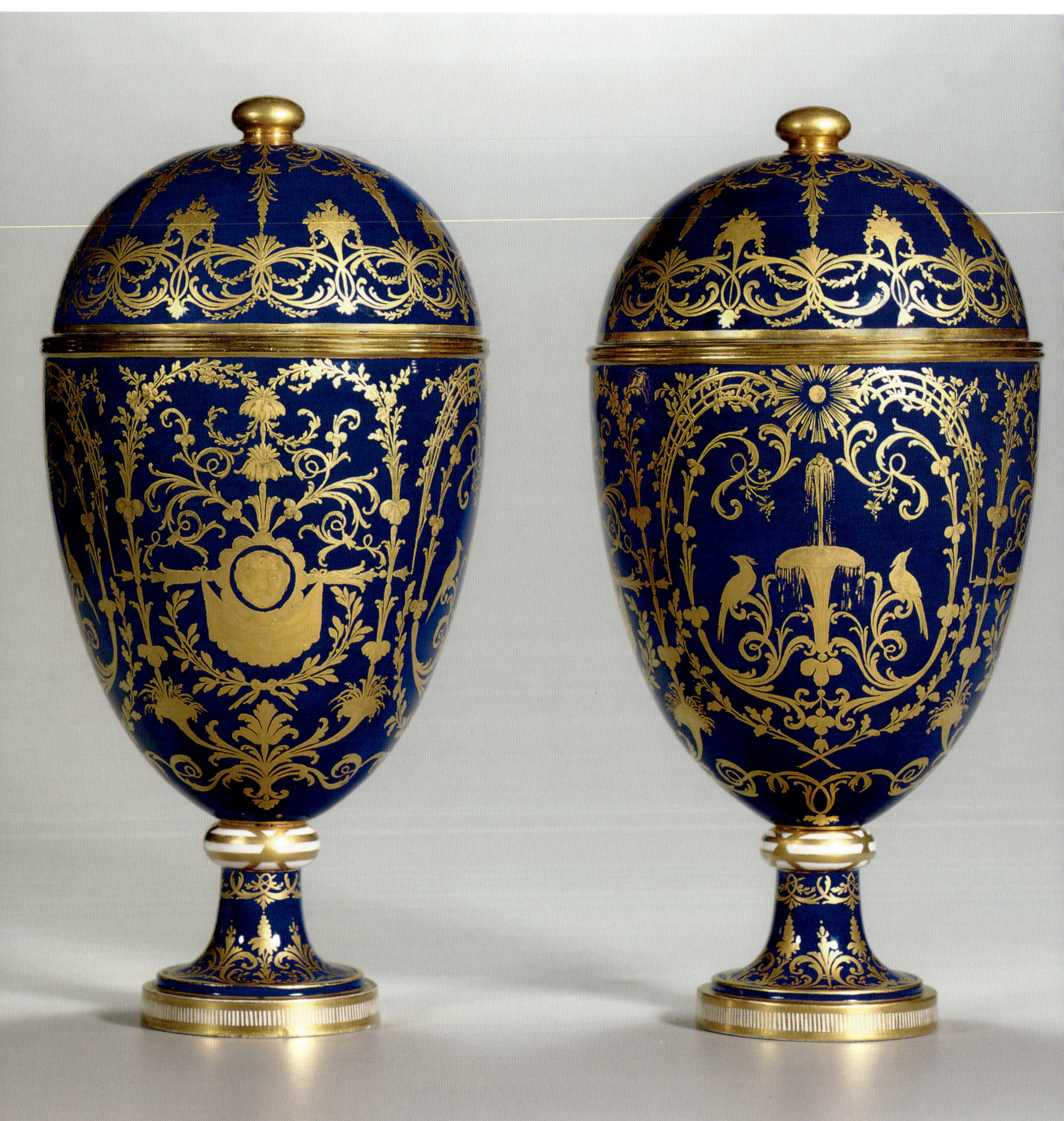

Fig. 25 (cat. 14): Pair of egg-shaped vases possibly for Grand Duke Paul and Grand Duchess Maria Fedorovna, ca. 1782

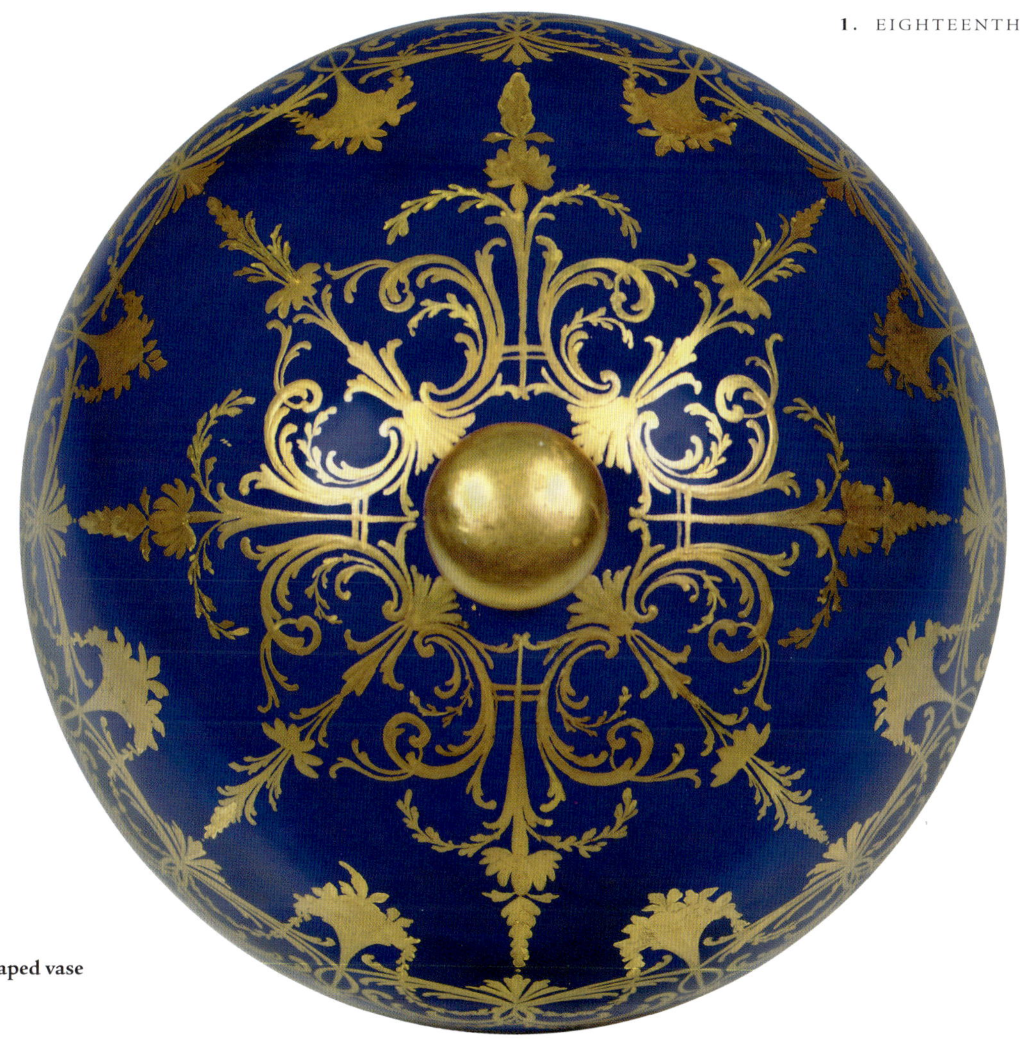

Detail of fig. 25, lid from one egg-shaped vase

the Wallace Collection as well as another of the same model with a *bleu nouveau* ground and *oeil-de-perdrix* pattern with a medallion of Louis XV after Edmé Bouchardon in the British Royal Collection.[43] This almost certainly is the pair referred to in the factory records of 1774, which mention that Louis XVI and Marie Antoinette were represented in biscuit on another pair of egg-shaped vases,[44] marking the year of their coronation.

The oviform vases in fig. 25 have cobalt blue grounds and are decorated on all sides with finely executed gilding and detailed with tooling. Birds flanking a fountain feature prominently on one side, whereas the other sides have marks surrounded with garden arabesque decorations. When Grand Duke Paul of Russia and his wife Maria Fedorovna visited France in 1782, the couple—traveling incognito as the comte and comtesse du Nord—visited the Sèvres factory[45] and received many Sèvres pieces from Louis XVI as diplomatic gifts, including a sumptuous dressing table set in *beau bleu* with Etruscan-style figures in gold and jeweling and raised enamel decoration in imitation of precious stones (on view at Pavlovsk Palace). In addition, the imperial couple charged the Russian envoy, Prince Bariatinskii, with selecting and purchasing additional pieces for dispatch to their palace at Pavlovsk. These included two sets of egg-shaped vases. The first, still at Pavlovsk, are listed as "garniture de cinq vases oeufs, lapis, montes en bronze" (egg-shaped vases with imitation lapis decoration with bronze mounts). The second, "vases oeufs beau bleu et or" (egg-shaped vases in *beau bleu* and gold), could very well be a reference to the pair of vases illustrated here.[46]

Considering the tremendous amount of royal patronage at Sèvres, it is surprising that Queen Marie Antoinette did not order a table service until 1781 and that the first three she commissioned are striking in their simplicity of decoration, all with white grounds and floral motifs.[47] Perhaps the relative modesty of the services can be attributed to the queen's desire to live a simpler, calmer life on the fringes of the highly official existence she had to live at Versailles. The pastoral pursuits of Marie Antoinette, aside from their

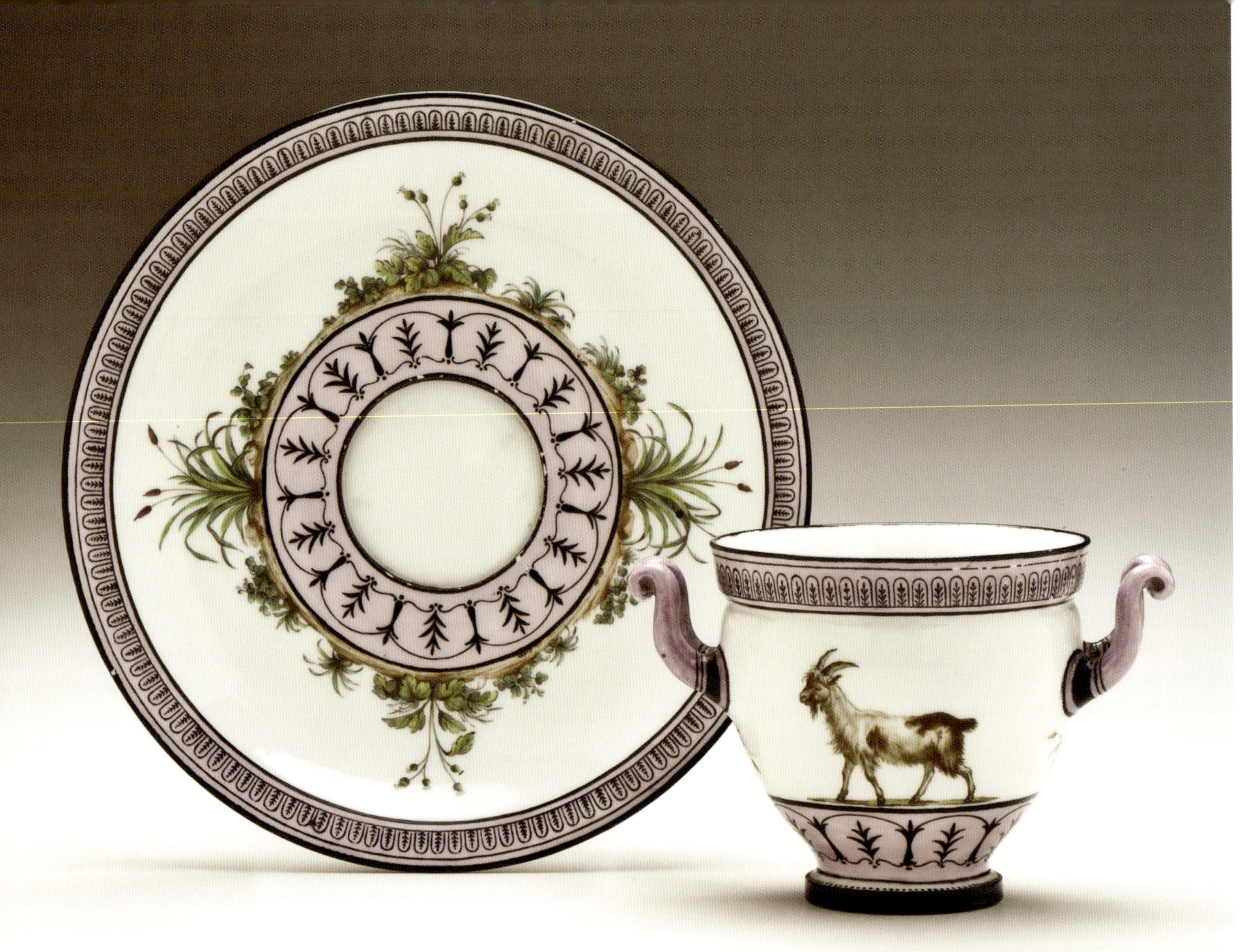

Fig. 26 (cat. 21): Cup and saucer for Queen Marie Antoinette's Dairy at Rambouillet, 1786–7

hedonistic aspect, have also been imbued with a tragic sense as they harbinger the end of an era that was brought about by the French Revolution.

In 1785 Sèvres began a service for the queen's dairy at the château de Rambouillet, a property that Louis XVI had acquired a couple of years earlier from the duc de Penthièvre. Painter Hubert Robert (1733–1808) took over the decorative project of the milk dairy. He designed the building and its furniture, which was executed by Georges Jacob (1739–1814), and asked Sèvres to design a porcelain service. As supervisor of the Sèvres factory, the comte d'Angiviller saw this as an opportunity to put forth the most modern interpretation of classical antiquity. He asked Boizot to design new forms and called on painter and engraver Jean-Jacques Lagrenée (1739–1821) to conceive the decoration. Lagrenée, who had lived in Italy and visited the ruins at Herculaneum, came back to Paris inspired by the examples of classical antiquity he had seen and intent on reforming the taste of the factory and bringing it up to date. Instead of gilded cartouches and richly colored backgrounds, for this service Lagrenée chose instead a white background and narrow colored friezes with "Etruscan" designs in soft colors to frame images of milk-yielding animals such as cows, goats, and lambs in green pastures. The term *étrusque* reflects the taste for classical antiquity which was particularly emphasized at Sèvres after 1785 when King Louis XVI acquired for the factory a collection of Etruscan vases from the collector Dominique Vivant, Baron de Denon, the French ambassador to Naples (from about 1776 to 1785). This collection gave artists a new opportunity to research and copy pieces from antiquity at first hand. The cups are direct copies of classical cup models called "*étrusque*" at the time (fig. 26). The service was unique for its style and use, and originally comprised about sixty-five pieces. Only seventeen are known to exist today, and only three cups and saucers have been identified to date.[48] The service was delivered to the château de Rambouillet in May of 1788, barely a year before the taking of the Bastille.[49]

Revolution

The last decade of the eighteenth century was characterized by crisis and turmoil. The Revolution and the establishment of the First Republic temporarily marked the end of royal patronage at Sèvres and brought many changes at the factory. The workforce was politically divided and political denunciations among workers created a climate of mistrust and discontent. There was a lack of direction in the administration, with new regulations implemented and then soon thereafter abandoned, and constant changes in the upper levels of management. In 1790 the management raised the question of selling the factory in order to pay debts, but King Louis XVI decided to keep Sèvres running at his own expense. After the fall of the monarchy, the National Convention decreed in 1793 that the factory was "one of the glories of France" and that it should be preserved.

At this time of upheaval, the manufactory certainly could not depend on royal commissions and purchases from the French aristocracy. Efforts were concentrated on attracting French and foreign dealers who would sell the porcelain abroad. The yellow service with birds and "Etruscan" borders was one such service sold to a dealer for export (fig. 27). Its austere decoration reflected the Republican spirit of the time.

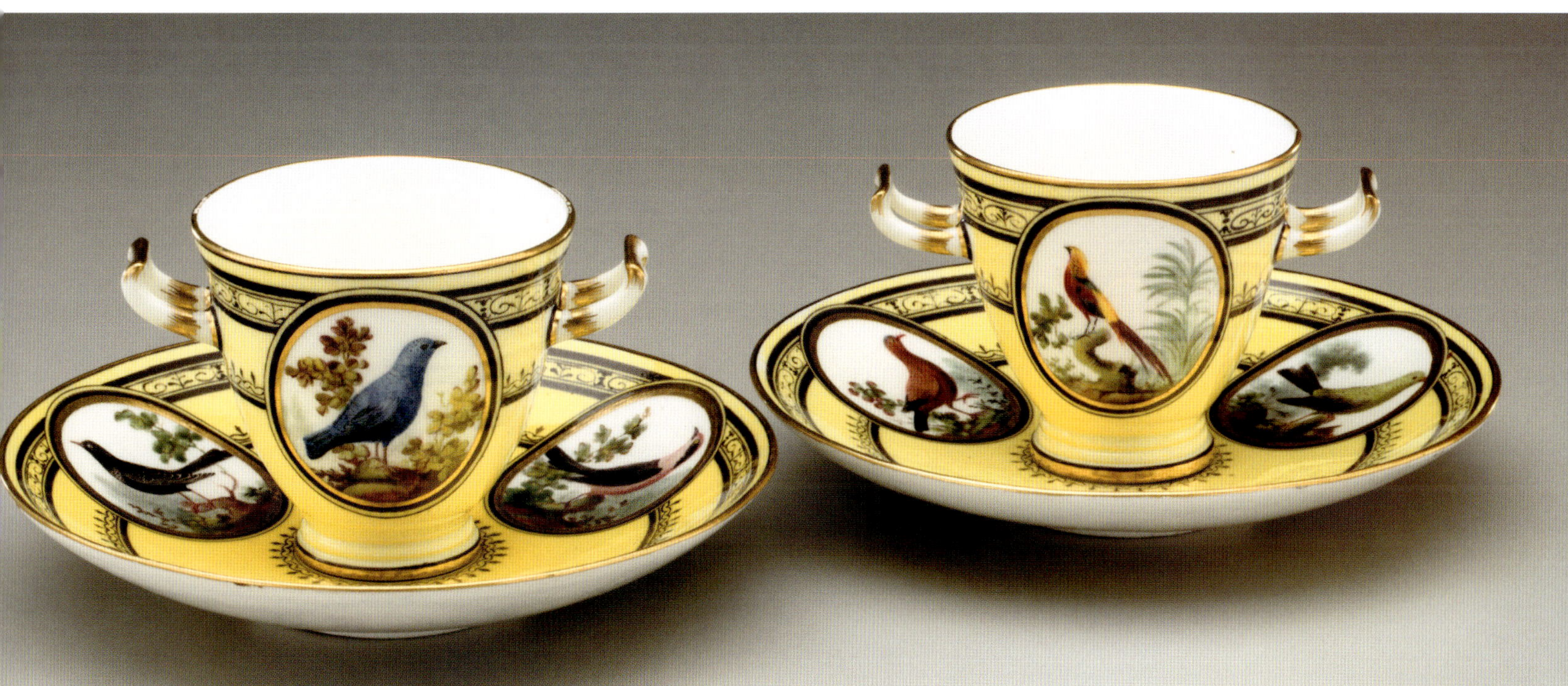

Fig. 27 (cat. 26): Two yellow "Etruscan" cups and saucers with birds after Buffon's *Histoire naturelle des oiseaux*, 1793–94

Both soft-paste and hard-paste porcelain were used for the components of this service, since in those turbulent years the factory had to make do with what was available. The birds are based on François-Nicolas Martinet's illustrations for the comte de Buffon's (1707–1788) celebrated ornithological compendium *Histoire naturelle des oiseaux,* published in ten volumes from 1770 to 1783. The cups were a Hillwood museum purchase of 2005 to match two saucers, already in the collection (24.130.8 and 24.130.9). They are also based on "Etruscan" examples provided by Vivant Denon and similar in form to the model devised for Marie Antoinette's dairy at Rambouillet in 1786 (see fig. 26).

Royal marks and Revolutionary marks both appear on this service and on other pieces dating from the same period. By order of the National Convention in 1793, a mark reading Sèvres and the initials *RF* (for République Française) replaced the royal cipher of intertwined Ls. The coexistence of these two marking systems can be explained by the fact that a complete change of marks might have jeopardized sales abroad as foreigners were accustomed to the old marks. Since the Revolution was mostly an internal matter, or so it was thought, it is not surprising that for export purposes, commercial interests came before politics.

Viewed in this light, it should not be surprising that such expensive and lavish wares as the black chinoiserie bottle cooler were produced in the midst of the Revolution (fig. 28). They were clearly earmarked for the export market, one that had to be nurtured if it was to survive. This cooler relates to

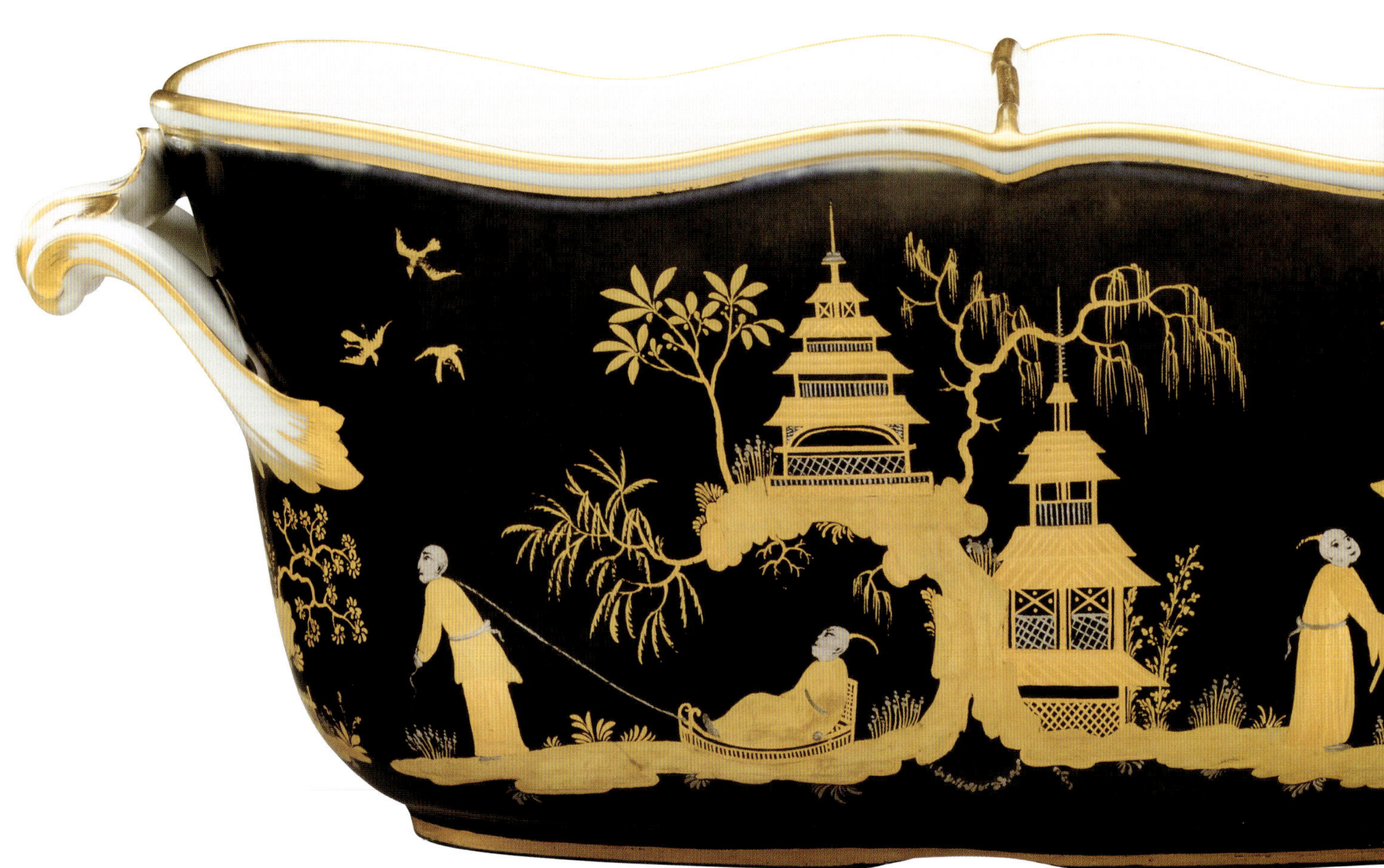

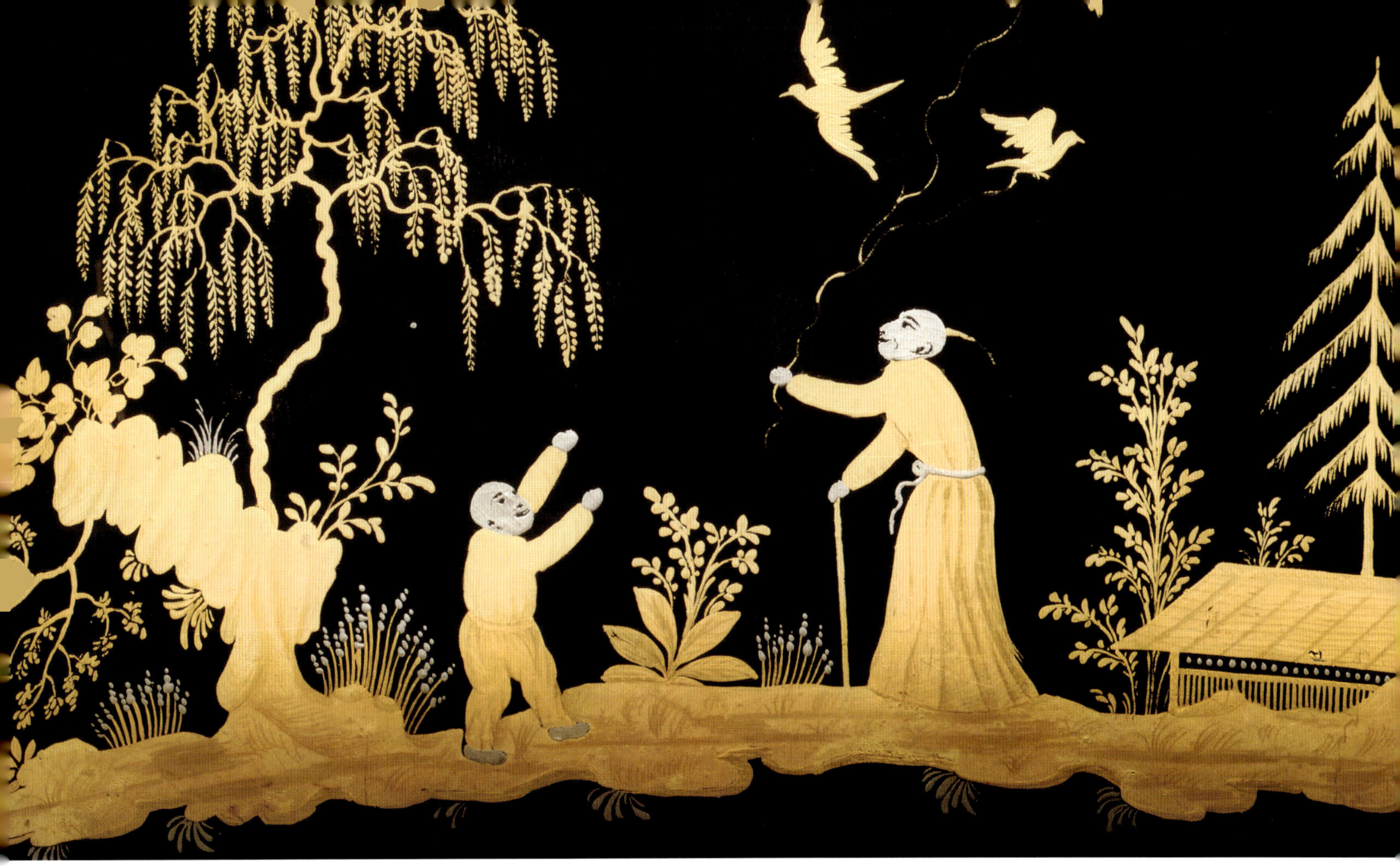

Detail of fig. 28 (reverse), chinoiserie figures

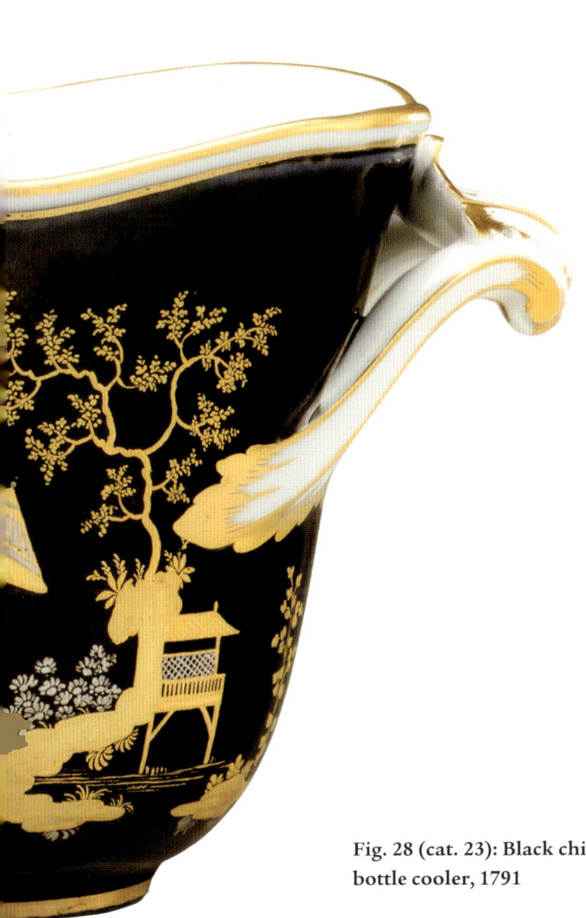

Fig. 28 (cat. 23): Black chinoiserie bottle cooler, 1791

a group of wares produced for a very short period between 1790 and 1792, which imitated Chinese *famille noire* grounds. At Sèvres, the black ground color was achieved by applying several coats of a deep blue-black enamel color which, when fired, would give the appearance of a highly polished black lacquer. The use of platinum in combination with matte and polished yellow gold is particularly noteworthy, as are the playful scenes evoking the early Rococo chinoiserie style of painter Jean-Baptiste Pillement (1728–1808). In this decoration, there is a clear reference to lacquer-paneled Chinese and Japanese furniture that was so much in vogue in France in the eighteenth century.

For the domestic market, a parallel production of pieces imbued with the French Republican spirit coexisted with more traditionally decorated wares. Numerous pieces painted with allegorical symbols of Liberty, Equality, and Reason, as well as Masonic symbols and emblems extolling Republican virtues were sold on French soil. An excellent example is the Revolutionary teapot (fig. 29). The Phrygian cap or bonnet was a symbol of liberty associated with the freeing of Roman slaves and was adopted by French revolutionaries, and the

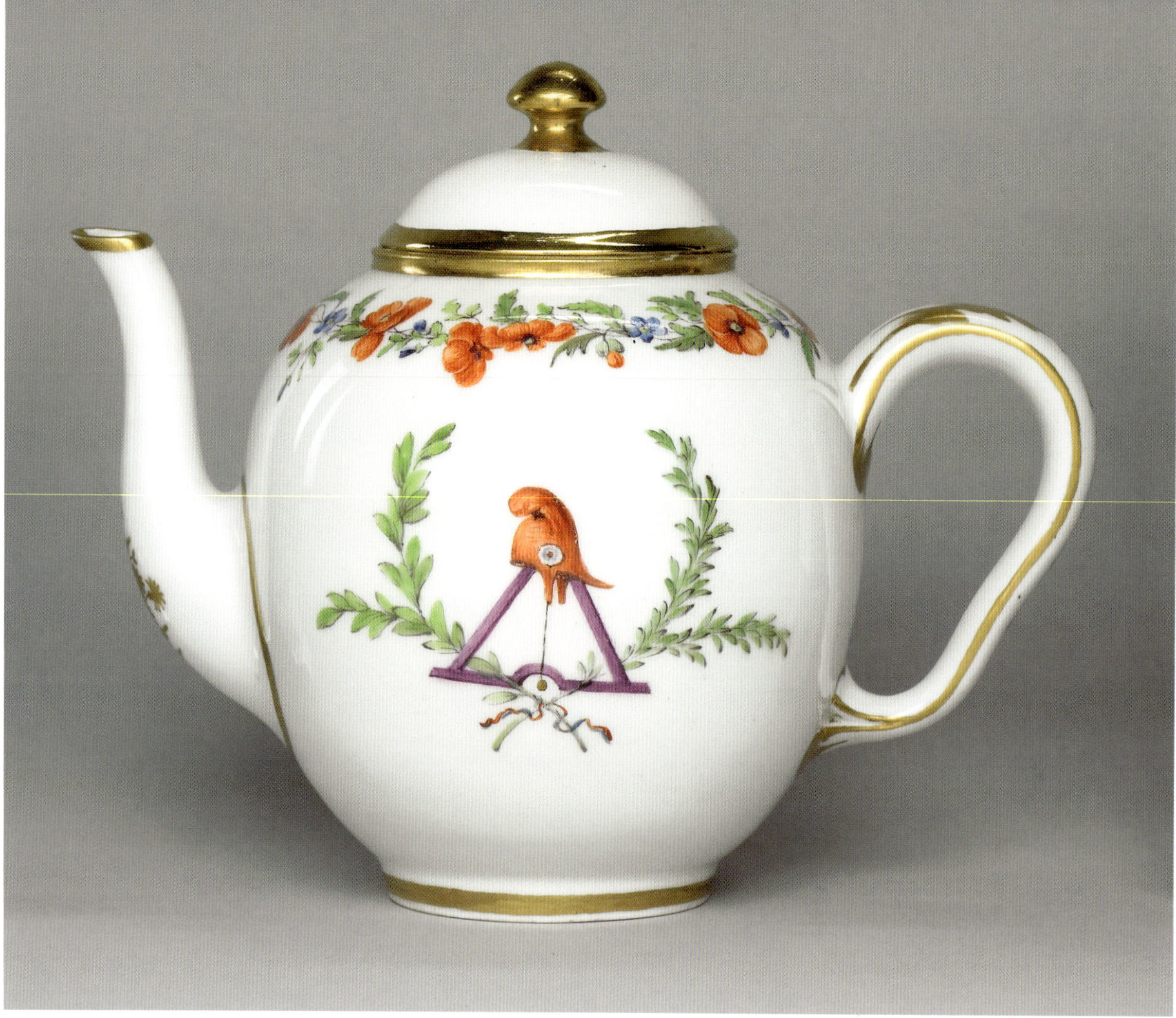

Fig. 29 (cat. 22): Teapot with Revolutionary symbols, 1795

level depicted with it represents equality of all men and justice for all. In 1794 a dealer observed that "employees have received orders not to let any piece out before putting the attributes of liberty on it. This measure might be good for the nation, but if it continues to be applied to every object, it will become impossible to export them, because this type of merchandise is difficult to sell in other countries."[50]

NOTES

1. Decree of the King's Council of July 24, 1745. T. Préaud and A. d'Albis, *La Porcelaine de Vincennes* (Paris, 1991), p. 21.
2. Few sales occurred in the early years of the factory before 1747 when the factory began to offer dealers in Paris a ten percent discount on their purchases. (For a full account of the subject, see Aileen Dawson's article, "Some Thoughts on the Clientele of the Vincennes/Sèvres Factory in the Eighteenth Century," *French Porcelain Society Journal*, vol. III, 2007, pp. 36-44.)
3. Still in 1750, almost half of the approximate hundred workers were women modeling flowers. T. Préaud, *Sèvres Porcelain* (Washington, D.C., 1980), p. 17.
4. Orry de Fulvy had been an obstacle in the affairs of numerous tax collectors and financiers, including the Pâris brothers, who were close friends of Madame de Pompadour and her family.
5. In 1753 King Louis XV, in the face of the factory's dire financial situation and its potential dissolution, made a dramatic gesture of support by acquiring one-fourth of the new company's stock and granting it the use of his royal monogram as the factory mark.
6. In M.L. de Rochebrune, "La Passion de Madame de Pompadour pour la porcelaine," in X. Salmon et al., *Madame de Pompadour et les arts* (Paris, 2002), p. 407.
7. For a detailed account of the development of enamel colors for porcelain, see A. d'Albis, "Les débuts de la peinture figurative sur porcelaine," *Salon International de la Céramique de Collection et des Arts du Feu*, 1999, pp. 62-72.
8. See G. Sadde, "Jean-Claude Duplessis: la liberté du style rocaille," *L'Estampille/L'Objet d'Art*, June 2004, pp. 42-51.
9. The marquis d'Argenson, who mistakenly thought this service was intended for the King of Saxony, commented, "L'on établit rue de la Monnaie un magasin royal pour cette porcelaine. On y voit un beau service que Sa Majesté envoie au roi Auguste de Saxe, comme pour le braver et l'insulter, lui disant qu'on a surpassé même sa fabrique." Quoted from Christian Baulez's chapter, "Une terrine et un plateau-corbeille du service 'bleu céleste' de Louis XV," in C. Baulez, *Versailles, Deux siècles d'histoire de l'art* (Paris, 2007), p. 309.
10. A "pot à oglio et plateau Ière grandeur" was sold for 1,320 livres to Lazare Duvaux in 1756 (Archives of the Manufacture Nationale de Sèvres [hereafter MNS archives], registre Vy2, fol. 12). On December 7, 1756 there is an entry in the Duvaux account books for a sale to "M. le Cte d'Egmont - Un grand pot á oille couvert avec son plat en blue-céleste, peint á fleurs, les cartouches en or, 1.320 l(ivres)." I am grateful to Tamara Préaud, archivist at Sèvres, for this information.
11. "30 Xbre 1758 ... Vente au compant faite á Versailles.... A Monseigneur le duc d'Orléans ... 1 Cuvette Mahon (roze) ... 480 (livres)." (MNS archives, registre Vy3, fol. 9.)
12. Letter discovered by Bernard Dragesco and reproduced in a special issue of the journal published by the Société des Amis du Musée National de Céramique, *Mélanges en souvenir d'Elisalex d'Albis* (Paris 1999), pp. 79-80.
13. This model was originally called "pot à eau et jatte 'feuille d'eau'" in production since 1756. This set is the largest size of the three made.

14. There is a green example with flowers at the Musée des Arts Décoratifs in Paris, a pink example also with flowers at the J. Paul Getty Museum in Los Angeles, and an incomplete *bleu céleste* example that was sold at Christie's London, July 5, 2004, lot 91.
15. His career has been recently studied by Marie Laure de Rochebrune in "Charles Nicolas Dodin, Miniature Painter at Sèvres," *Antiques*, October 2000, pp. 524–33.
16. "2 Vazes Elephants Rozes et Verds Chinois 360......720 {livres}" MNS series Vy3, fol. 115.
17. Of the twenty-five pieces recorded by Dodin decorated in this style, twenty-three of which are still known, fourteen belonged to Madame de Pompadour and four to the king; see M.L. de Rochebrune's essay in the exhibition catalogue *Madame de Pompadour et les arts* (Paris, 2002), p. 444.
18. Lord Clark later confessed that "I also gave some examples of bad taste, and this I rather regret as I have now become quite fond of them, and if anyone offers me a Sèvres elephant vase on my birthday, I will accept it with pleasure." (quoted in R. Savill, *The Wallace Collection: Catalogue of Sèvres Porcelain*, London, 1988, vol. I, p. 162, note 43.)
19. It has recently been ascertained that green ground wares appeared at Vincennes as early as 1753, as proved by a bowl *(jatte)* in the Yves Mikaeloff collection bearing the date letter *A* for that year, as well as a few mentions of green ground pieces in the article "Vincennes, 1753, le premier fond vert," *Connaissance des Arts*, July 1988, pp. 84–7.
20. The service was delivered to the king via the art dealer Lazare Duvaux. About a third of this service survives in the Hermitage Museum, but the circumstances of its transfer to the Russian imperial court have not yet been clarified. (For a full account see O. Villumsen Krog, "Service Diplomatique," *Connaissance des Arts*, November 1993, pp. 152–61 and D. Peters, *Sèvres Plates and Services of the Eighteenth Century* (Little Berkhamsted, 2005), vol. II, pp. 295–8.)
21. See L. Courajod, ed., *Livre-Journal de Lazare Duvaux, marchand-bijoutier ordinaire du roy (1748–58)* (Paris, 1965), entry 3068: "S.M Le Roy; Livré á M. l'abbé Cte. De Bernis, ministre des affaires étrangères, pour S.M. Danoise - un service de porcelaine de France, en vert, peint à figures, fleurs et oiseaux ... ounze glaces au tain taillés en rond suivant les jattes du fruit, 120 l(ivres)."
22. Boucher had five *Livres de Groupes d'Enfans* edited by different publishers.
23. The king first became aware of courtesan Jeanne Becu in the spring of 1768 and instantly succumbed to her charms. To obtain the nobility title that was necessary to become the official mistress, Jeanne was hastily married to the brother of her procurer, comte Guillaume du Barry in September of that same year. Madame du Barry was officially presented at court on April 22, 1769.
24. See Chistian Baulez's entry in the *Revue du Louvre*, 1996, cat. no. 12, p. 94. I am thankful to John Whitehead for this reference.
25. D. Peters, *Sèvres Plates and Services*, vol. II, pp. 387–90. Peters notes the list of sales to Madame Lair which included a "seau ovale à liqueur." These wares lack description, but in view of their high cost and the particular service components, Peters has linked them with a group of surviving 1767–8 items with Chantilly-like trellis grounds, putti, and trophies. Peters has also linked these pieces, somewhat dated in style, to a group of plates ("Enfant(s) Colorées") sold on July 1, 1759 to an unidentified buyer. He also points out that it is likely that the service that Louis XVI bought on April 16, 1791 described as "Miniature et Mozaïque" is in fact a supplement to the 1768–70 purchases.
26. C. Dauterman, "Sèvres Figure Painting in the Anna Thompson Dodge Collection," *The Burlington Magazine*, November 1976, p. 754.
27. C. Arminjon and N. Blondel, *Objets civils domestiques: vocabulaire* (Paris, 1984), p. 150.
28. C. Le Taillandier, "Une bouillotte en porcelaine bordelaise," *Sèvres, Revue de la Société des Amis du Musée National de Céramique*, no. 17, 2008, p. 53.
29. For a full account of *bouillottes* see J. Munger, "A Bouillotte in the Museum of Fine Arts, Boston," *Mélanges en souvenir d'Elisalex d'Albis* (Paris, 1999), pp. 103–9.
30. Ibid., p. 106.
31. MNS archives, registre V3, 6,f, in A. Dawson, *French Porcelain: A Catalogue of the British Museum Collection* (London, 1994), p. 144.
32. For a detailed account of Madame Adélaïde's artistic patronage see Jennifer Milam's chapter "Matronage and the Direction of Sisterhood: Portraits of Madame Adélaïde," in *Women, Art and the Politics of Identity in Eighteenth-Century Europe* (Burlington, VT, 2003), p. 130.
33. See C. Baulez, *Versailles, deux siècles d'histoire de l'art* (Paris, 2007), pp. 1–4: "Deux vases de Sèvres de la grande chambre du roi."
34. "4 pots à oglio, épis de blé, #900....3,600 [livres]."
35. I am indebted to Mme. Tamara Préaud for this information.
36. Quoted in S. Schama, *Citizens: A Chronicle of the French Revolution* (New York, 1989), p. 43.
37. In 1765 Beaujon acquired a complete Sèvres table service. A garniture of green vases with flowers and gilt bronze mounts adorned his *cabinet de toilette* in his Parisian residence (see J. Coural, *Le Palais de l'Elysée: Histoire et Décor*, Paris, 1994, p. 38).
38. See note by John Whitehead on object file.
39. Louis-Philippe Parizeau, *7ème Suite de différents sujets* (Paris, 1781).
40. E. Ducamp, *Pavlovsk: The Palace and the Park, The Collection* (Paris, 1993), vol. 2, pp. 147–8.
41. These were identified by Pierre Verlet from a 1792 inventory taken at Versailles. Verlet also attributed the mounts to Thomire from a bill he submitted to the factory in 1784 for the "Garniture de vases à bouc, fonte, modele en cire, monture, dorure au mat" (quoted in G. de Bellaigue, *Sèvres Porcelain from the Royal Collection*, London, 1979, p. 42).
42. "2 vases bas relief" sold to the comte d'Artois in 1786 for 1,500 livres each (MNS archives, registre Vy,10, fol. 115).
43. See R. Savill, *Wallace Collection*, vol. I, pp. 343–5.
44. In 1774 Tristan *le jeune* was paid for a model of "vase oeuf du Roy" and for medallions of the king and queen (see R. Savill, *Wallace Collection*, p. 347, note 7); for the one in the British Royal Collection see G. de Bellaigue, *Royal Collection*, no. 115.
45. This visit is discussed by P. Ennès in "The Visit of the comte and comtesse du Nord to the Sèvres Manufactory," *Apollo*, March 1989, pp. 150–6, 220–2. "Etat des Porcelaines choisies par son Excellence Le Prince Bariatinsky pour les Comte and Comtesse du Nord": MNS archives, registre Vy8.
46. "Etat des Porcelaines choisies par son Excellence Le Prince Bariatinsky pour les Comte and Comtesse du Nord": MNS archives, registre Vy8.46.
47. A simple service with scattered roses and cornflowers ("service double filet bleu, roses et barbeaux") was the first order of 1781; a slightly more ornate one ("cartels en perles en roses et barbeaux") was also delivered to the queen in that same year; in 1782 Marie Antoinette took delivery of a third simple service with a range of pearls and cornflowers ("range à perles et barbeaux") and the last one before Rambouillet's was the most elaborately decorated with gold friezes and floral sprays and of the same design as one sent to Gustave III of Sweden ("service riche en couleurs et riche en or").
48. Two other examples—one yellow and one green—survive at the Musée National de Céramique at Sèvres and in the Didier Cramoisan collection, respectively; see P. Arizzoli-Clémentel and X. Salmon, *Marie Antoinette* (Paris, 2008), p. 240.
49. For a full account of this service see Selma Schwartz, 'The Sèvres Porcelain Service for Marie-Antoinette's Dairy at Rambouillet: An Exercise in Archeological Neo-Classicism" *French Porcelain Society Journal*, vol. IX, 1992, pp. 1–35.
50. X. de Chavagnac and G. de Grollier, *Histoire des manufactures françaises de porcelaine* (Paris, 1906, p. 222).

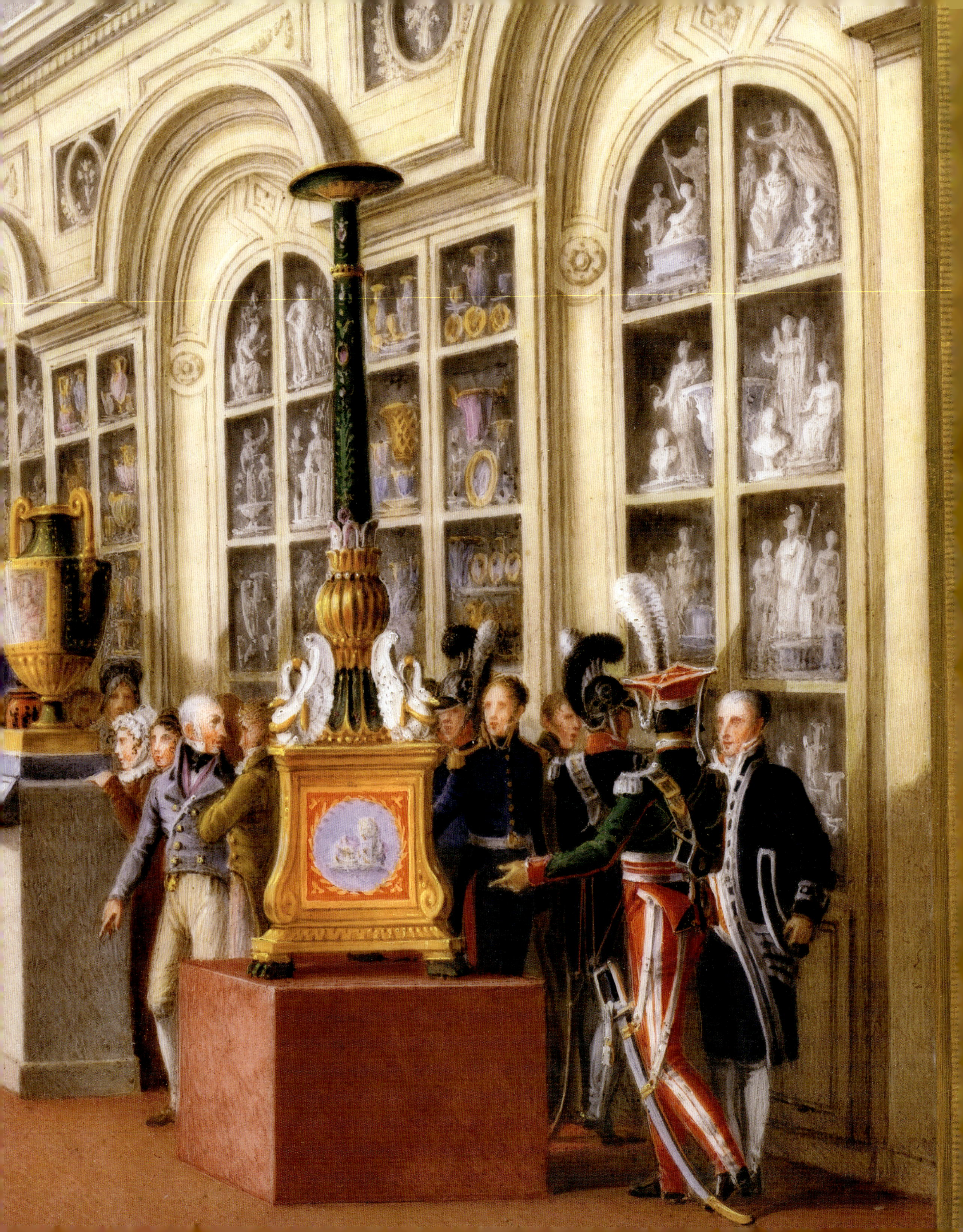

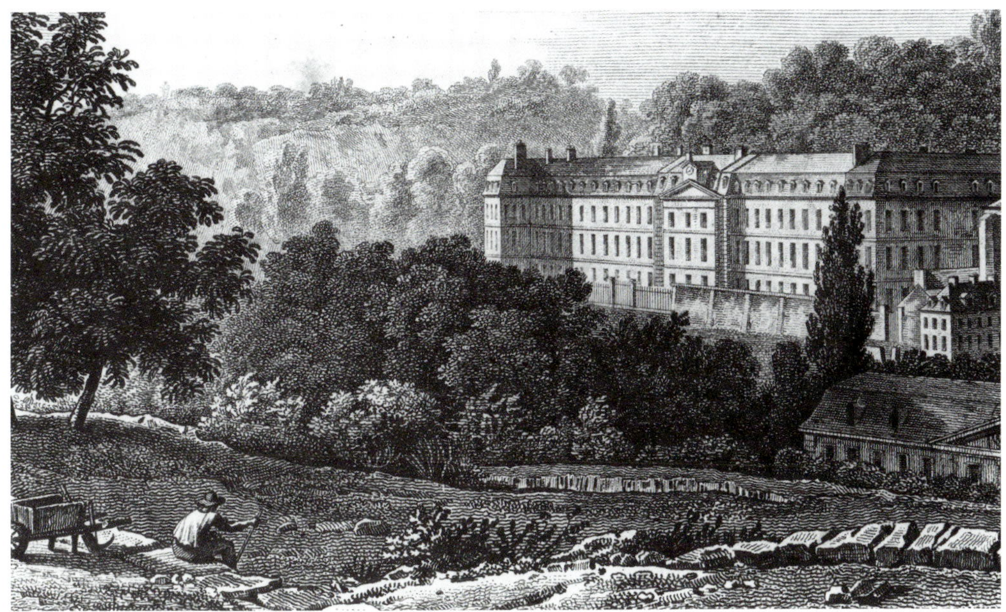

CHAPTER TWO

The Nineteenth Century

The French Revolution of 1789 triggered cataclysmic shifts in the social and political fabric of Ancien Régime society. The patronage of the monarchs and the aristocracy waned as many were killed or banished. Sèvres, in order to survive, had to shift gears and cater to the affluent bourgeoisie and the foreign market.

The gradual recovery of the factory after the Revolution began with the appointment of Alexandre Brongniart (1770–1847) as director in 1800. Throughout his lengthy tenure of forty-seven years, Brongniart reinvigorated the factory by breathing fresh life into it. His voracious search for new porcelain techniques and his flair for innovative decoration are manifest in the productions of his period.

Brongniart, son of an architect and nephew of a scientist, was a cultivated man in the fullest sense of the word. He was a mining engineer, who also studied the natural sciences. He became a member of the scholarly Societé d'Histoire Naturelle, and was well versed in

ABOVE

Fig. 30: View of the Sèvres manufactory (detail) from an engraving by Fortier and Dupard after A.E. Michallon

OPPOSITE

Detail of fig. 44, tray from the tea and coffee service *L'Art de la porcelaine*, 1816

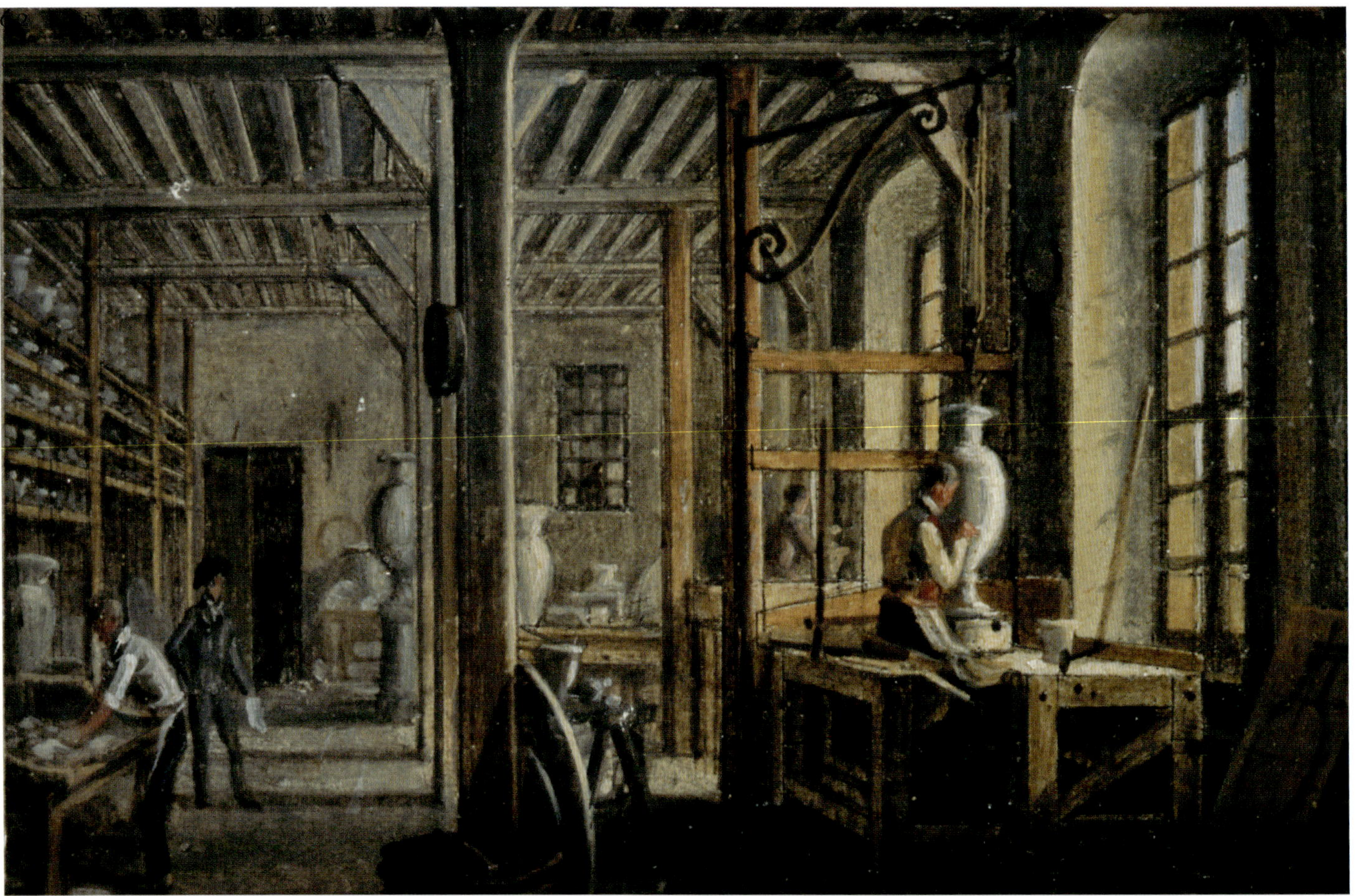

Fig. 31: Drawing showing the throwers' workshop for the *Art de la porcelaine* service by Jean-Charles Develly, 1816; gouache on paper

chemistry, mineralogy, and botany. With his inordinate talent, insatiable curiosity, and interest in all aspects of the manufactory, he restored Sèvres' finances and enhanced the reputation of the factory as the most technically and stylistically advanced in Europe.

Despite financial needs, Brongniart never placed much importance on achieving commercial success. His primary goal was to maintain Sèvres' hegemony through the manifest superiority of its designs and decorations, above the rivalries and competitive disputes of the private factories. His vision to make of the factory a model and a leading center of ceramic research would ensure that Sèvres continued to be the indisputable leader in the field: "It is not for its contributions to the general market in porcelains that Sèvres has influenced the ceramic industry.... By making waves in the luxury market the [Sèvres] factory is able to elevate the reputation of French porcelain at large. It is thus that, despite making pieces that nobody buys, the factory has rendered great service to the trade in porcelain."[1]

Brongniart formed the core of what is now the Musée National de Céramique in Sèvres, adjacent to the factory, by collecting a wide range of glass and ceramics from all over the world.[2] Following his idea of making the factory a laboratory of the ceramic industries for others to learn from, he published in 1841–4 a multivolume treatise on ceramics, *Traité des arts céramiques*, encapsulating the knowledge he had gathered throughout his career.

His tenure also had some downsides, most notably the unforeseen consequence of unleashing an industry of fakes. In order to clean up storage space and realize some additional cash for the factory, Brongniart ordered the sale of a huge amount of leftover stock of old-fashioned shapes and rejects. What he did not anticipate was that some less than reputable decorators and dealers would buy these blanks by the wagonload and decorate them in the Sèvres manner, often giving them spurious marks to deceive the public. The two massive sales of undecorated stock of 1826 and 1840 have repercussions even today. The number of faux Sèvres porcelains that have made their way into collections and the marketplace since those sales is staggering, with virtually no collection, private or public, untouched by fakes. At the time, however, this initiative enabled Brongniart to buy good supplies and raw materials and hire back talented artists whose skills had been sought by rival factories. In 1804 Brongniart made the difficult decision to stop production of soft-paste porcelain and to concentrate on hard-paste instead.

First Empire

Brongniart's beginnings at Sèvres coincided with the founding of the First Empire. When Napoleon crowned himself emperor in 1804, he inherited a series of royal residences which had been stripped bare during the Revolution. The emperor set about furnishing them as elegantly as possible through subsidies and incentives to French industry and manufacturers. No country, except Great Britain, could compete with France in matters of commerce and industry with its newly instituted mercantile policies. In the luxury arts France became the undisputed leader of a style that exerted influence throughout Europe. Sèvres was included in the emperor's Civil List in 1808, and just as the Bourbon monarchs had done before, Napoleon commissioned lavish services from Sèvres as well as elaborate presentation pieces which he sent to foreign rulers and dignitaries. On average, the emperor bought about eighteen percent of the total production for his own purposes and for use as gifts.[3]

In this new political era, the gracious, highly sculptural forms of the eighteenth century were abandoned and replaced with a new repertoire of simpler forms with large, uninterrupted fields ready to receive decorations that proclaimed the emperor's glory. However, the instructions of Napoleon's administration to the factory were vague, with the most recurrent of them being the dislike for nudity in favor of historical subjects.[4]

The white of the porcelain so beloved in the eighteenth century for its simple luminosity and translucency was completely obscured with color grounds, heavy gilding, and scenes in emulation of easel painting. Transcribing scenes and accomplishments from the emperor's life occupied the best figure painters of the period. Despite this fact, subjects directly related to Napoleon's military campaigns were scarce, with preference given to general subjects and landscapes. Initially, imperial Rome was the model. This was soon supplemented, from 1799, with elements from Egyptian art. Just as most artistic expressions of the Empire functioned as a coded discourse to communicate certain political notions, Sèvres embedded political and social messages into its ceramics. However, the artistic merit of these porcelains resided in their capacity to transcend these messages and avoid becoming merely propagandistic.

Dominique Vivant, Baron de Denon (1747–1825), one of the most gifted and universal men of the period and a vigorous proponent of a return to classicism, became a central figure during the Empire.[5] Napoleon and Empress Joséphine took Vivant Denon under their wing and put him in charge of organizing military parades and, more importantly, directing the Musée du Louvre. Vivant Denon studied engraving and accompanied Napoleon on his Egyptian campaign (1798–9) along with a group of French experts in the fields of science, engineering, and art. Napoleon's campaign in Egypt was a tactical disaster, but it yielded a number of satisfactory archeological and scientific results. The scholar Vivant Denon sketched many ancient Egyptian sites and objects which would become the basis of the first serious account of Egyptian archeology and a source of inspiration for designers in France and beyond. The "Egyptomania" unleashed by the Egyptian campaign yielded a new vocabulary of ornamentation with a profusion of sphinxes, animal-head human figures, lotus flowers, winged sun disks, and hieroglyphics, which populated all sorts of furnishings and decorative objects. The cup and saucer in fig. 32, a small compendium of Egyptian symbols, is one such example of the new aesthetic.

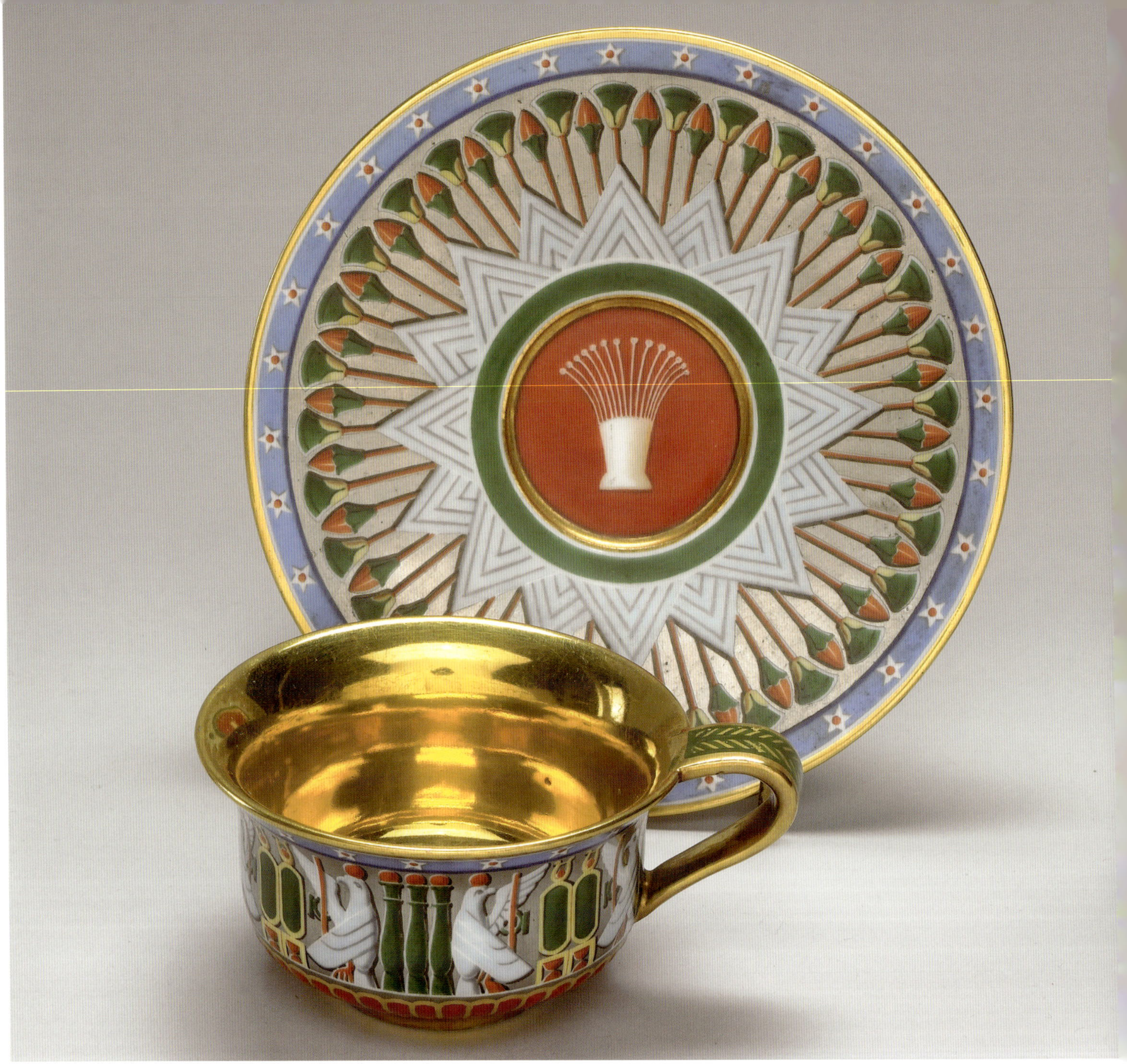

Fig. 32 (cat. 28): Egyptian Revival cup and saucer, 1813–14

The grandiose Egyptian Service, created at the factory in the course of 1804–6, reclaimed the importance of porcelain services at state level (fig. 33). The startling combination of blue, gold, and sepia tones was utterly novel. Jacques-François-Joseph Swebach (1769–1823) decorated the monochrome scenes in the main pieces and was granted the unusual privilege of signing them on the front. The source was Vivant Denon's *Voyage dans la Basse et Haute Égypte* (1802). The borders in *beau bleu* with gold were designed by renowned architect Théodore Brongniart (1739–1813),

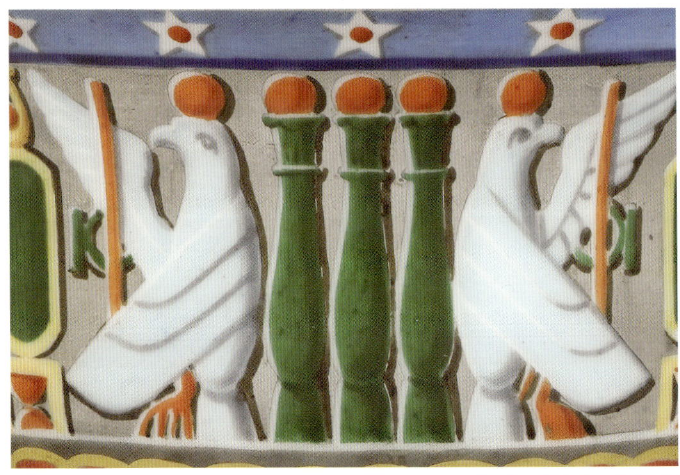

Detail of fig. 32, Egyptian motifs on cup

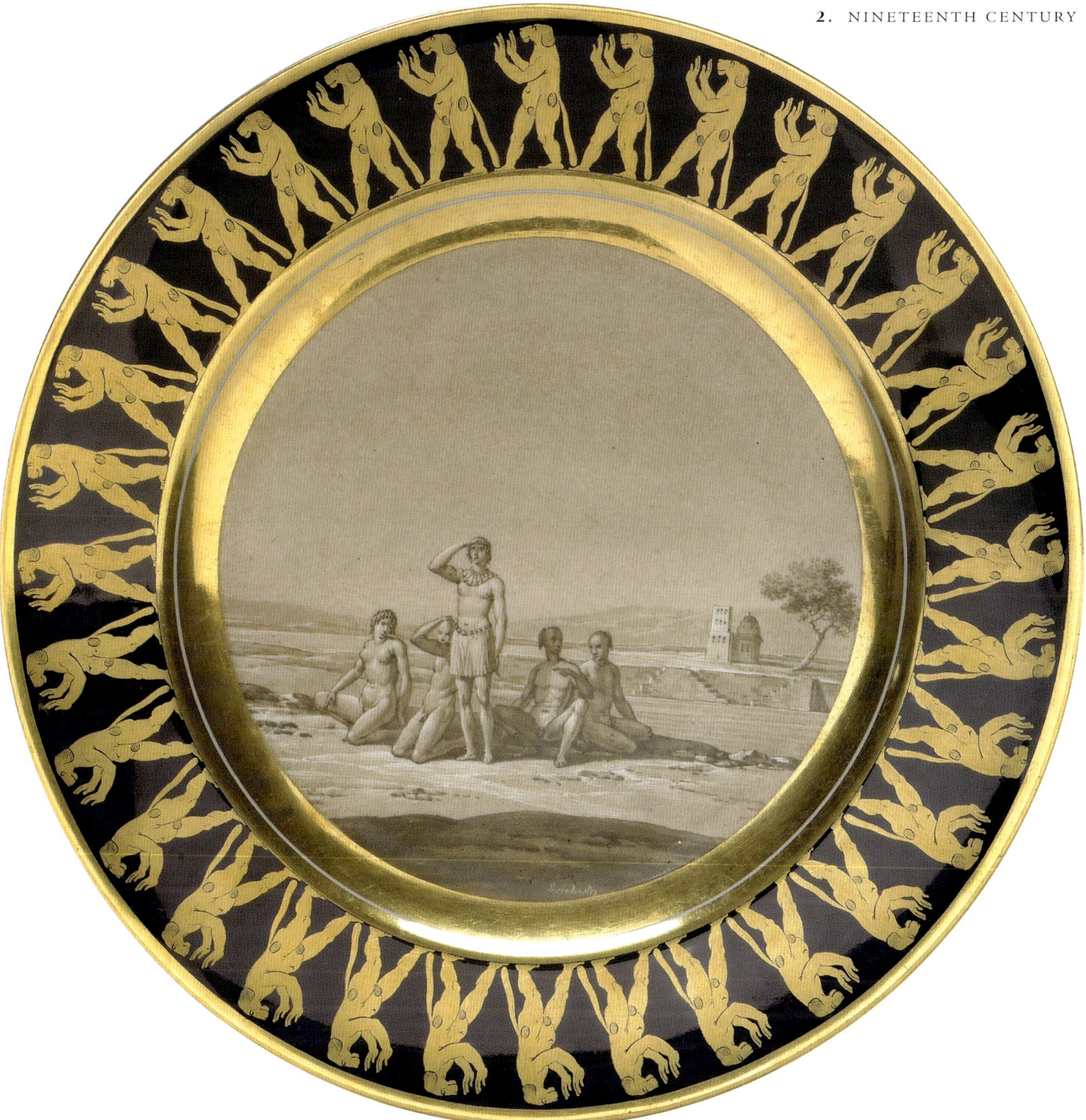

Fig. 33 (cat. 29): Plate from the first Egyptian Service, 1804

father of the famed Sèvres director. This Egyptian Service was presented to the Russian emperor Alexander I (reg. 1801–25) after the signing of the Treaty of Tilsit in 1807. In 1832 Nicholas I had it transferred to Moscow along with the *Service Olympique* to be used in grand banquets in the presence of the emperor.[6]

Empress Joséphine monitored the progress of this Egyptian Service's fabrication with great interest. Her love for it is signaled by the fact that at the time of her divorce from Napoleon in 1809, when the emperor offered her 30,000 francs of Sèvres porcelain, she immediately asked for a similar service. Her requested service, however, was not completed and delivered to Malmaison until April 1812. By then Joséphine had had a change of heart, and finding the service too severe she returned it to the factory where it remained for six years. All was not lost as the subsequent king eventually used Joséphine's commission as a diplomatic gift. After the Battle of Waterloo in June 1815, the first Duke of Wellington settled in Paris as commander of the army occupying France. In March 1818, King Louis XVIII hosted a dinner for the duke at which the subject of porcelain was discussed. As the Bourbon king wanted to remain on friendly terms with the man who had ensured his restoration to the throne, he ordered the Egyptian service to be delivered to the Duke of Wellington the following day.[7]

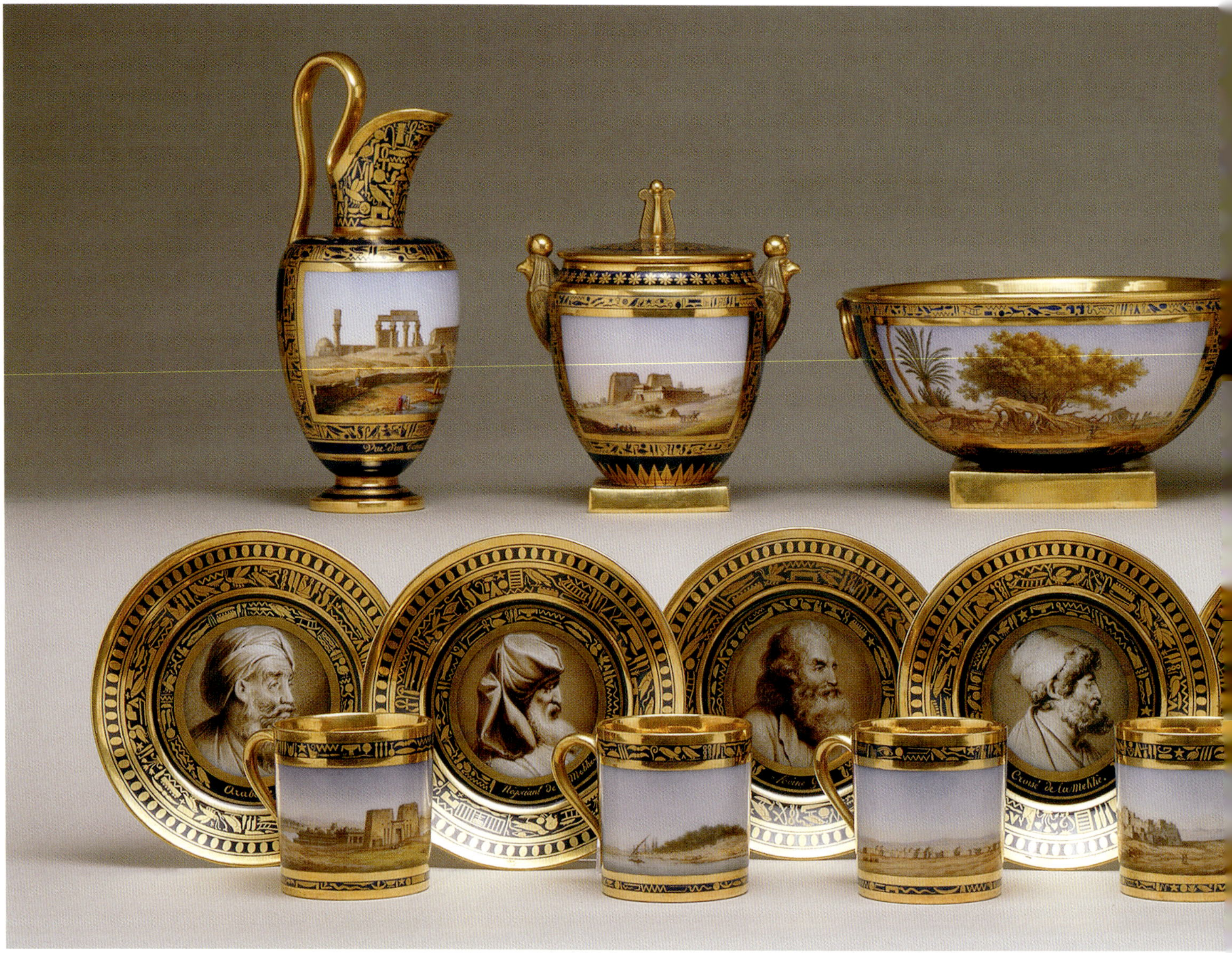

Fig. 34 (cat. 27): Egyptian tea and coffee set presented by Napoleon to the duchesse de Montebello, 1810–12

This grand coffee and tea service is another example of Egyptian design with imperial connections (fig. 34). It was a gift from Napoleon to the duchesse de Montebello, widow of Maréchal Jean Lannes, one of Napoleon's best generals who had died on the battlefield in 1809.[8] Maréchal Lannes had participated in the Egyptian campaign so the subject was particularly fitting. The views of Egypt are combined with a gallery of startling portraits of Egyptian popular types such as a merchant, a monk, or a journeyman. The teapot, slop bowl, and sugar bowl are forms based on designs by Vivant Denon, who was also responsible for the panoramic landscape scenes of almost photographic quality.[9] This is not surprising as it is known that, during the campaign,

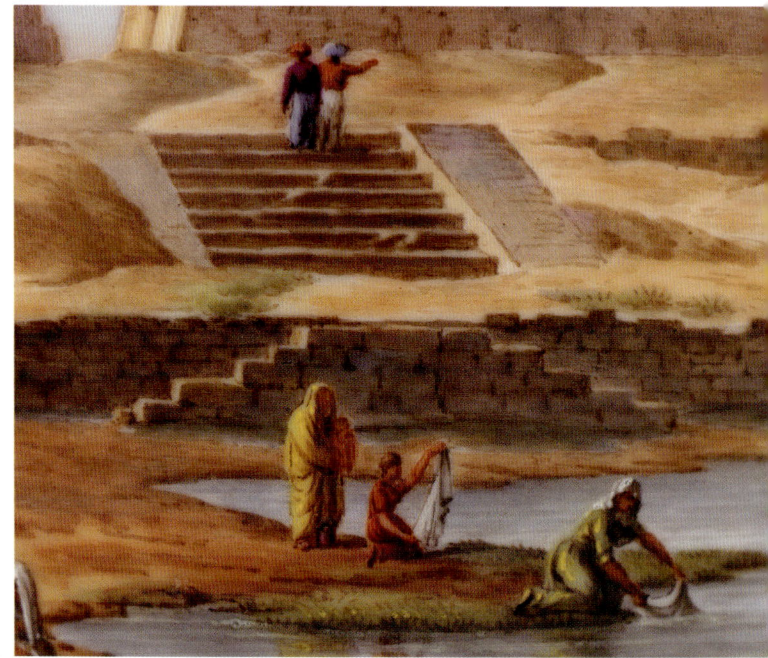

Detail of fig. 34, view of a temple in Hermontis

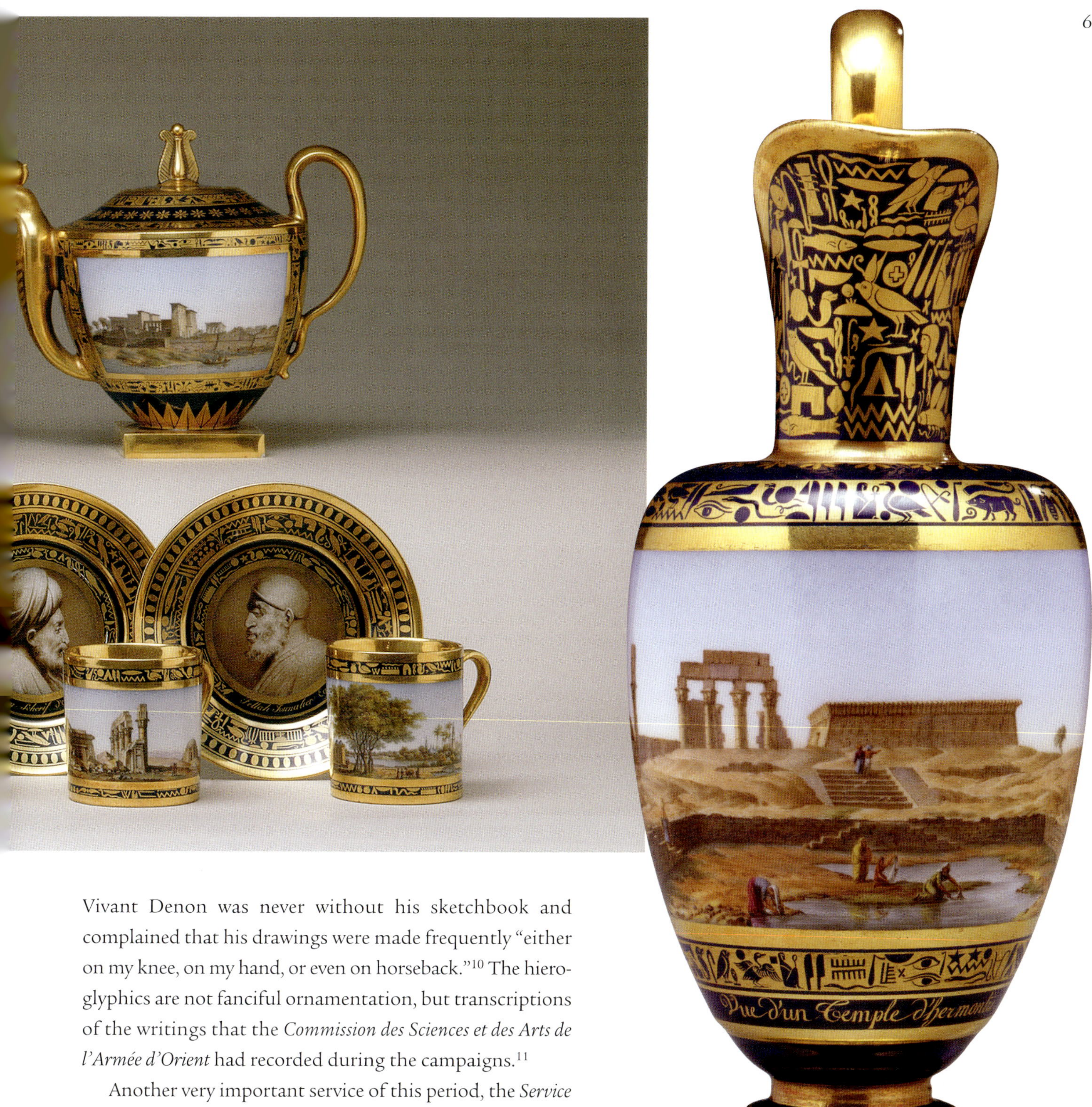

Detail of fig. 34, milk jug with view of a temple in Hermontis from the Egyptian tea and coffee set for the duchesse de Montebello

Vivant Denon was never without his sketchbook and complained that his drawings were made frequently "either on my knee, on my hand, or even on horseback."[10] The hieroglyphics are not fanciful ornamentation, but transcriptions of the writings that the *Commission des Sciences et des Arts de l'Armée d'Orient* had recorded during the campaigns.[11]

Another very important service of this period, the *Service Iconographique Grec*, dates from the end of the Empire. The *trompe l'oeil* decoration in imitation of cameos illustrates the prevailing love of antique carved gems, the emperor's interest in the ancient classical world, and Brongniart's studies in mineralogy. The proliferation of decorations imitating hard stones and antique cameos in sardonyx, agate, or carnelian is manifest in many important services and decorative pieces of the first quarter of the nineteenth century. The expansion of the factory's palette allowed for the subtle effects required to imitate cameos with enamel colors.

Two services of identical characteristics were produced in the years 1808–13.[12] The first was a gift from Napoleon to his uncle, the Cardinal Fesch, in 1811 on the occasion of the baptism of the King of Rome (the son of Napoleon I and

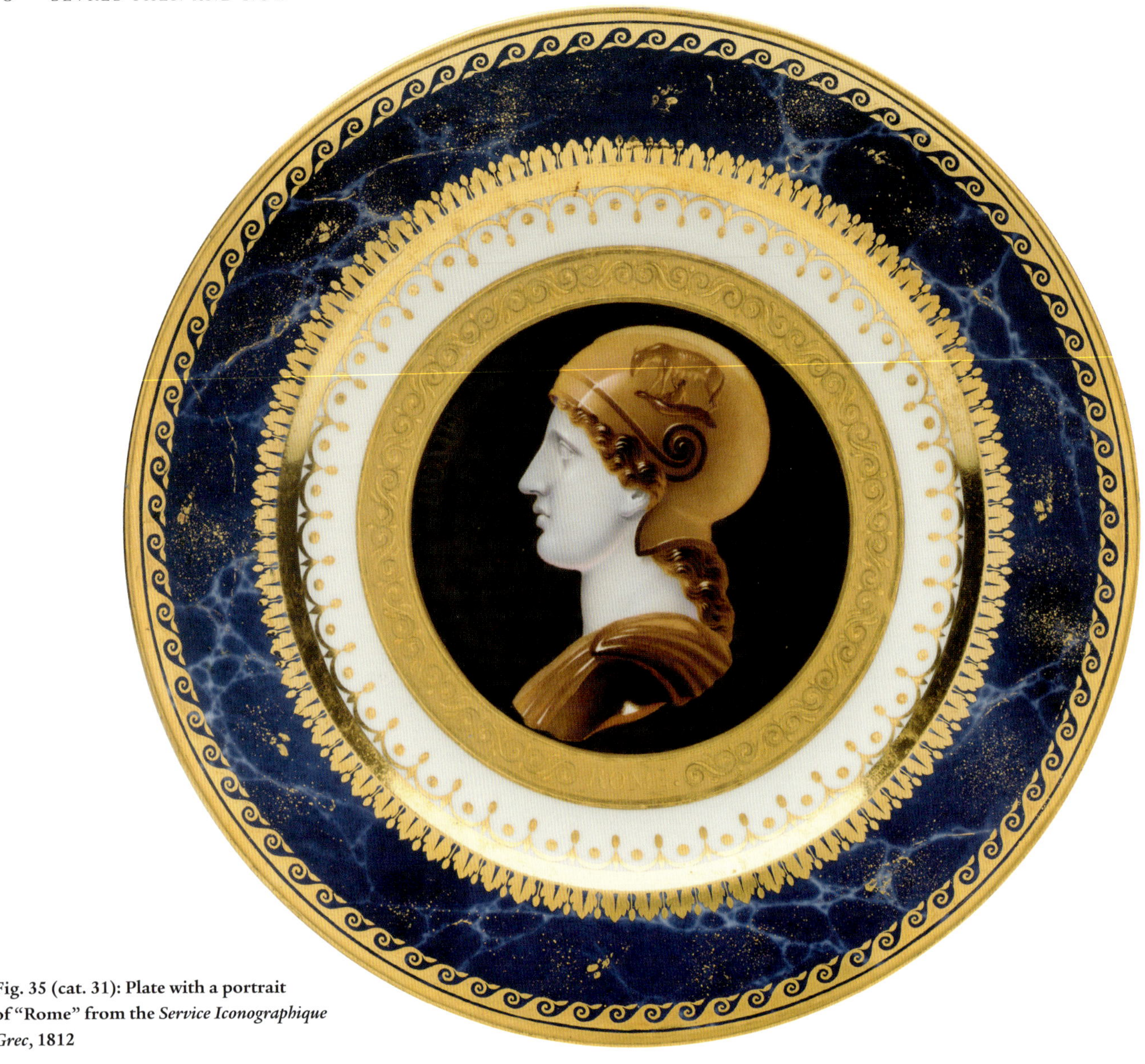

Fig. 35 (cat. 31): Plate with a portrait of "Rome" from the *Service Iconographique Grec*, 1812

Marie-Louise, his second wife). The two plates (figs. 35, 36), the basket (*corbeille basse*) (fig. 37), and the sugar bowl (*sucrier à têtes d'aigles*) (fig. 38) are part of the second *Service Iconographique Grec*. This service was commissioned by the Ministry of Foreign Affairs in 1812 and not finished until after the fall of the Empire in 1817. It was delivered to "the court of Rome" on September 17, 1819. This vague reference indicates a high-ranking recipient in the Vatican. Whether it was meant for presentation to Pope Pius VII, from whom Napoleon received the imperial crown to set upon his head at his coronation, or another member of his circle still has to be determined. The circumstances surrounding the dispersal of this service are also unknown.[13]

The numerous baskets that form part of this service are an indication of the changing fashions in table settings. In 1810 Empress Joséphine had rejected the large biscuit centerpiece to go with the Egyptian Service, as it was deemed too heavy, and ordered her architect Louis-Martin Berthault (1770–1823) to design some baskets instead.[14] The iconographical source for the classical portraits in the *Service Iconographique Grec* is the noted archeologist E.Q. Visconti's publication *Iconographie ancienne ou Recueil des portraits authentiques des empereurs, rois et hommes illustres de l'antiquité* (with supplements in 1817 and 1824). Factory painters may have had access to the preparatory drawings for this album provided by Visconti, who was curator of the

OPPOSITE
Fig. 36 (cat. 31): Plate with a portrait of "Pallas" from the *Service Iconographique Grec*, 1812

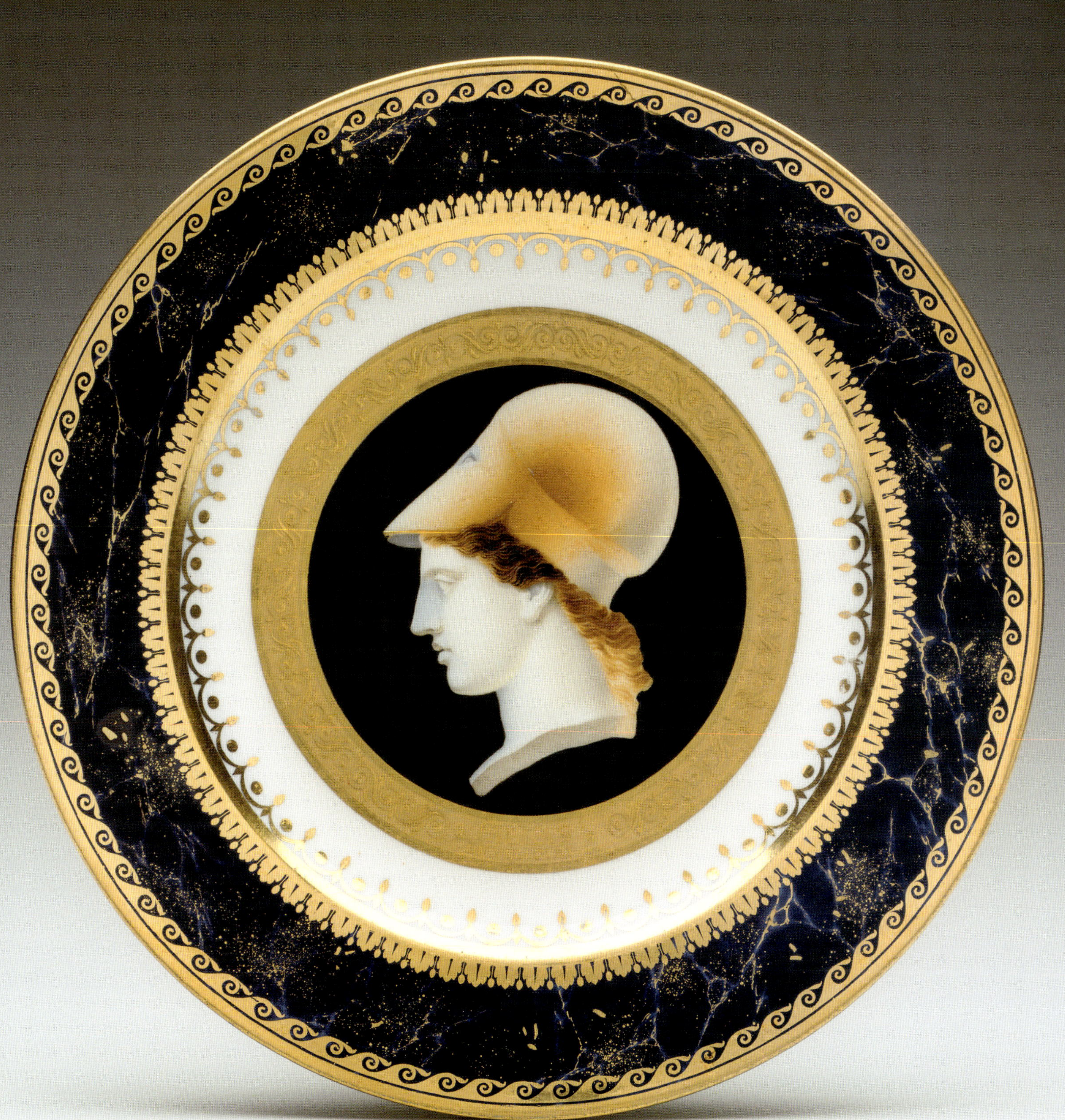

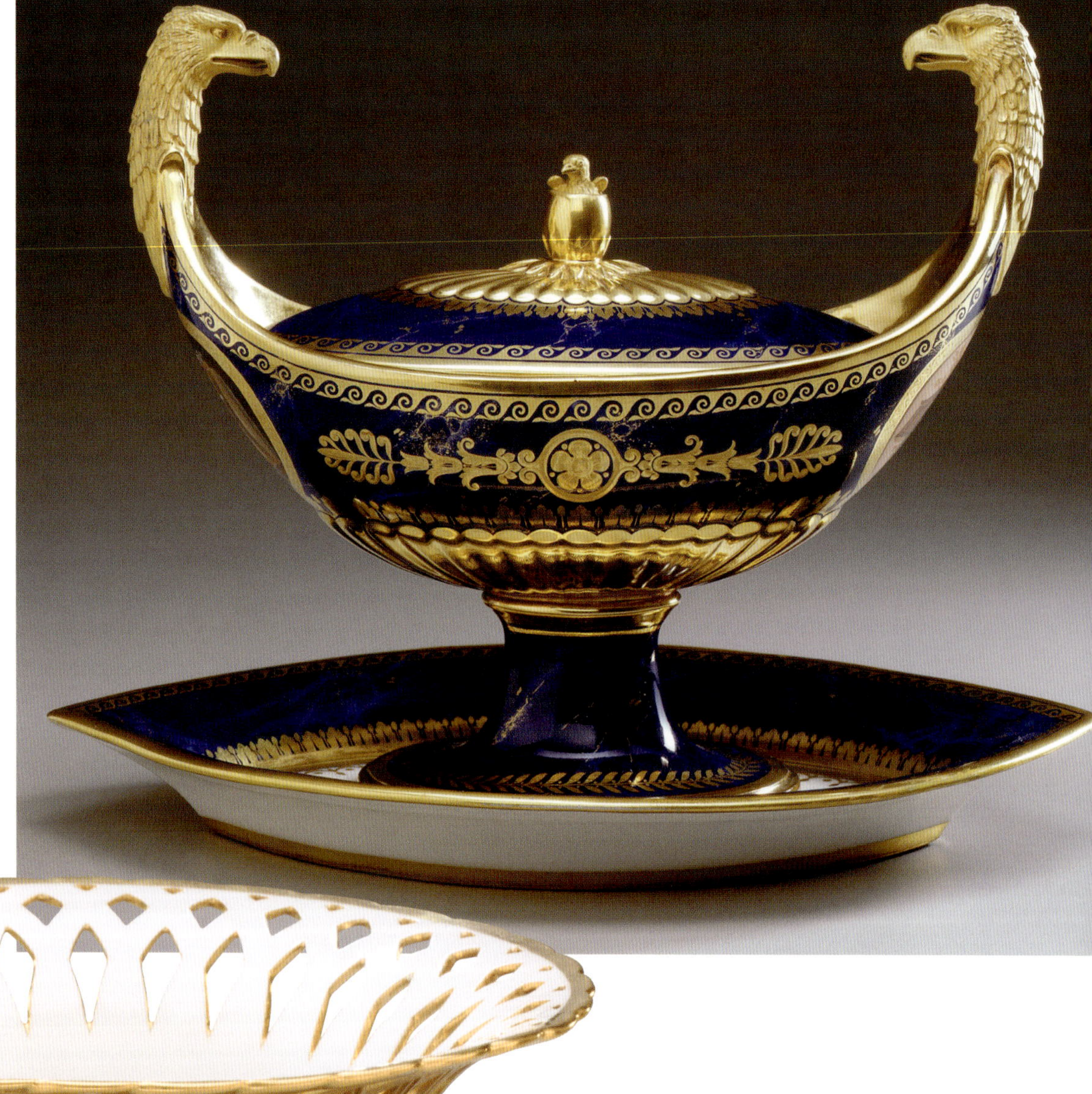

RIGHT: **Fig. 38 (cat. 32): Sugar bowl with eagle heads from the *Service Iconographique Grec*, 1817**

BELOW: **Fig. 37 (cat. 33): Basket from the *Service Iconographique Grec*, ca. 1813**

Musée des Antiques in Paris, while he was working on this compilation. In addition to examples exhibited at the museum, Napoleon offered a wealth of medals and portrait busts from classical antiquity to draw from. The choice of characters represented seems quite arbitrary for the service mixes Greeks and Romans, as well as emperors, poets, renowned scientists, philosophers, and deities from classical mythology.

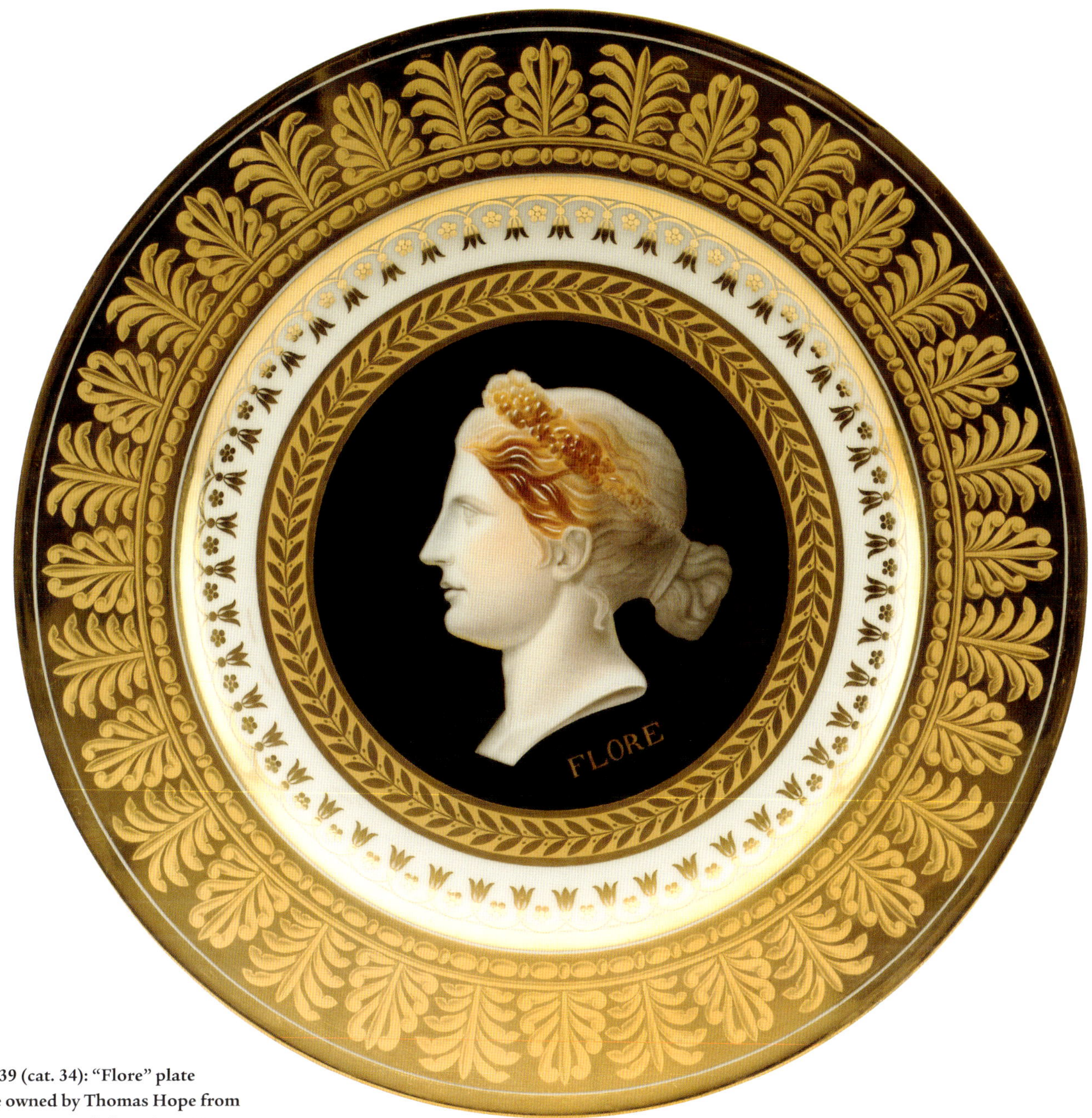

Fig. 39 (cat. 34): "Flore" plate once owned by Thomas Hope from the *Service à marli d'or*, 1813–14

In addition to the dinner services with elaborate decoration, intended for the emperor and his family, as well as for the high dignitaries of his court and foreign rulers, the manufactory's best painters were regularly handed plates to decorate as they saw fit, with figures, landscapes, cameos, flowers, and other motifs. The plates in figs. 39 and 40 fall into this category. They have solid gold-ground borders burnished with palmettes and, in each center, a profile in the cameo manner—one inscribed "Flore" and the other "Pallas." Plates like these were identified in the factory records as "Service pittoresque à marly d'or." When the painters had decorated a sufficient number of these plates to form a set, they would be supplied as such. For example, there are *marli d'or* plates at Malmaison from the collection of Prince Eugène de Beauharnais, Joséphine's son, who was viceroy of Italy during much of Napoleon's reign.

These are two of four plates purchased by Thomas Hope directly from Sèvres.[15] Thomas Hope (1769–1831) was one of the foremost connoisseurs of his age. He championed archeological Neoclassicism, and his houses—Duchess Street in London, near Cavendish Square, and Deepdene in Surrey—were famous for their advanced neo-Egyptian interiors.

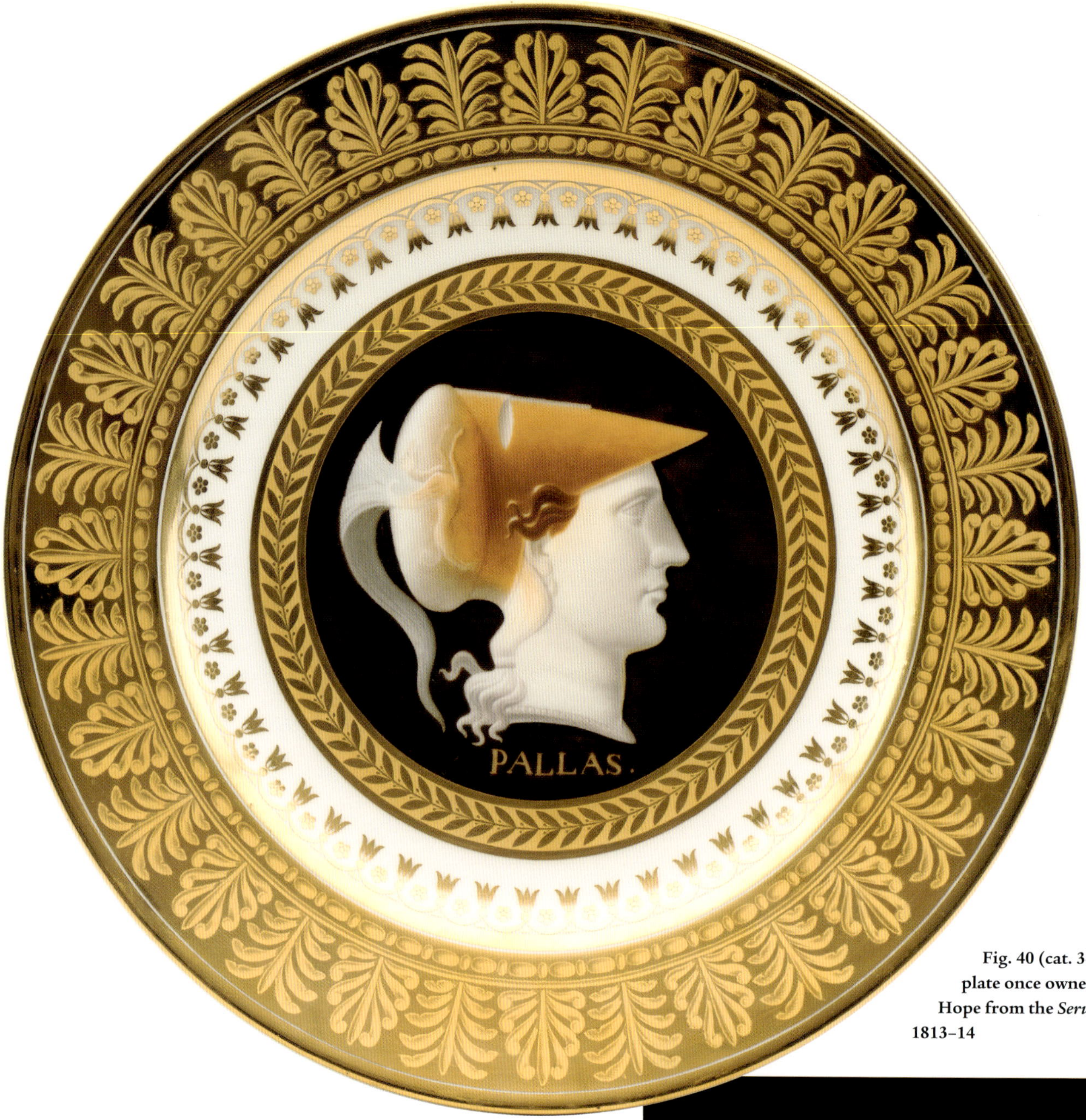

Fig. 40 (cat. 34): "Pallas" plate once owned by Thomas Hope from the *Service à marli d'or*, 1813–14

The name "Clumber" is inscribed on the back of each frame and the original factory sticker price is glued to the back of each plate.[16] It is extremely unusual for the Sèvres factory's original price label to remain on an object, as porcelain is normally washed (see cat. no. 34 in checklist of entries for image). The explanation for this must be that the plates were framed soon after they were purchased and never used or washed up. Their lavish decoration made them more suitable for display than for use at the table, and it is likely that it was Thomas Hope who had them framed (fig. 41). This is wholly consistent with his predilection for furniture and decorations in the antique taste.

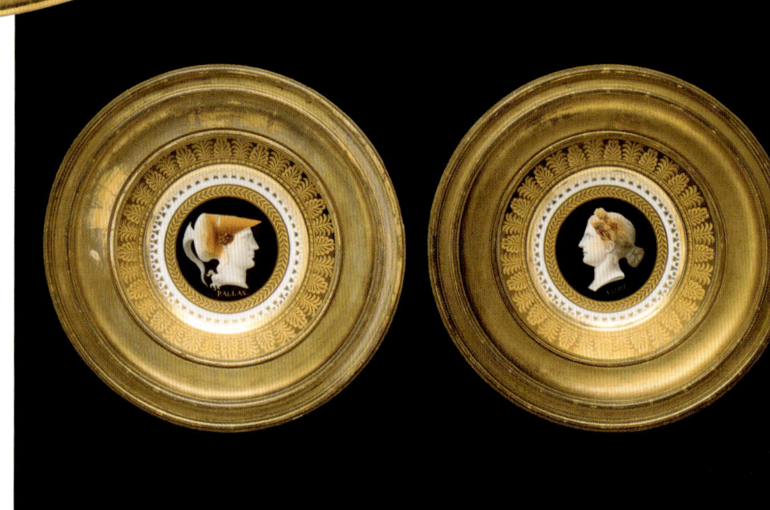

Fig. 41: "Flore" and "Pallas" plates in their frames

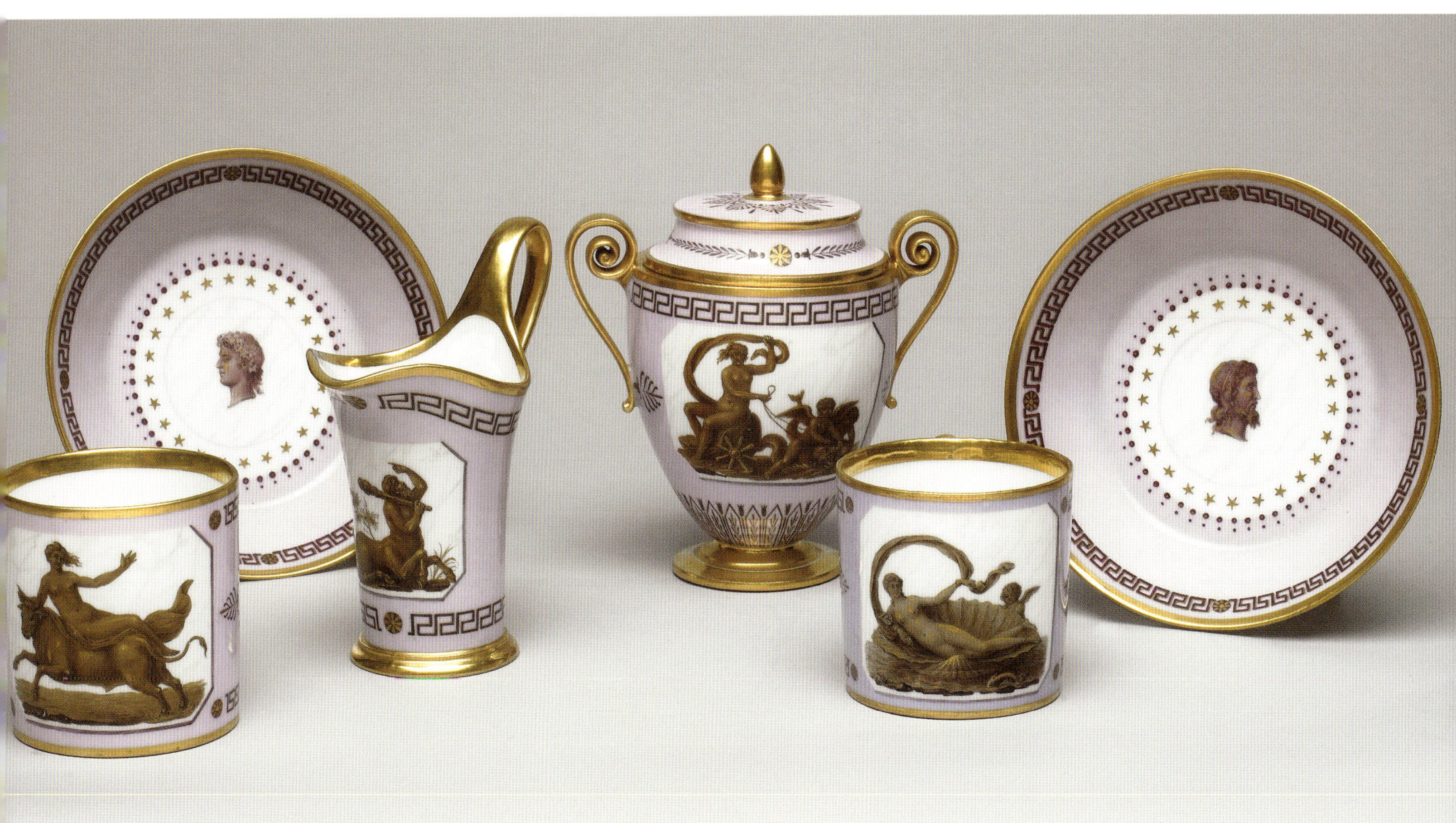

Fig. 42 (cat. 30): Pieces from a tea set presented by Napoleon to his sister Paulina Bonaparte, 1805

Hope had a room for the display of Greek vases on shelves, which was engraved for illustration in his book of 1807, *Household Furniture and Interior Decoration Executed from Designs by Thomas Hope*.

The interior decoration mavericks of the Empire, Charles Percier (1764–1838) and Pierre-François-Léonard Fontaine (1762–1853), established the basis for the most fashionable decorations after the Revolution in France and abroad. New interiors furnished with furniture from the prestigious workshop of Jacob-Desmalter, bronzes by Pierre-Philippe Thomire, and new color schemes were all the rage. The mauve ground color of the coffee and tea set in fig. 42 was quite popular during the Empire when a new palette of audacious and sometimes strident colors was introduced and combined in hitherto unseen ways. Madame Récamier, legendary hostess and saloniste, had her bedchamber upholstered in a similar color. Her bedroom, the creation of esteemed architect Louis-Martin Berthault (executed by the famous team of Percier & Fontaine, ca. 1798), was widely published and visited by a host of artistic and literary personalities during her lifetime.

The tea set belonged to another legendary woman and famous beauty of the First Empire, Paulina Bonaparte. Paulina had recently become the young widow of Victor Leclerc, one of Napoleon's most important generals and was remarried in 1803 to Prince Camillo Borghese, a member of one of the most powerful Roman families with influences both over church and state, and owner of one of the most impressive art collections of the time. The marriage was unsuccessful and Paulina left Rome and returned to Paris in 1805. There she lived in the hôtel de Charost (now the residence of the ambassador of Great Britain in Paris), which she had purchased a couple of years earlier, and decorated in the latest styles with the aid of Percier and Fontaine and the furniture firm of Jacob-Desmalter. Napoleon gave this mauve tea set to his sister in 1805, presumably to go with the décors she was so feverishly engaged in selecting. Decorated with "Pompeian" subjects, the figures are painted in gold against a color ground with incised outlines. This technique, referred to as *figures étrusques* in the eighteenth century (see figs. 21 and 22), was reintroduced at this time. In this nineteenth-century version, the outline incisions have been replaced by shadows painted in brown or burnished gold. The mauve color was also the color of choice for Paulina's boudoir at the hôtel de Charost.[17]

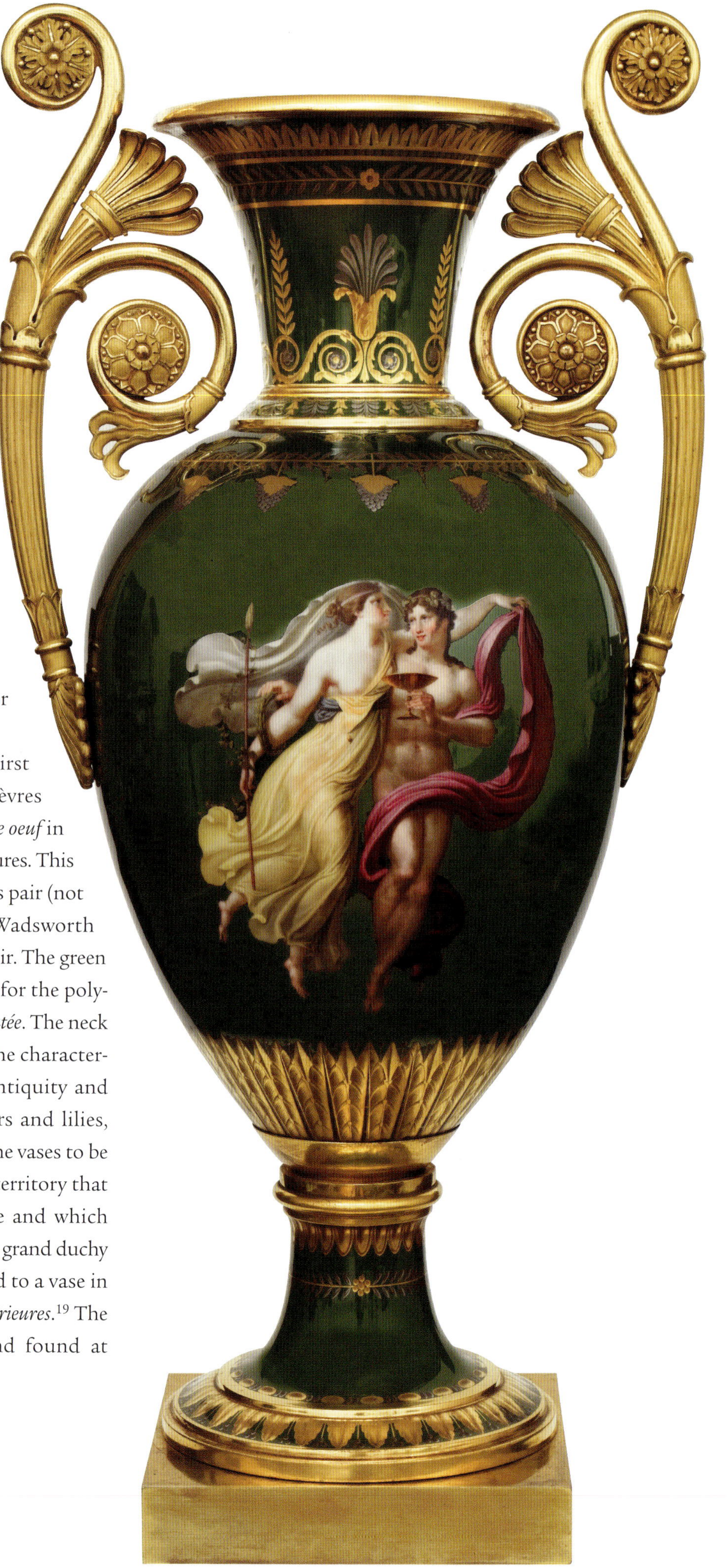

The other quintessential color of the First Empire, *vert de chrome*, was formulated at Sèvres around 1807. It is the ground color of the *vase oeuf* in fig. 43, one of a pair decorated with classical figures. This example depicts Bacchus and Ariadne, while its pair (not illustrated but also in the collection of the Wadsworth Atheneum in Hartford) depicts Flora and Zephir. The green ground was scratched precisely to leave room for the polychrome decoration in a technique known as *gratée*. The neck and shoulder of the vase are decorated with the characteristic repertoire of elements from classical antiquity and Egypt: anthemia, ears of wheat, lotus flowers and lilies, grapevines and rosettes.[18] Napoleon ordered the vases to be sent to Louis I, Prince of Hesse-Darmstadt, a territory that was part of the Confederation of the Rhine and which Napoleon had elevated from a landgraviate to a grand duchy in 1806. The design of the vases may be linked to a vase in Percier and Fontaine's *Recueil de décorations intérieures*.[19] The floating figures are reminiscent of the kind found at

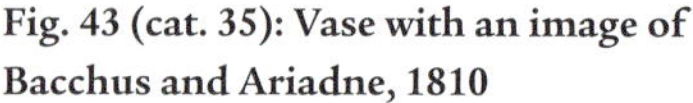

Fig. 43 (cat. 35): Vase with an image of Bacchus and Ariadne, 1810

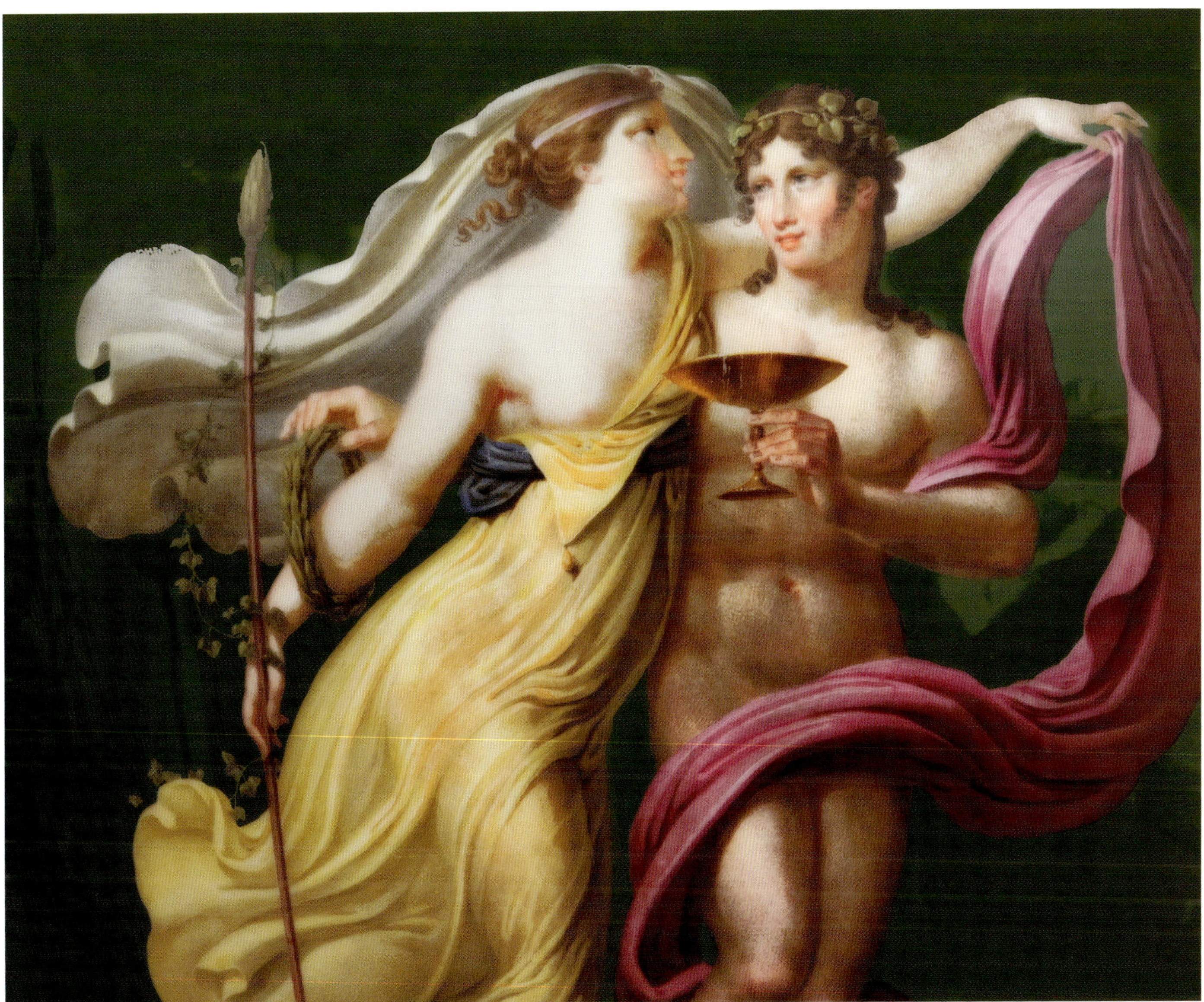

Detail of fig. 43, painting of Bacchus and Ariadne

Herculaneum and Pompeii and adopted in neoclassical decorations from the late eighteenth century through the First Empire when Pompeiian rooms were popular. It also bears comparison with the *Service Olympique* commissioned by Napoleon in 1806, which was decorated with mythological subjects and included some floating gods.[20]

At the fall of the Empire, Prussian forces occupied Paris in 1815 and took over the factory, initially for the purposes of establishing an ambulatory. Brongniart was asked to draw up a list of all objects for sale and to transfer them to Paris. He fortunately lagged on the order and avoided a disastrous dispersal. However, several pieces related to Napoleonic history were transferred to Berlin.

Bourbon Restoration

Napoleonic France may very well have been defeated, but the returning Bourbons and royalist *émigrés* set out to restore the glory of France after the "unfortunate" Napoleonic intermission. Louis XVIII (reg. 1814–24), the former comte de Provence and Louis XVI's brother, began a program of renovating the royal residences and commissioning all kinds of luxury wares to furnish them. Since this initiative was continued by his brother and successor, Charles X (reg. 1824–30), the Bourbons maintained their support of the royal porcelain factory.

The tray in fig. 44 depicts the royal visit of Louis XVIII to the sales room at the Sèvres manufactory on June 25,

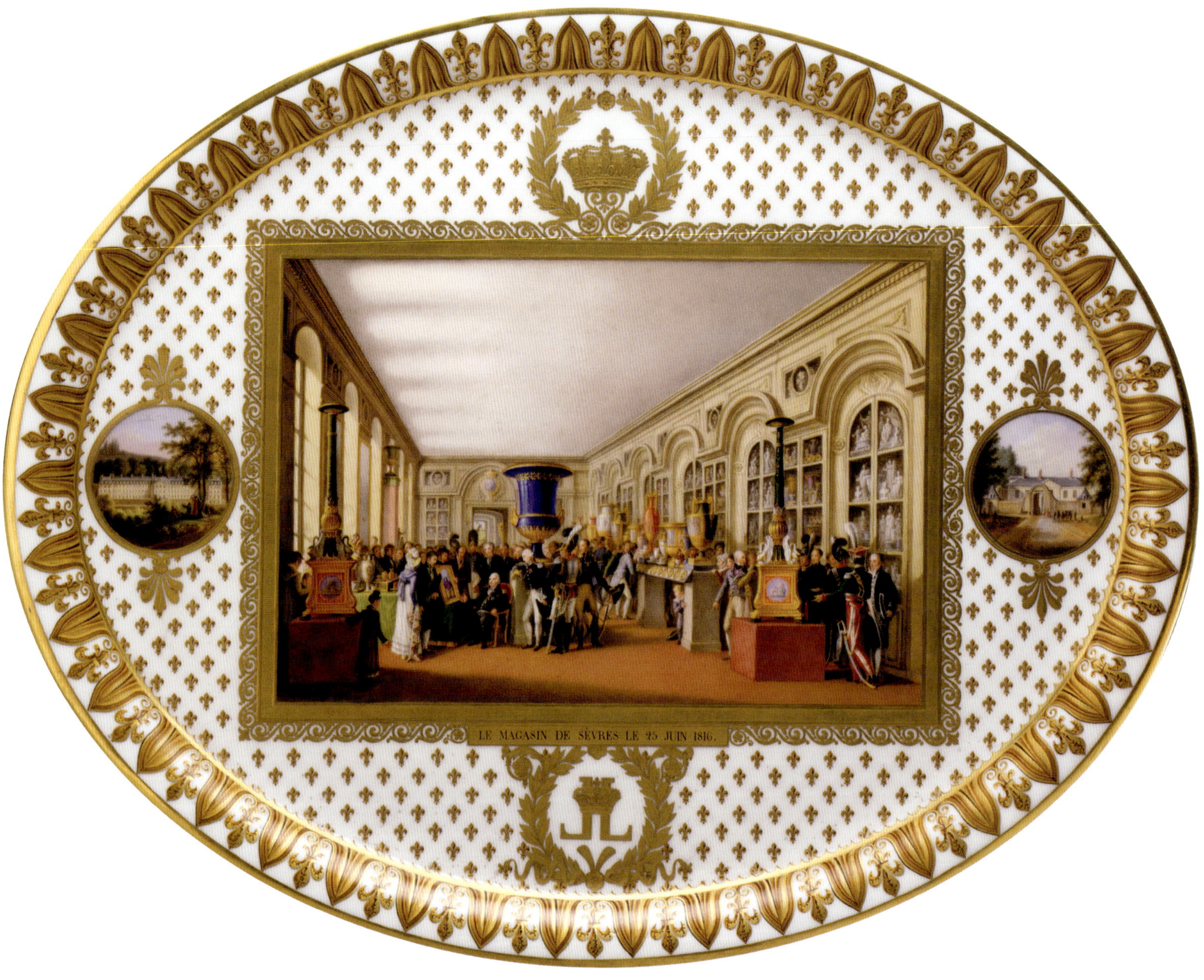

Fig. 44 (cat. 36): Tray from the tea and coffee service *L'Art de la porcelaine*, 1816

1816. The king, seated in an armchair, is reviewing the latest productions, accompanied by Brongniart, who is right behind him. A worker is presenting a porcelain plaque depicting *La Belle Jardinière* after Raphael, while the woman who painted it, Marie Victoire Jacquotot, is standing next to him. A large *vase "Médicis"* centers the composition. To its left, one can appreciate some of the larger vases on show while the cases are laden with biscuit figures and table service wares. Surrounding the scene are areas of white covered with the fleur-de-lis. At the top and bottom are the royal crown and the king's cipher, respectively. Flanking the cartouche on the sides are round medallions with external views of the Sèvres manufactory. Sèvres factory painter Jean-Charles Develly (1743–1849) made preparatory sketches of the royal visit, which served as the basis for the decoration of this piece. The tray was part of a tea set, *Les travaux de la manufacture de Sèvres*, while the rest of the pieces were decorated with scenes relating to porcelain making (see fig. 31).

The classical themes formulated during the Empire were retained under the Bourbon Restoration, with slight modifications. During those politically conservative times, less compromising imagery prevailed. A wave of naturalistic decoration of flowers and birds swept the production. Flower painting served to demonstrate the broad range of the manufactory's palette, which can be appreciated in the rich fruit and floral wreath on the *vase floréal* with African birds in fig. 45.

Detail of fig. 44, painting showing King Louis XVIII sitting in an armchair

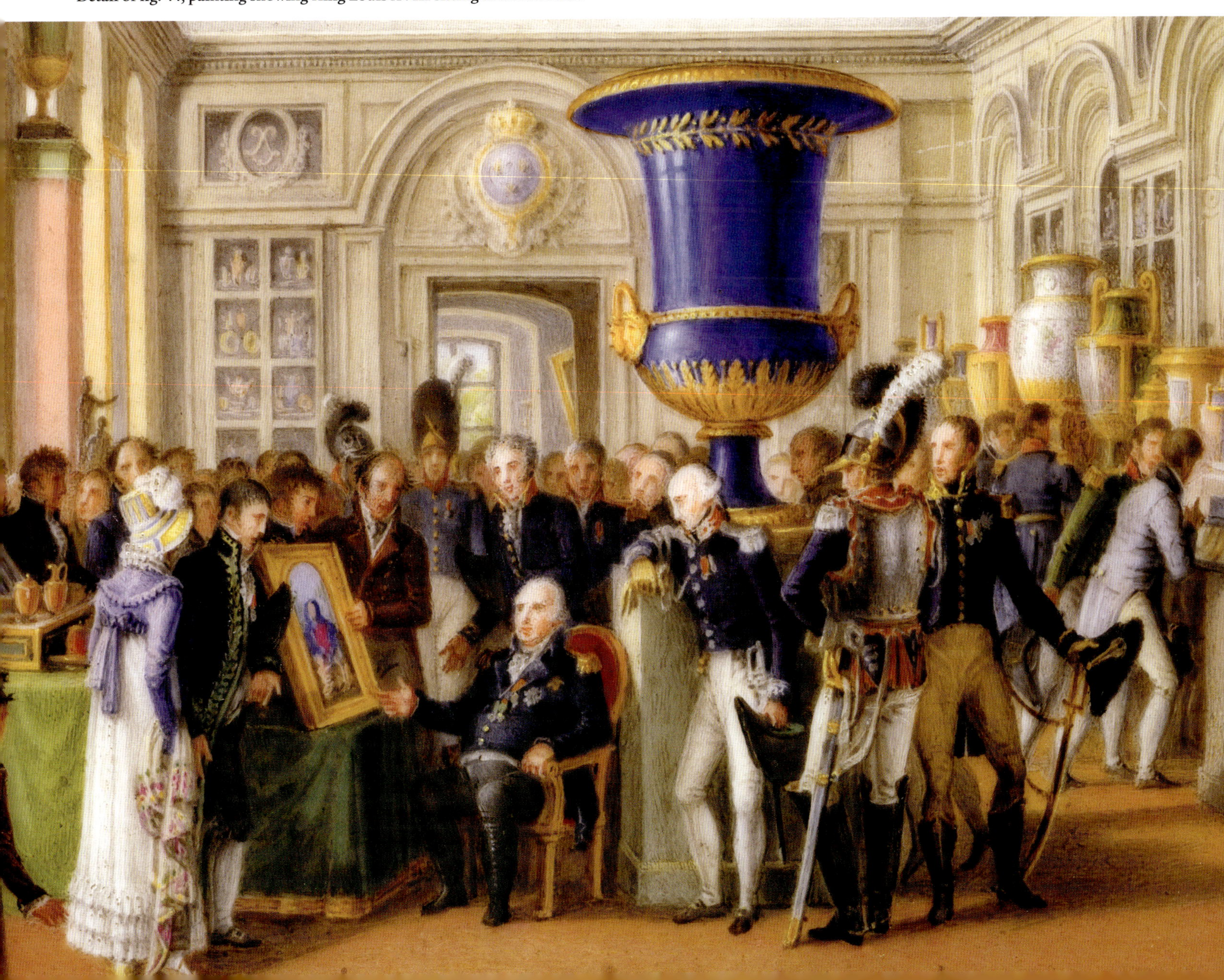

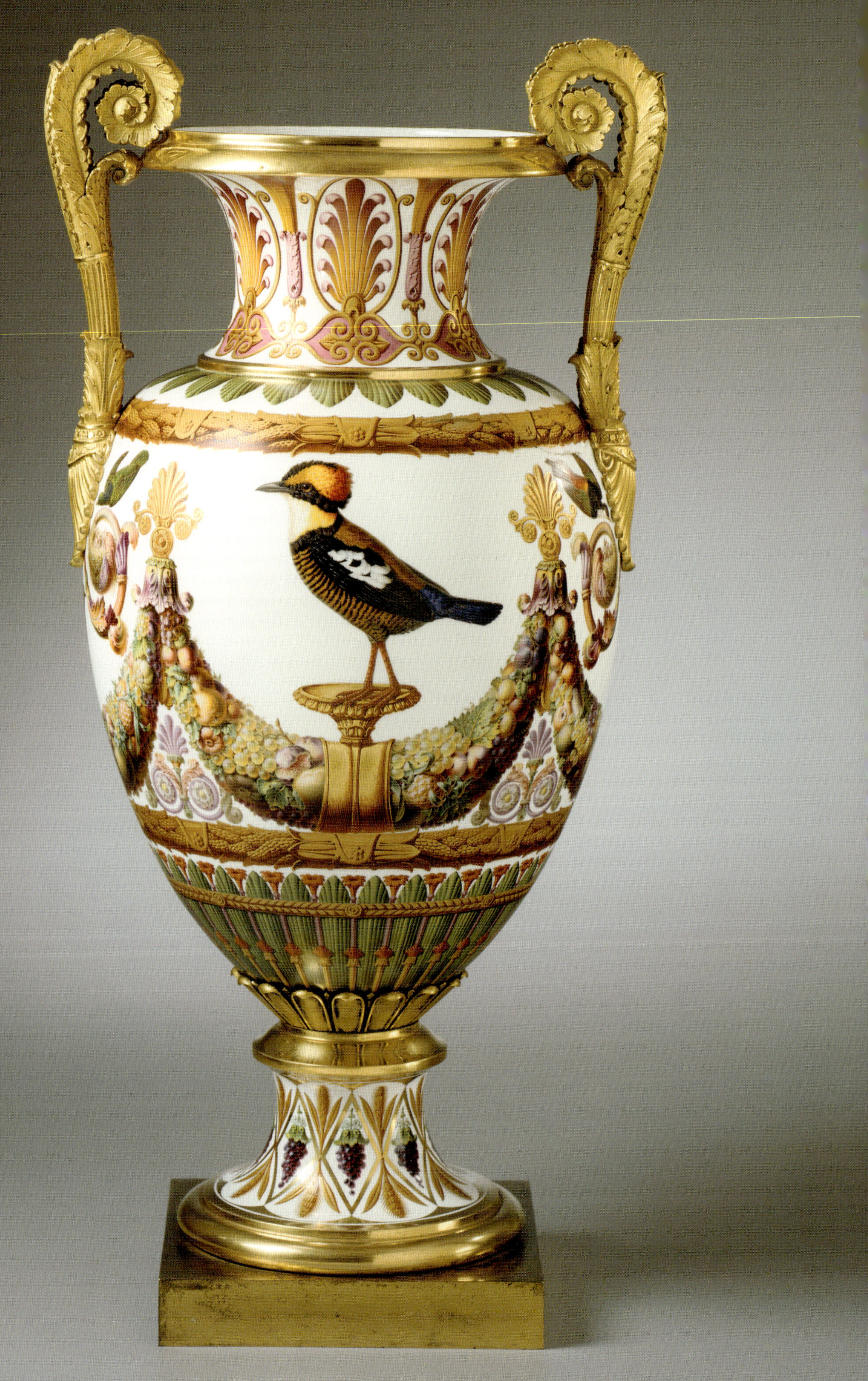

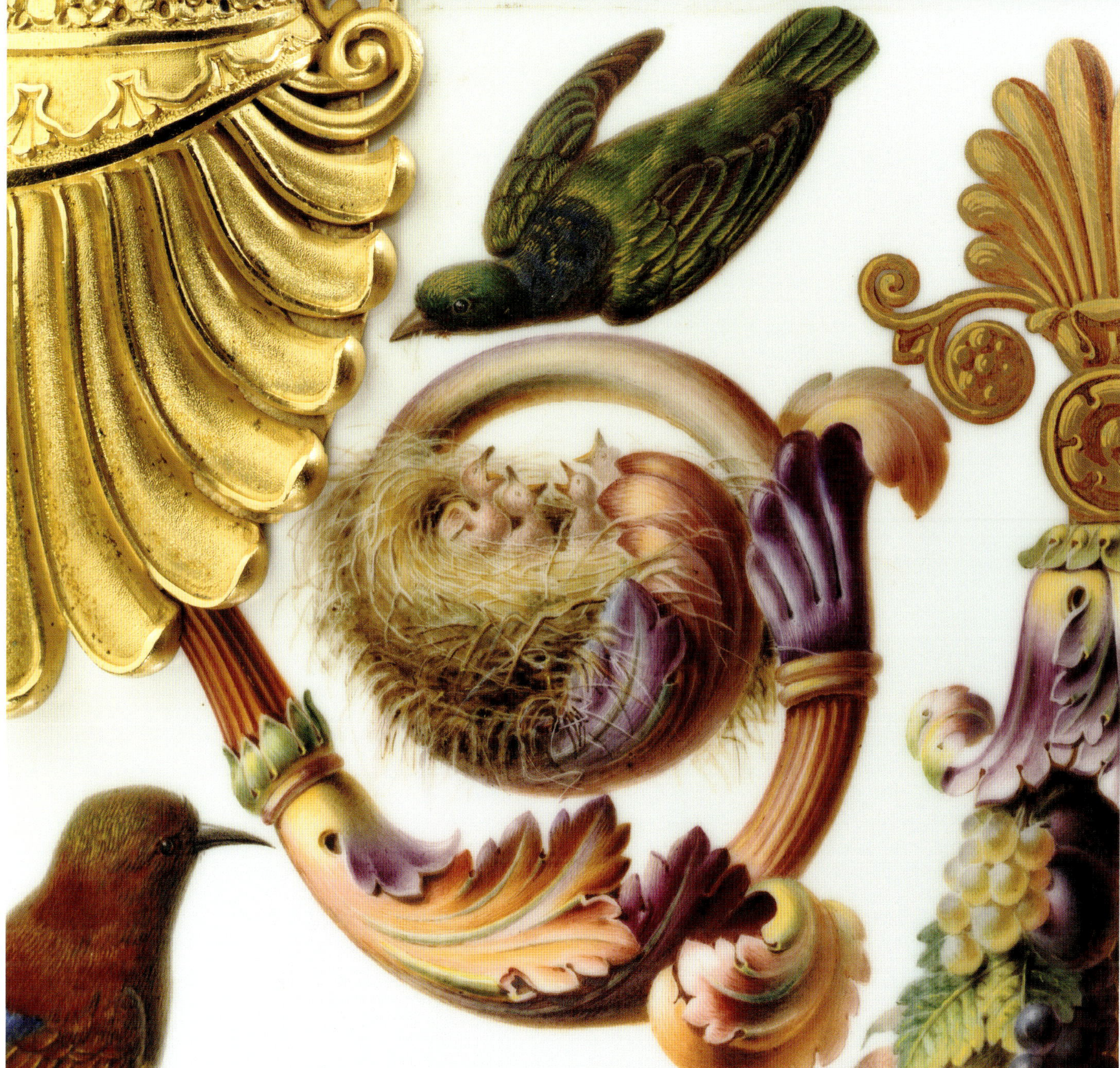

Detail of fig. 45, painting of baby birds in a nest

One of the main traits of the Sèvres factory—the extraordinary variety of its productions—was fostered to an even greater extent during the first half of the nineteenth century when new designs for ninety-two different vases and eighty-nine different cups were created, including the variations in their handles and feet.[21] The *vase floréal* was one of those new shapes. Two African bird vases, almost identical to this vase, were shown at the annual exhibition of products of French industry at the Louvre in 1823.[22] That year, Brongniart, concerned at the prospect that simple porcelains might drown in a mass of ceramic objects displayed by other makers, decided to exhibit only show pieces like this vase. Sometimes the royal commissions dictated the themes of decoration, particularly when there was a need to convey certain political notions, but in other cases, such as with animals, birds, and plants, the choice was left entirely to Brongniart's discretion. The decoration of this vase responds to the Sèvres director's fervent interest in the natural sciences and, in particular, the study of ornithology. Interestingly, it is one of the few pieces of the period to show any white ground. For the decoration of this vase Brongniart called upon Madame Knip (1781–1851), a noted painter of birds in watercolors on vellum.[23] The two vases sent to the

OPPOSITE
Fig. 45 (cat. 37): Vase with African birds, 1822

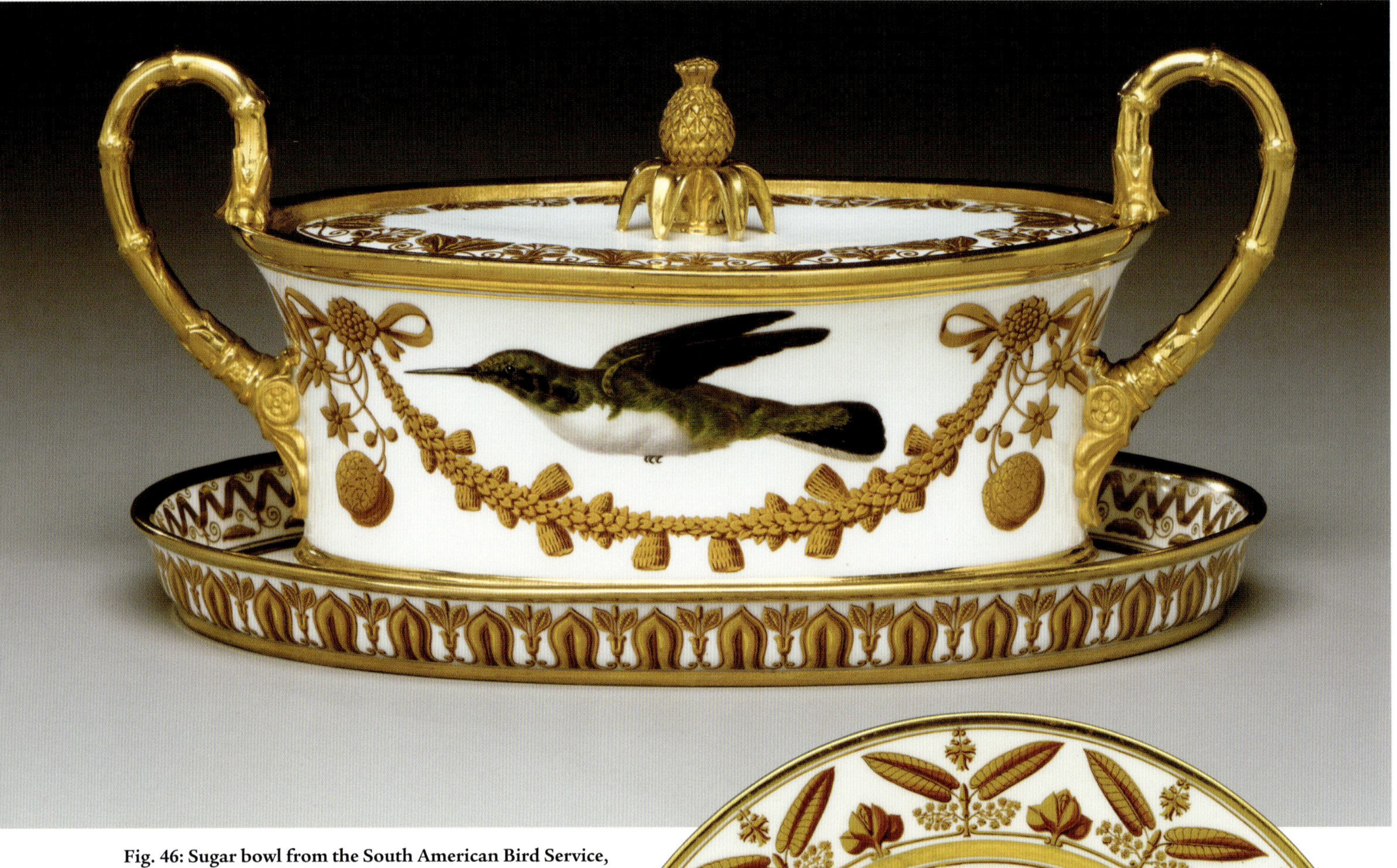

Fig. 46: Sugar bowl from the South American Bird Service, 1819–21

Louvre exhibition were subsequently delivered to the duc d'Angoulême. A third, with a hair crack on the shoulder, probably Hillwood's example, remained at the factory and was sold at a discounted price of 2,500 livres.[24] It is the only known extant example today. A drawing of the vase exists in the factory archives.

Thematic decorations were another characteristic of this period. Brongniart conceived themed sets of vases, *déjeuners*, and dinner services with detailed decorative programs.

Scientific research, the systematic organization of the natural world, and the exploration of remote corners of the planet are at the heart of some of the decorative schemes carried out at Sèvres during the Restoration.

Fig. 47 (cat. 45): Plate from the South American Bird Service, 1819–21

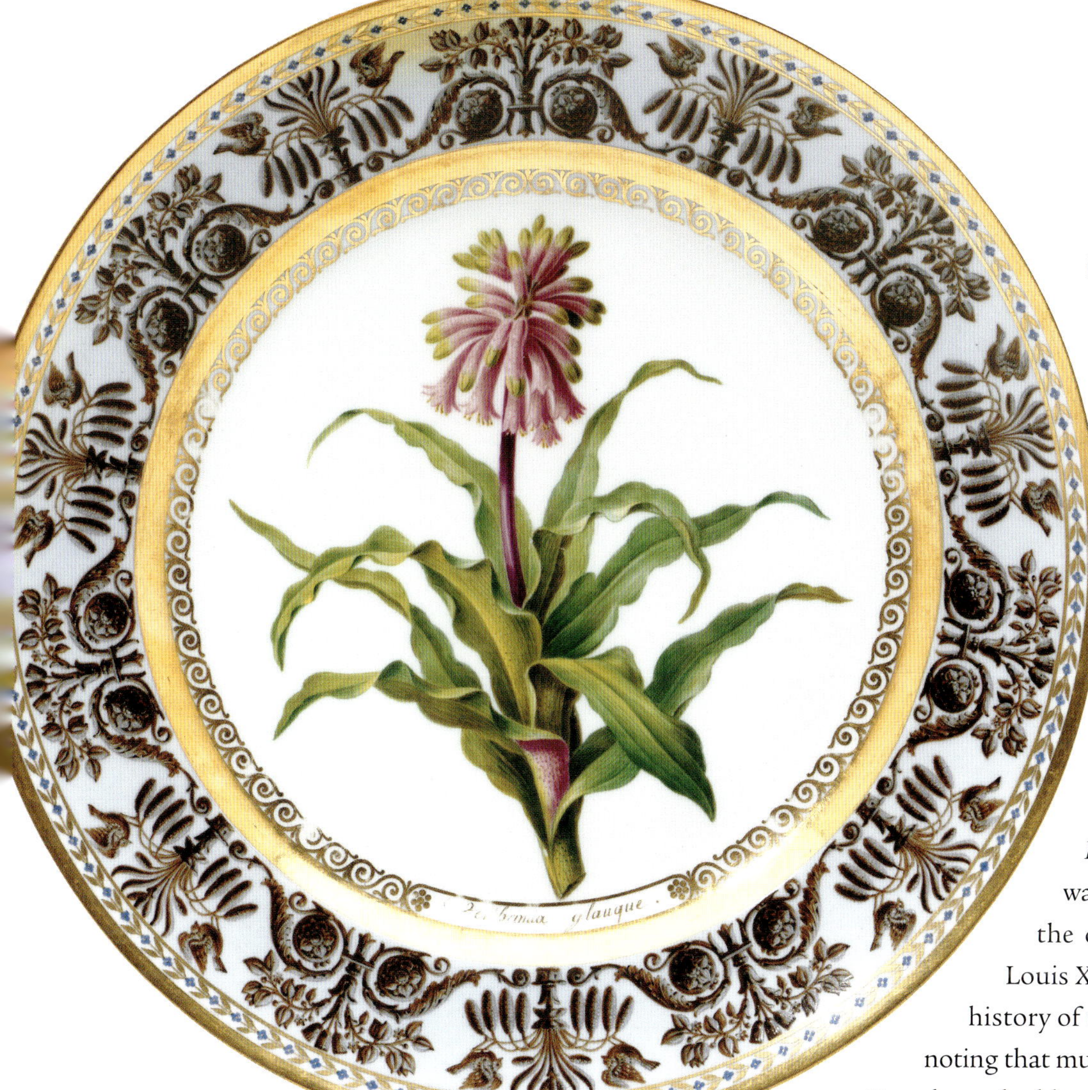

Fig. 48 (cat. 38): Plate from the *Service des Liliacées* intended for King Louis XVIII at the Palace of the Tuileries, 1821

The South American Bird Service is a case in point (figs. 46, 47). Madame Knip was again called on to undertake this project and to draw the birds from stuffed examples at the Muséum d'Histoire Naturelle and then paint them onto porcelain at her own studio. This process involved the pieces traveling back and forth from the painter's studio to the factory's kilns. The ornamentalist, Jean-Charles-François Leloy (active 1816–44), created borders with botanical plants specific to each bird's habitat as well as the perches on which each bird stands. In a scientific vein, the name of each bird is written on the front. This dessert service took three years to produce. In 1821 it was sent to the Louvre's annual exhibition. By order of King Charles X, it was delivered in 1826 to the duchesse d'Angoulême, the only surviving daughter of Louis XVI and Marie Antoinette.[25]

The lily plate in fig. 48 is the only plate known to date from a Sèvres service decorated with lilies and identified from the factory records as the *Service des Liliacées*. Begun in 1819, the service was delivered to the Tuileries Palace in the course of 1820–1 for use at King Louis XVIII's table. Part of the subsequent history of this service is gleaned from a letter noting that much of the glass and porcelain for the French royal table was destroyed at the Tuileries during the July 1830 revolution.[26] The plate is decorated with a bright pink flower identified in the border as *Veltheimia Glauque*, or Western Cape Sand Lily, a species native to Africa. The source for this flower and the others that decorate this service was Belgian painter and botanist Pierre Joseph Redouté's celebrated work, *Les Liliacées*, published in eight volumes in 1802–16. The Sèvres factory used the same source in the decoration of a service for Empress Joséphine in 1802–5, part of which is now in the collection of the Museum of Fine Arts, Boston.[27] The border ornamentation in brown heightened with gold and set against a pale blue ground was designed by Leloy and is known from a drawing in the Sèvres factory archive.[28] The border is notable for being among the earliest examples of transfer-printed decoration used in a full service.

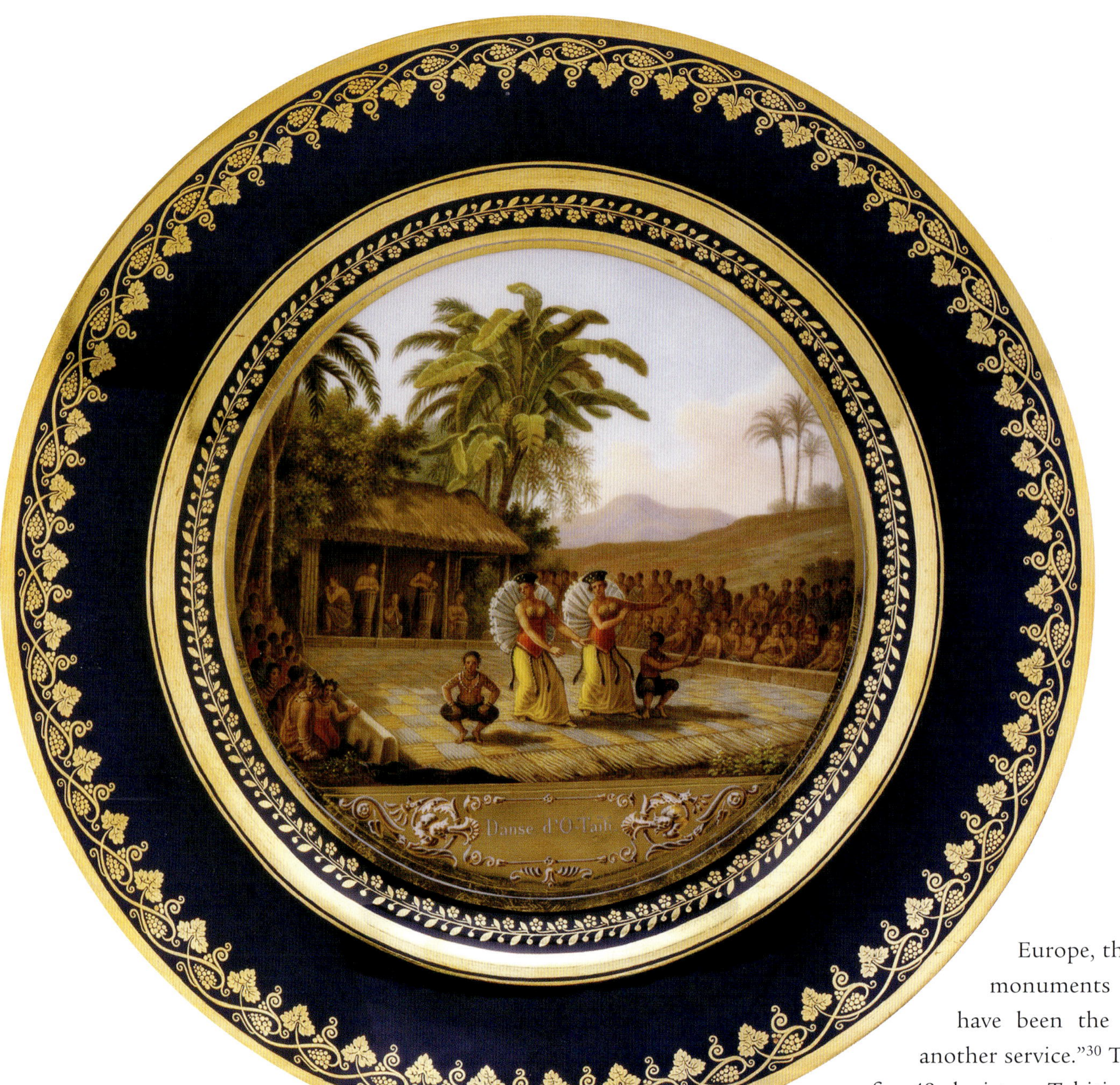

Fig. 49 (cat. 39): "Dance on Tahiti" plate from the *Service des vues de pays hors d'Europe*, 1820

Travel to distant lands captured people's imaginations, while explorations and travel books proliferated at this time. The sources for the decoration of the *Service des vues de pays hors d'Europe* were a variety of drawings provided by several artists, many of which are preserved in the factory's archives.[29] The service features emblematic sites of places outside Europe, "views of remarkable locations in Asia, Africa, the two Americas, the South Sea islands, but not of Europe, the sites and monuments of which have been the subject of another service."[30] The plate in fig. 49 depicts a Tahitian dance as recorded in a factory drawing by Jean-Charles Develly. Fabricated in the course of 1819–29, the service comprised seventy-two plates, part of which was purchased by the duc d'Angoulême in 1821.

The *Service des arts industriels* is well documented.[31] Production on this service began at the time of the coronation of Charles X (1824) around the iconographical theme of industries, some artistic—porcelain-making, iron forging, glass-making, or tapestry weaving— but others non-artistic such as beer-brewing, tobacco-manufacturing or bread-making. Contemporary interest in the subject had been generated by the *Exposition des produits de l'industrie française*

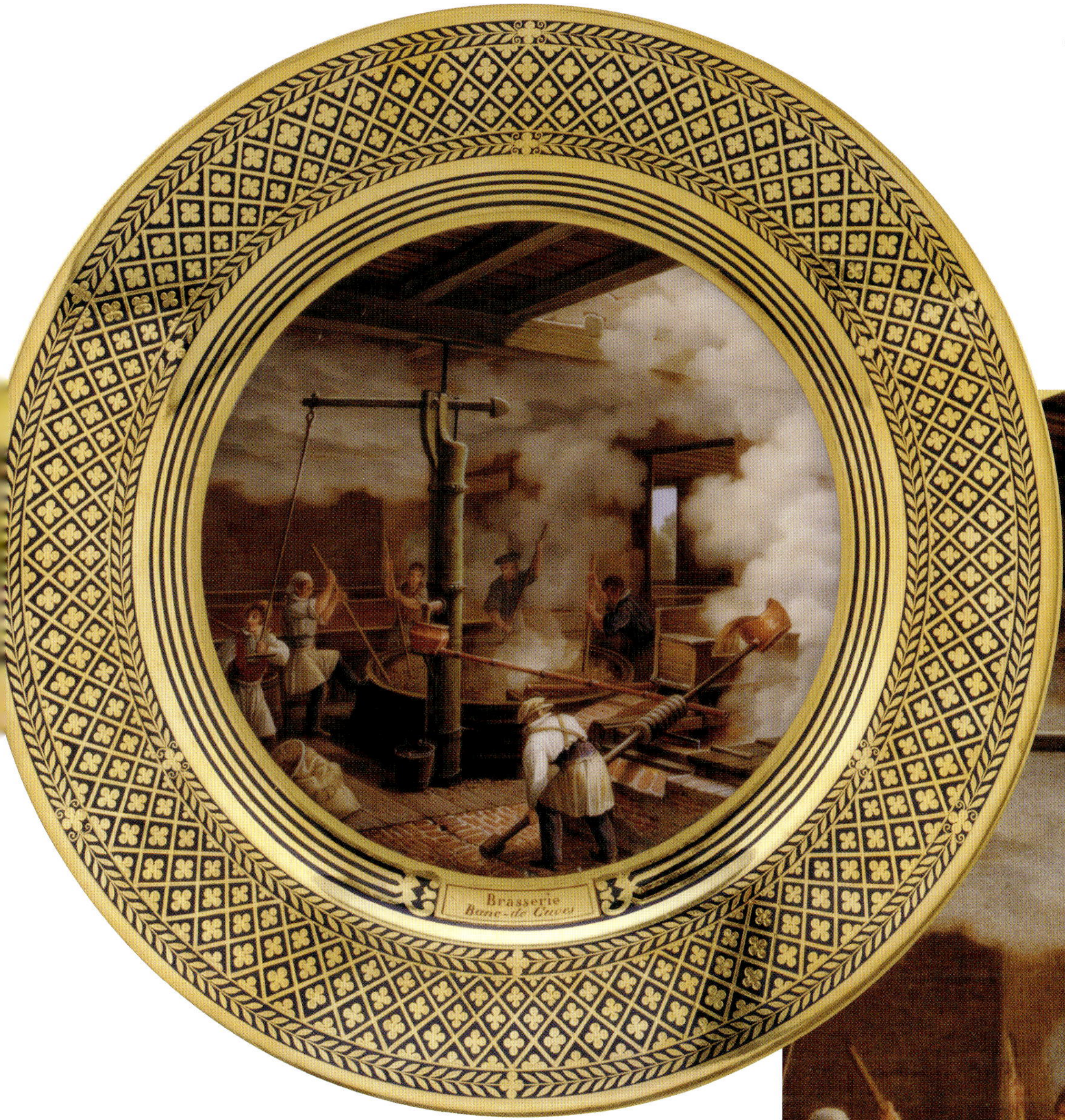

Fig. 50 (cat. 40): "Beer Brewery" plate from the *Service des arts industriels*, 1827

held at the Musée du Louvre in 1819. Develly, one of the most accomplished and prolific artists at the Sèvres factory, spent fifteen years on the project drawing scenes from life rather than working from engravings. His detailed compositions offer us a window into the state of industrial production of the 1820s. The plates are all inscribed with the scenes they represent, such as the one in fig. 50 depicting the steaming interior of a brewery, and some are signed on the front by Develly. Once the service was almost completed, it was exhibited at the 1828 New Year's exhibition. In 1838 King Louis-Philippe sent the original service, with an additional supplement amounting to 108 plates, to the Austrian chancellor Prince von Metternich, who had been the Austrian ambassador in Paris under Napoleon.

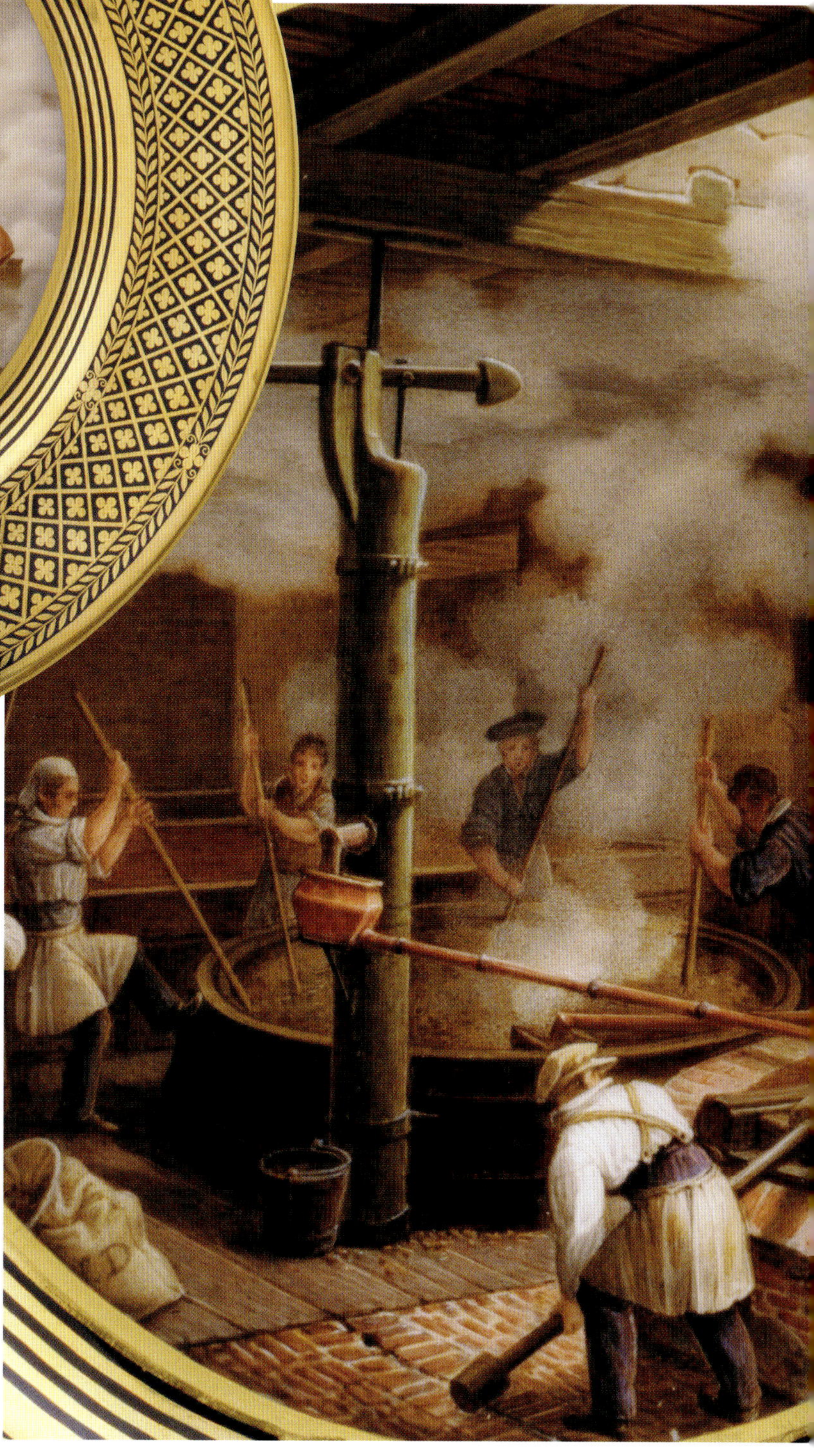

Detail of fig. 50, workers stirring a large fermenting vat with poles on "Beer Brewery" plate

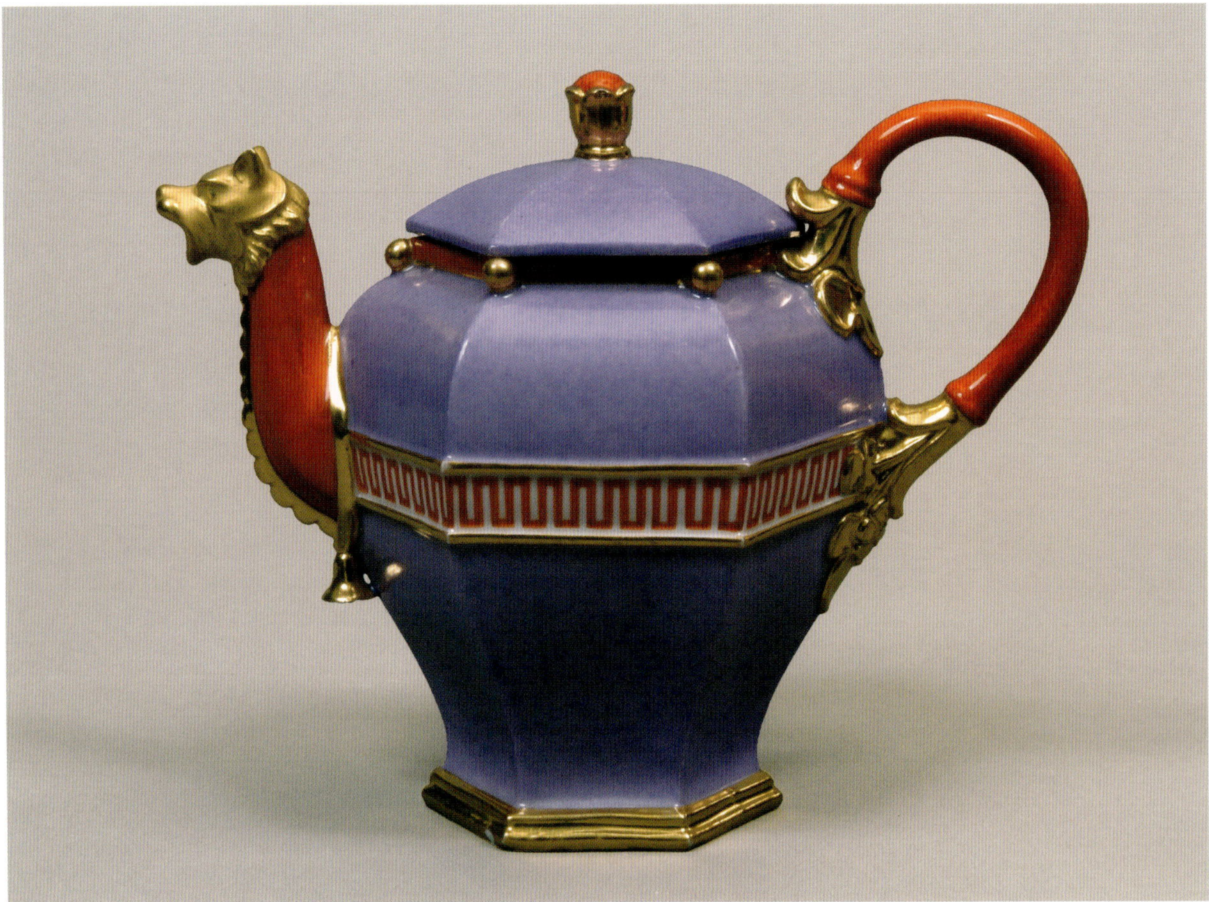

Fig. 51 (cat. 41): Chinese-style teapot designed by Alexandre-Évariste Fragonard, ca. 1818–21

The fascination with China, uninterrupted since the beginnings of the factory, took a new turn during the Restoration. The interest in Chinese wares must have prompted Alexandre-Évariste Fragonard's (1780–1850) design for the *théière chinoise* in 1818 (fig. 52). Some examples of his design were simply decorated with solid fields of color, such as the *théière* in fig. 51. This same form was reissued in 1827 with richer decoration (fig. 53). Sold separately, rather than as part of tea sets, these teapots were relatively inexpensive yet immensely decorative.

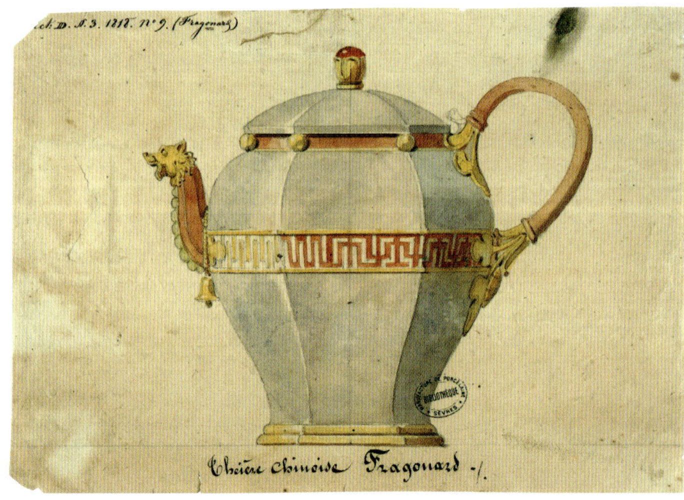

Fig. 52: Design and decoration for a teapot called *"théière chinoise"* by Alexandre-Évariste Fragonard, 1818; watercolor and pencil on paper

The influence of Romanticist currents is revealed in the Gothic Revival of the 1820s and 1830s. The curious round Gothic Revival plates are part of a peculiar commission from one of the most finicky and fastidious clients the factory ever had, Ernst I, Duke of Saxony-Coburg-Saalfeld. In 1818 the duke ordered a series of pieces to use for tea, coffee, or light lunches, including butter dishes and plates. In his characteristic punctilious manner, the duke specified new designs of

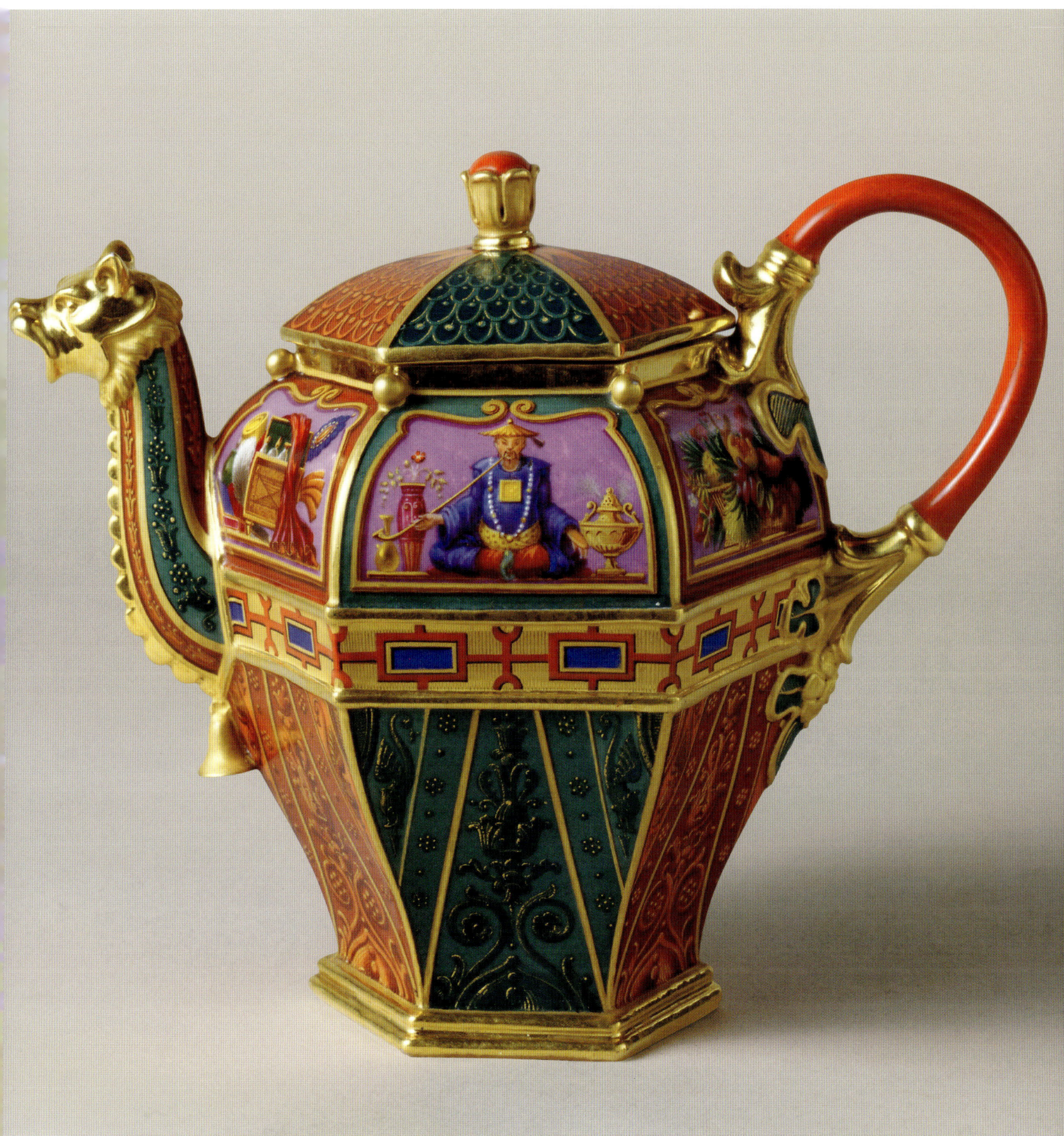

Fig. 53 (cat. 42): Chinese-style teapot designed by Alexandre-Évariste Fragonard, 1827

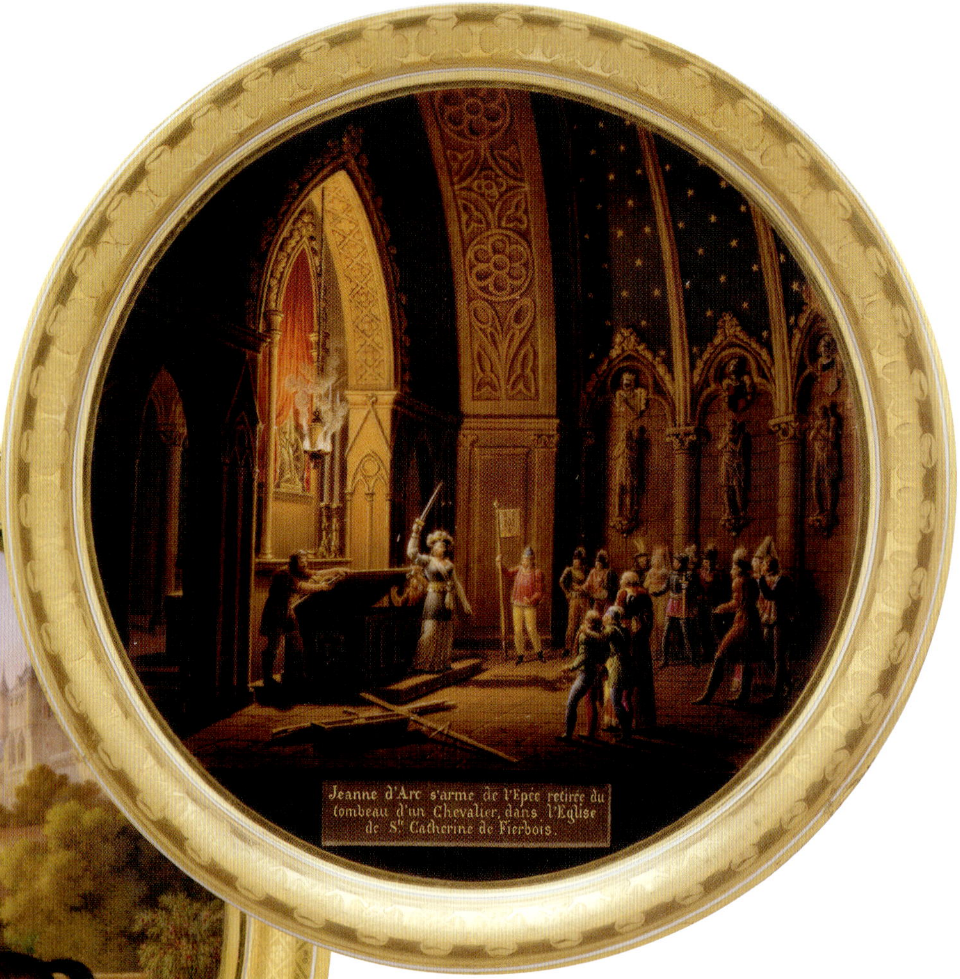

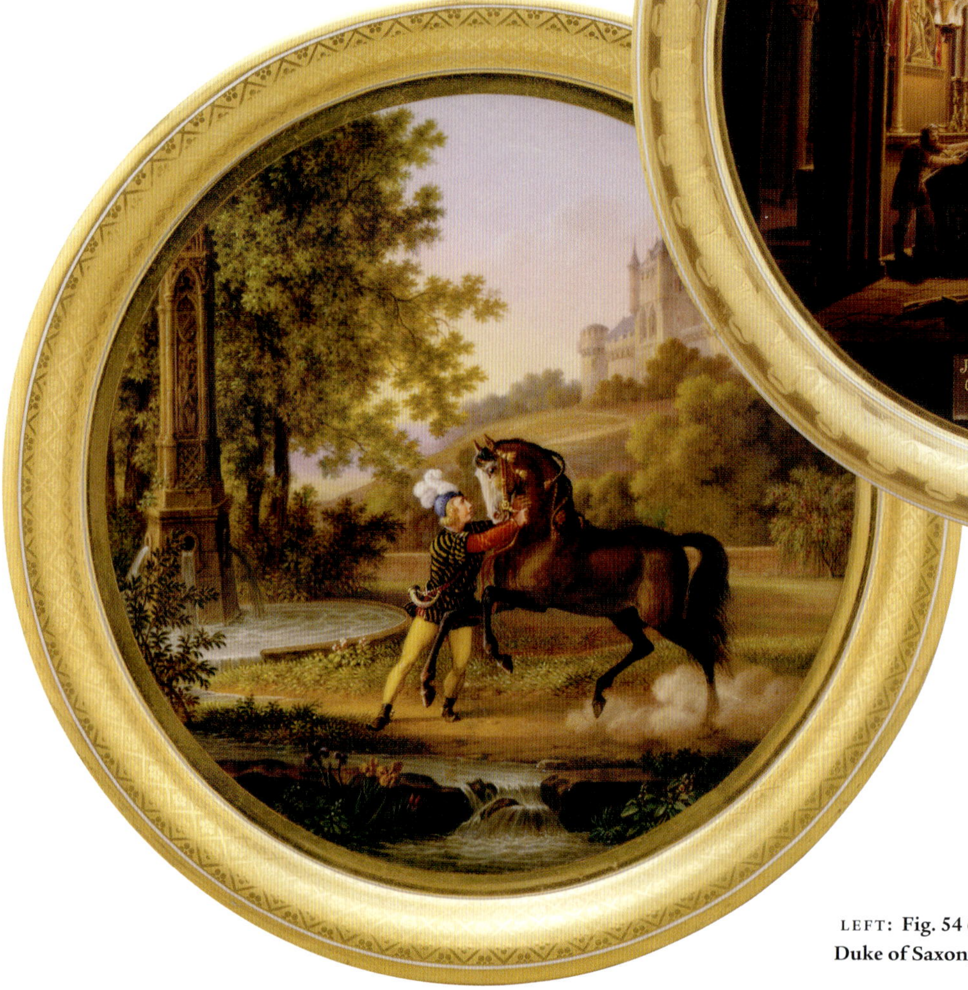

ABOVE: **Fig. 55 (cat. 43): "Joan of Arc" plate designed for the Duke of Saxony-Coburg-Saalfeld, 1818**

LEFT: **Fig. 54 (cat. 44): "Page Leading a Stallion" plate designed for the Duke of Saxony-Coburg-Saalfeld, 1818**

plates suitable for *tartines* (open sandwiches) but also for "anchovies, for fruit or godelettes, even little pickled pork, waffles and so forth...."[32] He also gave precise descriptions of the subject to be depicted—"a spirited stallion held by a fourteenth-century page with a jacket in black velvet with transverse golden bands, a crimson waistcoat, tight saffron yellow chamois hose, and four very short gold spurs. The steed has a lustrous and silky Persian coat, which can be fawny brown in color. The extremities and the insides of the hind quarters in black ..."—and specified that Jean-Charles Develly should paint it (fig. 54).[33] Another choice was "the interior of a chapel, very Gothic, very dark, lit only with the sanctuary lamp in the manner of Steinwerg."[34] Brongniart wrote back and said that they did not have any picture by Steinwerg in Paris, and suggested an image by Claude Roman, a painter versed in Gothic subjects.[35] He also proposed animating the church interior with an episode from the life of Joan of Arc in which the heroine draws a sword from the tomb of a cavalier in the church of St. Catherine of Fierbois (fig. 55).

July Monarchy

The July Monarchy represents the most eclectic moment at the factory. The works of this period successfully demonstrate the versatility of the factory's artists when it came to working in various historical styles. Gothic, Renaissance, and Chinese ornamentations complement the classical repertoire of traditional subjects. In the eyes of some contemporary critics, this eclecticism was interpreted as a blatant decadence of taste and disregard for composition,[36] but others viewed it as a new awareness of history, styles, and design. The catalogue of the opening *Exposition des produits de la manufacture de porcelaine du roi* of 1832 stated that Sèvres "should choose from every age and every nation whatever was the very best, whatever displayed in all its purity the character of the period and country which was to be copied or imitated... [and] thus attain the variety that so appeals to all manner of people."[37]

Louis-Philippe d'Orléans, the first modern sovereign of France and president of the constitutional monarchy, was also the last King of the French. In the creative arena, his reign tried to reconcile artistic traditions with a need to modernize production. His most important act of patronage was the restoration of the château de Versailles. Besides favoring historical paintings, Louis-Philippe promoted portraiture. He amassed a collection of 30,000 historical portrait engravings and commissioned portraits of himself by painters such as Horace Vernet, Eugène Lami, Ary Scheffer, and Franz Xavier Winterhalter. His image on the center of the vase in fig. 56 conveys the impression of an accessible monarch, as does the portrait of his wife Marie-Amélie in its pair (not illustrated but also in the collection of the Walters Art Museum in Baltimore); both were painted after works by Franz Xavier Winterhalter. Ten pairs of such *vases "Étrusque Caraffe,"* decorated with portraits of the royal

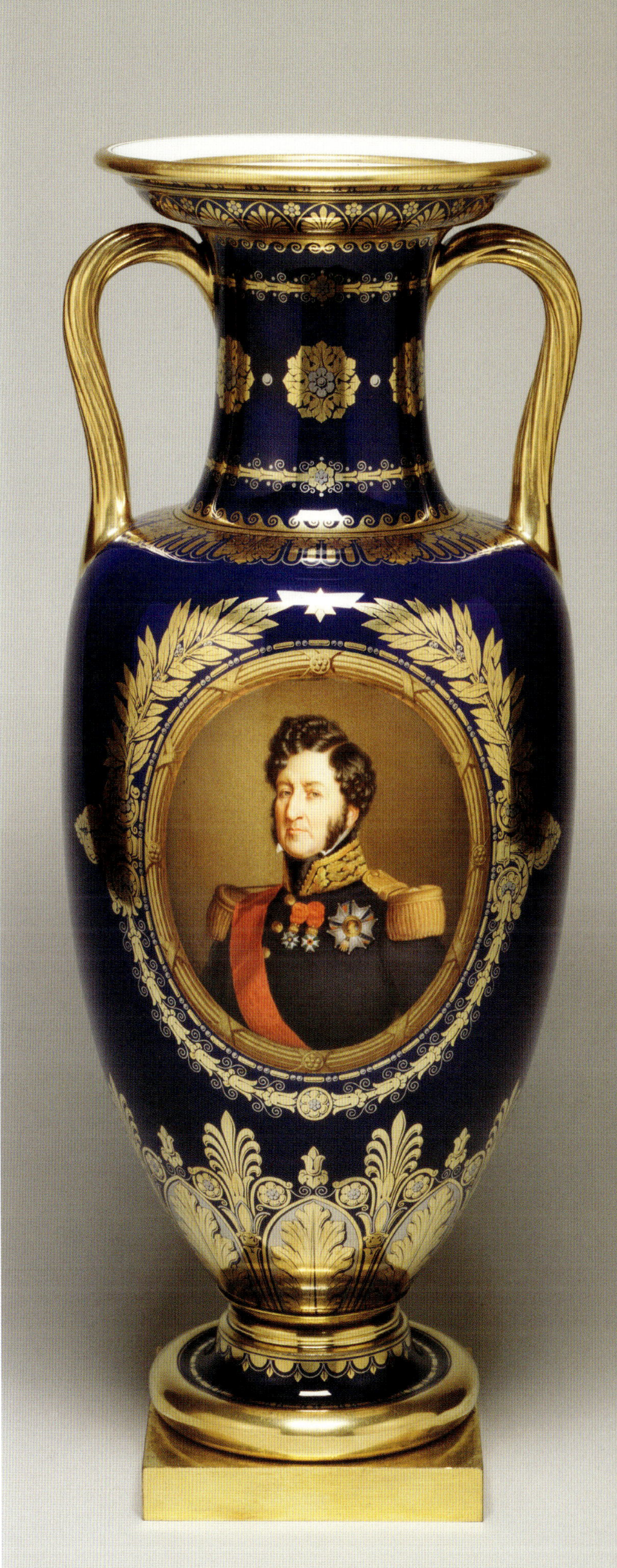

Fig. 56 (cat. 46): Vase with a portrait of King Louis-Philippe, 1844

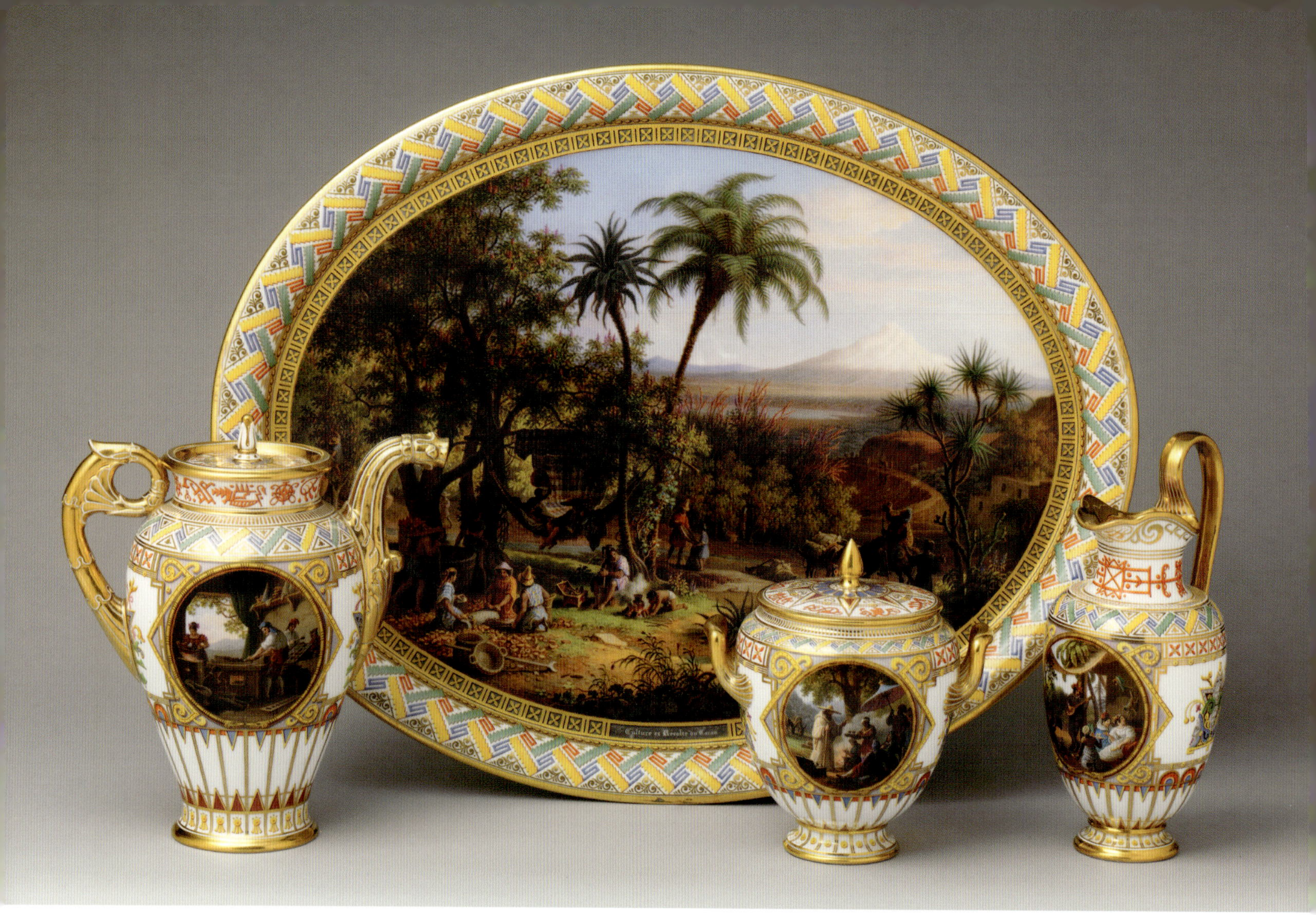

Fig. 57 (cat. 48): Partial coffee set depicting the cultivation and harvest of cocoa, 1836

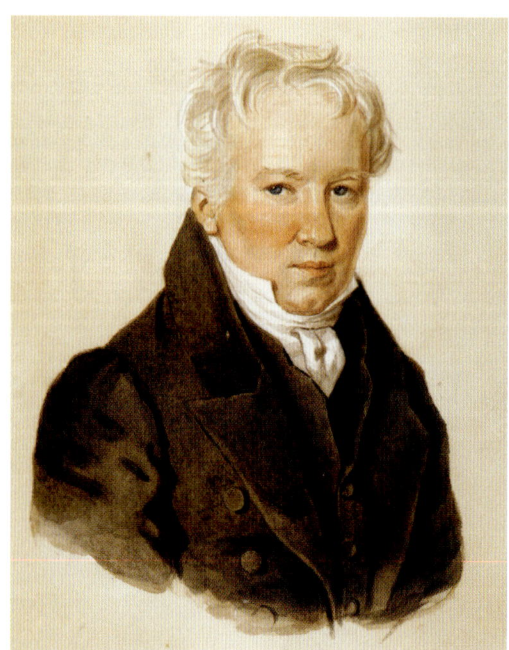

Fig. 58: Portrait of Baron Humboldt from the Middleton Watercolor Album, ca. 1820; watercolor on paper

couple and intended as presentation pieces, were produced between 1833 and 1847.

The taste for exotica continued during the reign of King Louis-Philippe. The attraction that far-away cultures exerted in society is evident in the choice of subject for the decoration of this tea and coffee set, called *déjeuner "Culture et récolte du cacao"* (fig. 57). Each piece of this set depicts a stage in the cultivation and harvest of cocoa in South America. The scenes were adapted by Develly from the work of naturalist Alexander von Humboldt (1769–1859) (fig. 59). The vivid hues of the borders are in direct contrast with the earthy tones of the scenes and are copied from engravings of Mayan antiquities published by Humboldt in *Vues des Cordillères* (1801) (fig. 58).[38] Unusual for Sèvres, this is one of two identical sets—a first set was presented as a gift to the distinguished Spanish politician and ambassador to London and Paris, the marqués de Miraflores, in 1835, while this other set was delivered to Queen Marie-Amélie in 1837.

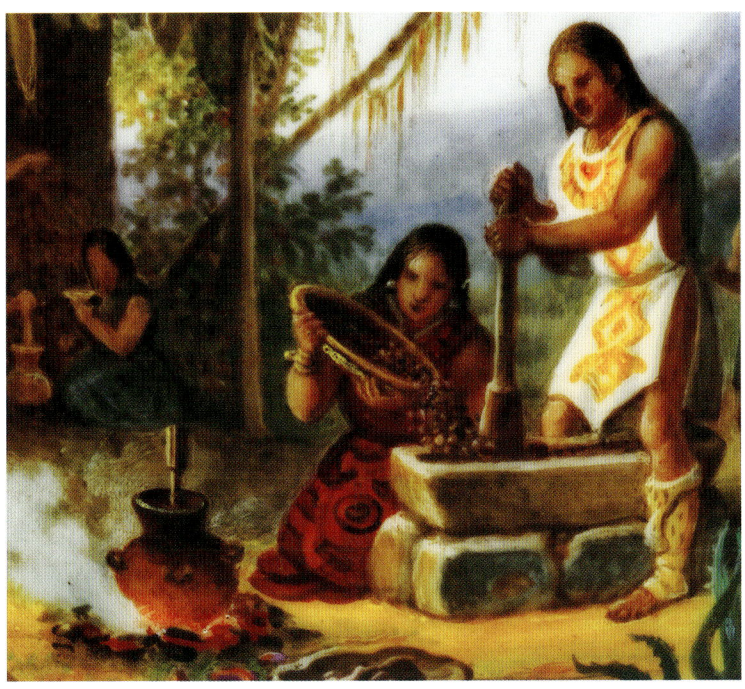

Detail of fig. 57, painting of natives grinding coffee on reverse of coffee pot

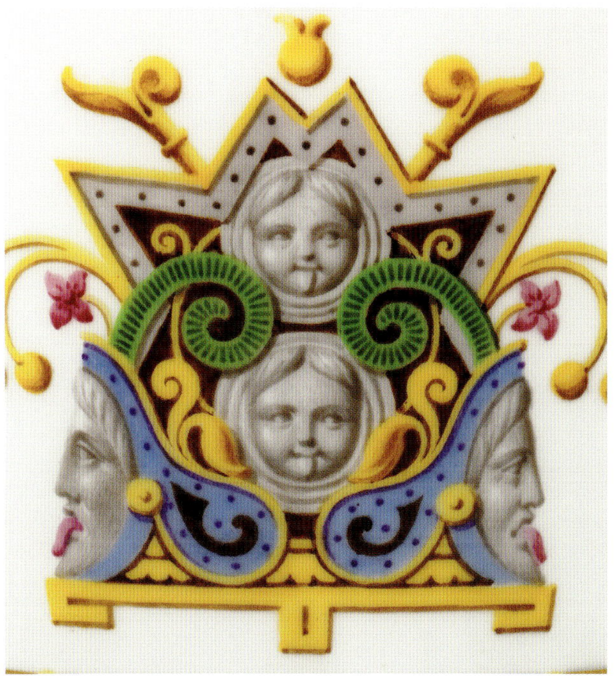

Detail of fig. 57, ornament on milk jug

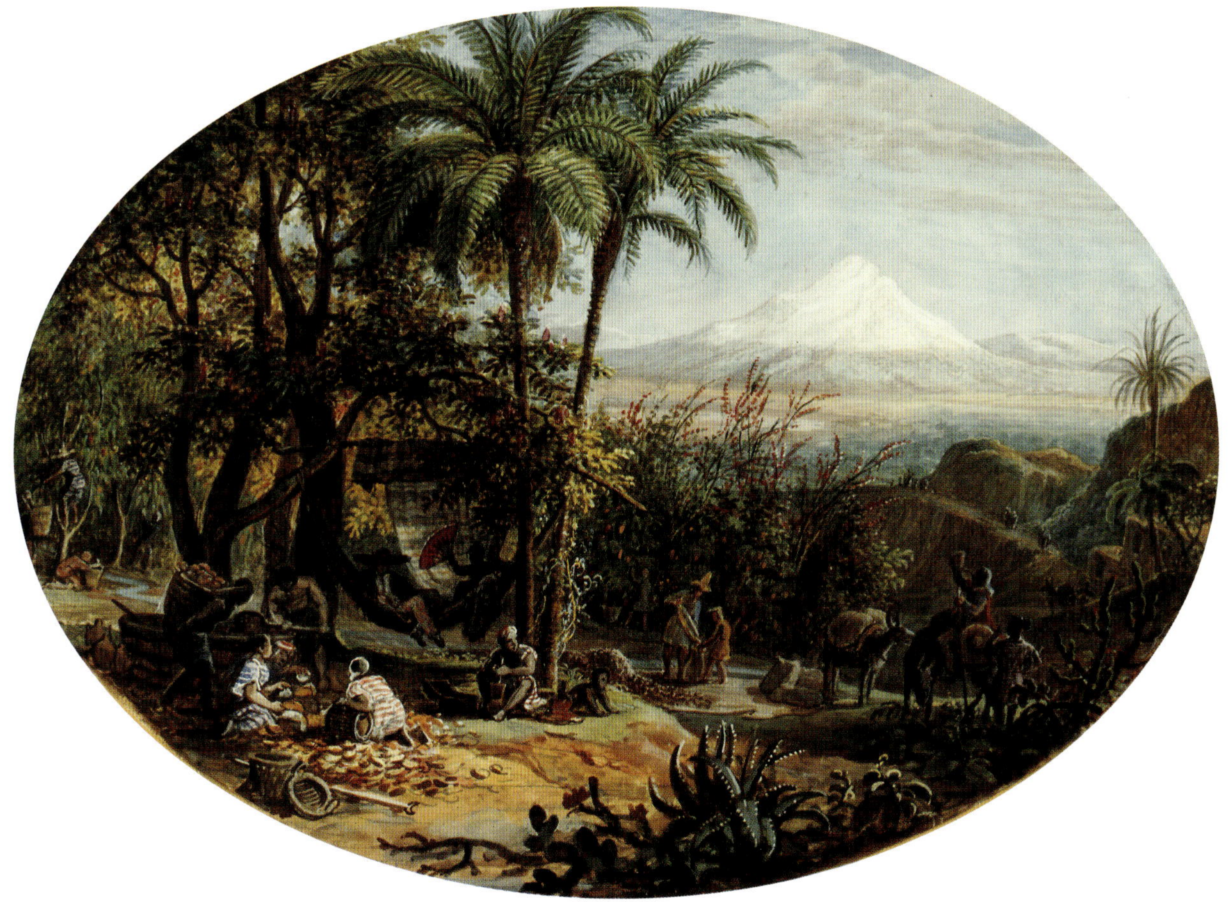

Fig. 59: Decoration for a tray from the *déjeuner "Culture et récolte du cacao"* by Jean-Charles Develly, 1816; gouache on paper glued to heavy paper

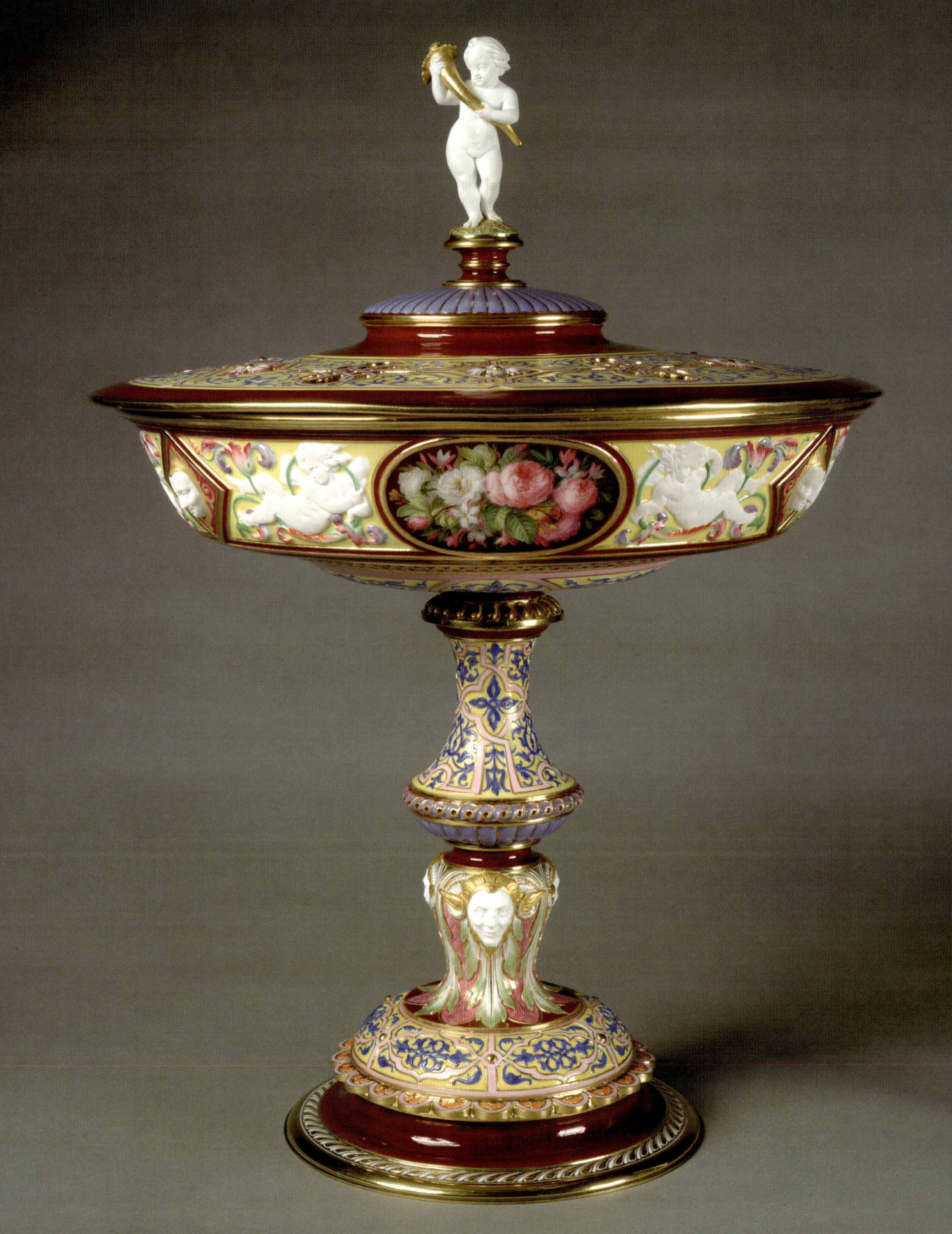

During this period, features characteristic of other media were transposed to the ceramic medium. Saint-Porchaire pottery, Palissy ware, Hispano-Moresque pottery, niello, damascene work, jewelry, and Limoges enamels, to name a few, were emulated in the decoration of porcelains.

Among the wider range of styles available, however, the Renaissance reigned supreme. The Mannerist decorations of the château de Fontainebleau built for François I in the 1520s served as a source of inspiration. Sèvres also experimented with a revival of Palissy-style wares by producing a range of pieces with rich polychrome and naturalistic aquatic animal and reptile reliefs. In 1845 the factory opened a new atelier dedicated to painting *en grisaille* in imitation of Limoges enamels. The factory also reinterpreted the intricate brown, beige, and white patterned earthenwares produced in Saint-Porchaire during the second quarter of the sixteenth century. In 1855 Sèvres opened a workshop for the chasing of bronze mounts, and another for the production of faiences. Here they created pieces inspired by Renaissance maiolica and Middle Eastern wares.[39]

The shape and design for the covered tazza in fig. 60 known as *coupe "Cassolette,"* has a direct link to the Renaissance with its colored glazes based on Renaissance earthenwares. The tazza and its cover are ornamented with a wide variety of decorative motifs plucked from Renaissance enamels and pottery: acanthus leaves, tracery, strapwork, scrollwork and the small putto at the top carrying a cornucopia among others. The design reflects a general fascination for the Renaissance, but also Brongniart's particular interest in the period and the techniques of Renaissance enamels and pottery. The tazza was acquired in 1846 by Queen Marie-Amélie, and soon thereafter was presented to an unknown recipient. It is one of four pieces of the same design made at Sèvres, modeled by Hyacinthe-Jean Regnier (1803–1870)[40] and decorated by François-Huber Barbin, with flowers by the hand of Jacques-Nicolas Sinsson.

The *vases "Adélaïde"* in fig. 61 illustrate the fascination with Renaissance artisans, techniques, and ornamental vocabulary. One of the pair features full-size portraits of famous French Renaissance goldsmiths, enamelers, potters, and maiolica painters, including Pierre Courtois, Jean Court, Suzanne Courtois, Léonard Limousin, Pierre Reymond, and

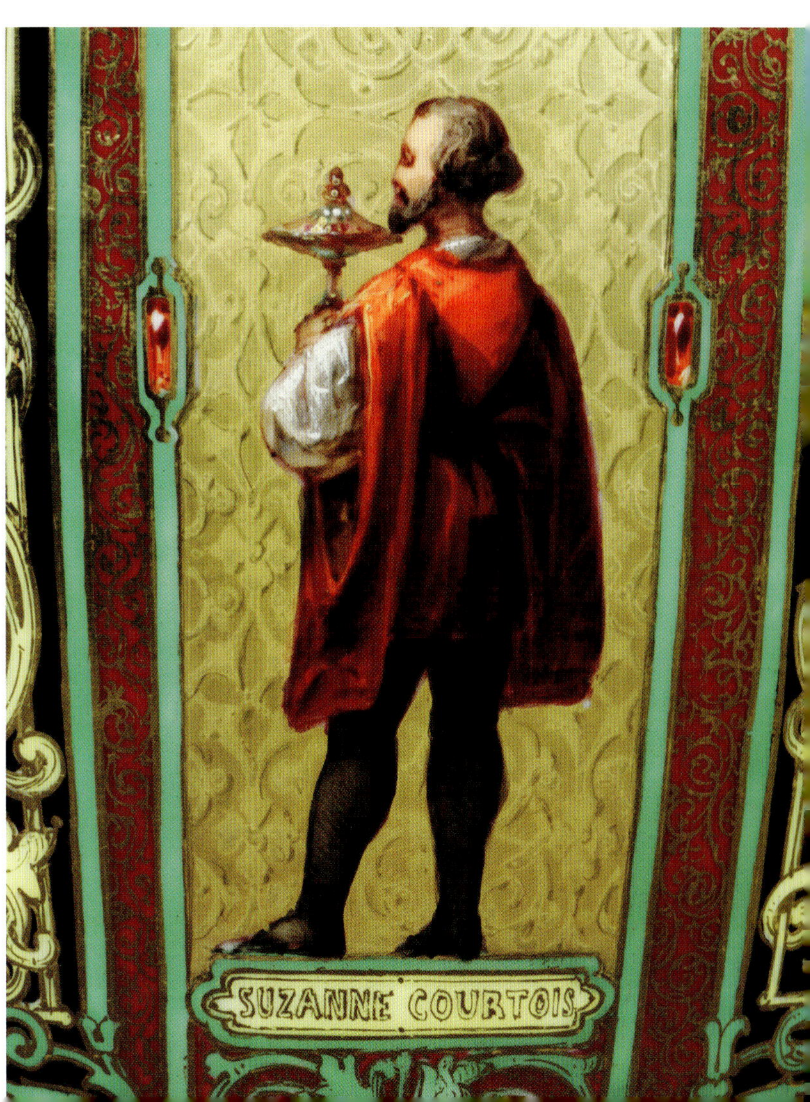

OPPOSITE
Fig. 60 (cat. 50): Renaissance Revival covered cup (*coupe "Cassolette"*) acquired by Queen Marie-Amélie, 1844

RIGHT: **Detail of fig. 61, portrait of the enamel painter Suzanne Courtois on one *vase Adélaïde***

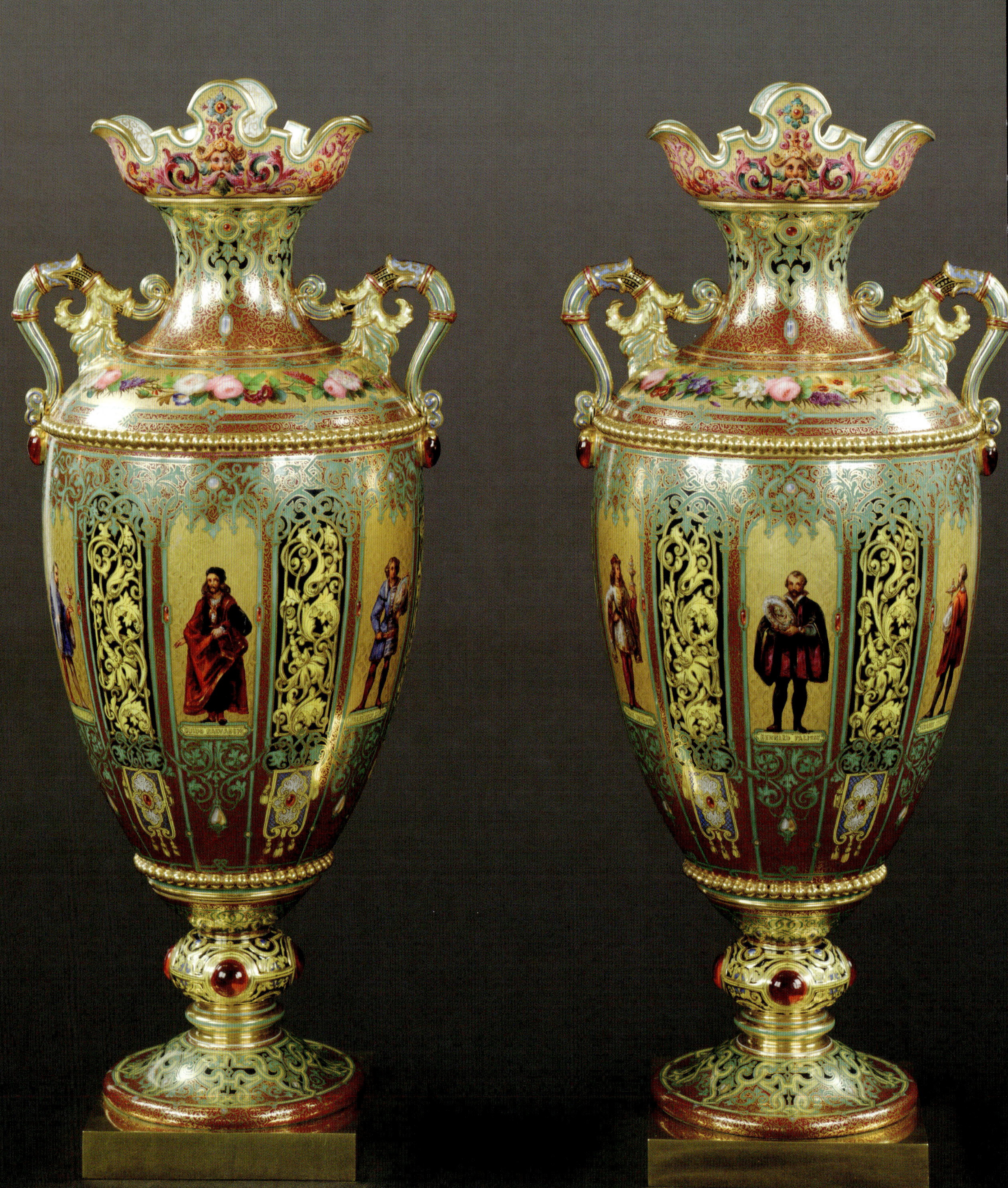

renowned ceramist Bernard Palissy, shown within architectural niches. Its pair features maiolica painters and decorative artists of the Italian Renaissance: Orazzio Fontana, Giorgio di Gubbio, Luca della Robbia, Francesco Zanta, Francesco Francia, and Guido Salvaggio—not a maiolica painter, but a character from Ludovico Ariosto's *Orlando Furioso*. The Sèvres artist Alexis-Étienne Eugène Julienne (active 1837–49) was in charge of the main decoration. The patterned background, in purplish brown and gold, bears resemblance to Moresque tracery and damascene work.[41] The bands of gold beads at the top and bottom of the central section and the large faux cabochon jewels at the bottom of the vase are an allusion to Renaissance jewelry techniques and can be seen in many other Louis-Philippe period wares. The vase was named after the sister of Louis-Philippe, Adélaïde, and was first put into production in 1840. Oddly enough, despite its neo-Renaissance decoration, the shape relates more to late Japanese Satsuma wares than to Western prototypes. This pair was at the Louvre exhibition of 1842. They were sent to the king at the closing of the show in 1843 to be later presented to an undisclosed recipient.

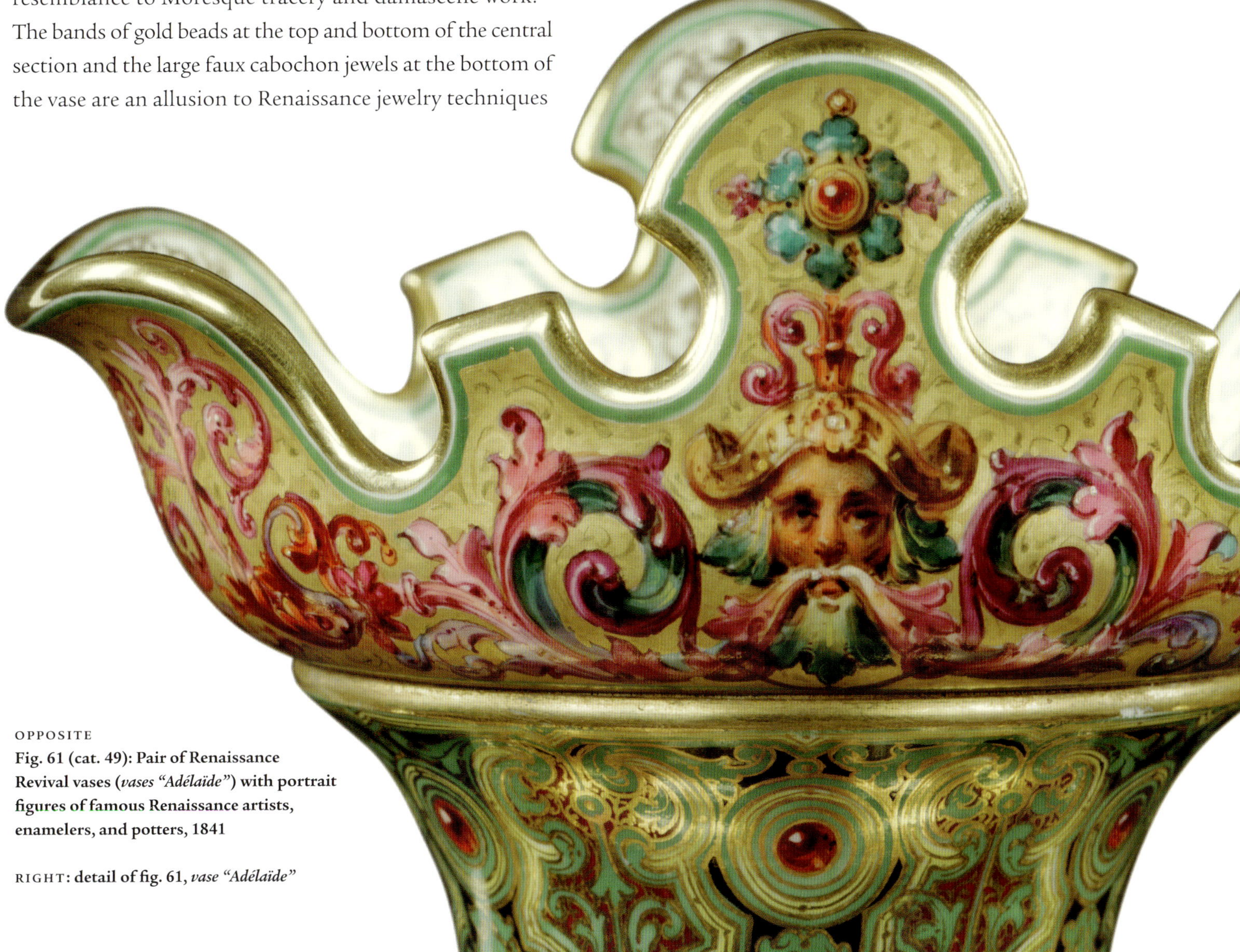

OPPOSITE
Fig. 61 (cat. 49): Pair of Renaissance Revival vases (*vases "Adélaïde"*) with portrait figures of famous Renaissance artists, enamelers, and potters, 1841

RIGHT: **detail of fig. 61, *vase "Adélaïde"***

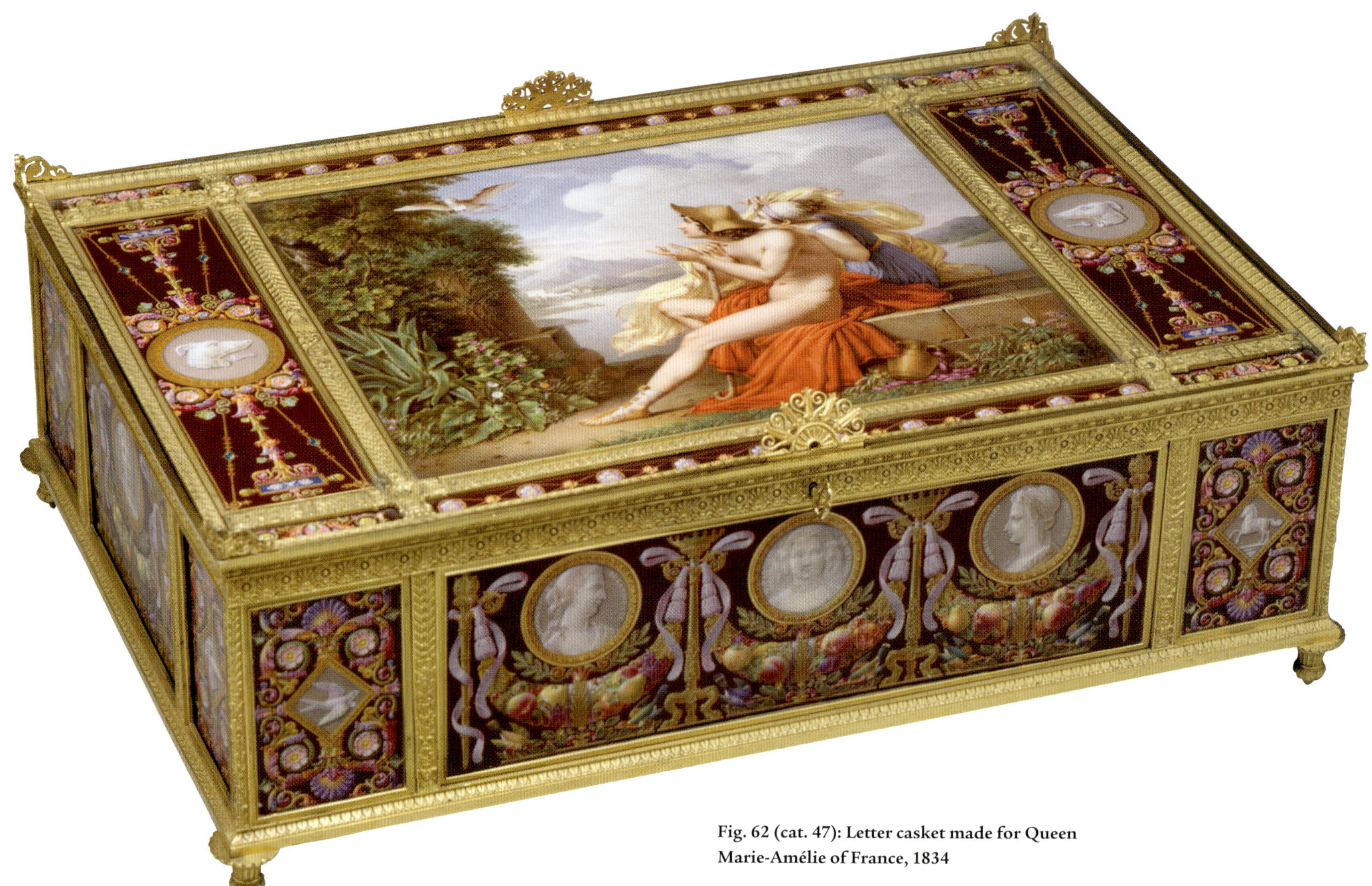

Fig. 62 (cat. 47): Letter casket made for Queen Marie-Amélie of France, 1834

In contrast to the fanciful and historicist decorations of many wares of this period, the letter casket quotes from a more modern neoclassical source for its main decoration (fig. 62). The large porcelain plaque on the cover depicts *The Dove and the Passer-By* after a line drawing by Anne-Louis Girodet done to illustrate Anacreon's *Odes*.[42] In keeping with the epistolary theme, the sides feature portraits of celebrated letter writers from history: Madame de Sévigné, Lady Montague, and Madame de Lafayette at the front, Sobieski, St. Evremont and Pope Clement XIV at the back, and Cicero and Pliny the Younger on the sides. The porcelain plaques are bound with delicate gilt bronze fittings which cost as much as the compensation given to the porcelain painters. The coffer was shown at the annual exhibition at the Louvre in 1832 and was delivered in 1834 to Queen Marie-Amélie, who greatly enjoyed such caskets.

In the 1840s, the increasing conservatism of the so-called July Monarchy obscured King Louis-Philippe's image as a liberal king. His intransigent opposition to parliamentary reform helped to provoke an insurrection that led to his abdication in February 1848 and his subsequent exile to England.

Second Republic (1848–1852)

The period between the fall of the monarchy on February 24, 1848 and the proclamation of the Second Empire on December 2, 1852 is marked by a desire to bring in new styles and fresh artists to the Sèvres manufactory. After the death of Brongniart in 1847, the new director, Jules-Joseph Ebelman, undertook a complete reform of the factory up until his own death in 1852. His most notable initiative was the replacement of many old employees with a new generation of artists.

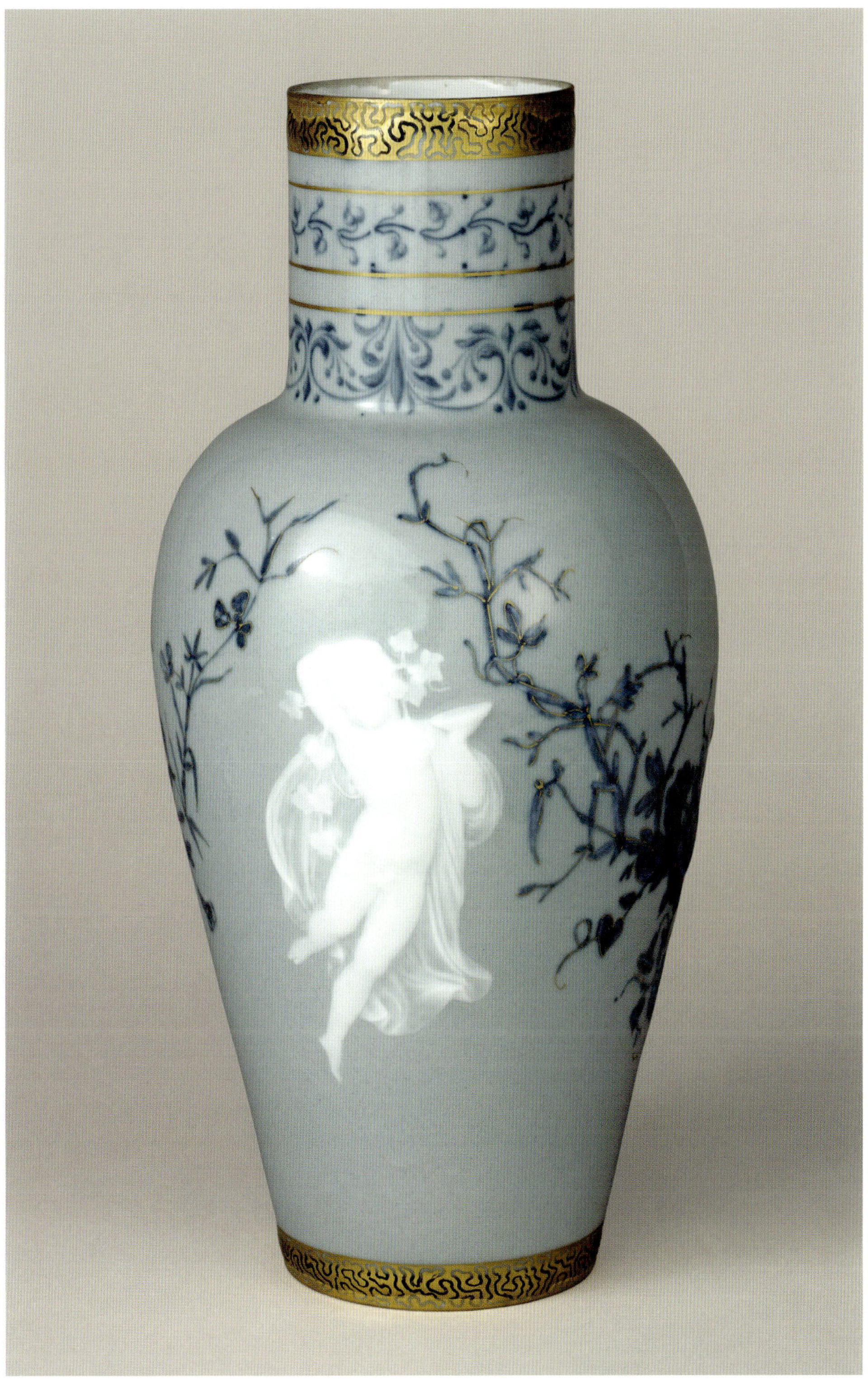

Fig. 63 (cat. 51): ***Vase "Ly"*** **with celadon ground and** ***pâte sur pâte*** **decoration, 1850**

In 1848, at the proclamation of the Second Republic, the manufactory's newly appointed Council of Improvement (*Conseil de perfectionnement des manufactures*) set out to refresh the styles. In stylistic terms, the council decided to better adapt decorations to shapes by casting away perspectives and miniature figural and narrative paintings in favor of all-round decorations. Novel forms decorated in monochromes or soft color palettes are characteristic of this time. The *vase "Ly"* is a good example of the new tendencies, as well as the investigation into Chinese glazes and enamels (fig. 63). The Chinese influence translated into the creation of monochrome and celadon hues. Celadon, a new color presented at the 1850 *Exposition des produits des manufactures*, delighted visitors and instantly became fashionable.

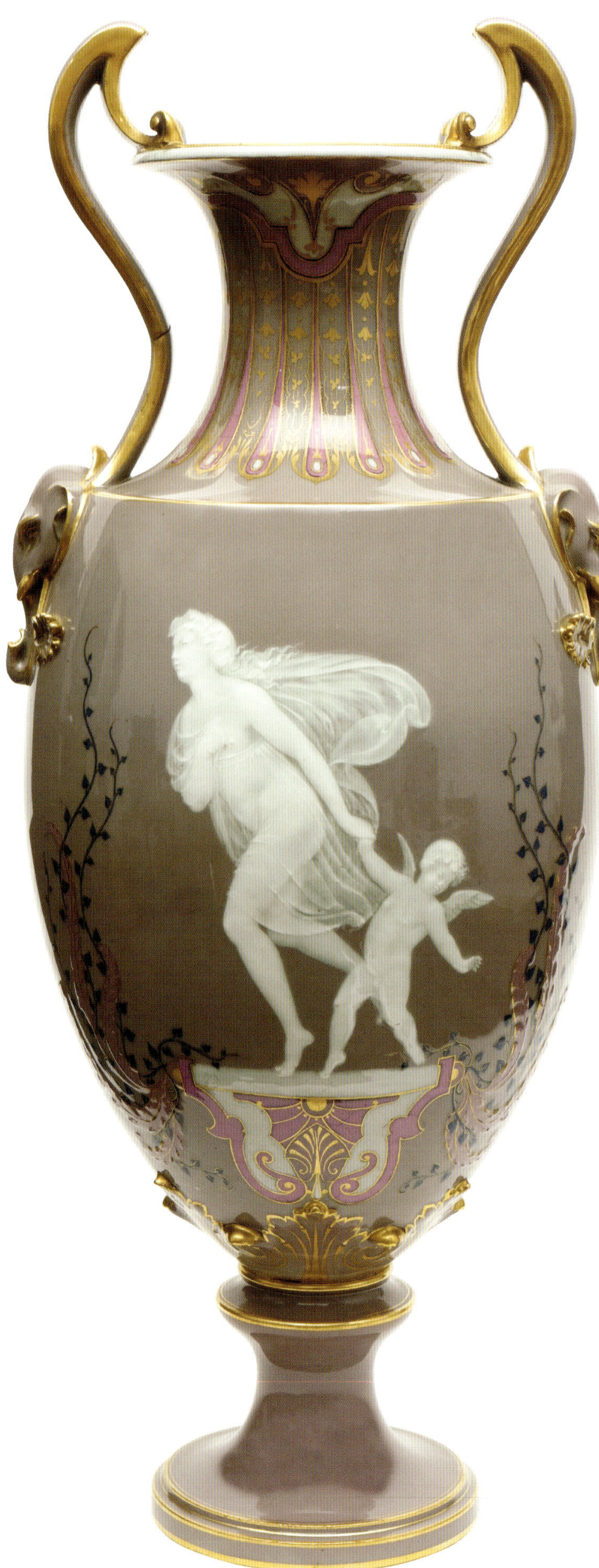

During this period, subtle effects were achieved with the newly developed technique of *pâte sur pâte* (see figs. 63, 64 and 66), in which a liquid clay was applied over a low-fired colored body and then covered with a high-fired glaze. The liquid clay was built up in several layers and thicknesses in order to achieve a sense of translucency and subtle relief. Potter Louis-Emmanuel Solon (1835–1913), who later took this technique to the famous British ceramic factory at Minton, was its main practitioner.[43]

Second Empire (1852–1870)

Shortly after Louis Napoleon's election to the presidency in 1848, he began to use the prestige attached to his family name to undermine the Republic. This led to the proclamation of the Second Empire in 1852. At this time, the Sèvres manufactory became incorporated into the household of the emperor. Physicist and chemist Henri-Victor Regnault (1810–1878) directed the factory until his retirement in 1871. This was not a very exciting period in an aesthetic sense. Regnault, absorbed by chemical experimentation, abandoned the artistic aspects of production.[44] The most notable achievements occurred in the technological arena, especially in the experiments with high-fired colors, colored pastes, and *pâte sur pâte*.

The *vase ovoïde tronqué* in fig. 64 was created at the end of the Second Empire by chief designer Joseph Nicolle (active 1856–71).[45] The elephant heads at the end of the handles are a vague nod to the *vases à têtes d'éléphants* of the Ancien Régime (see fig. 9). The most intriguing aspect of this vase is the changing color of its grayish-green paste, which, depending on how the light strikes it, could also appear to be pinkish brown. Solon, master of the *pâte sur pâte* technique, was responsible for the design and execution of

Fig. 64 (cat. 52): Vase made of *caméleon* paste with *pâte sur pâte* decoration, 1869

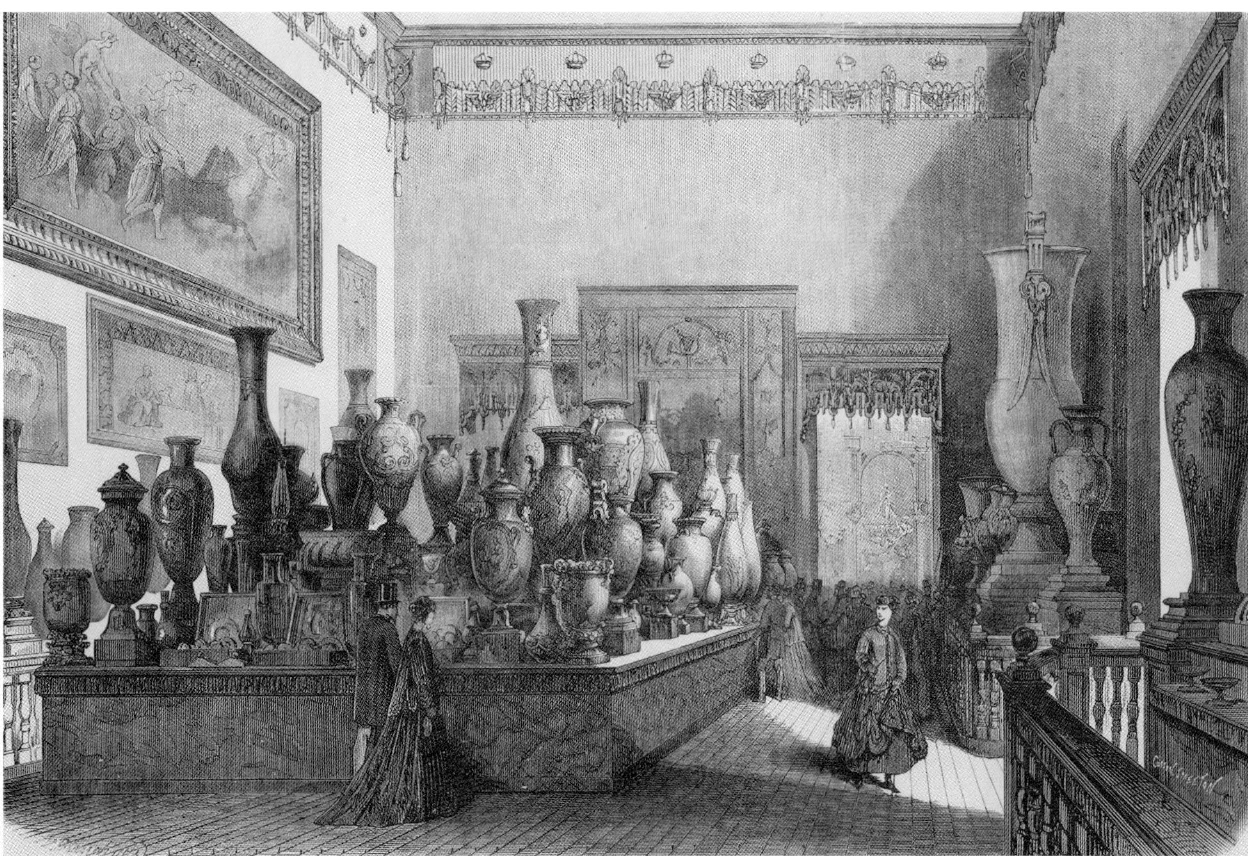

Fig. 65: View of Sèvres vases exhibited at the 1867 Paris Universal Exposition; published in the April 1867 issue of *L'Illustration*

the pseudo-classical decoration of a thinly veiled female figure and mischievous putti, so characteristic of his productions. The academic style of painting is reflected in the figural decorations of vaguely classicizing, scantily clad figures and putti floating in mid-air. Most decorations were characterized by their softness and lack of depth.

The Second Empire was marked by fast industrial changes all over Europe, which inevitably affected the modes of production in the ceramic industries. Many opted for mass production with the aid of new machinery, like steam machines that facilitated the preparation of the paste and more accurate kilns and advancements in cheap and quick decorating techniques such as the chromolithograph process. Sèvres opted to continue production with their traditional techniques and to put out a limited production of great quality. Unlike the ceramic manufactories at Berlin, Meissen, or Minton, which were forced to diversify their production and show a profit to survive, Sèvres, depending on national subventions, was the only factory that could afford the costly technological and artistic research needed to keep renewing its styles. In this period, Sèvres worked almost exclusively for the emperor and members of his circle.

The Sèvres factory participated in numerous expositions during the Second Empire: London in 1851, Paris in 1855, London again in 1862, and the Paris Universal Exposition of 1867 (fig. 65). The noted writer and historian, Prosper Merimée (1803–1870), in a report on the 1862 exhibition, commented on the general lack of inspiration that afflicted most of the artistic expressions of the time. He also remarked on the general weakness of all artistic productions shown, and criticized the absence of a characteristic style and the derivativeness that, he felt, reigned supreme. He linked the mediocre creations of the artists of the time with the lack of original ideas in the applied arts and ornamentation. The absence of a clear stylistic direction and the formulaic reconstitution of the past would inevitably lead, in his opinion, to an art of pure imitation without any French modern character.[46]

The nostalgia for the Ancien Régime and the Empress Eugénie's interest in the Louis XVI period gave impulse to the reestablishment of soft-paste productions and the revival of decorations and forms from the eighteenth century (see fig. 67). However, these never attained the freshness and depth of colors of the eighteenth-century originals.

Third Republic and *fin-de-siècle* Production

The factory endured the difficult times of the Franco-Prussian War and the collapse of the Second Empire. In 1875, with the proclamation of the Third Republic, Regnault resigned from his position as director at Sèvres. The last quarter of the nineteenth century was a period of unrest at Sèvres, and difficult moments threatened the closure of the manufactory. The instability is reflected in the frequent change of directors during this period.[47]

Théodore Deck's (d. 1891) tenure as director, though short, was significant. Deck had played an important role as member of the new Council of Improvement set up in 1871 to lay down the new technical and aesthetic directives for the factory. He modernized production with the introduction of *grosse porcelaine*, a highly malleable paste which allowed direct engraving and bas-relief. Capable of resisting sudden changes in temperature and the elements, it was well suited to the outdoors. Thus Sèvres began to create grand decorative schemes for the indoors and outdoors. The rest of the production was sent mainly to the ministries, embassies, and other official sites, with very little sold to retailers.

With its participation in the Universal Expositions in Paris in 1878 and 1889, and the exhibition of the Union Centrale des Arts Décoratifs in 1884, Sèvres strived to maintain its reputation as the leader in the field of fine porcelains, foster public interest, gain international prestige, and set standards for others in the industry to follow. During his tenure at the factory, chemist Alphonse-Louis Salvetat (active 1846–80) began trials for a new hard-paste composition that could fire at lower temperatures than the preexisting hard paste and could emulate Chinese glazes and achieve particular enamel effects. This paste was only perfected after Salvetat's retirement, when in 1884, Georges Vogt (active 1879–1909) and Charles Lauth (active 1879–87) succeeded in making the new body which had been so sought-after. The *pâte Lauth-Vogt*, or *pâte nouvelle*, fired at a lower temperature (1280 versus 1410 degrees centigrade), allowed for a much wider range of colors which melted into the glaze, permitted the use of crystalline and *flambé* glaze effects and achieved translucent enamels in relief (see figs. 71–72, and 74–75), all features which became fashionable in the 1880s and beyond.

The Council of Improvement at Sèvres, which operated for roughly two decades from 1872 to 1890, defined the aesthetic and technical orientations of the factory's output. The council's initial assessment singled out some problematic aspects of the factory's pieces, such as the languid forms and decorations without logical order[48] and the neglect of the painters' and sculptors' artistic education. The council was led by ornamentalist and talented sculptor Albert-Ernest Carrier-Belleuse (1824–1887). In its attempt to reform production, the council created a school in the factory to train future workers and decorators and instruct them in the principles of design and ornamental decoration. The main goal was to simplify production by rendering forms more basically and without many parts requiring assembly during and after firing. The council also instituted a competition, the *prix de Sèvres*, opened to participants from inside and outside the factory.

The final report issued in 1875 continued with the recommendations established by the 1848 council, to abandon perspective for decoration and most of the genres used to date, and reinforced the principle that decoration should always respect form. Acknowledging that Sèvres still held a position of indisputable superiority, the council suggested that the factory put emphasis on the education and instruction of its artistic force as the main way to improve production.

Carrier-Belleuse was appointed director of the Sèvres factory from 1871 to 1895 and was also art director in 1875. His prestige as a sculptor, his ability to coordinate a large atelier, and his year spent across the English Channel creating models for the factory at Minton made him the ideal choice to assume the responsibility of reorienting the entire production.[49] Carrier-Belleuse's creations fall into two types—simple

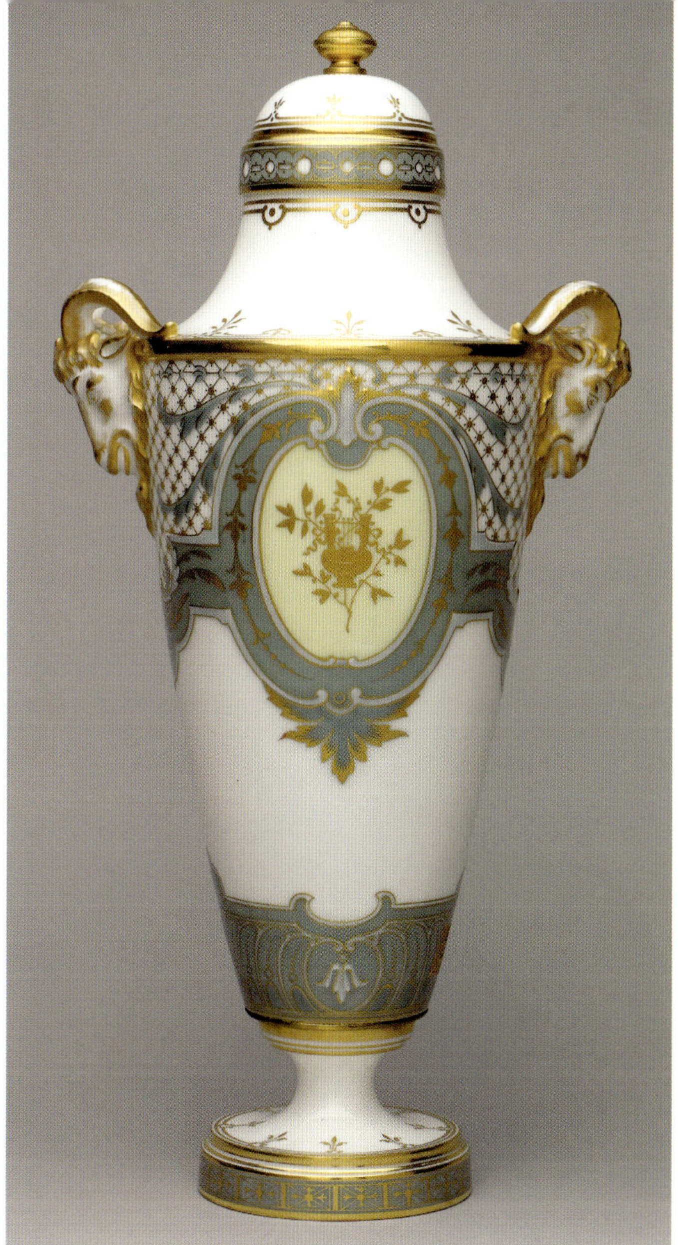

At the 1878 Paris Universal Exposition, the exhibition of Japanese ceramics and particular stonewares ignited the creative spirit of several French ceramists, who advanced a new era of French pottery and used the medium to express a fresh *fin-de-siècle* sensibility. *Japonisme*, or the trend for Japanese influence on artworks of the West, was not a style adopted officially at Sèvres, a sign that the factory was too classically disposed to move in such a different direction.[50] The plate from the *Service Lobé* reflects only timidly a

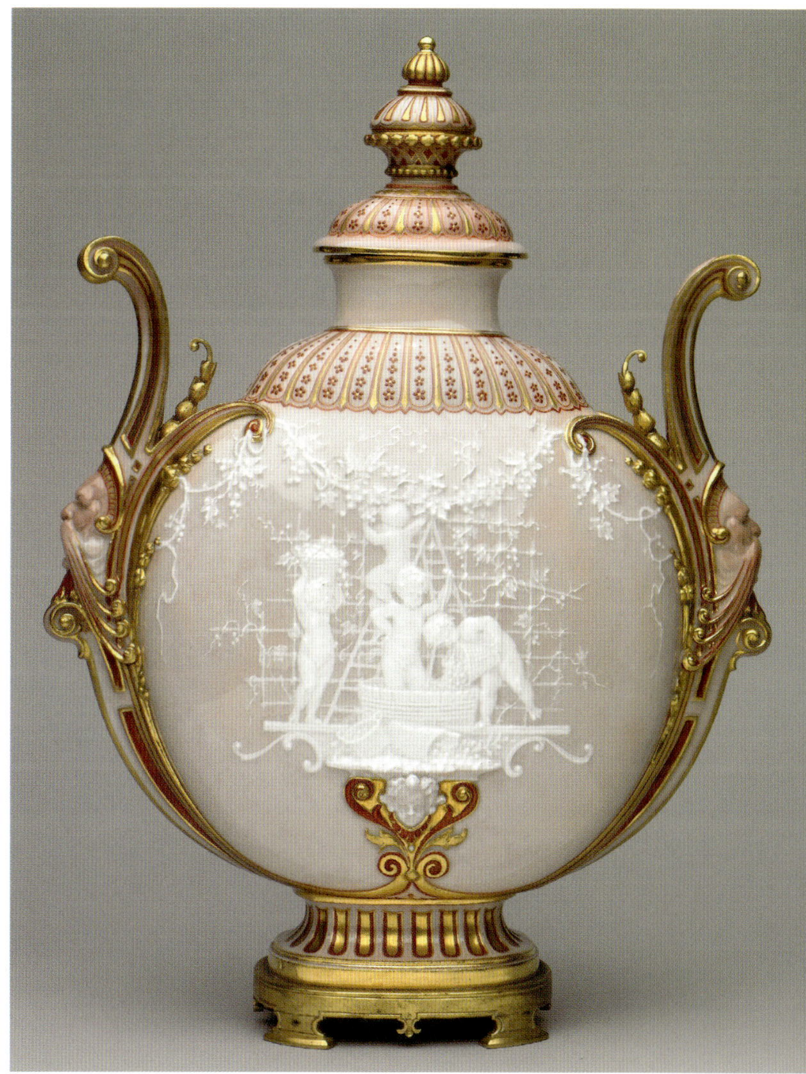

ABOVE: Fig. 67 (cat. 53): *Vase "Boizot"* designed by A.-E. Carrier-Belleuse, 1882

RIGHT: Fig. 66 (cat. 54): Pink and gold flask (*gourde "d'Asti"*) designed by A.-E. Carrier-Belleuse, 1885

forms with ample areas for decorators to fill and more elaborate forms with sculptural details, in particular in the neo-Renaissance style. The pink and gold flask with classical-inspired *pâte sur pâte* figural decoration and heavily modeled handles, called *gourde "d'Asti,"* is an excellent example of the latter style (fig. 66). Carrier-Belleuse's *vase "Boizot"* of 1882 pays tribute to the shapes designed by the talented Louis-Simon Boizot in the 1770s (see fig. 22), while its decoration with delicate lattice work and neo-Rococo cartouches denotes a *fin-de-siècle* design sensibility (fig. 67). Today, some of these forms may appear heavy and overdecorated, but at the time they signified a radical change of style.

Fig. 68 (cat. 55): Plate with Japanese-influenced design from the *Service Lobé*, 1888

Japanese flavor in the stylization of its floral decoration and its asymmetrical composition (fig. 68).

As art and studio potters began affirming their status and consolidating a market for their work in the early 1890s, Sèvres followed the trend and actively entered the growing market for art pottery. Thanks to the enormous financial resources supplied by the French state, Sèvres was uniquely positioned to employ exceptionally skilled artists and artisans such as Leonard Gebleux, Ernest Chapelet, Albert Dammouse, and Émile Belet to develop new materials and techniques for ceramic production. Sèvres was to become one of the most influential forces in the French art pottery renaissance.

At the close of the century and at the instigation of the Council of Improvement, Sèvres had managed to shift gears and abandon almost entirely the use of polychrome figural and landscape painting for a more ornamental decoration better suited to porcelain. A new generation of artists had been raised in the spirit of creating decorations more respectful of form and shape.

NOTES

1. "Ce n'est pas par la porcelaine que la Manufacture mettra dans le commerce qu'elle conservera son influence sur l'industrie.... Il suffit qu'elle fasse de bruit en Europe par ses produits de luxe, pour que sa réputation s'attache à toute la porcelaine française. C'est ainsi que la Manufacture de Sèvres, en faisant des pièces que personne n'achète, a rendu de grands services au commerce de la porcelaine." (G. Lechevallier-Chevignard, *La Manufacture de porcelaine de Sèvres*, Paris, 1908, p. 133.)
2. A. Brongniart and D. Riocreux published and illustrated a descriptive catalogue of the museum in 1845.
3. Data drawn from a lecture given at Sèvres by Tamara Préaud on the subject of "Sèvres Ceramics of the First Empire" (October 15, 1998).
4. See T. Préaud, "Brongniart and the Imperial Iconography at the Manufacture de Sèvres," in *Symbols of Power: Napoleon and the Art of the Empire Style, 1800–1815* (Paris and New York, 2007), p. 70.
5. Before the Revolution, Vivant Denon had been an attaché at the French embassy in St. Petersburg and served as a diplomat in Sweden and Naples where he amassed a collection of classical antiquities. His involvement with Sèvres dates from the year 1785 when his collection of "Etruscan" vases was acquired by the king and deposited at Sèvres to provide inspiration for new shapes like the "Etruscan" cups in figs. 26, 27.
6. Nathalie Kazakevitch, "Porcelaine de Sèvres: le service égyptien en Russie," *Sèvres, Revue de la Société des Amis du Musée National de Céramique*, no. 4, 1995, p. 25.
7. This service is presently at Apsley House in London, the former home of the Duke of Wellington.
8. Lannes received the title of duc de Montebello in 1808, eight years after defeating the Austrians under General Ott at Montebello. He participated in military campaigns throughout the Directory, Consulate, and Empire and was a close friend of the emperor. See S. Wittwer, ed., *Refinement and Elegance: Early Nineteenth-Century Royal Porcelain from the Twinight Collection, New York* (Munich, 2007), pp. 226–8.

9. Drawn from Vivant Denon's *Voyage dans la Basse et la Haute Égypte*.
10. Quoted from C. Truman, "Emperor, King and Duke," *The Connoisseur*, November 1979, p. 149. These drawings were subsequently engraved by Baltard, Fournier, and Petit for the book *Voyage dans la Basse et Haute Égypte.*
11. The Commission des Sciences et des Arts was a special unit of Napoleon's army comprised of notable scholars, architects, artists, and scientists that was charged with documenting various aspects of Egypt.
12. The first mention of a service with these characteristics (service "fond bleu lapis têtes imitant le camée...") was intended for the Palace of St. Cloud, but was never delivered. Very possibly, these pieces formed the core from which the Cardinal Fesch service grew (see H. de la Verrie, *Le Service Iconographique Antique du cardinal Fesch*, Paris, 2007, pp. 34–5).
13. It is not known how and why the service was dispersed, but by 1888 over sixty-six pieces were offered for sale at the shop of James B. Pooley of Walnut Street, Philadelphia. Pooley sold the service to Mr. W. Weightman for $5,000. The name "comtesse de Nadaillac" inscribed at the bottom of the invoice might hint at the identity of its previous owner. (See Sotheby's New York, October 15, 1996, lot 506). Weightman's granddaughter sold part of the service at Sotheby's New York, October 15, 1996. The lots (506–517) comprised eighteen plates and one sugar bowl.
14. H. de la Verrie, *Service Iconographique Antique*, 2007, p. 49.
15. MNS archives, registre Vz2, fol. 112r. records the purchase on September 30, 1814 by Monsieur Hope of four "assiettes marly d'or têtes camées" at a price of 125 francs each, or 500 for the four. The reference numbers are 16.3 and 16.22.
16. Thomas Hope's granddaughter Henrietta Adela married in 1861 Henry Pelham-Clinton, 6th Duke of Newcastle. The Pelham-Clinton family seat was Clumber in Nottinghamshire. "Clumber" is also the name inscribed on the back of each frame. After World War I Clumber was emptied of its contents and was demolished in 1938.
17. For a comprehensive history of the hôtel de Charost see J.N. Ronfort and J.D. Augarde, *À l'ombre de Pauline: La résidence de l'ambassadeur de Grande-Bretagne à Paris*, (Paris, 2001).
18. Linda Roth lists the various artists and decorators involved on this pair of vases: M. Godin in charge of the ground color, M. Boitel of the gilding and platinizing, and Mlle. Le Grand and M. Durosey of the burnishing. The painting was executed by Georget and the gilt bronze mounts were supplied by Thomire (see L.H. Roth, "Neoclassical Variations at Sèvres: Early Nineteenth-Century Vases in the Wadsworth Atheneum, *French Porcelain Society Journal*, vol. XII, 1995, p. 8).
19. Ibid., p. 9.
20. The *Service Olympique* was a diplomatic gift to Tsar Alexander I of Russia at the signing of the Treaty of Tilsit in 1806. The majority of the pieces are at the National Museum of Russian Ceramics in Kuskovo as well as in the Kremlin in Moscow. For three plates and a brief discussion of this service, see S. Wittwer, *Refinement*, pp. 240–2.
21. T. Préaud, *The Sèvres Porcelain Manufactory: Alexandre Brongniart and the Triumph of Art and Industry, 1800–1847* (New Haven and London, 1997).
22. The exhibition catalogue lists two vases "floréal, fond bleu ciel" (light blue) decorated with birds by Madame de Courcelle Knip. The blue color must surely have been a catalogue error, for the three vases recorded all had a white ground (see MNS archives, feuilles d'appréciation, 1822, carton Pb 5).
23. Born Pauline de Courcelles, Madame Knip (1781–1855) was a bird illustrator. Her main work was the illustrations she provided for Anselm-Gaeton Desmarest's *Histoire naturelle des tangaras* (1807) and for C.J. Temmink's *L'Histoire naturelle des pigeons* (1811).
24. I thank Tamara Préaud for providing this information.
25. For a full account of this service see A. Odom and L. Paredes Arend, *A Taste for Splendor: Russian Imperial and European Treasures from the Hillwood Museum* (Alexandria, VA, 1988), pp. 226–7.
26. See a letter from Leduc, *administrateur des dépenses des gouvernements*, to the factory's administrator dated August 2, 1830, published by T. Préaud in *Versailles et les tables royales en Europe* (Paris, 1993), p. 218.
27. T. Albainy, "Flowers for the Empress: The Sèvres Service des plantes de la Malmaison et les liliacées," *French Porcelain Society Journal*, vol. III, 2007, pp. 191–210.
28. Illustrated in D. Ostergard, ed, *The Sèvres Porcelain Manufactory: Alexandre Brongniart and the Triumph of Art and Industry, 1800–1847* (New Haven and London, 1997), pl. 49.
29. Preserved in the "Portefeuilles" of the MNS archives. For a detailed account of this service see S. Wittwer, *Refinement*, pp. 322–30.
30. Ibid., p. 325.
31. A first extensive article was published by P. Ennès, "Four Plates from the Sévres Service des Arts Industriels," *Journal of the Museum of Fine Arts Boston*, 1990, pp. 89–106.
32. S. Wittwer, *Refinement*, p. 423.
33. Letter from Brongniart dated February 11, 1818 in the factory archives (quoted in S. Wittwer, *Refinement*, p. 423).
34. Ibid., p. 424.
35. Ibid., p. 423.
36. "Toutes les couleurs à la disposition de l'artiste se trouvent réunies sur la même piece; il n'y a plus ni harmonie, ni unité dans la composition ni dans la coloration" (George Vogt's words quoted in G. Lechevellier-Chevignard, *Manufacture*, p. 151).
37. Quoted from L.H. Roth, "Mixing Metaphors: The Renaissance Revival at Sèvres", *French Porcelain Society Journal*, vol. III, 2007, p. 102.
38. *Vues des Cordillères et monuments des peuples indigènes de l'Amérique* (1810–13), where Humboldt illustrated the landscape, human types, and art of ancient pre-Columbian civilizations in the first scientific book on the subject.
39. N. Blondel and T. Préaud, *La Manufacture nationale de Sèvres: parcours de blanc à l'or* (Charenton, 1996), p. 57.
40. Regnier also designed other similar Renaissance-inspired tazzas such as the "Benvenuto Cellini"—directly inspired by a famous work by the Renaissance goldsmith at the Louvre, the *coupe "Chevenard,"* and the *coupe "Henri II."*
41. For a detailed description of this vase and its pair see L.H. Roth, "Mixing Metaphors," pp. 216, 218–23.
42. Most of these drawings are at the Louvre. The one for *La Colombe et le Passant* is preserved at the Musée Girodet in Montargis (S. Wittwer, *Refinement*, p. 250).
43. The practice of working outside the factory was longstanding at Sèvres. Brongniart, who paid his workers little, compensated them by allowing them to decide how much work they would do for the factory and how much time they would spend working elsewhere.
44. G. Lechevallier-Chevignard, *Manufacture*, p. 157.
45. The shape was identified by Tamara Préaud, archivist at Sèvres, in a letter to Linda Roth, curator at the Wadsworth Atheneum (undated).
46. See G. Lechevallier-Chevignard, *Manufacture*, p. 160.
47. Numerous directors rapidly succeeded one another. Chemist Louis Robert—in charge of the glass and decorating ateliers—became director from 1870 to 1879. He was succeeded by chemist Charles Lauth—forced to resign in 1887 following his attempt to introduce some unpopular workplace reforms. Upon his resignation, potter Théodore Deck ran the factory for a brief three-year period, and was soon replaced by Émile Baumgart.
48. "formes souvent languissantes" and "décorations sans ordonnance" (quoted in G. Lechevallier-Chevignard, *Manufacture*, p. 163).
49. For a biography of Carrier-Belleuse, see June Hargrove, *The Life and Work of Albert Carrier-Belleuse* (New York and London, 1977).
50. Henri Lambert, designer and painter at Sèvres, was a fervent promoter of *Japonisme*. He worked on a faience dinner service at the Creil-Montereau factory but did not do any significant decorations in the Japanese style for Sèvres.

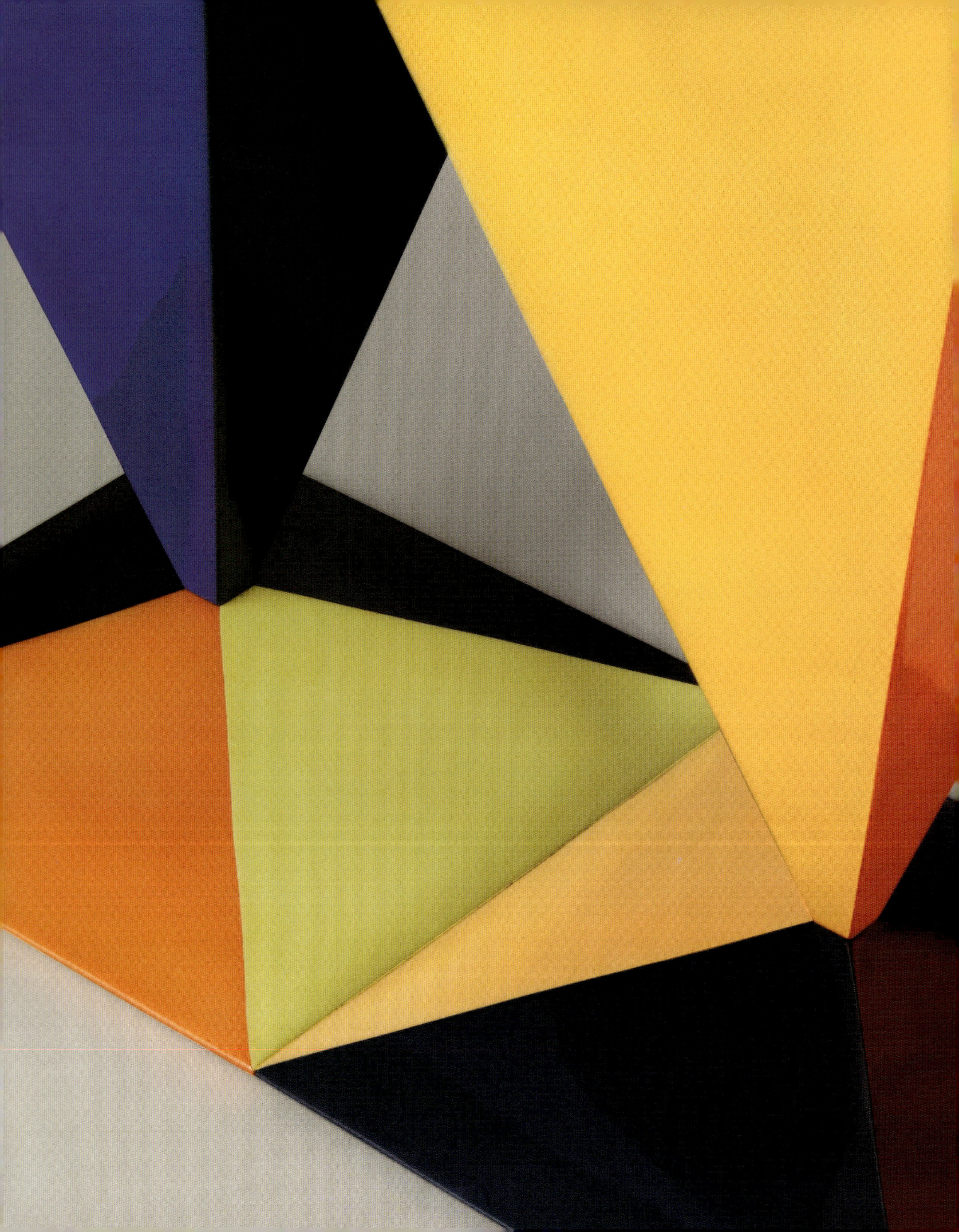

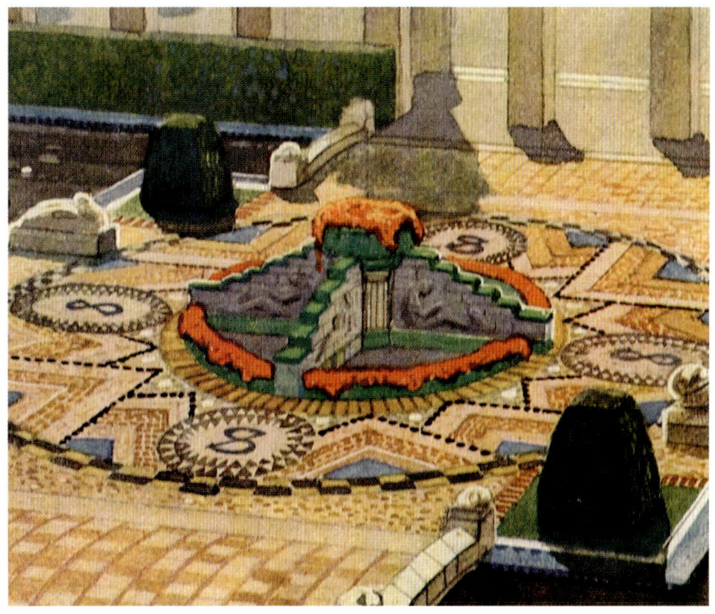

CHAPTER THREE

The Twentieth Century

The last decade of the nineteenth century was a time of drastic administrative reforms at the factory. Management did away with a cadre of full-time staff and began a process of hiring artists and artisans for specific projects or for limited periods.

The quick succession of artistic directors[1] explains the hesitant artistic style, apparent in some productions of the later years of the nineteenth century. Things changed with architect-decorator Alexandre Sandier's (1843–1916) appointment as artistic director in 1897.[2] Sandier surrounded himself with a group of creative collaborators—modelers, painters, and ornamentalists—and allowed them free rein to rejuvenate the production of a factory which, in the view of critics such as Victor Champier, seemed to be destined to "perpetually execute funerary urns for the cenotaph of Louis XVI...."[3]

ABOVE

Detail of fig. 78, Sèvres pavilion at the 1925 *Exposition internationale des arts décoratifs et industriels modernes*

OPPOSITE

Detail of fig. 103, "Reform" vase by Richard Peduzzi

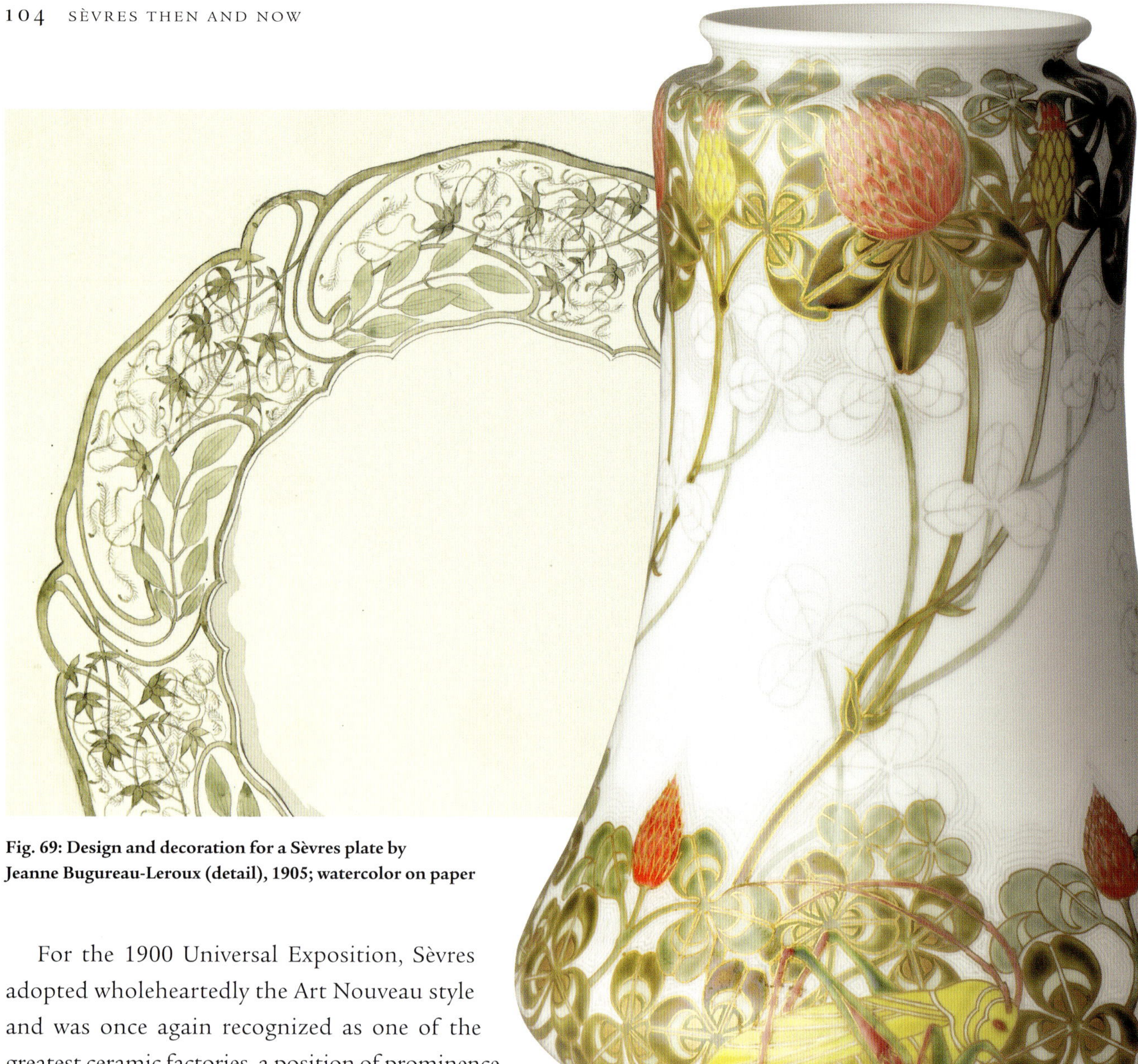

Fig. 69: Design and decoration for a Sèvres plate by Jeanne Bugureau-Leroux (detail), 1905; watercolor on paper

Fig. 70 (cat. 56): ***Vase du Bourget "B"*** **designed by Alexandre Sandier and decorated by Henri-Louis-Laurent Ulrich, 1895–1901**

For the 1900 Universal Exposition, Sèvres adopted wholeheartedly the Art Nouveau style and was once again recognized as one of the greatest ceramic factories, a position of prominence which it had not held since the fall of the Second Empire. Aiming to make an impact, Sandier and his collaborators designed a group of new forms characterized by flat, faceted linear or curvilinear surfaces and soft decoration, with which they had enormous success at the exposition. Molded vases with naturalistic motifs were also presented. Under Sandier's direction more than 300 new models appeared, grouped under different regional nomenclatures: Auxerre, Sens, de Neuilly, de Marnes, or du Bourget (figs. 70, 71, 72). The black cloud cast over the factory by critics like Champier began to be dispelled.

Figures, landscapes, and in general narrative scenes, disappeared. Decorations drew inspiration from the natural and animal world, stylized and free-flowing in accordance with the aesthetics of the period (fig. 69). Drawings were often provided by outside designers and carried out by hired artists. Shapes ranged in size from small and delicate to monumental, with large areas given over to decoration. Whether large or small, forms were often simple with no added casts or elaborate mounts. Colors were soft, as in the case of the *vase du Bourget "B"* by Sandier and Henri-Louis-Laurent Ulrich (active 1879–1925) with raspberry flowers and green leaves expressed in whiplash curves and lines (fig. 70). Layering glazes to create extremely complex layers of decoration was one of Sèvres' specialties.

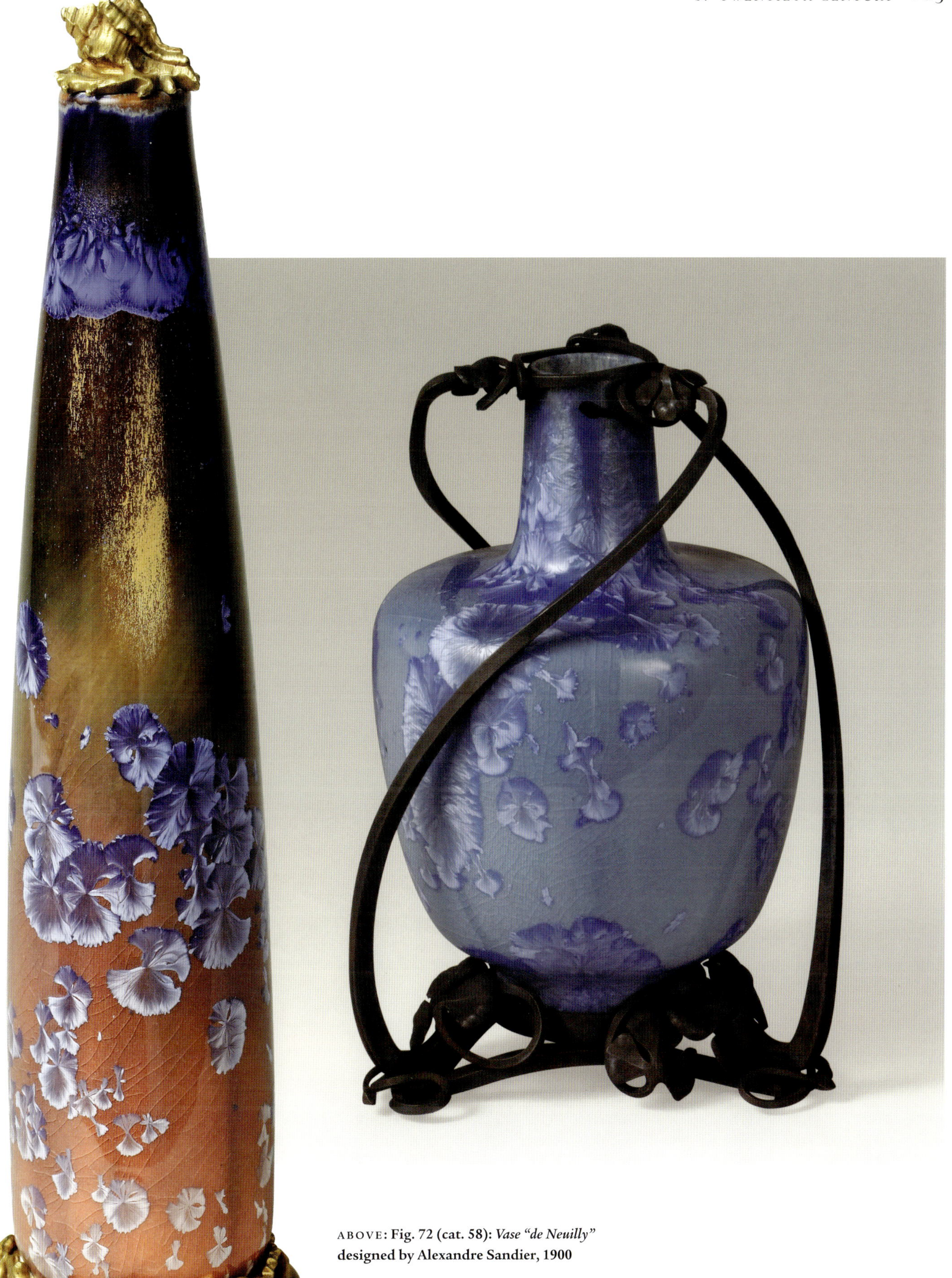

ABOVE: **Fig. 72 (cat. 58):** ***Vase "de Neuilly"*** **designed by Alexandre Sandier, 1900**

LEFT: **Fig. 71 (cat 57):** ***Vase "de Marnes"*** **designed by Alexandre Sandier, 1904**

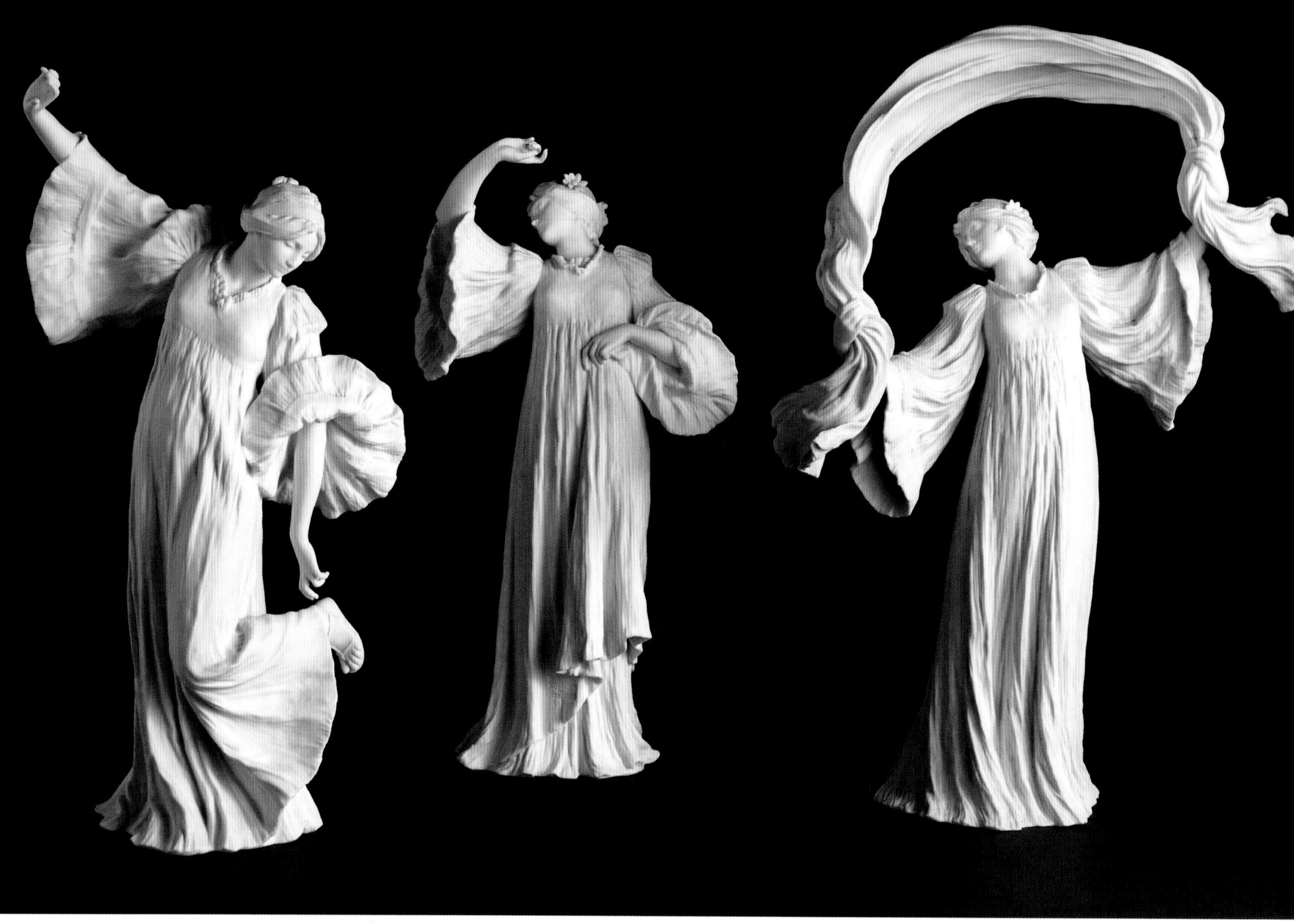

Fig. 73 (cat. 59): Three dancing biscuit figures from the *Jeu de l'Écharpe* centerpiece designed by Agathon Léonard, 1900

Around 1898 the experimentation with crystallized glazes yielded a delicate range of vases with soft gradations that evoked silk or precious stones. Examples of this technique can be appreciated in the *vase "de Marnes"* with crystallizations in beige and lilac and a gilt bronze base, or the *vase "de Neuilly,"* with a lotus flower base in gilt bronze and green/blue and ochre/blue crystallizations (figs. 71, 72).

The sculpture department was extremely active. The biscuit group of fifteen dancers from *Le Jeu de l'Écharpe* (the scarf dance) by Agathon Léonard (1841–1923) was sent to the Universal Exposition of 1900 (fig. 73). In this group, Léonard combined the rhythm of the dancers and the movement of the drapery to convey a sense of elegantly subdued dynamism. For the ensemble, Léonard was inspired by Loïe Fuller (1862–1928), a Chicago-born dancer who had awed Parisian audiences with her innovative free dances in which she transformed herself into natural elements (for example birds, flowers, fire, or clouds) and projected swirls of light onto her flowing, oversized silk costumes. With her performances, Fuller became the embodiment of Art Nouveau and a darling of the Symbolist movement, as well as of the Parisian intelligentsia.[4] The choice of subject again shows how much Sèvres was in tune with other contemporary expressions. The first *Jeu de l'Écharpe* set was offered as a sculptural ensemble to Tsar Nicholas II (reg. 1894–1917), who in turn bequeathed it to the Hermitage Museum. Taken by the results, the director of Sèvres decided it would be the perfect piece for the exposition and came up with the idea

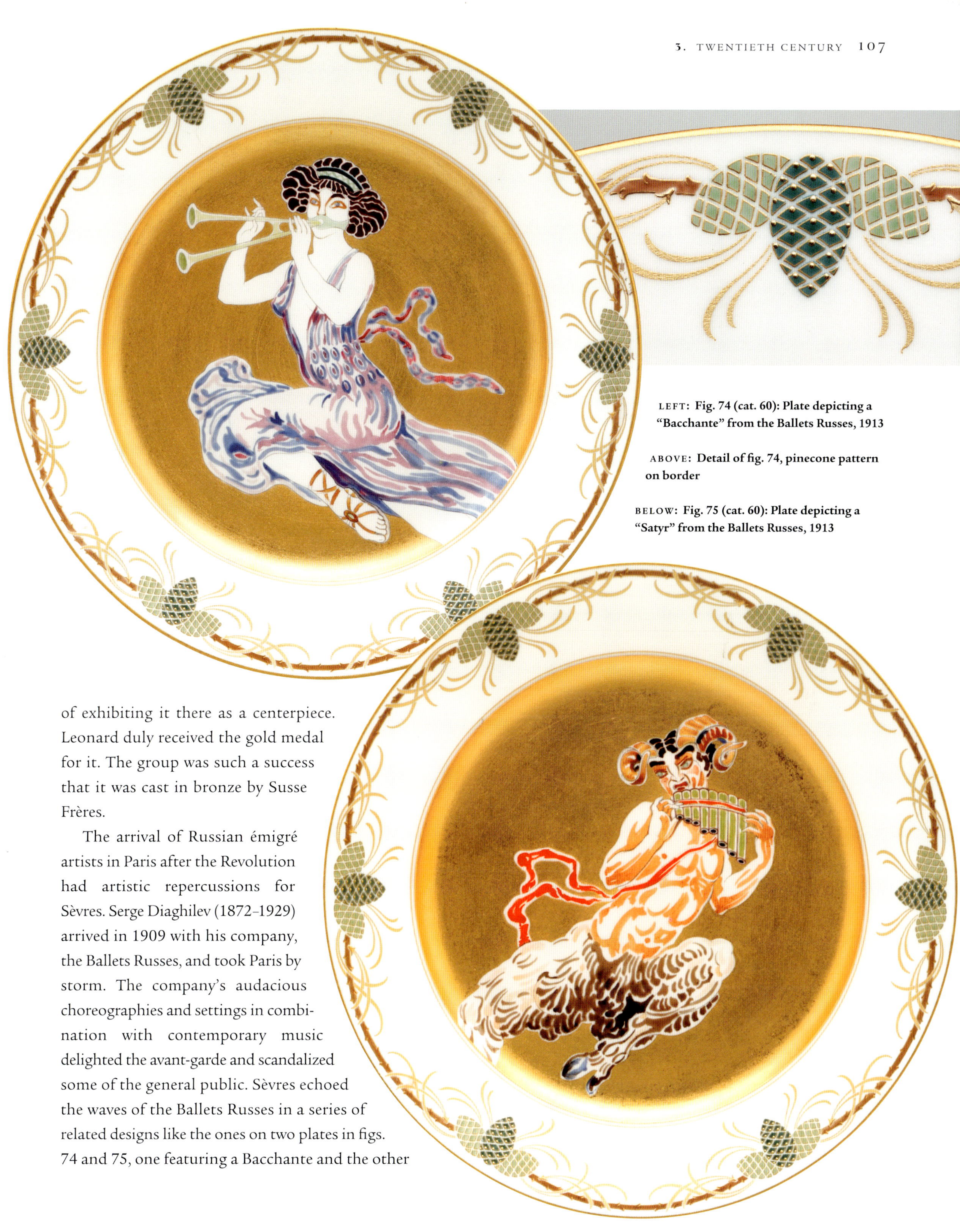

LEFT: **Fig. 74 (cat. 60): Plate depicting a "Bacchante" from the Ballets Russes, 1913**

ABOVE: **Detail of fig. 74, pinecone pattern on border**

BELOW: **Fig. 75 (cat. 60): Plate depicting a "Satyr" from the Ballets Russes, 1913**

of exhibiting it there as a centerpiece. Leonard duly received the gold medal for it. The group was such a success that it was cast in bronze by Susse Frères.

The arrival of Russian émigré artists in Paris after the Revolution had artistic repercussions for Sèvres. Serge Diaghilev (1872–1929) arrived in 1909 with his company, the Ballets Russes, and took Paris by storm. The company's audacious choreographies and settings in combination with contemporary music delighted the avant-garde and scandalized some of the general public. Sèvres echoed the waves of the Ballets Russes in a series of related designs like the ones on two plates in figs. 74 and 75, one featuring a Bacchante and the other

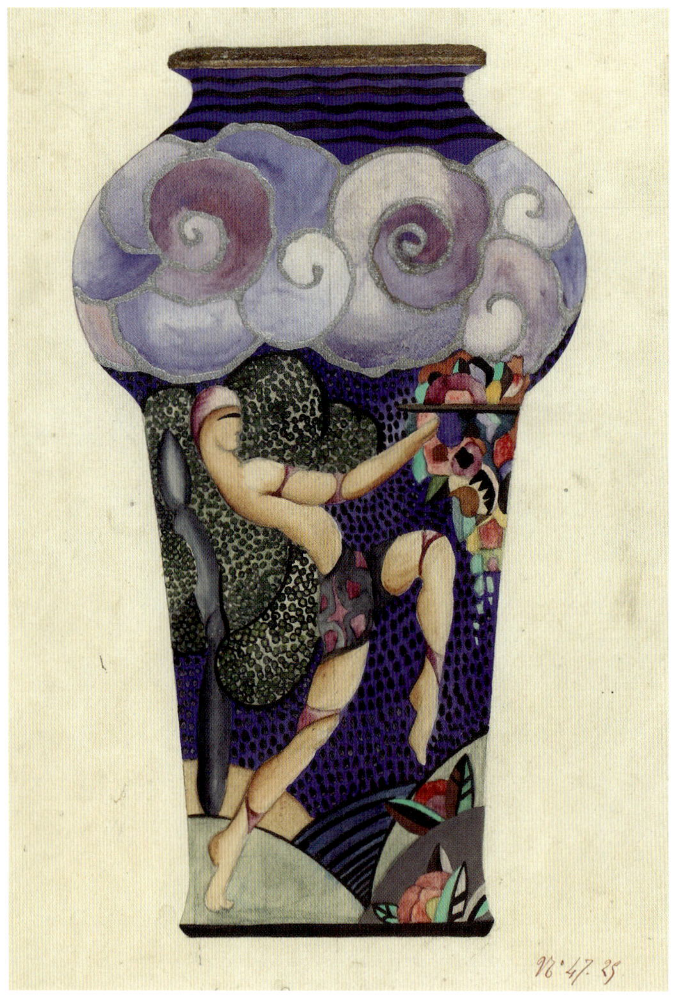

Fig. 76: Design drawing for *vase "Aubert" no. 64* by Odartchenko, 1925; gouache on paper

featuring a Satyr. The ballets *Daphnis et Chloë* (1912), *L'après-midi d'un faune* (1912) and the *Sacre du printemps* (1913) all premiered during the years when these plates were produced. Many of these ballets were designed by the talented scenographer Léon Bakst (1866–1924) and it is clear that the factory designer who worked on these plates, M. Maignan, must have drawn inspiration from Baskt's designs. Painter Louis-Jules Mimard (active 1884–1928) painted the figures and decorative borders of pine cones and needles on the plates. One of the peculiarities of these plates resides in the paste chosen—*pâte nouvelle*—a ceramic paste developed in the last quarter of the nineteenth century which allowed painting with raised enamel colors fired at high temperature, like Chinese enamels. Here, the unglazed ground left in its biscuit state contrasts quite strongly with the brilliance of the colorful painting. The Russian love of mixing strong colors, patterns, and flat decorations is captured on the Bacchante's dress. It is evident that these plates were intended for display rather than for dining ware.

At the outbreak of World War I Sèvres stopped production to concentrate on manufacturing gunpowder cases. But, after the war, the factory became once more a model for progressive ceramic art and a laboratory for many technical developments in the field of ceramics.

The appointment of Georges Lechevallier-Chevignard as director (1920–38), an ardent believer in the autonomy of the factory vis-à-vis the government, fostered a new period of financial independence and openness to the outside world. In the 1920s the factory opened its doors to a group of Russian collaborators who contributed to the modernization of the productions with their avant-garde vision and Cubist and Suprematist sensibilities. Work by these artists had been shown at the Soviet pavilion of the 1925 *Exposition internationale des arts décoratifs et industriels modernes*.[5] The figure in the center of Odartchenko's vase design in fig. 76 is a male dancer carrying a bunch of flowers. His figure is delineated with distinct segments for each body part, which stresses the muscular condition of the dancer. The rest of the vase is decorated with landscape sections in bright colors against a deep blue dotted ground. Schematic blue to lilac clouds adorn the shoulder of the vase. The vaguely Cubist fragmentary manner of representation and the colors of "Fauviste" intensity denote an artist *au courant* with the latest artistic tendencies and able to use them in a decorative idiom.

As director, Lechevallier-Chevignard revamped the factory's output in accordance with the new Art Deco style. He commissioned Félix Aubert (1866–1940), professor at the École des Arts Décoratifs, and designers Émile-Jacques Ruhlmann (1879–1933) and Henri Rapin (after 1873 – after 1939), to create new streamlined forms. The new geometric

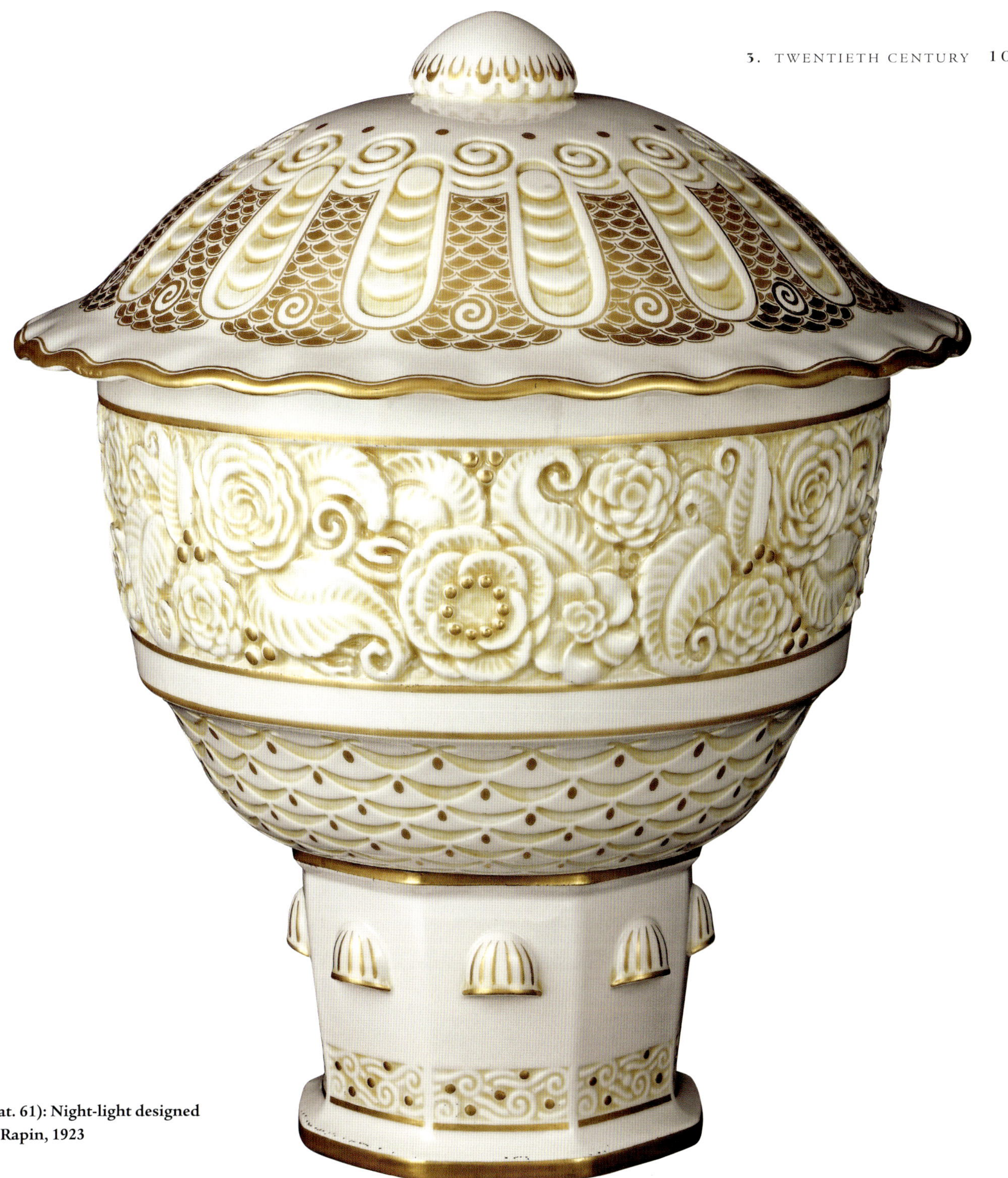

Fig. 77 (cat. 61): Night-light designed by Henri Rapin, 1923

shapes were translated into all kinds of wares. Striated, linear decorations became paramount whether incised on white wares or painted. Somber colors coexisted with vivid tonalities. The first occasion the public had to see the new products was at the 1922 and 1923 salons of the Societé des Artistes Décorateurs.[6]

Designers strived to be modern and in synchronicity with the interiors of contemporary architects and designers. Sèvres contributed to the new modern interiors by creating a line of small precious objects to go within them, as well as a range of decorative elements including lamps like the *veilleuse "Rapin"* which exposes the beautiful translucency of the Sèvres paste while at the same time embracing the modern currents of Art Deco with its raised surface of jagged lines and incised geometric designs simply picked out in black and gold (fig. 77). Its designer, Henri Rapin, had been director and professor at the École des Arts Décoratifs and a major contributor to the design of several pavilions at the 1925 Paris decorative arts exposition, including the garden at the Sèvres pavilions (fig. 78).

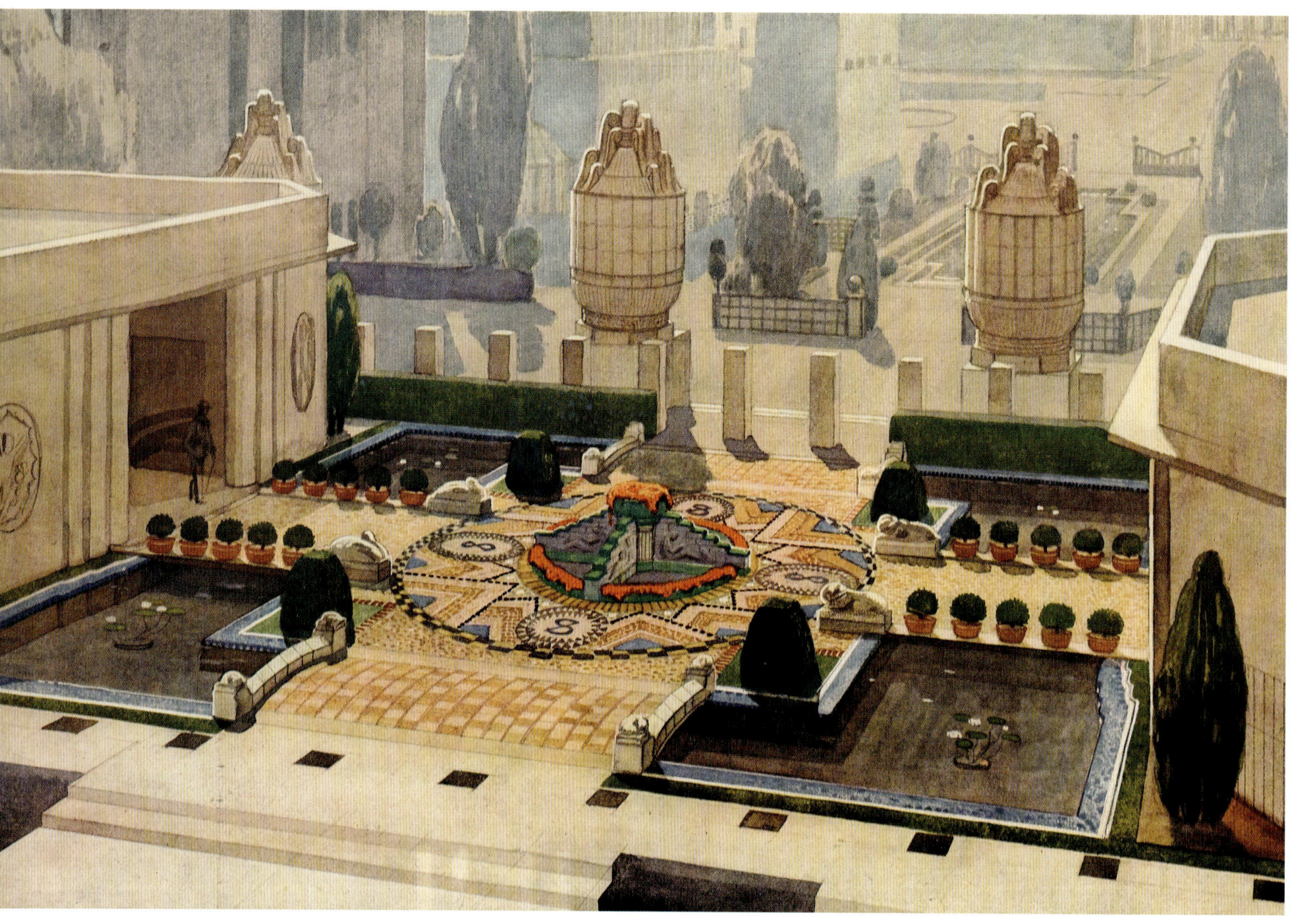

Fig. 78: Watercolor depicting the Sèvres pavilions and garden at the 1925 *Exposition internationale des arts décoratifs et industriels modernes* by Henri Rapin, published in the April 1925 issue of *L'Illustration*

The *vase "Ruhlmann"* is one of the vase forms created by the celebrated *ébéniste* and decorator Émile-Jacques Ruhlmann (fig. 79). The circumstances of the commission and collaboration are not well known, but Lechevallier-Chevignard must have contacted him in about 1925 at the time of the international decorative arts exposition in Paris where Ruhlmann's *Pavillon du collectionneur* was among the most visited of the fair. A tour de force, Ruhlmann's creation represented a lavish interior for a wealthy and discerning imaginary collector, which involved more than forty designers, artists, and craftsmen under his supervision. For Sèvres, Ruhlmann produced a few shapes based on the cone including a tall vase, a small flask, and this tall *coupe* on a round base. The vase was decorated by Anne-Marie Fontaine (active 1928–38), one of several women artists who joined the factory to create the ensemble for the 1925 exposition. Fontaine had received formal training as a designer. She also went to Vienna on a scholarship and this artistic exchange enriched her designs substantially. Fontaine was a versatile artist capable of conceiving decorations as well as graphic and textile designs, and for these reasons she was put in charge of publicity for the factory in the 1920s (fig. 80).

Sèvres used the 1925 exposition to confirm its status as a modern, yet non-industrial enterprise. At the fair, Sèvres constructed two pavilions connected by a garden where they

OPPOSITE: **Fig. 79 (cat. 63): vase designed by Émile-Jacques Ruhlmann and decorated by Anne-Marie Fontaine, 1926–7**

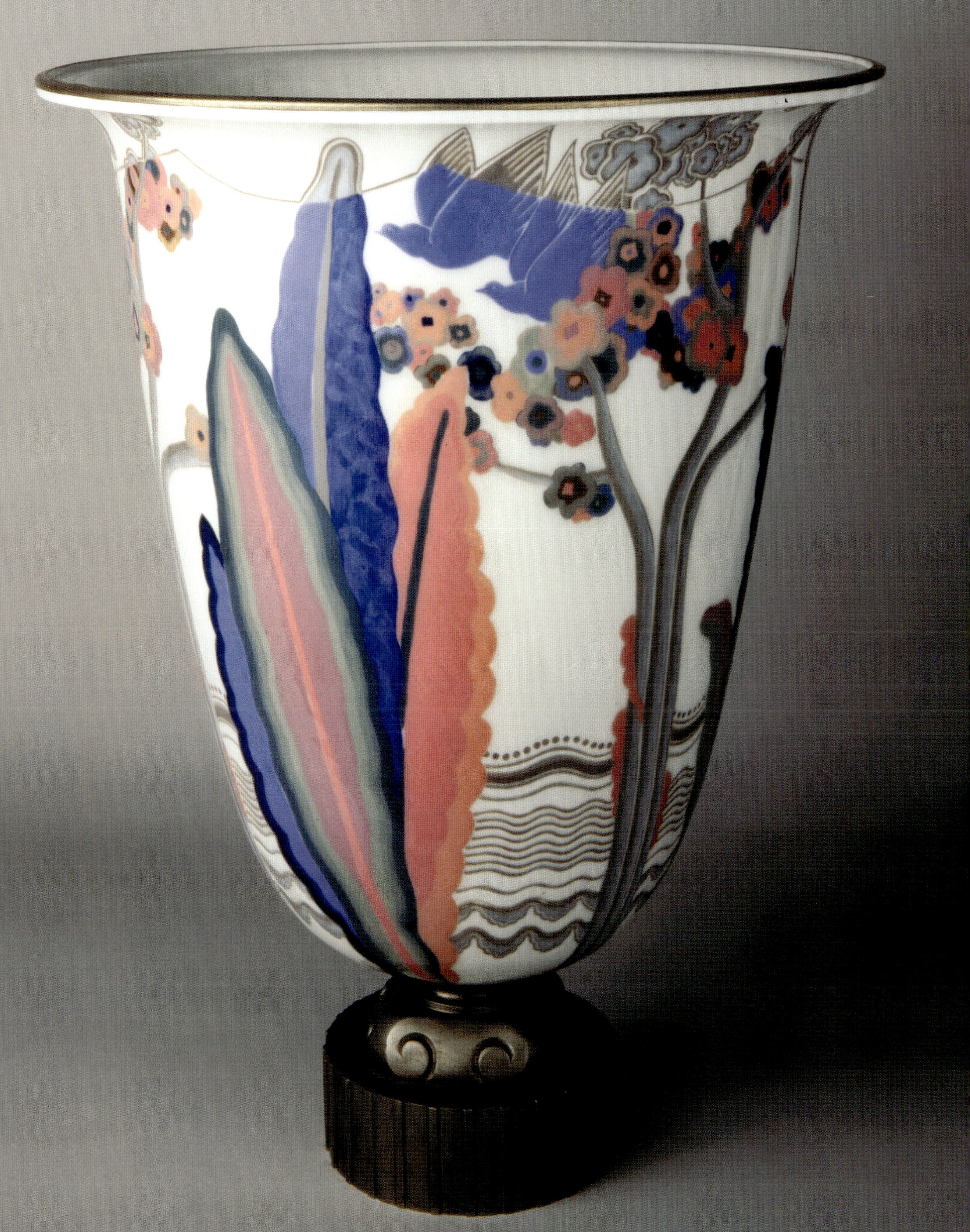

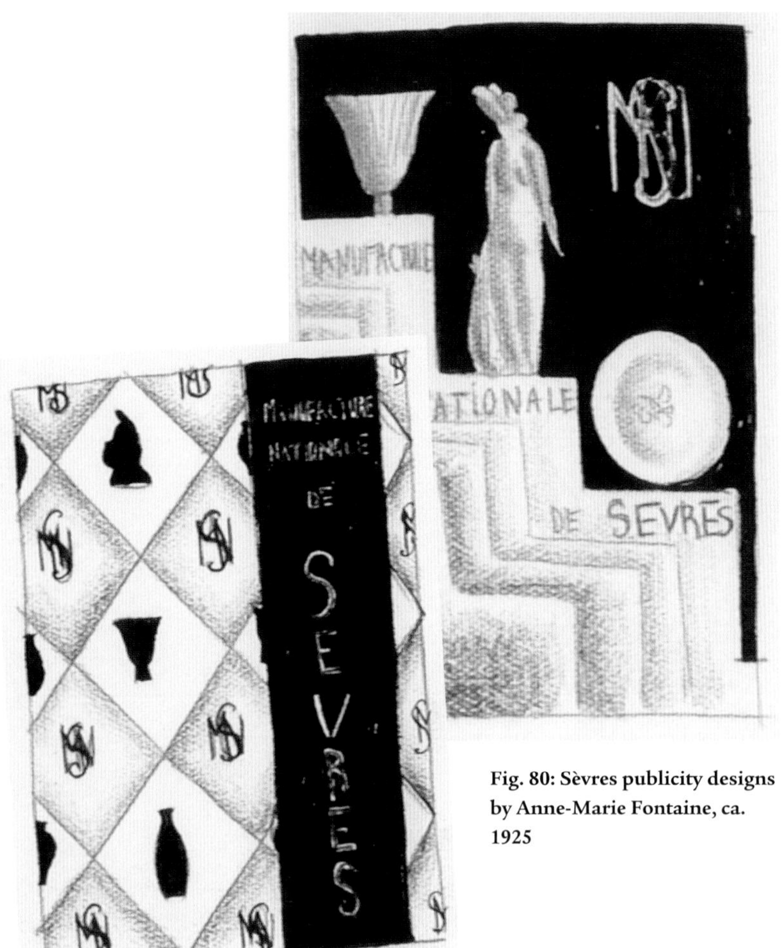

Fig. 80: Sèvres publicity designs by Anne-Marie Fontaine, ca. 1925

exhibited their creations in situ rather than in cases. The creations ranged from large architectural elements such as fountains, basins, and murals to small precious bibelots (fig. 78). The popular success obtained at the 1900 Universal Exposition made the factory more conscious of its potential role in the commercial arena. In the new marketplace, taste was sovereign, and fashion was ever changing. But for Sèvres, market demand was only one consideration. Sèvres stood alone with its artistic-driven, non-industrial production amidst a burgeoning group of independent ceramists and factories changing to adapt to the new times, to functionalism, and to the democratization of production serving a larger audience.

The turn of the century marked an upset in the hierarchy of ceramics that would affect production for the rest of the century. Porcelain prevailed as the main ceramic body, but the formerly lowly stonewares and low-fired earthenwares and *grès* gained popularity and respect, even in the high end market of Sèvres.

In 1924, in an attempt to serve a larger clientele, a faience workshop opened at Sèvres under the direction of Maurice Gensoli (1892–1972) and later under Louis Delachenal (1897–1966). Easier to fire and decorate, faience was a much simpler ceramic body. The process involved fewer steps at the decoration stage. The lower temperatures for firing allowed for a faster, more economical production at a time of crisis in the factory, which lost the annual subventions from the government in 1931. The faience workshops produced simple forms without glazes in monochromes or with a limited range of ochres and reds and very simple decoration. The distribution of the factory's output through a series of sales points in Paris helped ease the dire financial situation.

This was also a time of increased official commissions for embassies, presidential residences, and collectors' interiors; many of these porcelains are imbued with an official character since they are quintessentially representational. Lechevallier-Chevignard commissioned Ruhlmann, Rapin, and René Prou (1889–1947) to create new forms that would complement the repertoire introduced in the 1920s. Large-scale projects like the decorations of "paquebots" (grand vases for the *Île-de-France*, the swimming pool for the *Normandie*) or the court at the Universal Exposition of 1937, which involved the talented collaborations of architects and designers, were received with great acclaim.

Between 1925 and 1939 some new vases were created by factory staff, including Anne-Marie Fontaine, as well as freelance artists such as Maurice Prou (1861–1930) and Jean Beaumont. Animals and human figures now gradually reappeared as decorative elements along with ornamental compositions, as one can appreciate in the *vases "Prou,"* designed by René Prou and decorated by Madame Max Vibert, where women and children are at play in a dynamic and economical composition, leaving much of the white ground exposed (fig. 81). The tall cylindrical shape is

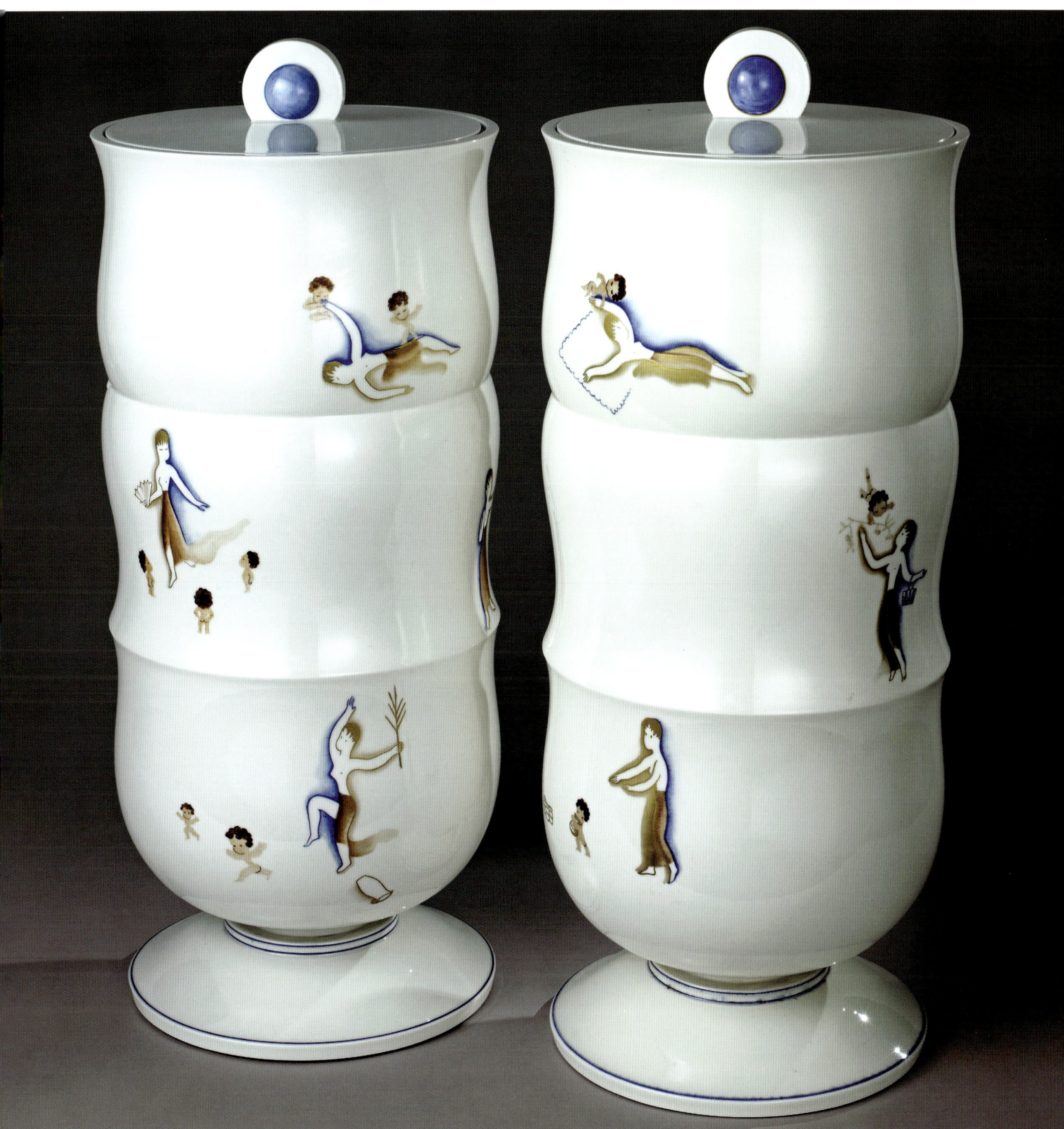

Fig. 81 (cat. 62): Vases designed by René Prou and decorated by Madame Max Vibert, 1935

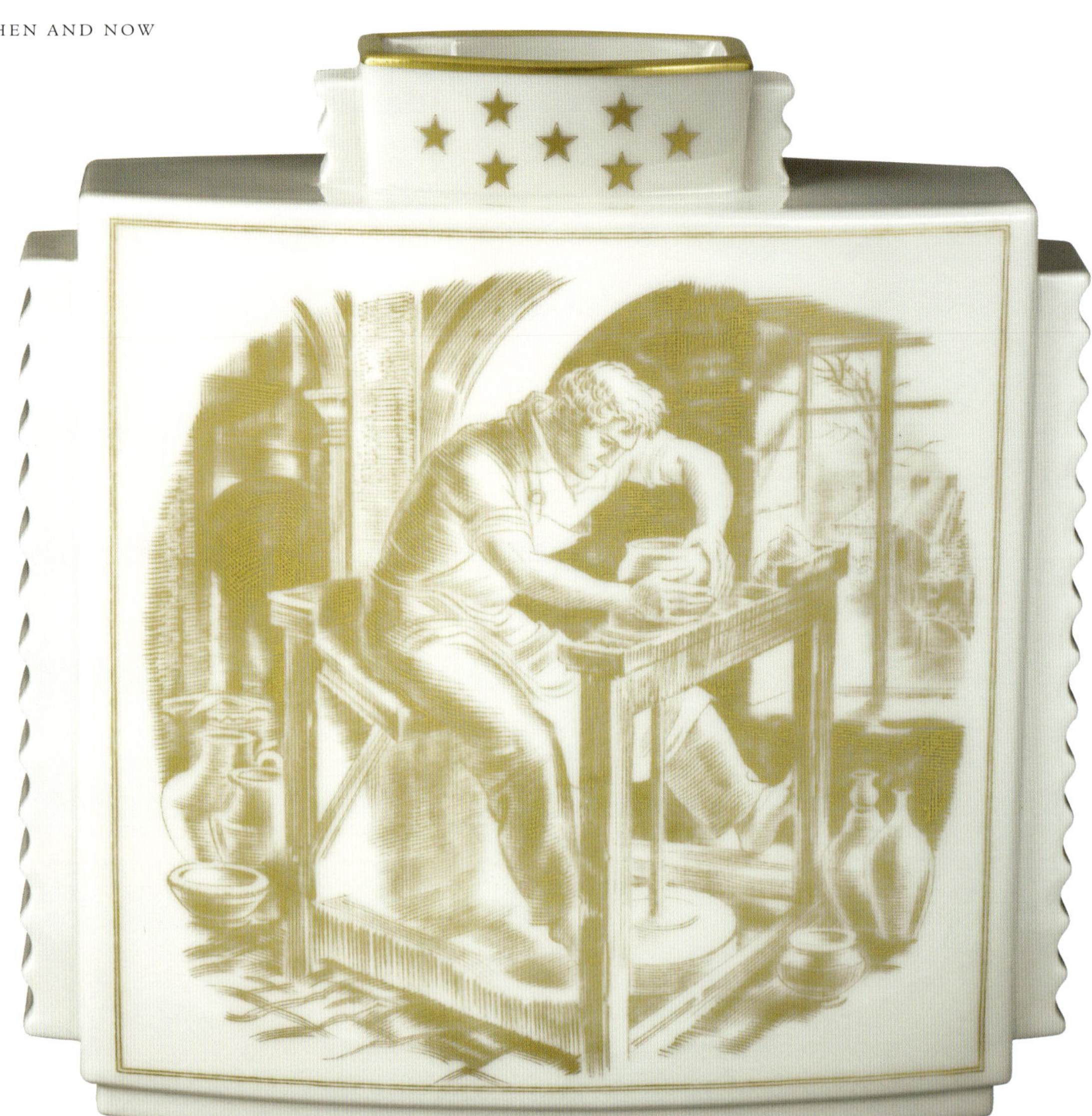

Fig. 82 (cat. 64): "Lallemand" vase picturing an artisan at work, 1944

animated by the movement of three curvaceous segments divided by an incised and a projecting line.

The decade of the 1940s was marked by war and by a clear intent to depart from previous styles. The artist Louis Desmarest, in a report to the Ministry of Education dated August 29, 1939, four days before France entered World War II, expressed his distate for the Art Deco and Art Nouveau styles and claimed the need to return to the high standards of production and artistic research of the 1880s.[7]

During World War II, sales and commissions ceased except for a service for the then chief of state, Marshal Pétain, and a few orders for the Germans during the Occupation. The vase in fig. 82 is one of these commissions. The front has an image of a potter at work at the turner's wheel after a drawing of *L'artisan* by Albert Decaris. A quote from Pétain on the back extols the virtues of artisan work, which demands "a physical effort of both mind and soul." In 1941 the Sèvres factory lost its autonomy and was annexed to the Mobilier National. In that same year the École Nationale Supérieure de Céramique (Advanced School of Ceramics) was funded separately as the factory's training department. Sèvres suffered great losses during the war. In 1943 the first English bombardment of the city destroyed the decorators' workshop. More than 10,000 pieces were broken and 250 prototypes were lost beyond recovery.[8]

In the 1950s Sèvres was faced with the dual challenge of reconstructing and upgrading the factory and revitalizing its ceramic production. Sèvres followed its own creative path away from emerging ceramic trends. The earthy and austere *grès* wares of many artist-potters closer to popular types or oriental models, or the colorful and primitive faiences of Picasso at Vallauris or Jean Lurçat at Sant-Vicens, had little

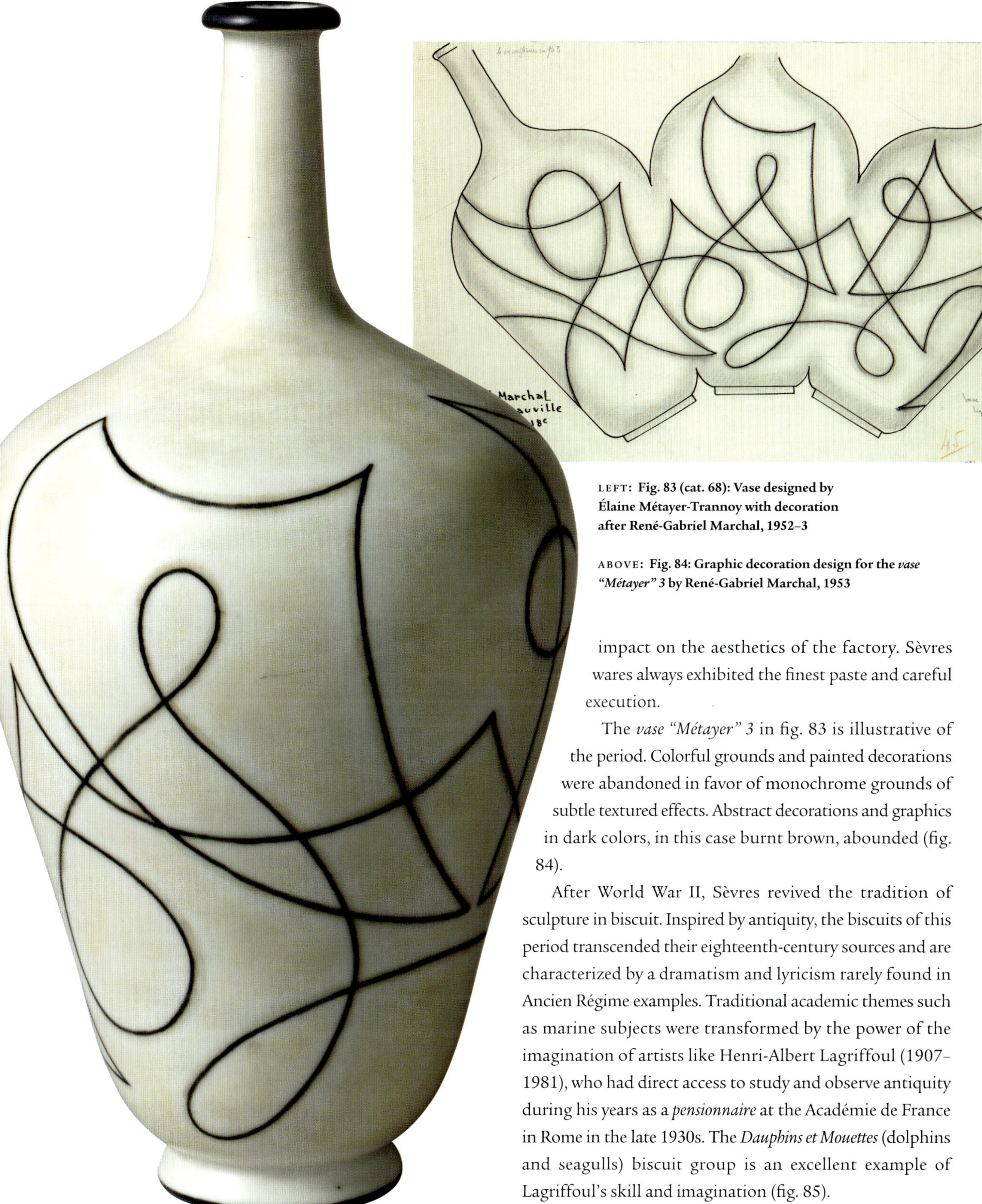

LEFT: **Fig. 83 (cat. 68): Vase designed by Élaine Métayer-Trannoy with decoration after René-Gabriel Marchal, 1952–3**

ABOVE: **Fig. 84: Graphic decoration design for the *vase "Métayer" 3* by René-Gabriel Marchal, 1953**

impact on the aesthetics of the factory. Sèvres wares always exhibited the finest paste and careful execution.

The *vase "Métayer" 3* in fig. 83 is illustrative of the period. Colorful grounds and painted decorations were abandoned in favor of monochrome grounds of subtle textured effects. Abstract decorations and graphics in dark colors, in this case burnt brown, abounded (fig. 84).

After World War II, Sèvres revived the tradition of sculpture in biscuit. Inspired by antiquity, the biscuits of this period transcended their eighteenth-century sources and are characterized by a dramatism and lyricism rarely found in Ancien Régime examples. Traditional academic themes such as marine subjects were transformed by the power of the imagination of artists like Henri-Albert Lagriffoul (1907–1981), who had direct access to study and observe antiquity during his years as a *pensionnaire* at the Académie de France in Rome in the late 1930s. The *Dauphins et Mouettes* (dolphins and seagulls) biscuit group is an excellent example of Lagriffoul's skill and imagination (fig. 85).

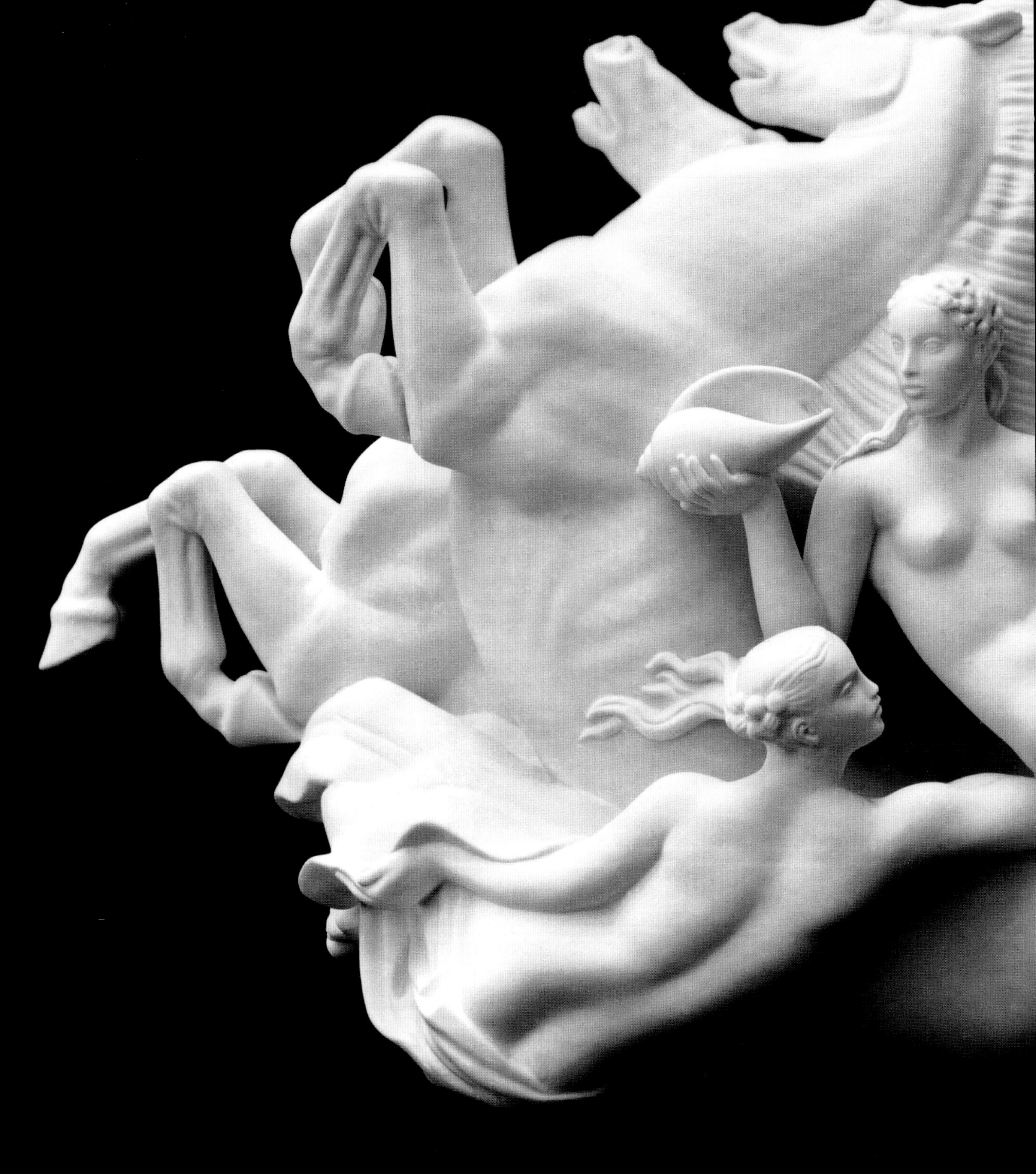

Fig. 85 (cat. 65): Central biscuit group from the *Dauphins et Mouettes* centerpiece, 1951–5

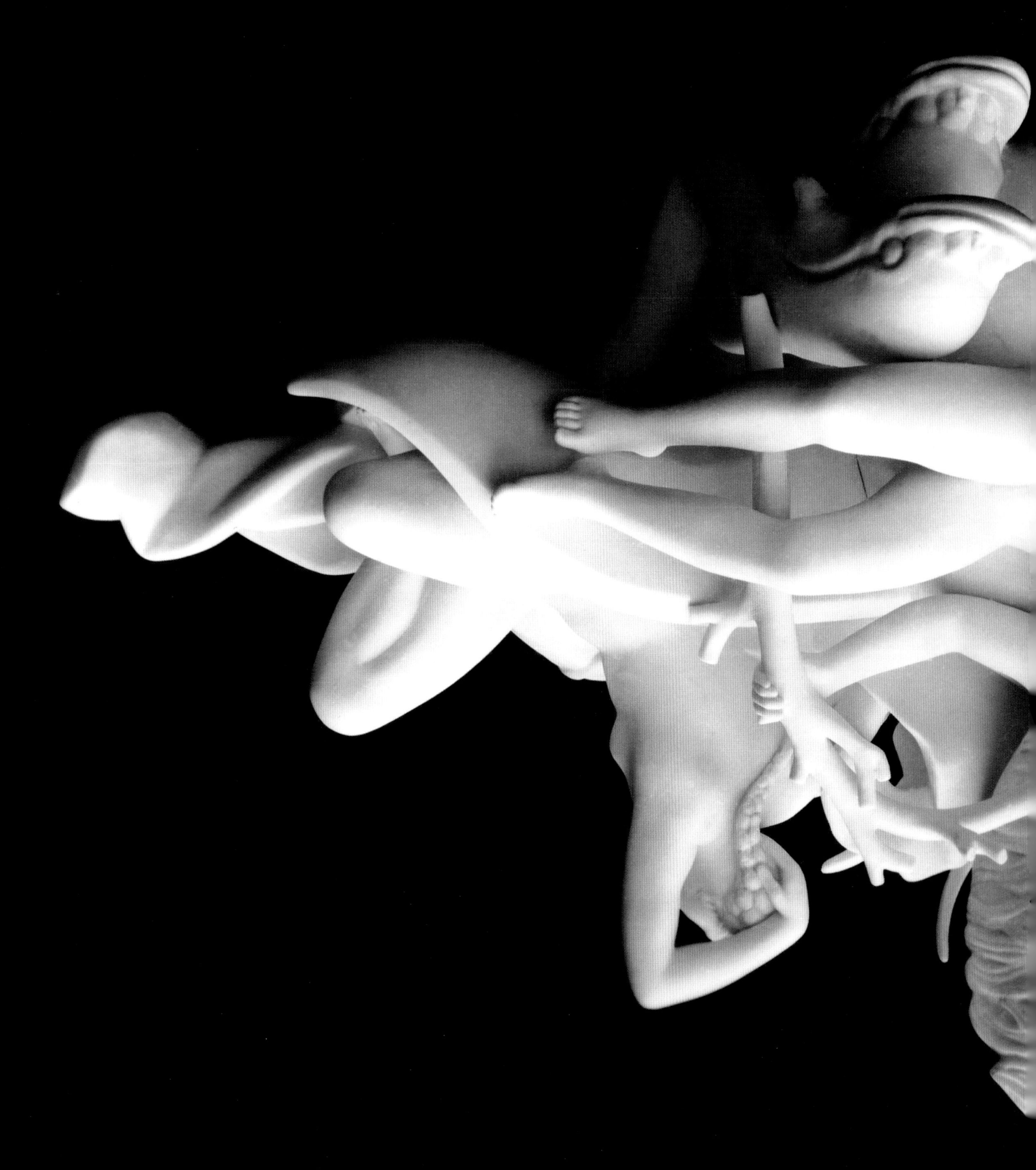

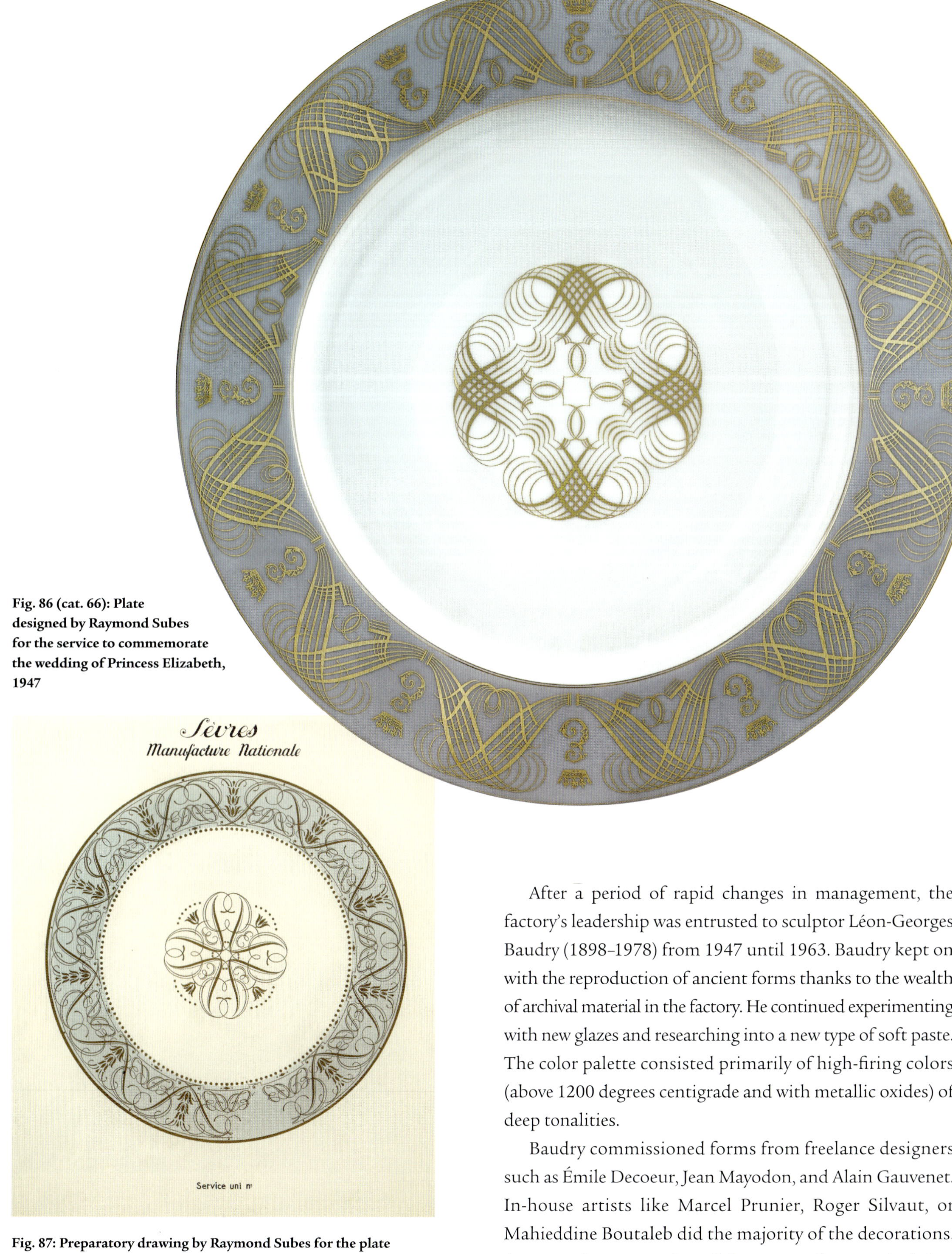

Fig. 86 (cat. 66): Plate designed by Raymond Subes for the service to commemorate the wedding of Princess Elizabeth, 1947

Fig. 87: Preparatory drawing by Raymond Subes for the plate illustrated in fig. 86.

After a period of rapid changes in management, the factory's leadership was entrusted to sculptor Léon-Georges Baudry (1898–1978) from 1947 until 1963. Baudry kept on with the reproduction of ancient forms thanks to the wealth of archival material in the factory. He continued experimenting with new glazes and researching into a new type of soft paste. The color palette consisted primarily of high-firing colors (above 1200 degrees centigrade and with metallic oxides) of deep tonalities.

Baudry commissioned forms from freelance designers such as Émile Decoeur, Jean Mayodon, and Alain Gauvenet. In-house artists like Marcel Prunier, Roger Silvaut, or Mahieddine Boutaleb did the majority of the decorations. Among the external collaborators, Raymond Subes

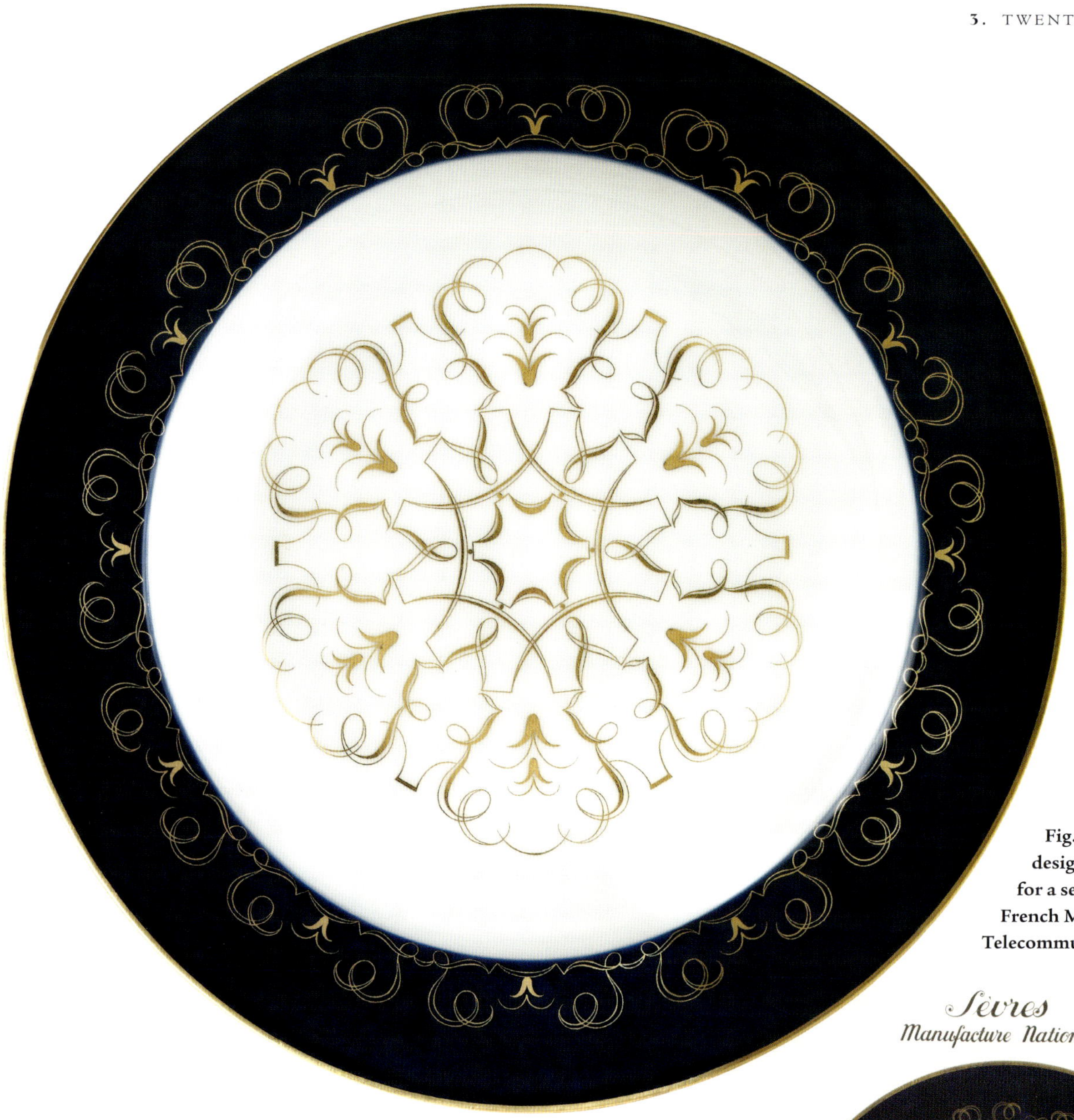

Fig. 88 (cat. 67): Plate designed by Raymond Subes for a service presented to the French Ministry of the Post and Telecommunications, 1947

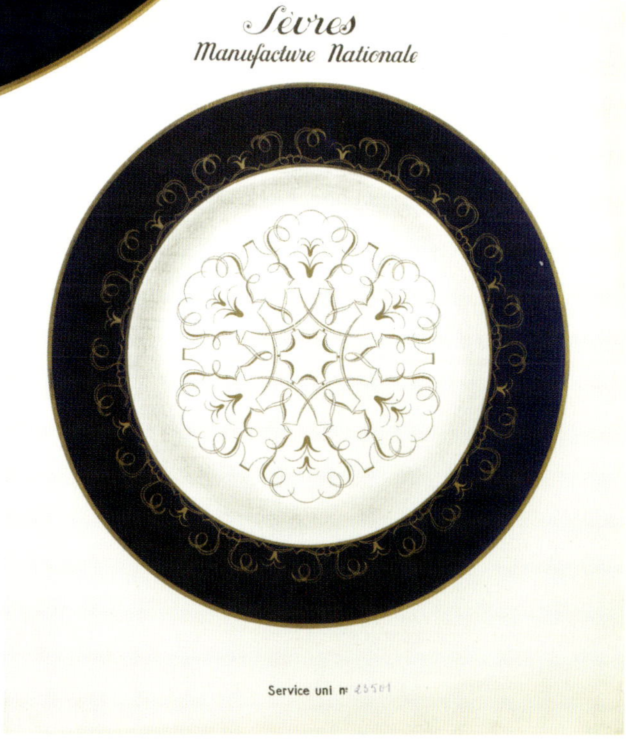

Sèvres
Manufacture Nationale

Service uni n° 25561

(1891–1970) should be singled out for his classical friezes and the services he designed in 1947 for the marriage of Princess Elizabeth of England (figs. 86, 87), the First Lady of Argentina, Eva Perón, and the French Ministry of the Post and Telecommunications (figs. 88, 89), where his characteristic forged iron curlicues are reproduced in graphic designs for porcelain.

In the mid-1960s contemporary artistic expressions had a brilliant forum at Sèvres under the directorship of Serge Gauthier (1964–76), who in tandem with the minister of culture, André Malraux, brought the factory closer to the contemporary scene. In an era of futuristic space-age-driven designs such as the Mirage IV, Concorde, and the new airport at Orly, porcelain—an old world material—was

Fig. 89: Design drawing by Raymond Subes for the plate illustrated in fig. 88

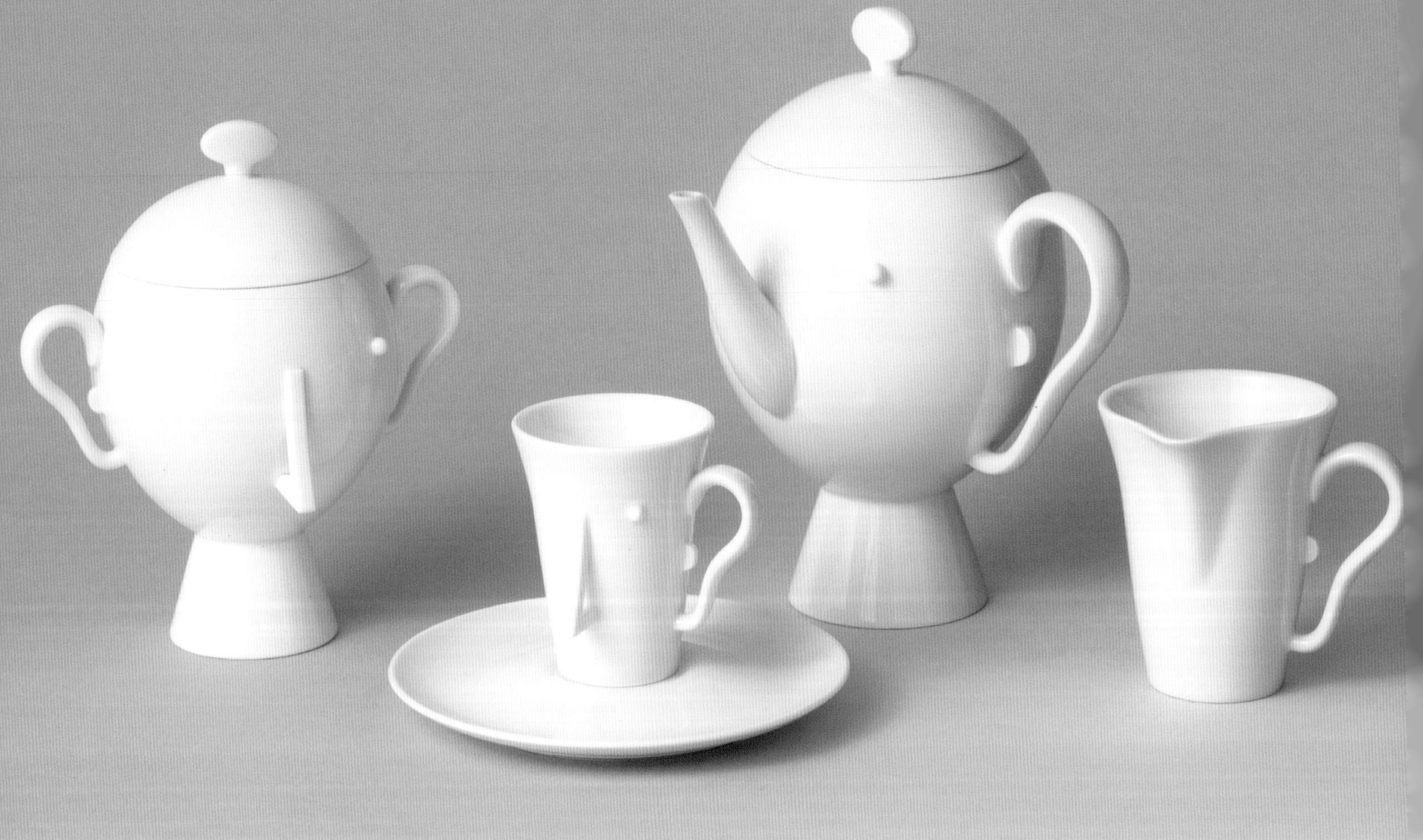

Fig. 90 (cat. 69): Coffee set with geometric faces designed by Robert Couturier, 1959–61

destined to suffer a serious drawback. Yet, the determination of Malraux and Gauthier to reform the factory and renew its production yielded great results, and they called on artists to meet the challenge of producing contemporary works in porcelain.

This was a period of real evolution of both forms and decorations. Robert Couturier (1905–2008) was a prolific collaborator with the factory in the 1960s. He designed a table centerpiece, prototypes for coffee and tea services, and anthropomorphic vases in *grès*.

The coffee service in fig. 90 also draws on the human figure for inspiration. The highly economic, yet expressive lines of the male heads on each piece betray the hand of a talented sculptor modeling ceramic with volumes and lines. The nakedness of the white porcelain enhances the clean forms of this figural coffee service. There is a humorous interplay of function and form in the design of this set. The handles are shaped as ears, the spout on the coffee pot takes the place of a nose, and the covers resemble traditional French berets. Inexplicably, the service did not go into production and remained a prototype until 2005 when Sèvres director David Caméo decided to produce it in a limited edition in collaboration with the Parisian gallery of Dina Vierny et Gaston. The twelve sets produced sold almost instantly.[9]

Celebrated sculptor and painter Jean Arp (1886–1966) initiated the practice of inviting established artists to work on specific projects at Sèvres (fig. 91). Unfortunately what Arp and Gauthier had envisioned as a long and fruitful collaboration was truncated by Arp's death. Nevertheless, the series of vases, called *Amphores de rêve*, is testimony to the highly expressive work that Arp carried out in ceramics (fig. 92). Arp humanized abstraction through his formal investigation into biomorphic forms when he began taking an interest in sculpture in the 1930s. For this series of vases, Arp quoted from one of his favorite subjects—variations on torsos which he had explored in sculpture from the 1930s onwards. His early studies served as a model for his later creations, such as this series of vases, through which he lyrically transposed the human torso into a formal, abstract synthesis.

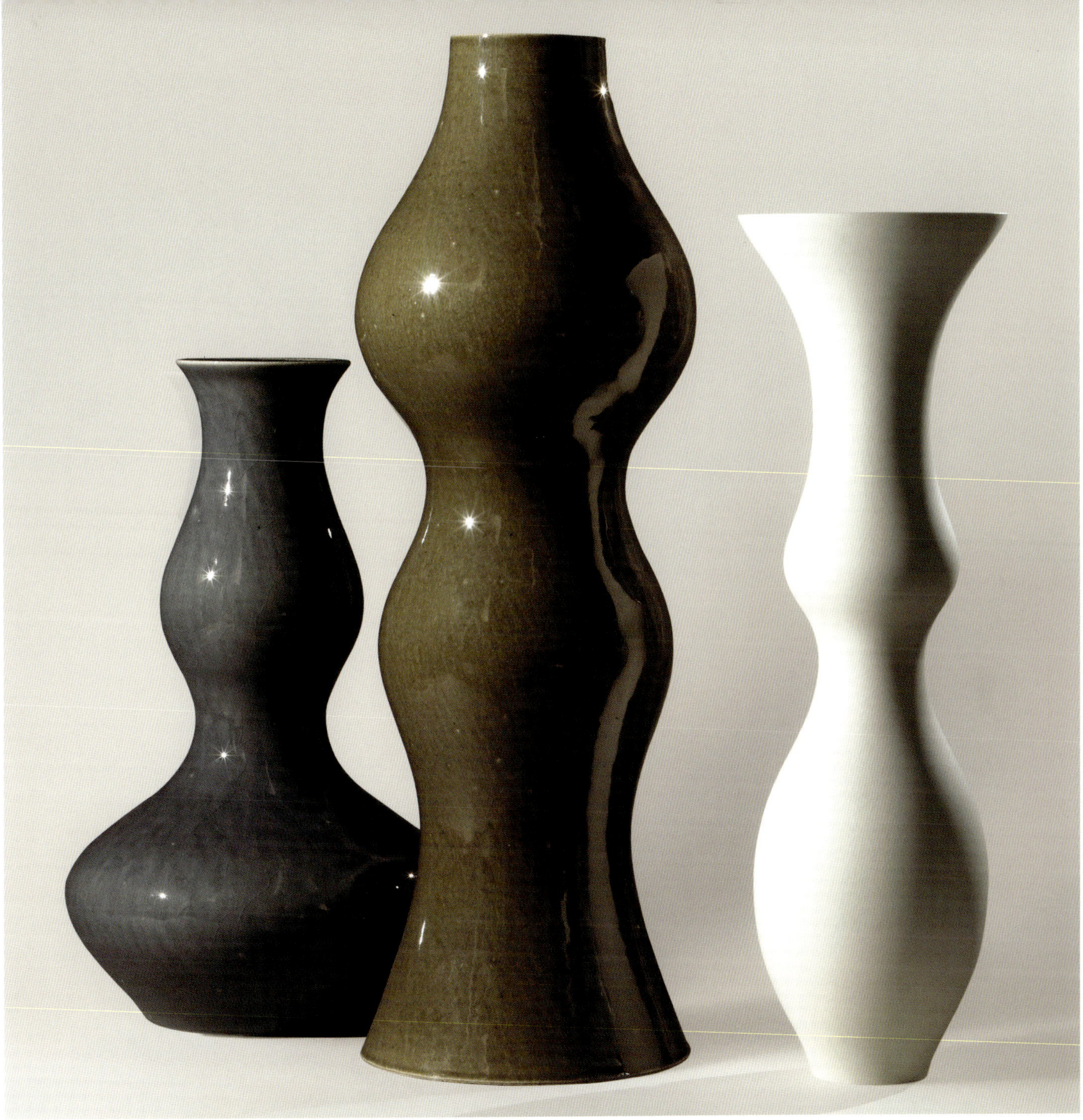

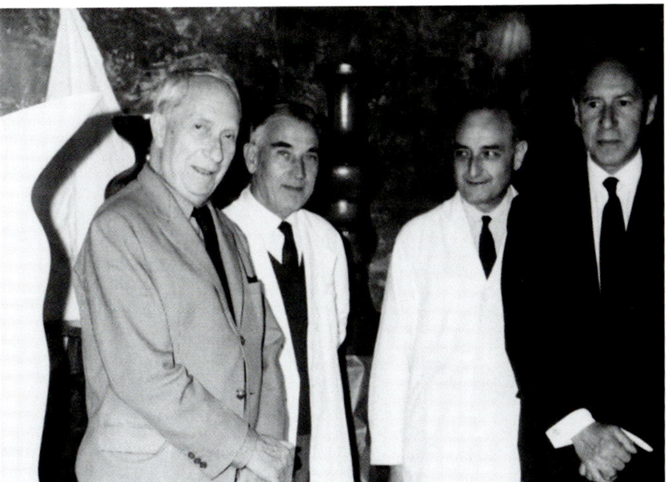

Fig. 92 (cat. 70): Three vases designed by Jean Arp from the *Amphores de rêve* series, ca. 1966

Fig. 91: Photo of Jean Arp (left), Roger Sivault, André Plantard, and Michel Seuphor at the Manufacture Nationale de Sèvres, 1966

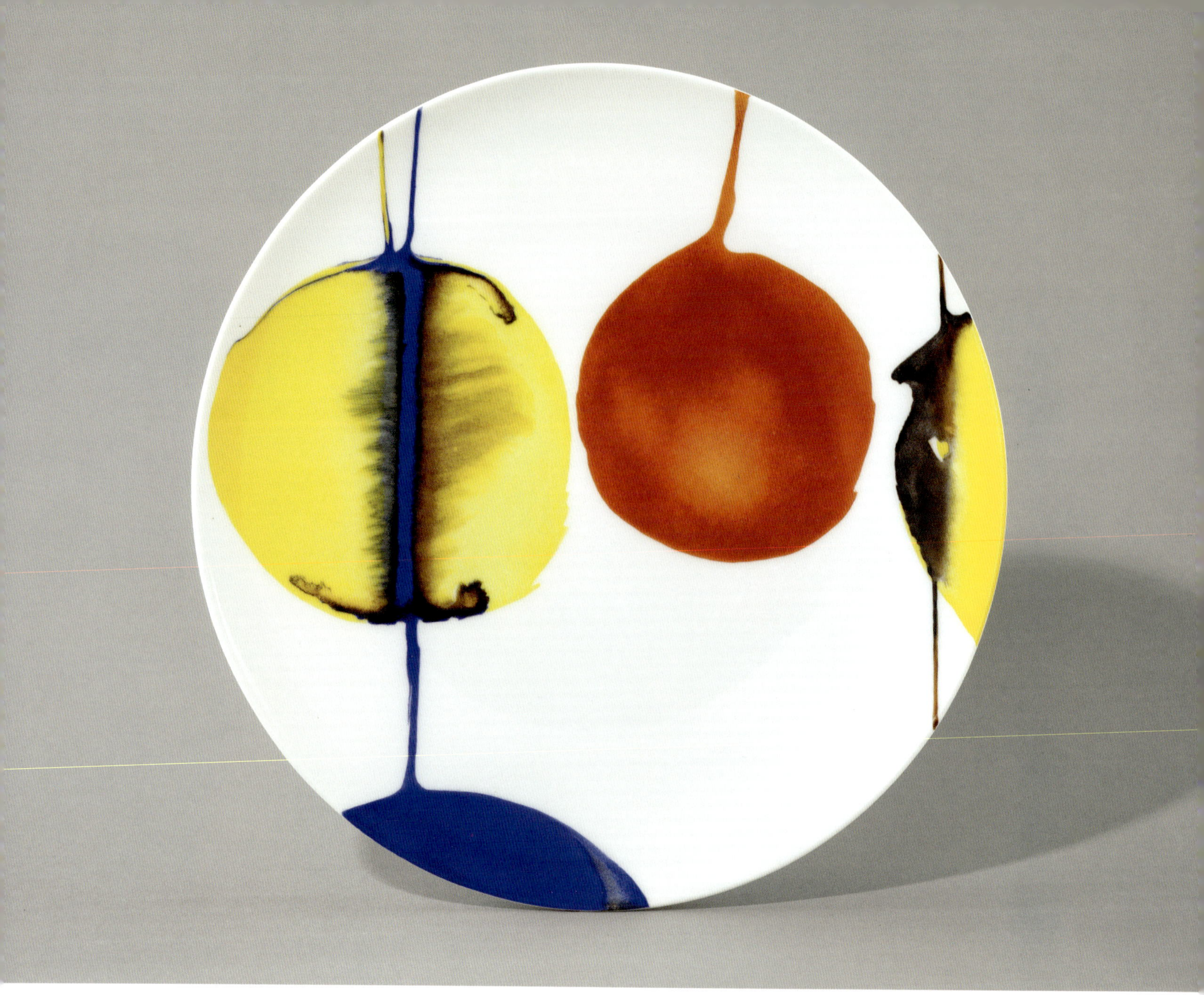

Fig. 93 (cat. 73): ***Diane*** **plate, decoration designed by Alexander Calder, 1969–70**

The renowned artists Alexander Calder, Serge Poliakoff, and Pierre Alechinsky were specifically called on to decorate *Diane* plates (figs. 93, 95). These artists brilliantly explored the possibilities of enamel colors and abstract compositions in the broad, continuous, and smooth surfaces of the *Diane* dishes. Calder created a service of plates with balloon-like configurations in bright colors, as well as designs for other projects at Sèvres (figs. 93, 94). As Poliakoff's wife Marcelle put it, "these Sèvres' dishes of Serge's are truly original works of art ... they are not decorations, they are veritable round paintings...."[10] (fig. 95).

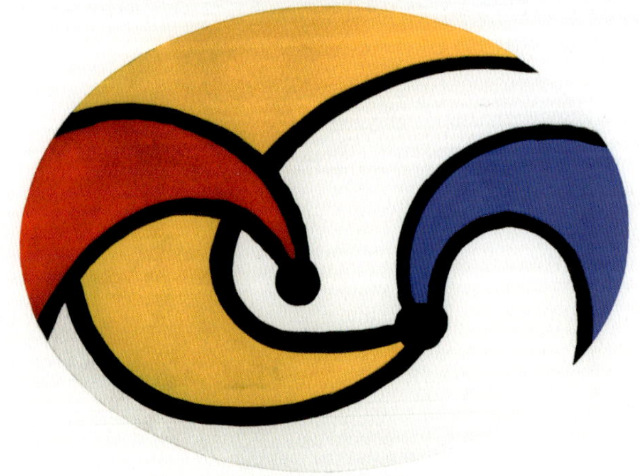

Fig. 94: Design for a tabletop by Alexander Calder, 1970; original pochoir after a gouache on paper from an edition of ten

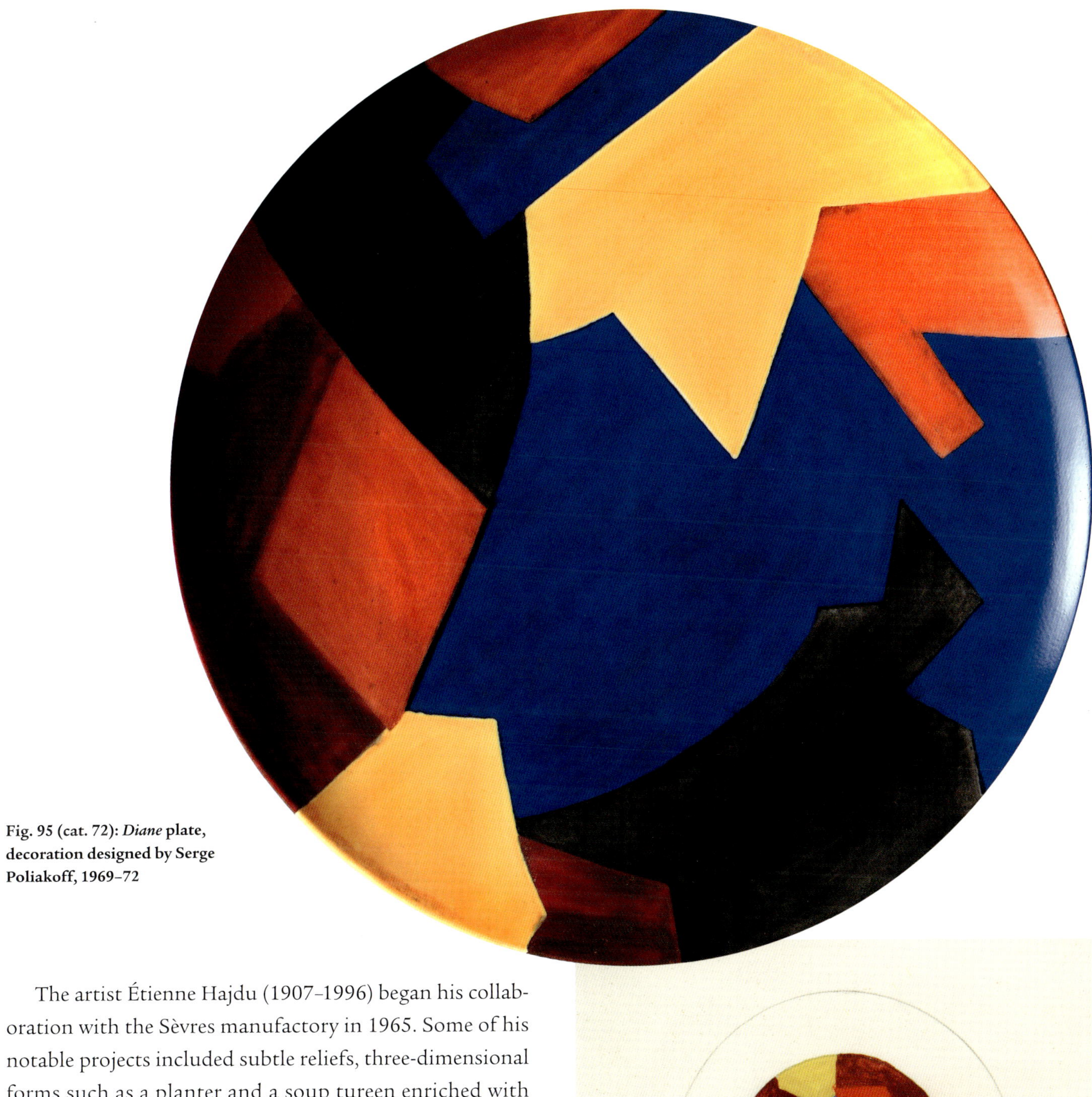

Fig. 95 (cat. 72): *Diane* plate, decoration designed by Serge Poliakoff, 1969–72

The artist Étienne Hajdu (1907–1996) began his collaboration with the Sèvres manufactory in 1965. Some of his notable projects included subtle reliefs, three-dimensional forms such as a planter and a soup tureen enriched with metal elements—genuine expressions of contemporary painting in ceramic. He was also asked to create a service for the Elysée Palace, the residence of the president of the French Republic. Hajdu effectively transcribed to porcelain his inks on paper, as can be appreciated on the plate in fig. 97. Sèvres director Gauthier had proposed continuing the tradition of experimenting with the color blue, the quintessential Sèvres color. Although this suggestion was not well received by Malraux, who spoke with tremendous disdain about the idea,[11] it was nevertheless followed through and incorporated into Hajdu's creations. For these plates Hajdu

Fig. 96: Design for a cake plate by Serge Poliakoff, ca. 1968; gouache on paper

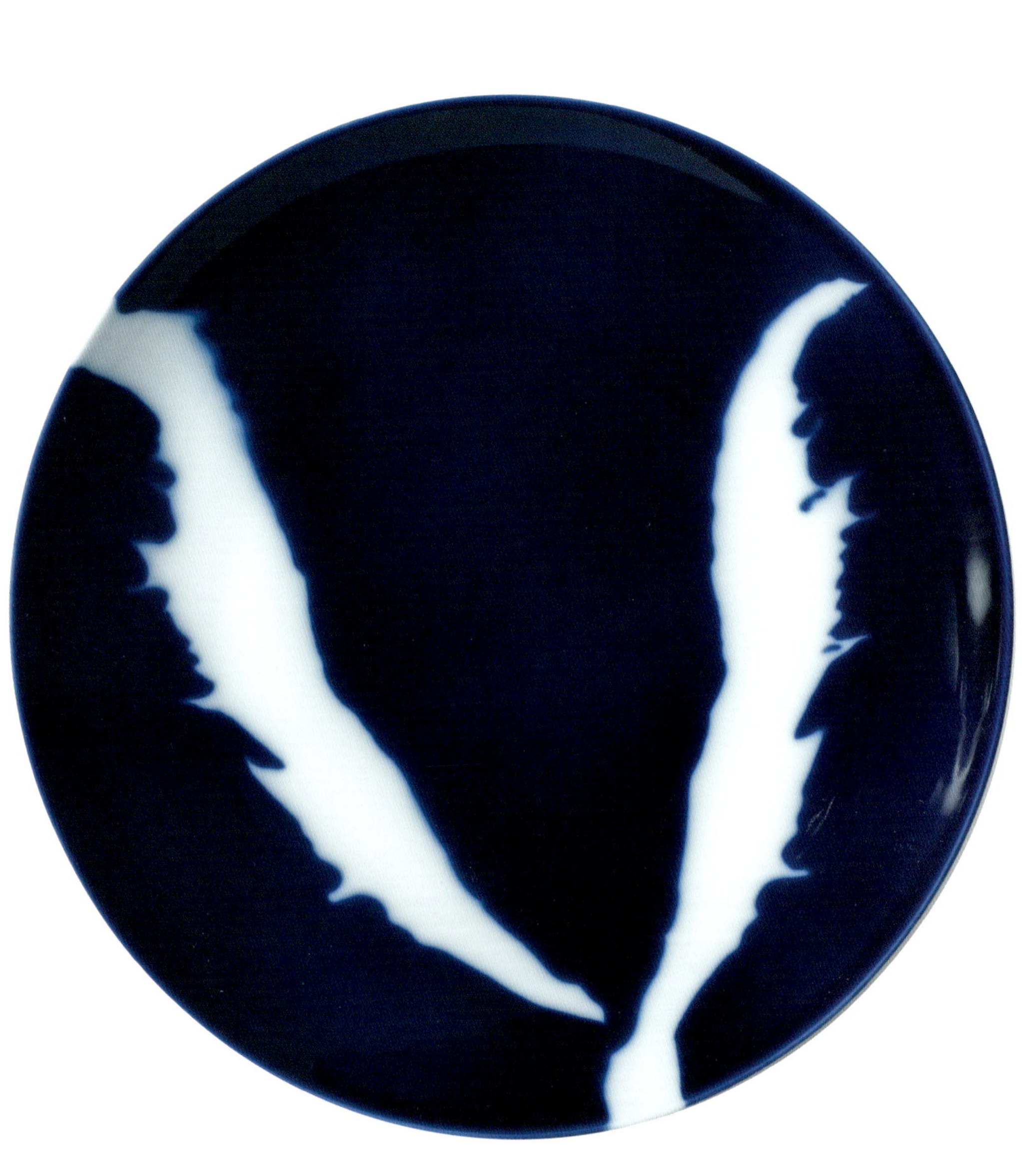

Fig. 97 (cat. 71): ***Diane*** **dessert plate designed by Étienne Hajdu, 1972**

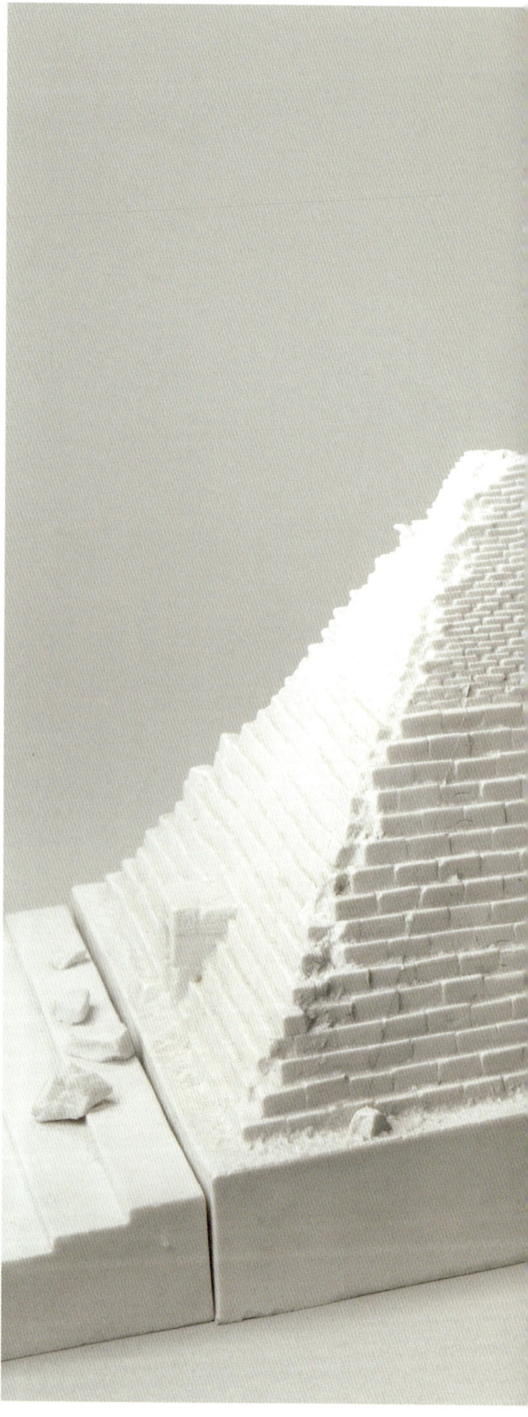

blew the cobalt blue around the concealed areas of his designs. Sometimes he worked with high-fired underglaze colors which he applied directly to the ceramic body leaving no chance for error.

In this period, biscuit was revived by artists like Hans Bischoffshausen, Arthur-Luis Piza, and animal sculptor François-Xavier Lalanne. One of the masterpieces in biscuit, created in the late 1970s by husband and wife team Anne and Patrick Poirier, is the sizeable *Ruines d'Égypte* centerpiece or *surtout de table* (fig. 98). The architectural subject for this architect and designer duo was alluring. The Poiriers, who defined themselves as "artists and archeologists," had

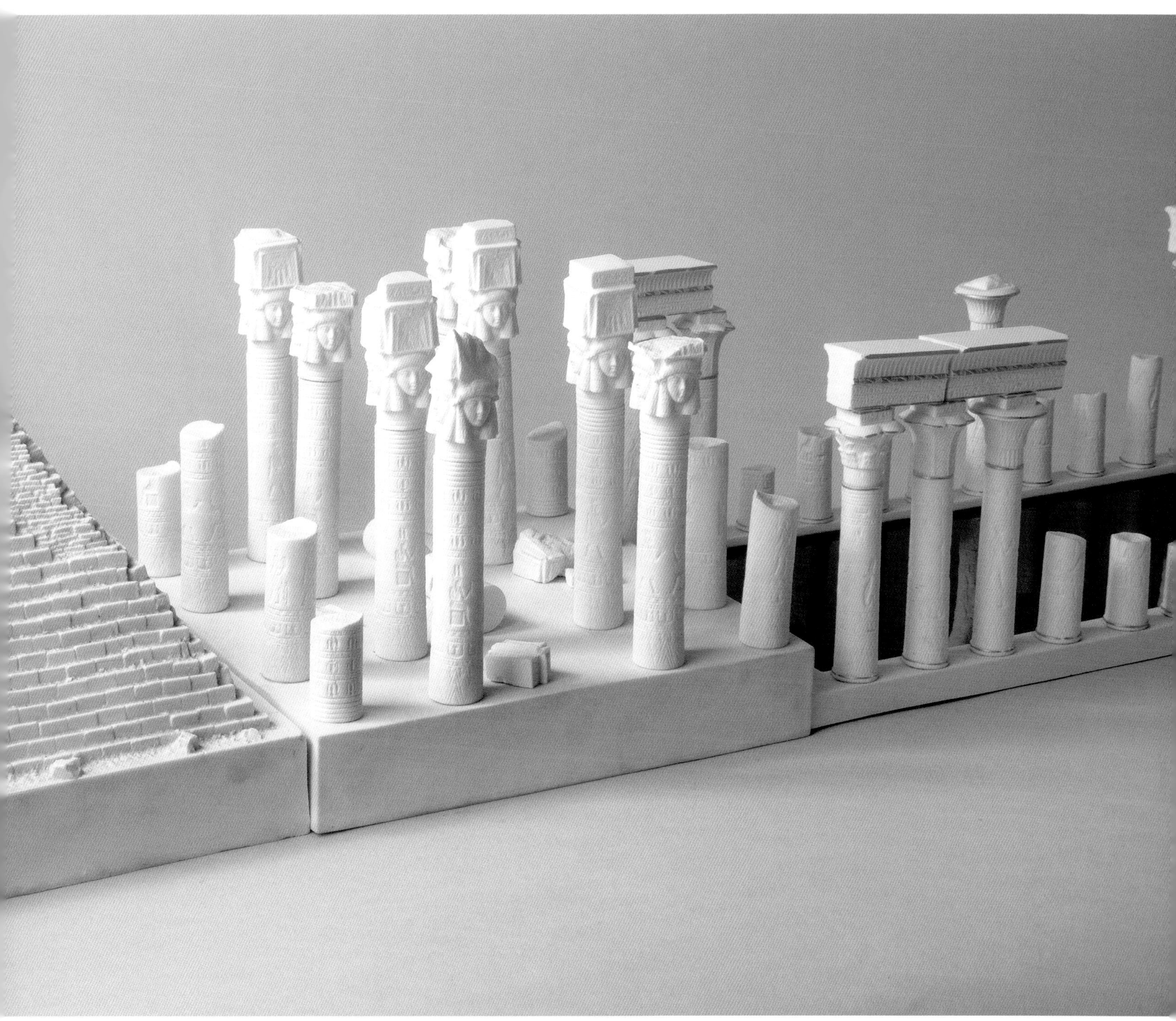

Fig. 98 (cat. 82): Large biscuit centerpiece called *Ruines d'Égypte* designed by husband and wife team Anne and Patrick Poirier, 1979

delighted in the study of the ruins of classical antiquity during their three years as *pensionnaires* (scholars in residence) at the Villa Medici in Rome.

The molds for the original Egyptian Service (1810–12) had been preserved at the factory since the nineteenth century and reused again in the 1930s to create a table centerpiece to send to Cairo. The Napoleonic Egyptian centerpiece was a reference, not a model to follow. The team downplayed the relevance of the colonnades, the temple of Memnon and the obelisks of the original centerpiece, and emphasized the importance of the central section with two basins in deep blue enamel—destined to be filled with water

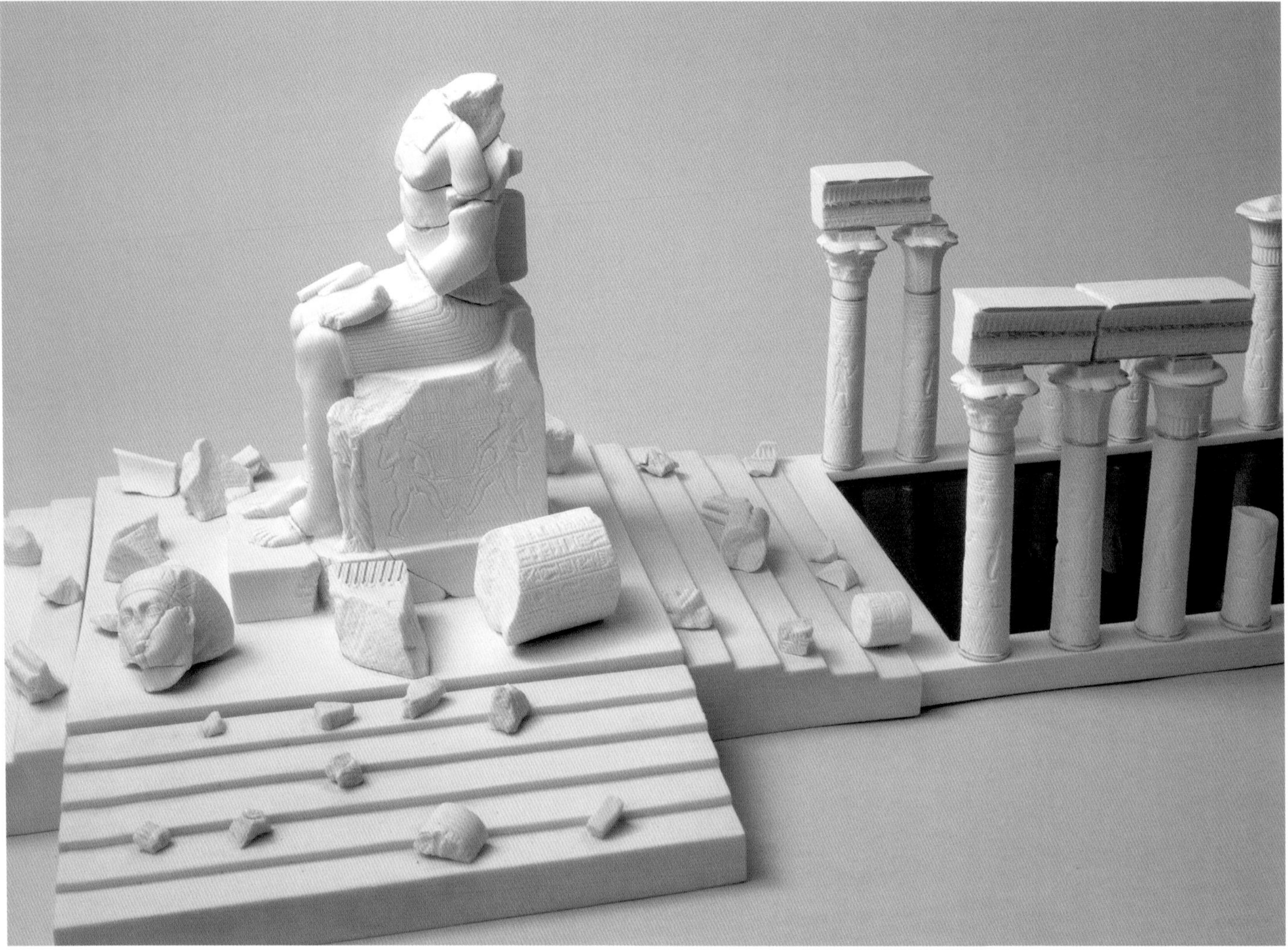

Additional view of fig. 98

and flower petals—as well as two ruined pyramids. The ensemble evoked the idea of the "dormant" or central piece of a table service that remained on the table throughout the various courses of a dinner *à la française*. For this project, the Poiriers immersed themselves in imaginary archeological subjects or modern *capricci*, that is, whimsical groupings of monuments from antiquity. The resurgence and reinterpretation in a contemporary idiom of the myths, legends, and allegories on which the Mediterranean civilizations rest is central to their work and beautifully echoed in this centerpiece. Their nostalgic reconstructions using broken, chipped, and ruined fragments are also illustrative of this sentiment.

In 1982, the creation of an experimental workshop at Sèvres, the Atelier Expérimental de Recherche et de Création, was another step in forging links with contemporary artists. This initiative had the dual purpose of strengthening the collaboration between the factory and ceramists at large, and opening the factory to the latest currents in the contemporary art scene. The experimental workshop invited ceramists to stay and work for a six-month period. Among those asked to participate in the 1980s were three notable Americans: Viola Frey, Adrian Saxe, and Betty Woodman.

Adrian Saxe (1943–) welcomed the unique opportunity of working in the Atelier Expérimental at Sèvres. In his words, "my real passion, however, is for mid-eighteenth century Sèvres. It is ambitious and complex, and for me it is the most satisfying technically and formally."[12] Saxe created this teapot design for Sèvres, which he altered with a range of decorations emulating wood and hard stone (fig. 99). His

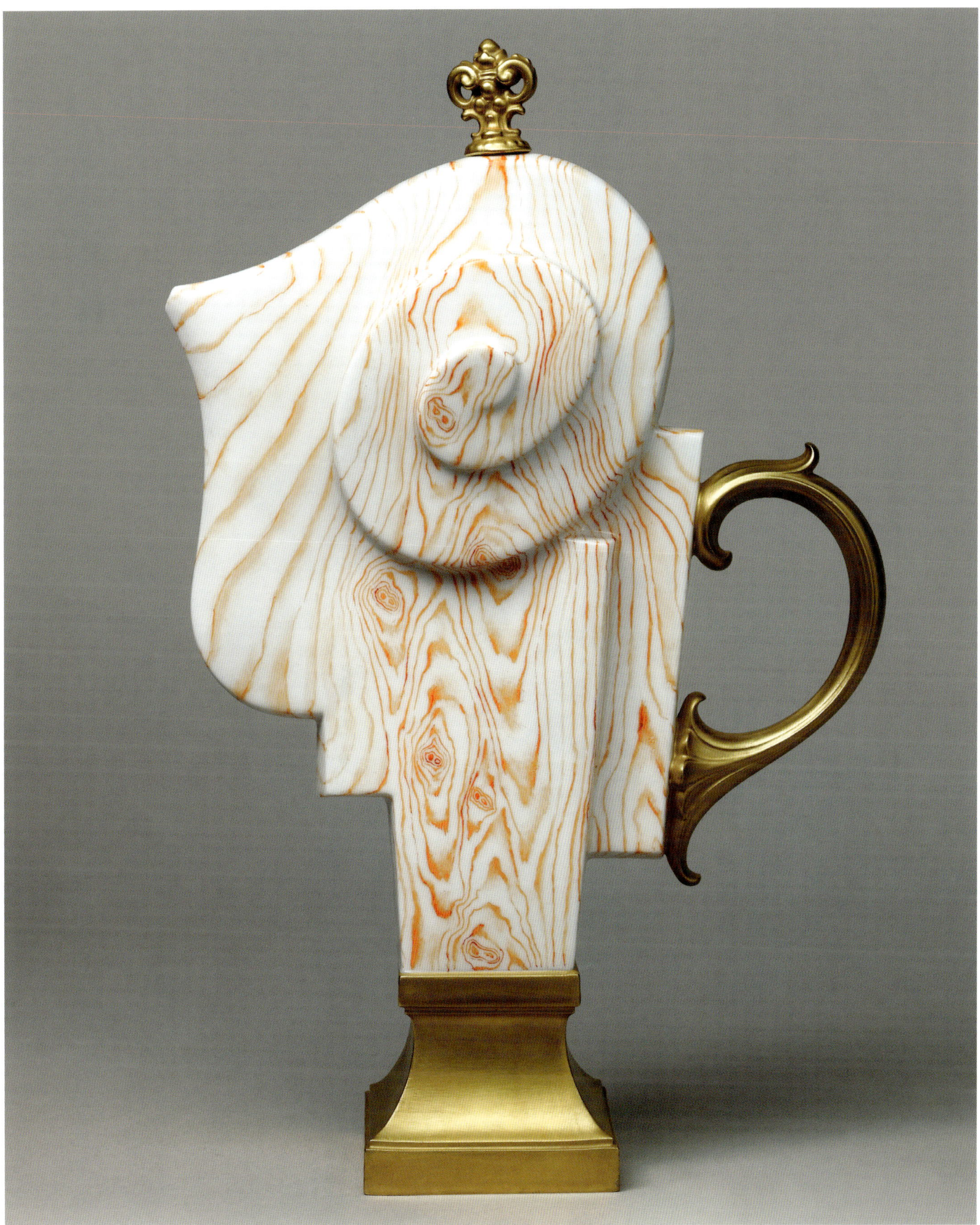

Fig. 99 (cat. 74): Teapot in the *crevette* pattern by Adrian Saxe, 1984–5

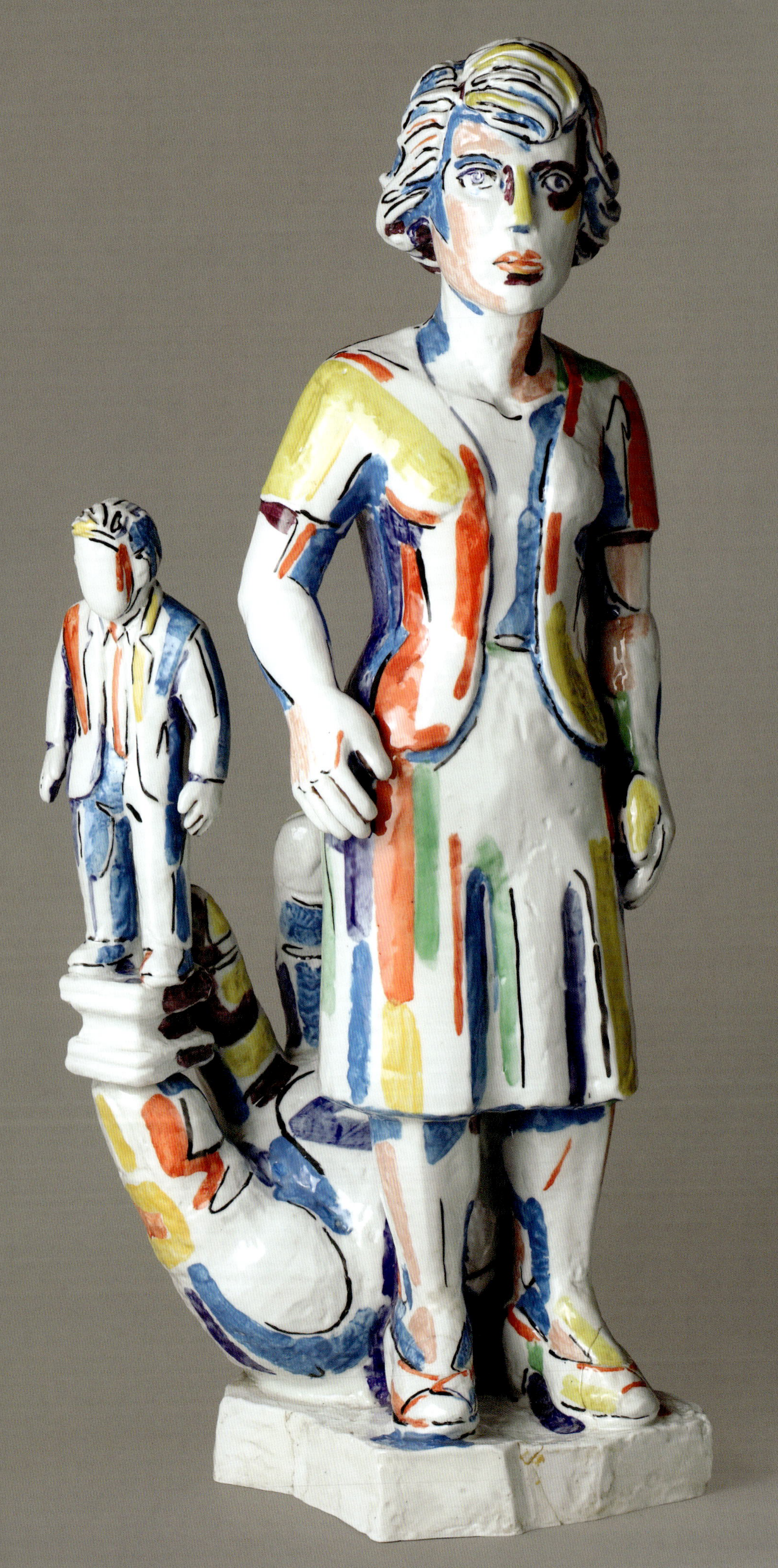

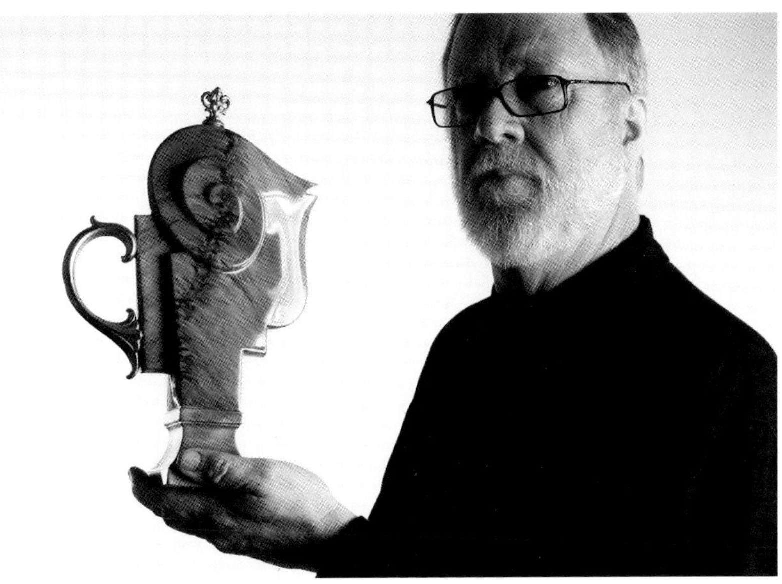

Fig. 100: Portrait of Adrian Saxe, 2004; photograph by GLCS II

postmodern precious ensembles draw from Western European influences. Saxe is one of the most important contemporary American ceramists (fig. 100). His work has been showcased in numerous national and international exhibitions, and it has been characterized by the French as "sculpture whose subject was pottery."[13] In his creations, Saxe is very connected to the realm of decorative art, which he transcends and comments upon with a certain dose of irony and humor. Renaissance and Baroque ewers come to mind when looking at this modern piece.

Viola Frey (1933–2004) was part of a group of sculptors in California who reclaimed ceramic as their preferred medium. Her leitmotiv of socially charged figurative sculpture came to the fore during her stint at Sèvres. The figural groups she created there were made in soft-paste porcelain (fig. 101). Just as soft paste had created many problems for the firing of sculpture in the eighteenth century, so it also presented difficulties for Frey. Frey worked with a new soft-paste body composition formulated by the then chief chemist of the factory, Antoine d'Albis. In order to make the paste more malleable and firmer when fired, nylon fibers were added. Frey has been called a visual anthropologist and an urban archeologist.[14] Almost life size, many of these figures present a contrast—women, often dressed in floral, colorful prints and decked with colorful accessories, are juxtaposed with men, prisoners in their suits and ties. For the painted decoration Frey used an eighteenth-century enamel palette of six colors (red, blue, green, black, light green, and brown).

Betty Woodman (1930–), recently the subject of a retrospective at the Metropolitan Museum of Art in New York (2006), has created her own formal language with her pictorial ceramics. Her work, as described by one *New York Times* art critic, "challenges and invokes the traditional elements of the vase and vesselhood so imaginatively that it lives in a class by itself."[15] In her pieces, Woodman has quoted Etruscan motifs, tricolor glazes of Chinese Tang ceramics, Mediterranean hues, and elements of classical antiquity. She playfully works in the two-dimensional and three-dimensional planes, establishing a dialogue of surface and form, tradition, and invention. She often fashions compositions of several pieces. These characteristics are well illustrated in the console and urn-shaped vase in fig. 102, which rotates on its base to offer two alternate views. The volute handles viewed from the front quote classical antiquity, while the flat front belies a rounded back occupied by a cylindrical vase. Modeled by the artist, the forms bear her direct imprint. Here, wildly colorful enamel colors on a

OPPOSITE
Fig. 101 (cat. 76): Figural group of a woman and a hand holding a Lilliputian man by Viola Frey, 1990

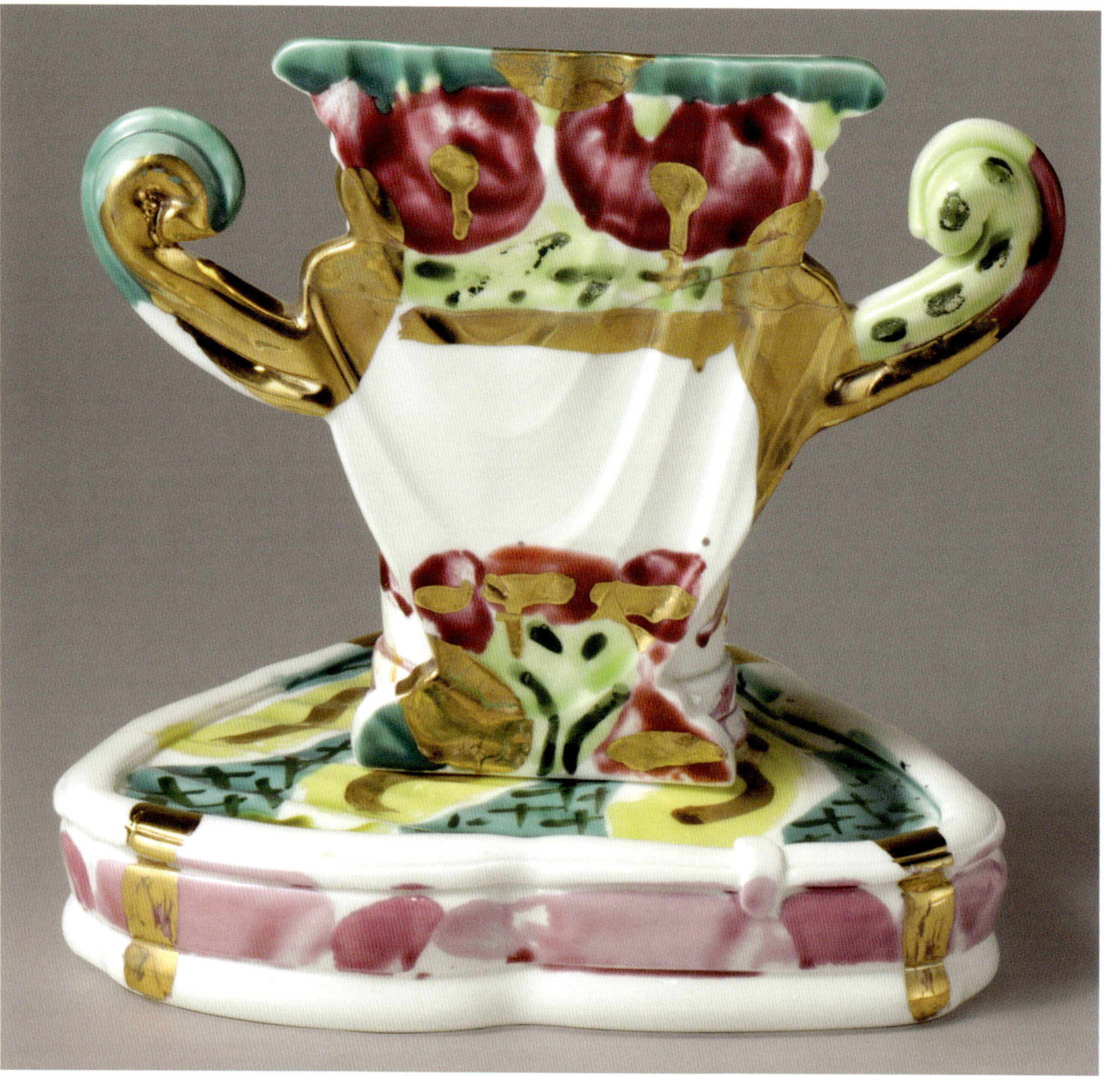

Fig. 102 (cat. 75): *Vase sur console* by Betty Woodman, ca. 1987

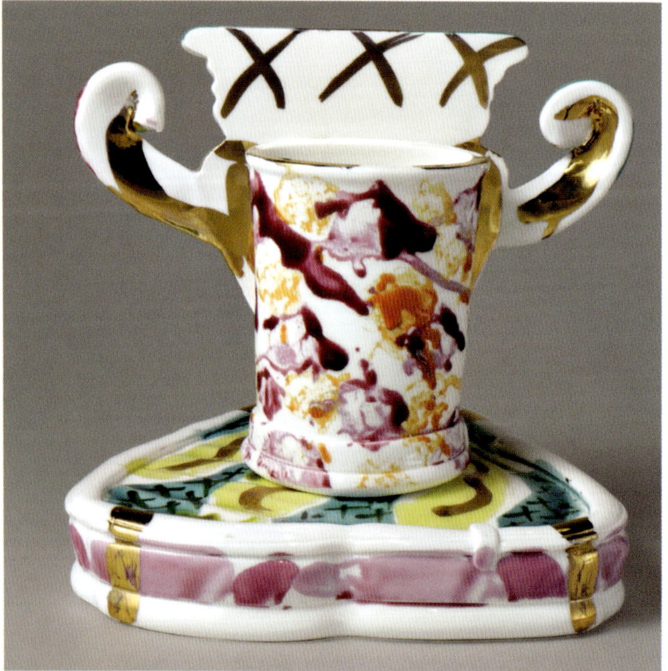

LEFT: Reverse of fig. 102, *Vase sur Console*

soft-paste body derive from her love of the Mediterranean cultures which have fascinated her throughout her career.

The most recent collaborations of the 1990s have allowed for a renewal in the factory's formal vocabulary as well as in its repertory of forms. Set designer, painter, and decorator Richard Peduzzi created the highly innovative "Reform" double vase for Sèvres in 1995 (fig. 103). Made of a soft paste, a variant of the paste used at Sèvres in the eighteenth century, the vase presented serious technical difficulties. Soft paste is not a very malleable clay and is therefore not easy to

OPPOSITE: Fig. 103 (cat. 78): "Reform" vase by Richard Peduzzi, 1995

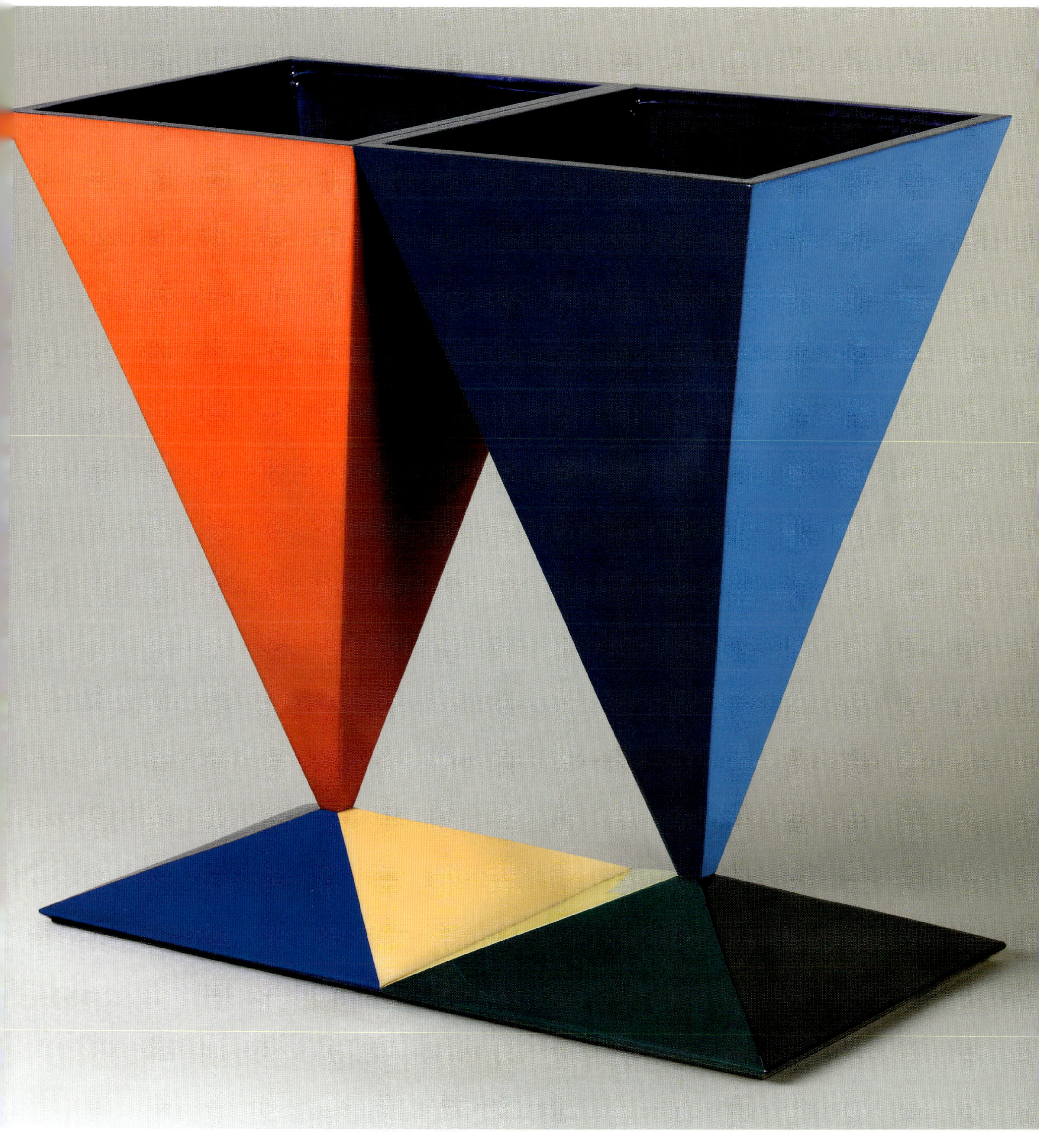

sculpt and shape, but it is, however, ideal for yielding wonderfully rich and deep colors. In this instance, the sharp angles were particularly difficult to render in porcelain. Despite all these obstacles, the result is a piece with precisely defined geometric lines—a tour de force which demonstrates the virtuoso skills of Sèvres ceramists. Its bright and colorful polychrome decoration of fifteen colors required multiple applications of glaze and six successive firings. In his characteristic borrowing from other periods, the turquoise blue is a modern reference to the *bleu céleste* or "heavenly blue" of the early ceramic productions of the eighteenth century (see fig. 6). Peduzzi once revealed in an interview, "I availed myself of everything I'd learned for my work as a set designer."[16] He is well known for his film and stage designs for director Patrice Chéreau. At the time of his collaboration with Sèvres, Peduzzi was director of the École Nationale Supérieure des Arts Décoratifs (1990–2002) and he designed exhibition spaces[17] as well as furniture for the Mobilier National. Until 2008, he was head of the Académie Française in Rome.

While most ceramic factories chose to abandon their hand turning wheels in favor of molding or mechanical pressing, Sèvres became the only workshop in the world to keep the tradition of turning shapes in a two-step process (*ébauchage* and *tournassage*), just as was done in the eighteenth century and based on technical drawings.[18] The *coupe "Excelsior"* is one of those startling modern pieces in which the color and form are supported by traditional techniques (fig. 104). The piece, hand-thrown and decorated inside and out with low-firing colors, is evocative of works by the Italian design collective Memphis Group. The designer of this piece, Mathilde Bretillot (1959–), became interested in Memphis design after her graduation from the École Camondo in Paris in 1984. In 1991 she joined the firm of Philippe Starck, where she spent ten years designing objects and interiors. In 1997, with fellow artist Frédérique Vallete, she created the interior design firm of Bretillot/Vallete. She and her partner stated that references, standpoints, and commitment are all essential elements of their work. Forms that combine clarity and a complex relationship with the context, like this *coupe* of

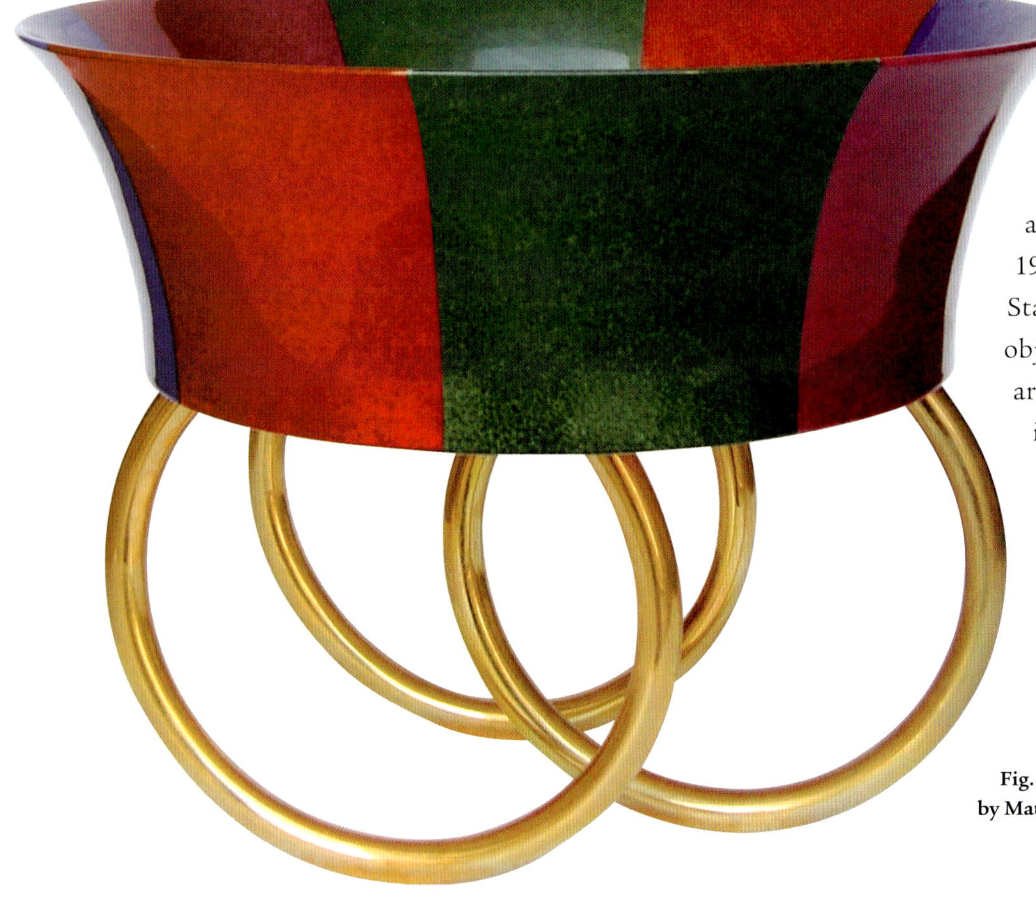

Fig. 104 (cat. 79): *Coupe "Excelsior"* by Mathilde Bretillot, 1996–7

straightforward form and a deceivingly simple ring foot, are a signature of her work. Continuing the tradition of the gilt-mounted pieces of the eighteenth and nineteenth centuries, the *coupe* sits on a gilt metal base in the form of three rings.

Pieces like Peduzzi's and Bretillot's are a salute to the color and decoration which the Memphis Group, with Ettore Sottsass (1917–2007) as its head, had proposed after years when color and decoration had been taboo. Sottsass designed a group of fourteen vases for Sèvres from 1994 to 1996 using different techniques and materials, some of them including marble or glass (fig. 105). Typical of his vases are the superpositions of shapes, the use of inverted forms (like Peduzzi's "Reform" vase), the change of scale, and the vivid color ranges. Sottsass received the invitation to collaborate with the factory as he was preparing for his retrospective at the Centre Georges Pompidou (1994). Previously he had worked with faience but never with porcelain, which he saw as an interesting challenge. Sottsass described his sentiments in working outside market dictates and galleries for this venerable institution in a most vivid and colorful way: "I had to design in the shadow of a long procession of distinguished ghosts: of powerful and capricious kings, great queens and cultivated and probably refined mistresses, a vast crowd of courtesans, intellectuals and thinkers. I had the feeling that the heritage of the Sèvres manufactory echoed the history of the whole nation, and not the fluctuations of the market."[19]

Just as monarchs, emperors, and presidents did in the past, the French state keeps up the tradition of commissioning pieces from their national ceramics factory. There is hardly a more symbolic element of official dining than a large table centerpiece or *surtout de table*. President Jacques

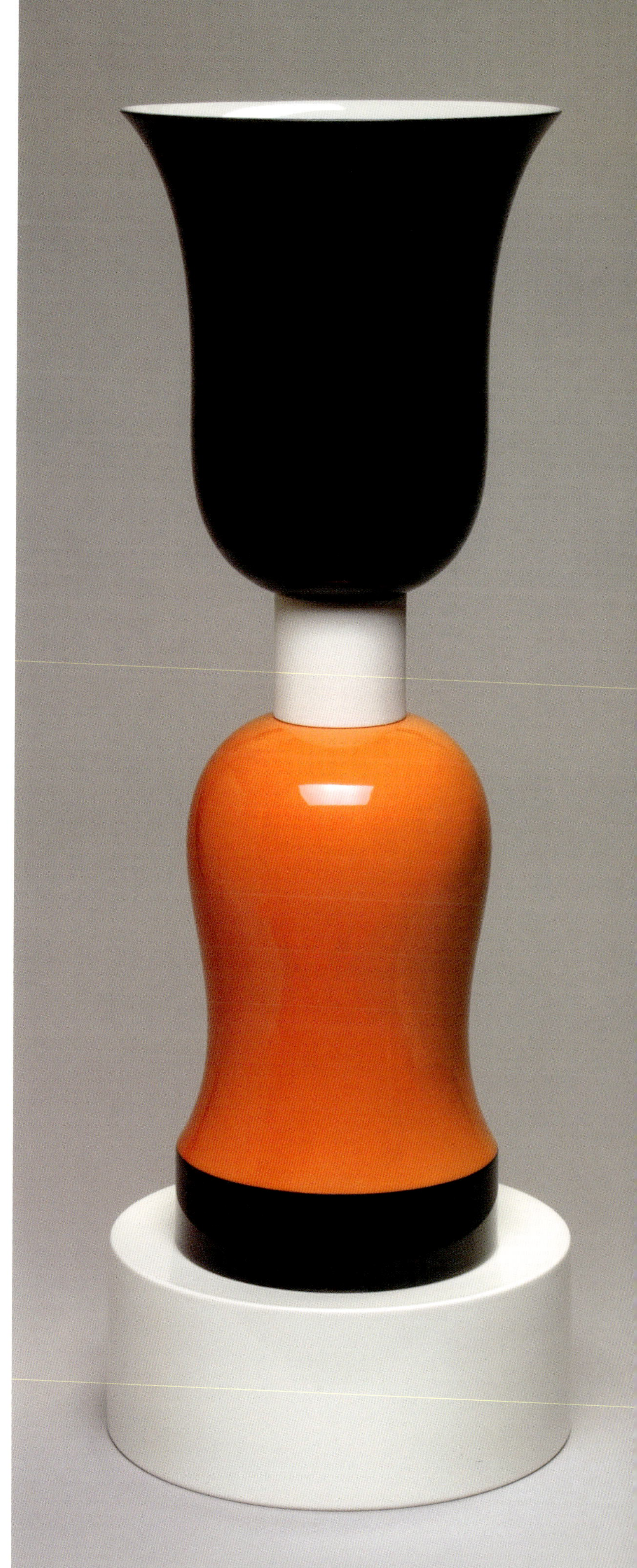

Fig. 105 (cat. 77): "Sybilla" vase (from a series of fourteen) by Ettore Sottsass, 1994–5

Chirac (1995–2007), faithful to the tradition, approached Sèvres when it came to ordering a new contemporary *surtout.* The project was opened to competition and granted to Catalan/Spanish sculptor Jaume Plensa (1955–). Plensa's composition consists of forty-eight spheres of different sizes reflecting the constellations of the southern and northern hemispheres (fig. 106). The ensemble is in two groups resting on wooden platforms and covered with a golden net. The balls are made of soft-paste biscuit, a material in constant use at Sèvres since it was developed in the 1750s. Each ball sphere is decorated with the name of the constellation and its position on the astral charts. The net helps hold the pieces in their particular arrangement. The work began in January of 2002 and, at the end of the year, the piece, the first grand official commission of the new millennium, made its way to the Elysée Palace. Plensa also created some presentation plates with an astral chart design to go with the centerpiece (figs. 107, 108). Artist Philippe Favier designed a table service to complement Plensa's centerpiece and presentation plates with shooting stars in gold against a cobalt blue ground.

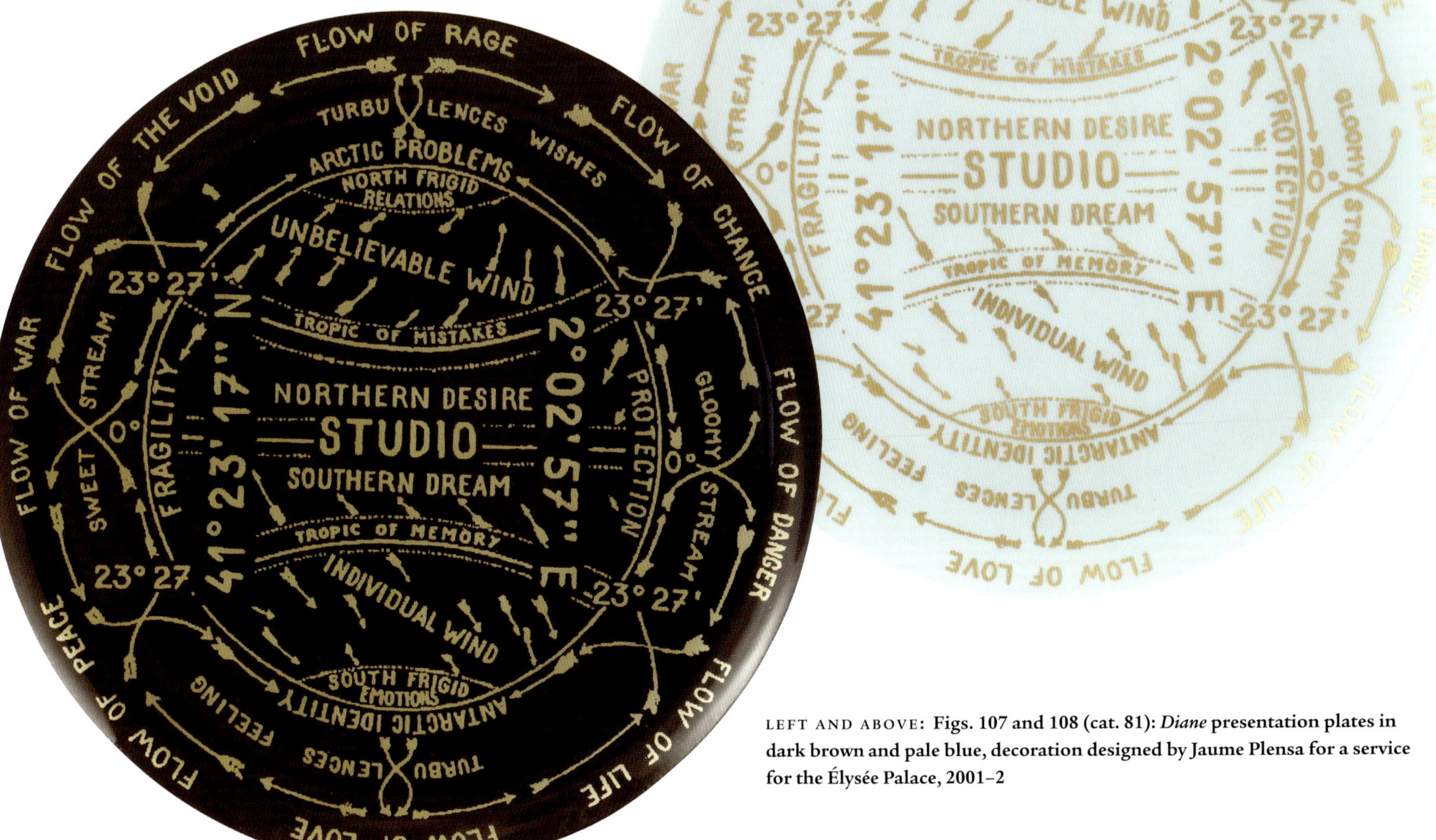

LEFT AND ABOVE: **Figs. 107 and 108 (cat. 81): *Diane* presentation plates in dark brown and pale blue, decoration designed by Jaume Plensa for a service for the Élysée Palace, 2001–2**

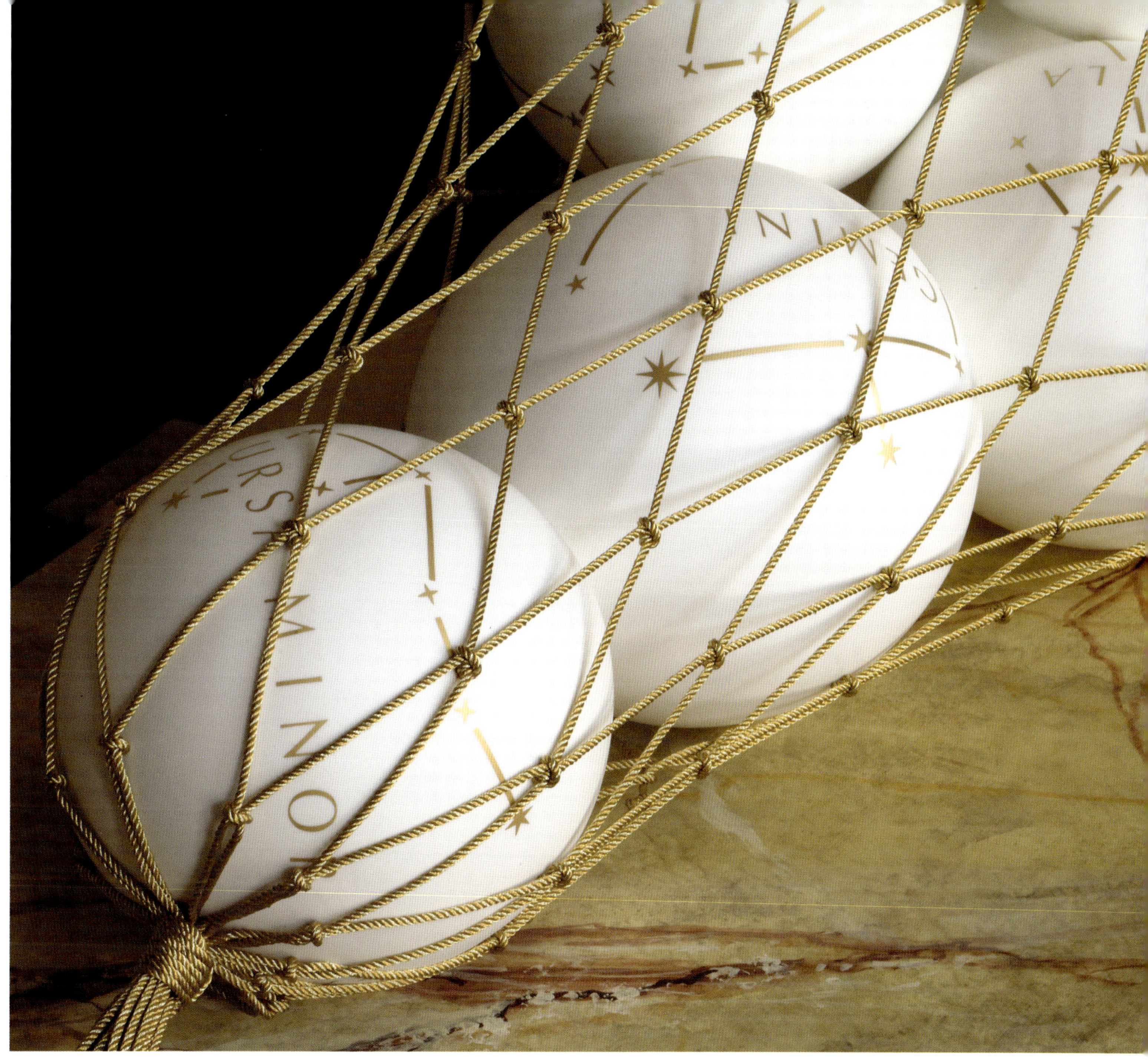

ABOVE: **Fig. 106: Centerpiece (detail) by Jaume Plensa for the Élysée Palace, 2002**

Sèvres in the twenty-first century continues to be atypical. Its idiosyncrasies please some and annoy others. How can a factory employing nearly 200 people produce only a few thousand pieces a year? Why does Sèvres refuse new technology such as laser cutting or isostatic pressing? Why do they still insist on throwing porcelain several centimeters thick before turning it repeatedly until down to the thickness of an eggshell? Sèvres has always been atypical in many ways. It was the first porcelain factory to be built with a total disregard for the proximity of clay deposits, wood supplies or water, but intentionally close to the seat of power—first royal, then imperial and finally national. It was created to serve the powerful, and it never had to worry about its balance sheet or about yielding profits.

Today the factory continues to fulfill its mission of collaborating with contemporary artists and balancing the adoption of technical innovations while keeping and transmitting its heritage of hand-crafted and artisan work. After three centuries, Sèvres is still producing ceramics at the very highest technical and artistic level.

NOTES

1. Jules Coutan, 1891–5; Jules-Clément Chaplain, 1895–7.
2. In 1866 Sandier crossed the Atlantic to work in the atelier of Russel Aturgis in Chicago. In 1871 he opened a decorator's establishment in New York City. In association with the firm of Herter Brothers, Sandier received the fabulous commission to decorate William Henry Vanderbilt's mansion. Back in Paris in 1882, royalty and aristocracy vied for his services. His most notable commission of that decade was the neo-Byzantine throne room for Carol of Romania. His love of ceramics was manifest in his collaborations with ceramic factories at Sarreguemines.
3. J.P. Midant, *Sèvres: la manufacture au XXème siècle* (Paris, 1992), p. 15.
4. Her admirers included poet Stéphane Mallarmé, writer Alexandre Dumas, sculptor Auguste Rodin, and scientists Pierre and Marie Curie.
5. For more detail on this subject read I. Lavrin, "Les artistes russes à Sèvres au temps des avant-gardes," *L'Estampille/L'Objet d'Art*, January 2008, pp. 60–67.
6. In 1923 Rapin orchestrated an exhibition of a dining table decorated with a table service in blue and gold by G.I. Claude and a lit centerpiece by Pierre-Émile Braquemond and glassware by Lalique. As a backdrop he used a case set with vases by Anne-Marie Fontaine and Henri Patou. (Midant, *Sèvres*, pp. 60–1).
7. Midant, *Sèvres*, p. 152.
8. Midant, *Sèvres*, p. 152.
9. D. Caméo, "Les Têtes à café de Robert Couturier," in *Manufacture Nationale de Sèvres: Années 50: l'effet céramique* (Paris, 2006), pp. 38–39.
10. Manufacture Nationale de Sèvres, *Sèvres: tradition et innovation* (Paris, 1999), p. IX.
11. Malraux to Gauthier; quoted in ibid., p. IX.
12. G. Clark, "Adrian Saxe: An Interview", *American Ceramics*, I, Fall 1982, p. 26. From *Going for Baroque: 18 Contemporary Artists Fascinated with the Baroque and Rococo* (Walters Art Gallery, Baltimore, 1996).
13. In the biography written by the Frank Lloyd Gallery that represents Adrian Saxe.
14. Nancy Hoffman Gallery.
15. G. Glueck, "Betty Woodman, Turning the Humble Vase into High Art," *New York Times*, April 28, 2006.
16. Quoted in J. Lambán et al., *Sèvres, 1740–2006* (Zaragoza, 2006), p. 365.
17. Peduzzi designed the Opera galleries at the Musée d'Orsay and the history galleries at the Louvre.
18. Wheel-throwing is a two-step process based on full-scale drawings mapped out by the draftsman. The first phase of rough shaping (*ébauchage*) consists of throwing the paste into a rough shape, which is left to dry before it is given its precise shape at the turner's wheel (*tournassage*) with the aid of a steel tool with a wooden handle and other measuring instruments; these lend the piece its desired profile and thickness.
19. Ettore Sottsass, *Sèvres, les temps d'un voyage* (Paris, 2006), p. 7.

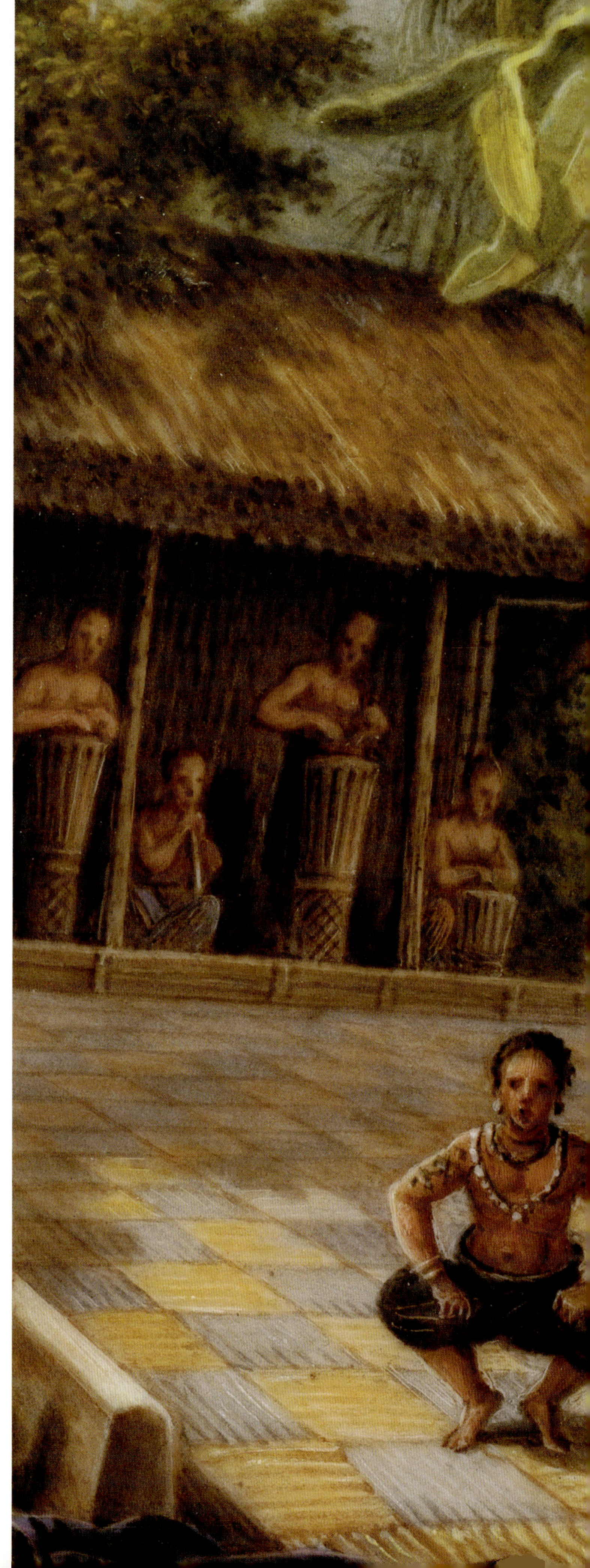

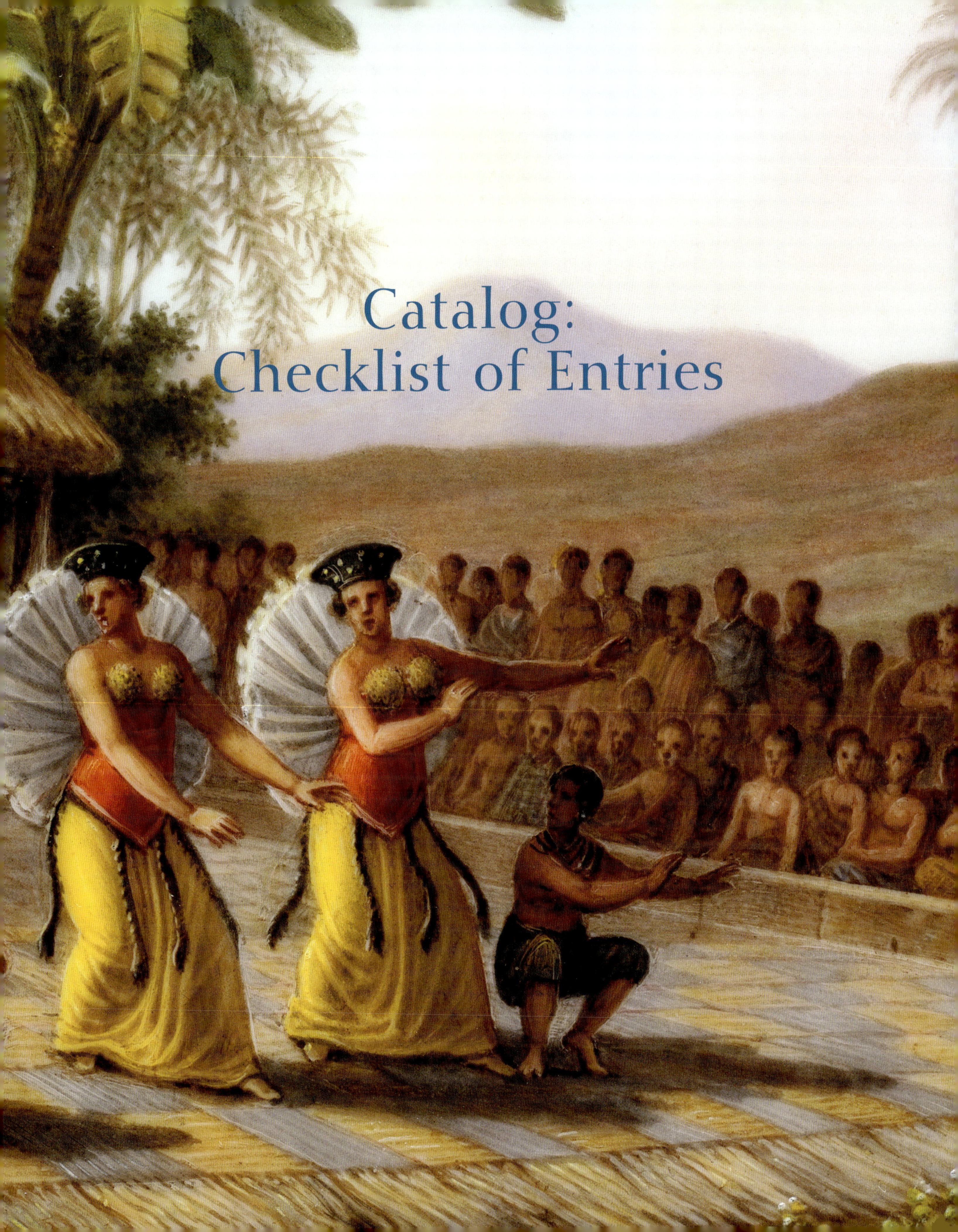

Catalog: Checklist of Entries

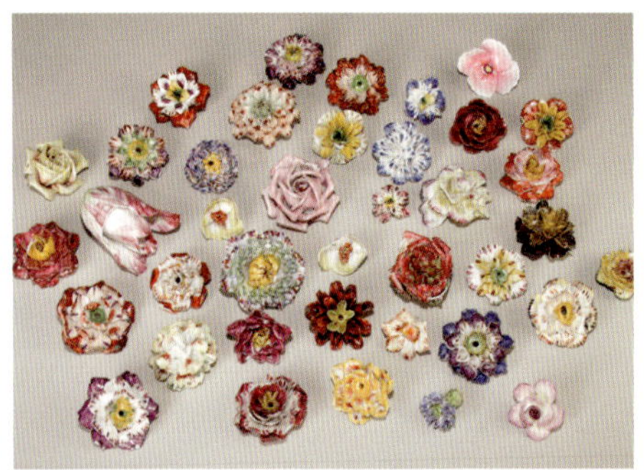

1 Group of Unmounted Flowers

Vincennes, ca. 1750
Soft-paste porcelain
Private Collection

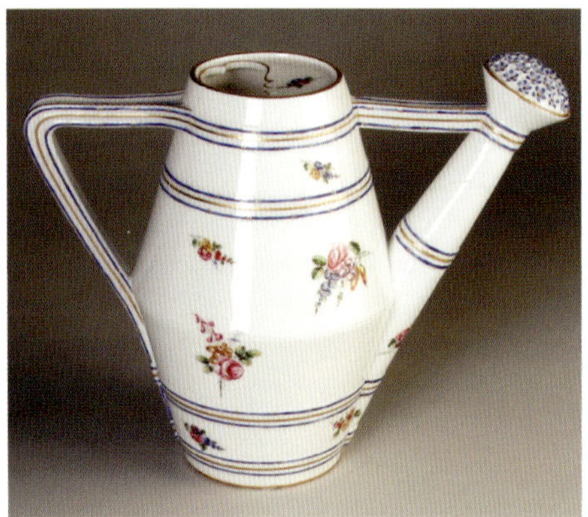

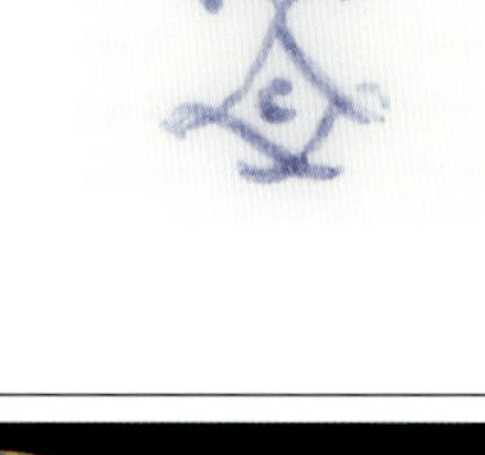

2 Watering Can

(arrosoir)

Vincennes, 1755
Soft-paste porcelain
H. 9 in. (23 cm)
Private Collection

MARKS: Crossed letters *L* with date letter *C* for 1755; painter's mark of sunburst in blue

PROVENANCE: T.H. Clarke Collection; Wilfred J. Sainsbury Collection; Sotheby's London, 1 March 1994, lot 85.

RELATED EXAMPLES: Only seven or eight examples of this form, four or five of the smaller size (under 20 cm) and three of the larger size, seem to have survived. Four examples of the smaller size are in the collections of the J. Paul Getty Museum, Los Angeles, the Gardiner Museum of Ceramic Art, Toronto, the David Collection, Copenhagen, and an English private collection. One of the two other extant examples of the larger size is in the collection of the Musée National de Céramique, Sèvres, and the other was sold at Christie's Monaco, 3 December 1989, lot 33.

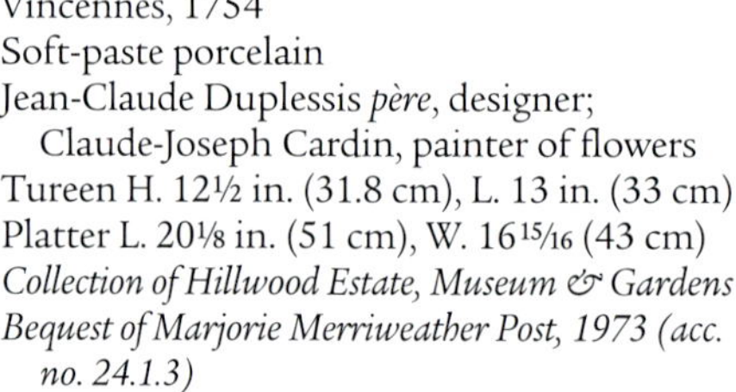

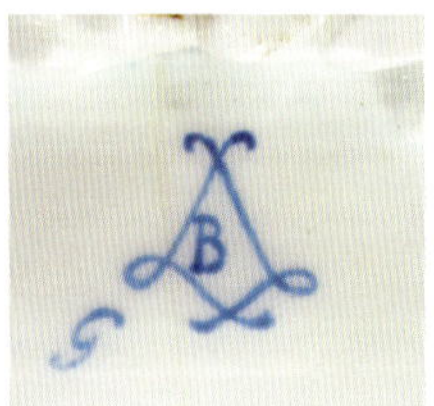

3 Tureen and Platter

(pot à oille "du roi" et son plateau)

Vincennes, 1754
Soft-paste porcelain
Jean-Claude Duplessis *père*, designer; Claude-Joseph Cardin, painter of flowers
Tureen H. 12½ in. (31.8 cm), L. 13 in. (33 cm)
Platter L. 20⅛ in. (51 cm), W. 16 15/16 (43 cm)
Collection of Hillwood Estate, Museum & Gardens Bequest of Marjorie Merriweather Post, 1973 (acc. no. 24.1.3)

MARKS (tureen): Crossed letters *L* with date letter *B* for 1754; letter *g*, possibly mark of Claude-Joseph Cardin, accomplished painter of flowers (active 1749–87)

PROVENANCE: Property of the comte d'Egmont, 1756; Rothschild family collection (London branch) and Madame Jacques Balsan (unverified); French and Company, New York, 1952

RELATED EXAMPLES: A *seau à verre*, or indistinctly referred to as *seau à liqueur* with the same marks and similar gilding pattern, from the Baron Mayer Amschel de Rothschild Collection at Mentmore, Buckinghamshire, was sold Sotheby's Parke-Bernet, 24 May 1977, lot 2011 and again at Sotheby's New York, 20 May 1989, lot 71.

PREVIOUS PAGE
Detail of central painting from fig. 49, "Dance on Tahiti" plate from the *Service des vues de pays hors d'Europe*, 1820

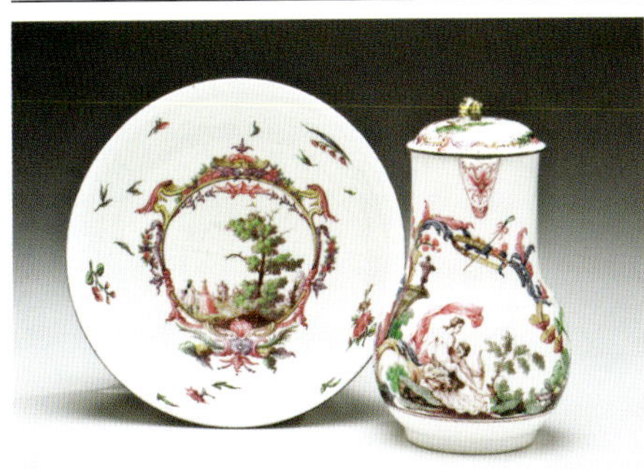

4 Ewer and Bowl

(pot à eau et jatte ronde)

Vincennes, ca. 1747
Soft-paste porcelain
Ewer H. 6⅜ in. (16 cm)
Bowl Dia. 7½ in. (19 cm)
Private Collection

MARKS: none

PROVENANCE: Collection of Madame de Polès, sold Paris, 17–18 November 1936, lot 73; sold Marc Ferri, Paris, 8 December 1995, lots 123 and 124

RELATED EXAMPLES: A similar ewer depicting a military scene and a marmite *(pot à bouillon)* with a similar goddess draped in purple cloth are in the collection of the Musée National de Céramique, Sèvres.

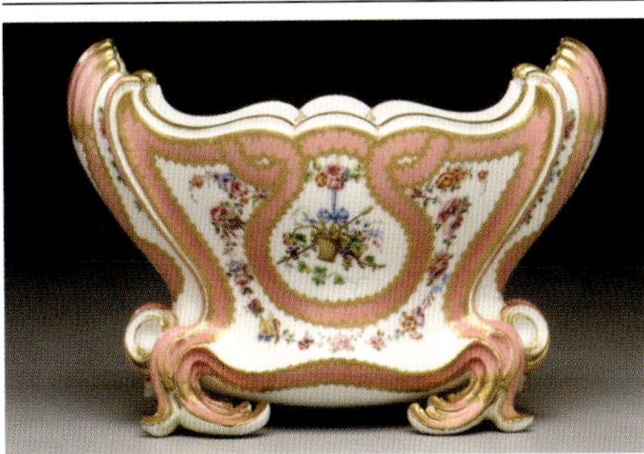

5 Vase

(cuvette "Mahon")

Sèvres, 1757
Soft-paste porcelain
Jean-Claude Duplessis *père*, designer; Philippe Parpette, painter of flowers
H. 8⅛ in. (20.6 cm), L. 11½ in. (29.2 cm)
Collection of Hillwood Estate, Museum & Gardens Bequest of Marjorie Merriweather Post, 1973 (acc. no. 24.91)

MARKS: Crossed letters *L* enclosing date letter *E* for 1757; letter *P* for painter of flowers Philippe Parpette (active 1755–7 and 1773–1806)

PROVENANCE: Sold to Louis-Philippe I, duc d'Orléans, 1758; René Fribourg collection, sold Sotheby's London, 4 May 1965, lot 173

RELATED EXAMPLES (of the largest size): Two *cuvettes Mahon*, one with pink and blue lattice ground with a peasant scene and one with turquoise blue ground, are in the collection of the Metropolitan Museum of Art, New York; a *cuvette Mahon* with pink and dark blue lattice and *vermiculé* ground and scenes after Flemish artist David Teniers the Younger is in the collection of the J. Paul Getty Museum, Los Angeles (72.DE.65); a blue and green example with a scene of peasants drinking is in the British Royal Collection; a green example with rustic landscape is in the David Collection, Copenhagen; a pink example with *La Chasse* after François Boucher is in the collection of Harewood House, Yorkshire; a similar green example is in the Rothschild Collection at Waddesdon Manor, Aylesbury; a pair with *rose marbré* and chinoiserie scenes is in the collection of the British Museum, London; a pair with *frizes colorées* is in the collection of the Indianapolis Museum of Art; and an example with *rose marbré* ground and *fête gallante* scene sold at Christie's New York, 5 May 1999.

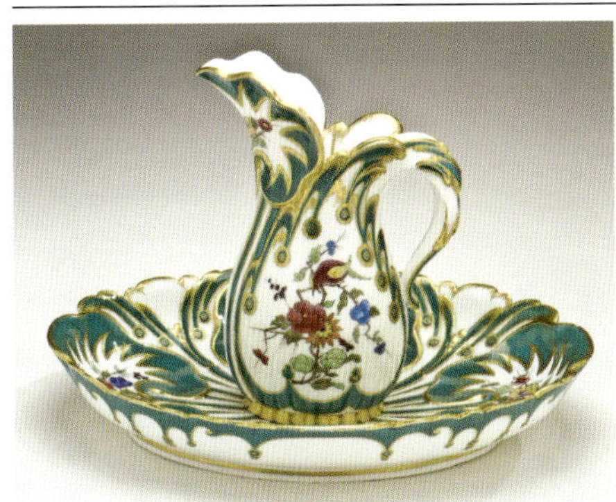

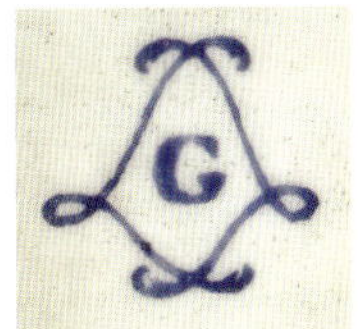

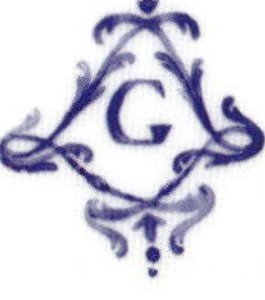

6 Waterleaf Ewer and Bowl

(broc et jatte à feuilles d'eau)

Sèvres, 1759–60
Soft-paste porcelain
Jean-Claude Duplessis *père*, designer
Ewer H. 7¼ in. (18.9 cm)
Basin W. 11⅞ in. (30.2 cm)
Private Collection

MARKS: (on each) Crossed letters *L* enclosing date letter *G* for 1759–60

PROVENANCE: The Portland Collection, Welbeck Abbey, Nottinghamshire, as of at least 1897; collection of their Graces the 9th Duke and Duchess of Portland; sold Henry Spencer & Sons Fine Art Auctioneers, Retford, 23 June 1970, lot 289; Windsor Antiques, Melbourne; Private Collection, Australia

RELATED EXAMPLES: Another waterleaf ewer and basin with a green ground is in the collection of the Art Institute of Chicago (1984.821a–b); an example with a pink ground is in the collection of the J. Paul Getty Museum, Los Angeles (84.DE.88); another example with green ground and flowers is in the collection of the Musée des Arts Décoratifs, Paris (inv. Gr. 228); and an incomplete example in *bleu céleste* sold at Christie's London, 5 July 2004, lot 91.

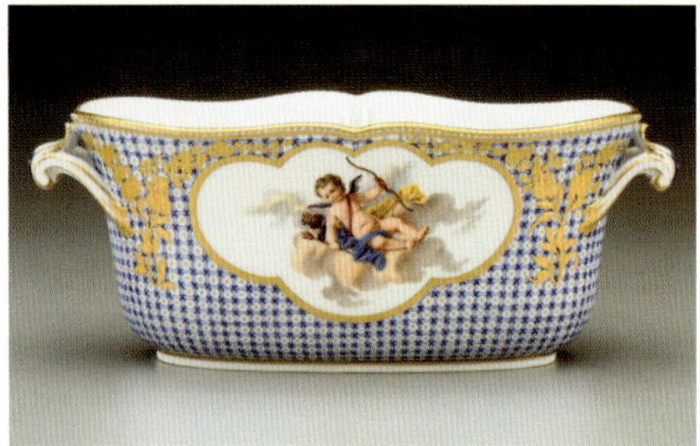

7 Bottle Cooler from a Service for King Louis XV

(*seau à liqueur ovale*)

Sèvres, ca. 1768
Soft-paste porcelain
Charles-Nicolas Dodin, painter (probably)
H. 4 11/16 in. (17.6 cm), W. 12 1/4 in. (31.1 cm)
Private American Collection

MARKS: none

PROVENANCE: Sold to Paris *marchand-mercier* Madame Lair in 1768; probably purchased by King Louis XV; sold Christie's London, 12 December, 1884; sold Christie's London, 6 April 1894, lot 68; sold Christie's London, 13 May 1898, lot 88; sold Christie's London, 11 March 1913, lot 77; Collection of Mrs. Alan L. Corley, sold Sotheby's Parke-Bernet, New York, 5–7 December 1974, lot 68; Christner Collection, sold Christie's New York, 9 June 1979, lot 213; Dalva Brothers, New York; Mingledorff-Mitchell Collection

RELATED EXAMPLES: An *écuelle* with cover and stand from this service is in the collection of the Victoria and Albert Museum, London (C.430&A-1921 and C.430B-1921); a *plateau triangle* is in Versailles; an ice cup dated 1773 and a cup and saucer from the Pompey Collection sold at Christie's New York, 23 May 2002, lots 24 and 25. A plate dated 1791 from the later additions ordered by Louis XVI is at the Musée National de Céramique at Sèvres.

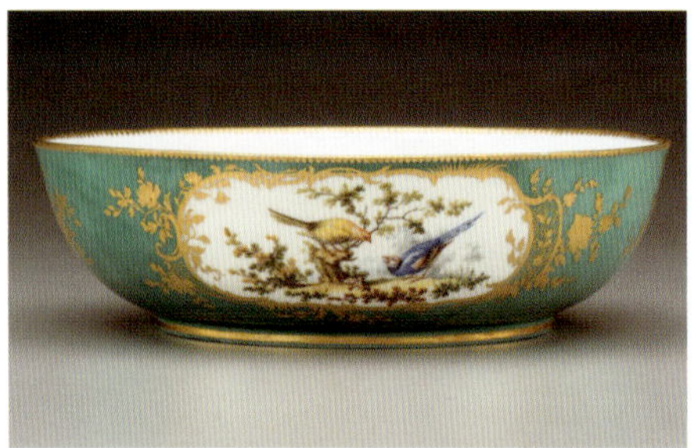

8 Green Fruit Bowl from the Service for King Frederick V of Denmark

(*jatte à fruits*)

Sèvres, 1756–7
Soft-paste porcelain
Louis-Denis Armand *l'aîné*, painter
Dia. 10 1/8 in. (25.7 cm)
Private American Collection

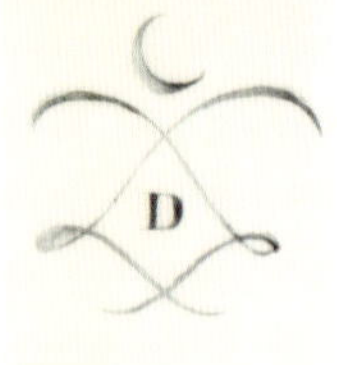

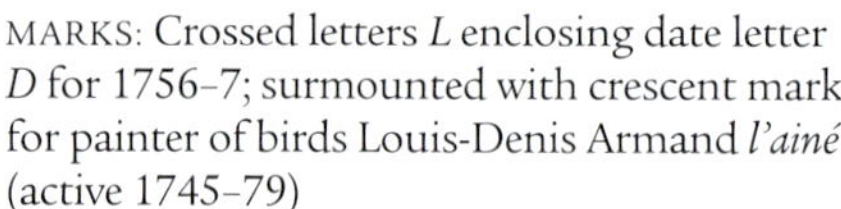

MARKS: Crossed letters *L* enclosing date letter *D* for 1756–7; surmounted with crescent mark for painter of birds Louis-Denis Armand *l'aîné* (active 1745–79)

PROVENANCE: Gift of Louis XV to King Frederick V of Denmark in 1758; Private Collection; Dragesco & Cramoisan, Paris, 2004; Mingledorff-Mitchell Collection

RELATED EXAMPLES: The majority of pieces from this Sèvres green service, bearing the date letter *D* for 1756, are in the collection of the State Hermitage Museum, St. Petersburg; a *pot à oille* is in the Forsyth Wickes Collection at the Museum of Fine Arts, Boston (65.1885abc); a *terrine* missing its plateau is in the collection of the Metropolitan Museum of Art, New York (inv. no. 50.211-182ab); another *pot à oille* from this service is in the collection of the Cleveland Museum of Art (acc. no. 1949.15a-b); and a number of green Sèvres pieces dating from circa 1756–8 are in the collection of the Victoria and Albert Museum, London.

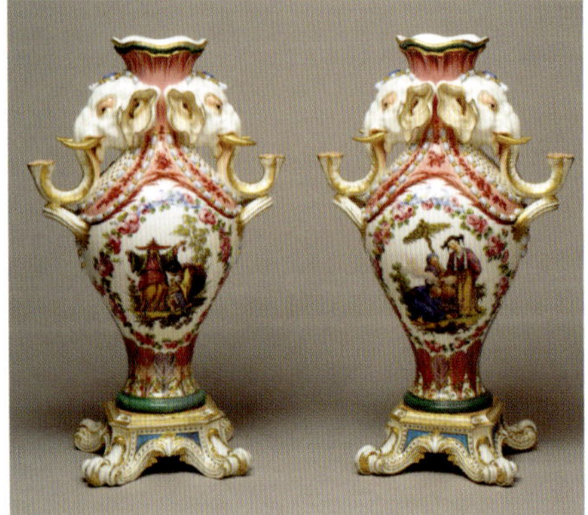

9 Pair of Vases

(*vases à têtes d'éléphants*)

Sèvres, 1760
Soft-paste porcelain
Jean-Claude Duplessis *père*, designer; Charles-Nicolas Dodin, painter (after engravings by Gabriel Huquier after François Boucher's series of paintings *Les Quatre Éléments*)
H. 12 1/4 in. (31.1 cm), L. 9 in. (22.9 cm)
Collection of the Walters Art Museum, Baltimore, Maryland (48.1796 and 48.1797)

MARKS: Crossed letters *L* in blue enclosing date letter *H* for 1760; letter *k* in blue for painter Charles-Nicolas Dodin

PROVENANCE: Possibly Madame de Pompadour; Collection of Alfred de Rothschild; Collection of Almina, Countess of Carnarvon, London; Collection of Arnold Seligman, London; Mrs. Henry Walters, 1941

RELATED EXAMPLES: There are several elephant vases on record. A related pair of elephant vases with green ground and putti (1757) are in the Wallace Collection, London, which are almost certainly a pair sold to Madame de Pompadour and inventoried in her Paris hôtel de Pompadour. Other pieces with similar chinoiserie painting by Dodin include: a pair of green ground triangular pot-pourri vases (1761) in the collection of the Detroit Institute of Arts (71.246A); a split garniture including a pink ground pot-pourri *vaisseau à mât* (P.48.418), two pots-pourris *à bobèches* and a pair of sconces in the collection of the Musée du Louvre, Paris; and two pots-pourris *fontaines* in the collection of the J. Paul Getty Museum, Los Angeles (78.DE.358). Two pots-pourris *à feuilles de myrte* are in the collection of the Walters Art Museum, Baltimore; and a *cuvette "Courteille"* with chinoiserie scenes and *rose marbré* ground is in the collection of the Metropolitan Museum of Art, New York.

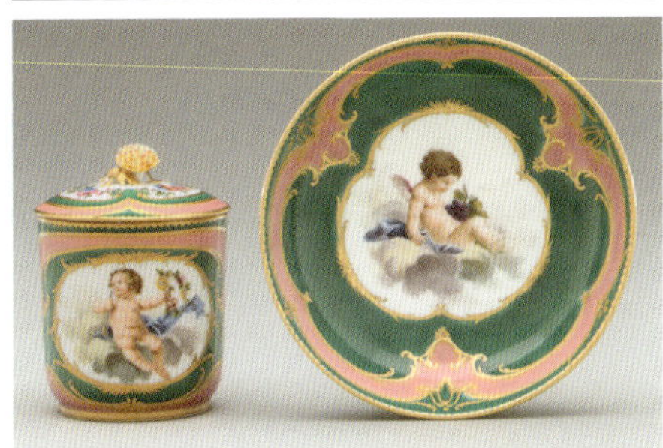

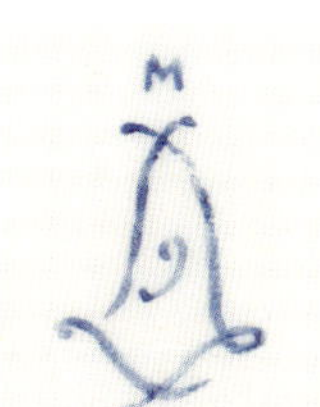

10 Pink and Green Cup and Saucer

(*gobelet couvert et soucoupe "Bouillard"*)

Sèvres, 1759–60
Soft-paste porcelain
Jean-Louis Morin, painter
Cup H. 3⅝ in. (9.2 cm)
Saucer Dia. 5⅛ in. (13 cm)
Private American Collection

MARKS: (saucer) Crossed letters *L* enclosing date mark *g* for 1759–60; letter *M* in blue for painter Jean-Louis Morin; (cup) Ghost of crossed letters *L*; dot in underglaze blue near rim

PROVENANCE: Mr. Deane Johnson, Bel Air, California, Sotheby's Parke-Bernet New York, 9 December 1972, lot 22; John R. Williams, Christie's New York, 21 October 2004, lot 948; Mingledorff-Mitchell Collection

RELATED EXAMPLES: A similar pink and green cup and saucer set featuring a cherub in clouds also painted by Morin is in the Wallace Collection, London (cat. no. C367); a few pink and green cups and saucers of similar form are in the collection of the Victoria and Albert Museum, London (including but not limited to C.1422-1919, C.1422B-1919, C.409-1921, and C.412-1921); a cup and saucer of the same form with a pink and green ground, but with pastoral trophy decorations (1759), is in the collection of the J. Paul Getty Museum, Los Angeles (72.DE.74); and a cup and saucer (1760) presenting the same scroll pattern in pink and green is in the collection of the Wadsworth Atheneum, Hartford, CT.

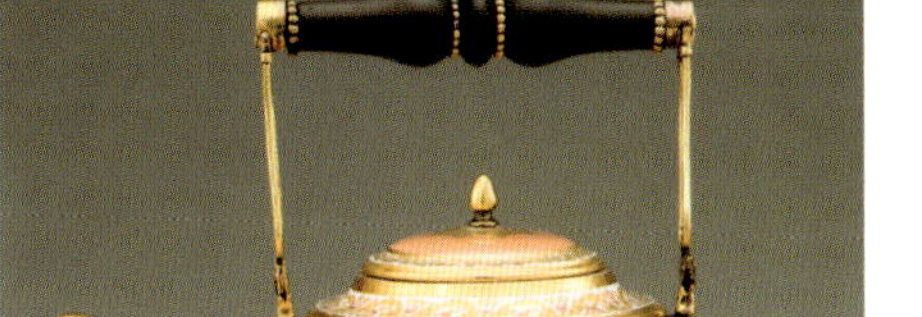

11 Tea Kettle

(*bouillotte*)

Sèvres, ca. 1778
Hard-paste porcelain, gilt bronze, wood
Jean-Jacques Dieu or Louis François Lécot, painter (probably); Henri-Martin Prévost, gilder
H. 7¼ in. (18.4 cm), W. 7½ in. (19 cm)
Private American Collection

MARKS: *HP* in gold for gilder Henri-Martin Prévost (active 1757–97)

PROVENANCE: Probably the example purchased by Madame Adélaïde in 1778; Mingledorff-Mitchell Collection

RELATED EXAMPLES: There are at least ten known Sèvres *bouillottes*. Examples include one with white ground and pink roses at the Wadsworth Atheneum, Hartford, CT (1917.1156); one with a dark brown ground and gold figures at the Art Institute of Chicago (1988.517a–b), one with a white ground and exotic birds at the Museum of Fine Arts, Boston (1975.658a–b); one with a brown ground sprinkled with gold and with gold and silver tone chinoiserie figures at the British Museum, London (Franks 385); and one with a *café au lait* ground with chinoiserie figures at the Musée National de Céramique, Sèvres (MNC 23.260).

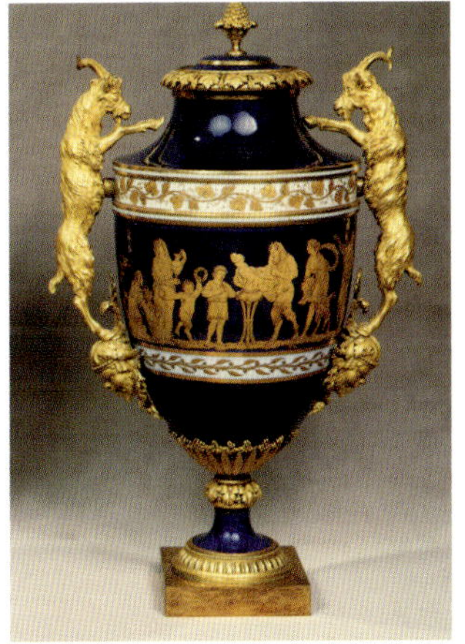

12 Covered Vase with Gilt Bronze Mounts (one of a pair)

(*vase "Boizot"*)

Sèvres, ca. 1782–4
Hard-paste porcelain, gilt bronze (ormolu)
Louis-Simon Boizot, designer (active 1773–1809); Pierre-Philippe Thomire, designer of bronze mounts
H. 17$\frac{5}{16}$ in. (44 cm)
Collection of the Walters Art Museum, Baltimore, Maryland (48.644)

MARKS: none, unless obstructed by base

PROVENANCE: Collection of Mme. Charcot Hendry, London

RELATED EXAMPLES: A pair of vases dated about 1782–4 and decorated with arabesques in polychrome colors was delivered to King Louis XVI at Versailles and is now in the British Royal Collection.

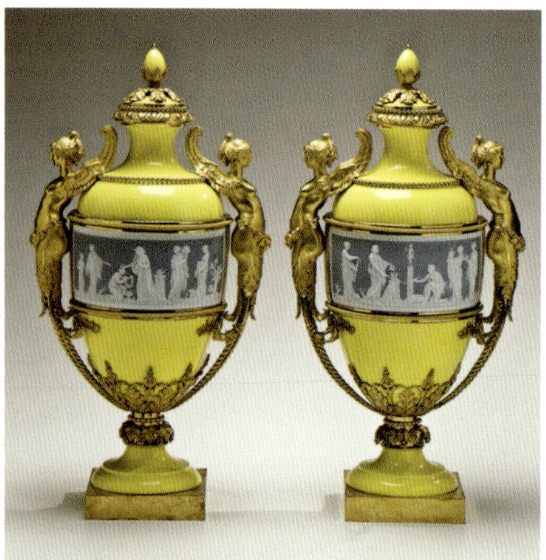

13 Pair of Yellow Vases with Gilt Bronze Mounts

(*vases "bas relief"*)

Sèvres, ca. 1786
Hard-paste porcelain, gilt bronze
Pierre-Philippe Thomire, designer of bronze mounts
H. (without cover) 16⅛ in. (41 cm)
Private Collection

MARKS: Both stamped *TH* with a fleur-de-lis for the Palais des Tuileries; one stamped *TU* below a closed crown with *9827* and the other stamped *TU 3971*

PROVENANCE: Charles comte d'Artois, brother of Louis XVI and later Charles X, King of France; Adélaïde Filleul, the comtesse de Flahaut, later comtesse de Sousa-Botelho; August-Charles-Joseph, comte de Flahaut de la Billarderie; Lady Emily Jane Mercer Elphinstone de Flahaut, Baroness Nairne; The Marquis of Lansdowne, Sotheby's, London, 8 December 2004, lot 39

RELATED EXAMPLES: An almost identical pair with a green ground and mounted as a candelabra is in the collection of the Musée du Louvre, Paris; a pair of vases and covers with a yellow ground delivered to the Princess of Asturias in 1783 is at the El Pardo Royal Palace, Madrid; and a pair with green ground and ram's mask handles ordered for the King of Sweden in 1784 is in the Swedish Royal Collection, Stockholm.

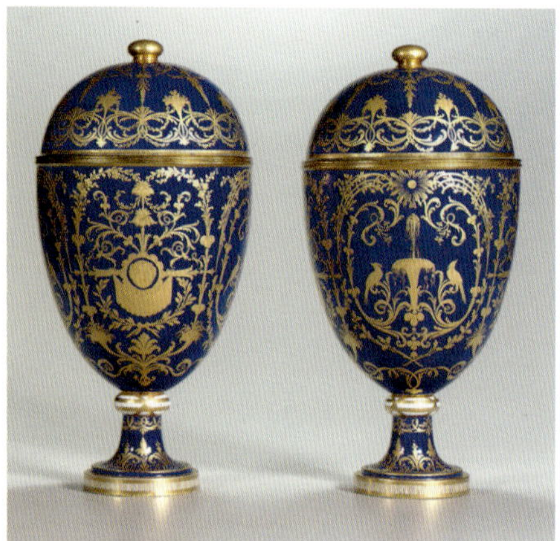

14 Pair of Egg-Shaped Vases

(*vases oeuf*)

Sèvres, ca. 1782
Hard-paste porcelain
H. 11¾ in. (29.9 cm)
Private American Collection

MARKS: none

PROVENANCE: Almost certainly the pair of "vases oeufs beau bleu et or" purchased by Grand Duke Paul and Grand Duchess Maria Fedorovna directly from the factory in 1782; University of Virginia Art Museum; Freeman's Philadelphia, sold 13 July 2006; Mingledorff-Mitchell Collection

RELATED EXAMPLES: A garniture of three egg-shaped perfume burner vases dated 1782 is in the collection of the Pavlovsk Palace, St. Petersburg; a pair of similarly shaped *bleu Fallot* vases with bundles of straw forming the handles at the sides and an egg at the top of each is in the collection of the J. Paul Getty Museum, Los Angeles (86.DE.520); and a pair of vases with *bleu Fallot* ground and *incrusté* flowers dated 1768 is in the collection of the Fine Arts Museums of San Francisco.

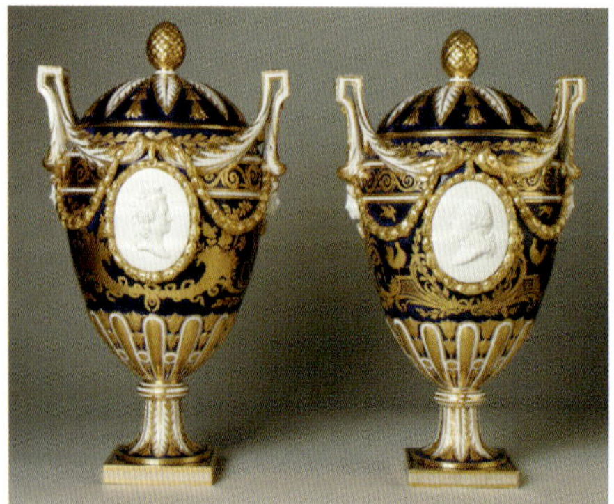

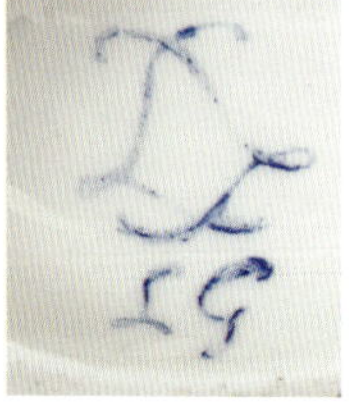

15 Pair of Egg-Shaped Vases with Medallions of Louis XVI and Marie Antoinette

(*vases oeuf*)

Sèvres, ca. 1774
Soft-paste porcelain
Étienne-Henri Le Guay *père*, gilder; models for medallions likely created by Louis-Simon Boizot (after official medals)
H. 16¾ in. (42.5 cm)
Private Collection

MARKS: Crossed letters *L* and letters *LG* for painter and gilder Étienne-Henri Le Guay *père* (active 1748–9, 1751–97)

PROVENANCE: Private Collection, Switzerland, sold Sotheby's Zurich, 24–25 November 1994, lots 121 and 143; Collection of W. Sainsbury; Private Collection

RELATED EXAMPLES: No identical examples have been identified to date. An egg-shaped pair of *vases à médaillon du roi* that are topped with a crown and feature a biscuit oval medallion with a portrait of Louis XV is in the Wallace Collection, London; and one vase, also with a crown-shaped cover and two similar biscuit portrait medallions of Louis XV, is in the British Royal Collection.

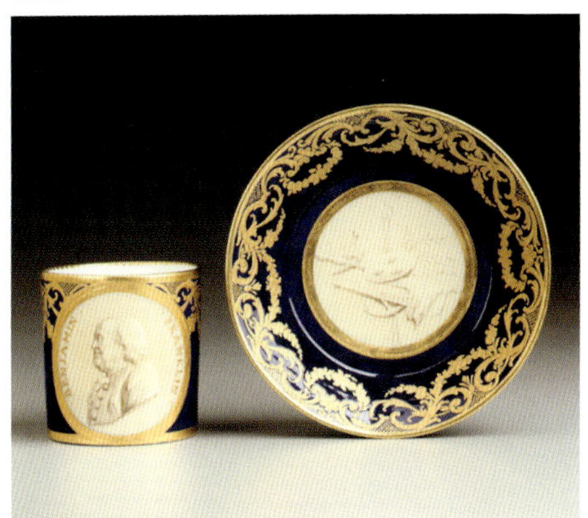

16 Cup and Saucer with Portrait of Benjamin Franklin

(gobelet "litron" et soucoupe)

Sèvres, ca. 1779
Soft-paste porcelain
Étienne-Henri Le Guay *père*, painter and gilder
Cup H. 2$\frac{15}{16}$ in. (7.5 cm)
Saucer Dia. 5$\frac{7}{16}$ in. (13.8 cm)
Collection of Hillwood Estate, Museum & Gardens Bequest of Marjorie Merriweather Post, 1973 (acc. nos. 24.151.1–.2)

MARKS: Both cup and saucer with crossed letters *L* and letters *LG* for painter and gilder Étienne-Henri Le Guay *père* (active 1776–1817)

PROVENANCE: Collection of Lord Henry Thyme, sold Christie's London, 21 June 1899, lot 160; gift of Joseph E. Davies to Marjorie Merriweather Post, 1950

RELATED EXAMPLES: One cup is at the Victoria and Albert Museum, London, one cup with a replacement saucer is in the Wallace Collection, London, and another cup and saucer set is in the Art Institute of Chicago. A hard-paste example is at the Philadelphia Museum of Art (1998-67-1a,b).

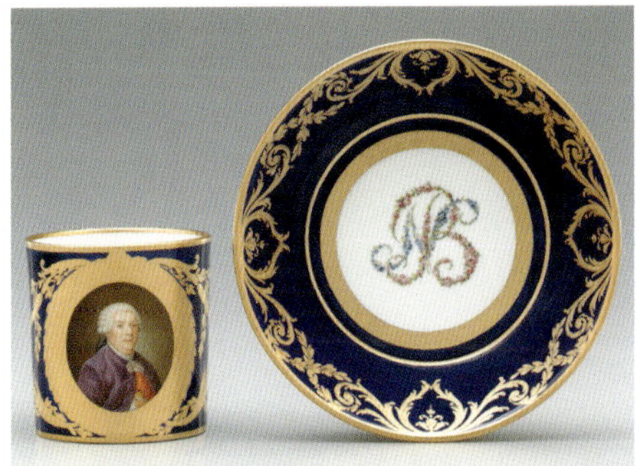

17 Cup and Saucer with Portrait of Nicolas de Beaujon

(gobelet "litron" et soucoupe)

Sèvres, 1782
Soft-paste porcelain
Étienne-Henri Le Guay *père*, painter and gilder; Pierre Massy, painter of cipher; Nicolas-Pierre Pithou *jeune*, painter of portrait
Cup H. 3 in. (7.6 cm)
Saucer Dia. 5$\frac{13}{16}$ in. (14.8 cm)
Collection of Mr. Dan Mingledorff and Mr. Richard A. Mitchell

MARKS: (cup) Crossed letters *L* and letters *LG* for painter and gilder Étienne-Henri Le Guay *père* (active 1748–9; 1751–97); (saucer) Crossed letters *L* enclosing date letters *EE* for 1782; scrolling letter *M·* surmounted on left side with crescent shape for painter Pierre Massy (active 1779–1803) and letters *LG* for Étienne-Henri Le Guay *père*

PROVENANCE: John Whitehead Works of Art

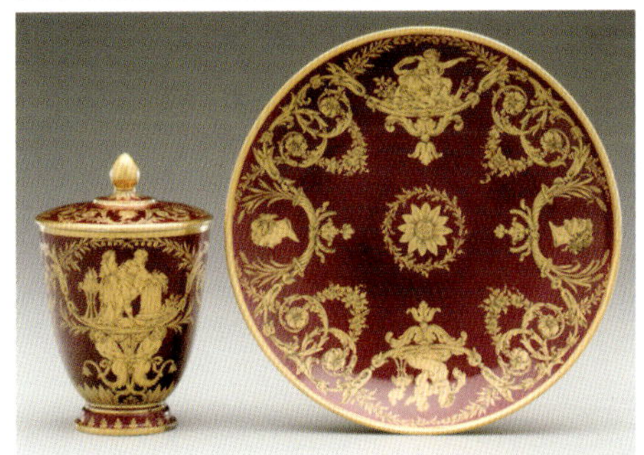

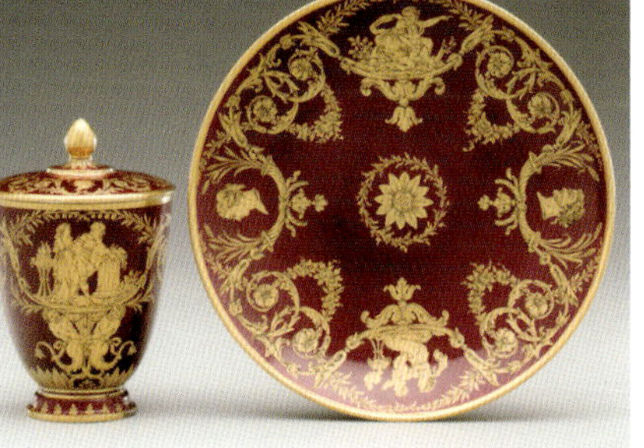

18 Covered Cup and Saucer with Gold Figures

(gobelet de la toilette et sa soucoupe)

Sèvres, 1784
Hard-paste porcelain
Pierre-André Le Guay *jeune*, painter (after designs by Philippe-Louis Parizeau)
Cup and Cover H. 4$\frac{15}{16}$ in. (12.5 cm)
Saucer Dia. 7$\frac{1}{4}$ in. (18.4 cm)
Private American Collection

MARKS: Crossed letters *L* enclosing date letters *gg* for 1784, all in gold; flaming torch in gold for painter Pierre-André Le Guay, *jeune* (active 1772–1817)

PROVENANCE: Klaber & Klaber, London, 2000; Mingledorff-Mitchell Collection

RELATED EXAMPLES: A covered cup and saucer of similar form with Revolutionary symbols dated 1794 is in the collection of the Musée National de Céramique, Sèvres (MNC 17.821); and a hard-paste *écuelle de la toilette* decorated in dark blue and gold in the "Etruscan" manner is in the collection of the Art Institute of Chicago (inv. no. 1993.343).

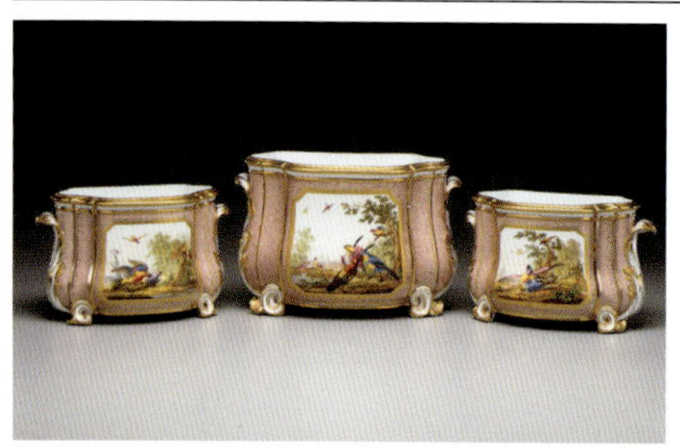

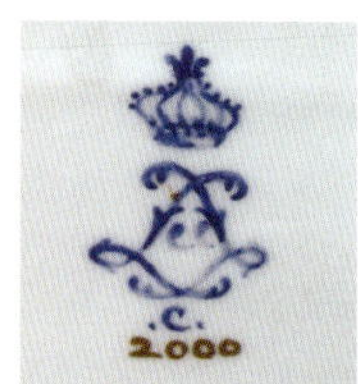

19 Garniture of Three Vases

(*cuvettes "Courteille"*)

Sèvres, 1782
Hard-paste porcelain
Philippe Castel, painter; Henri-François Vincent, gilder
Large vase (24.106.1) H. 7½ in. (19.1 cm), L. 11½ in. (29.2 cm)
Smaller vases (24.106.2–.3) H. 6 in. (15.2 cm), L. 9⅞ in. (25.2 cm)
Collection of Hillwood Estate, Museum & Gardens Bequest of Marjorie Merriweather Post, 1973 (acc. nos. 24.106.1–.3)

MARKS: All with crossed letters *L* surmounted by a crown to indicate hard-paste porcelain; date letters *ee* for 1782; *.c.* underneath for painter Philippe Castel (active 1772–97); *2000* for gilder Henri-François Vincent (active 1753–1806)

PROVENANCE: J. Rochelle Thomas, London, 1949

RELATED EXAMPLES: Although this shape was in almost continuous production from 1754 through the late 1780s, this is the only known three-piece garniture in a public collection. The distinctive pattern of pink *oeil-de-perdrix* is repeated in a pair of *vases jardin* (1779) destined for Louis XVI and now in the collection of the château de Versailles.

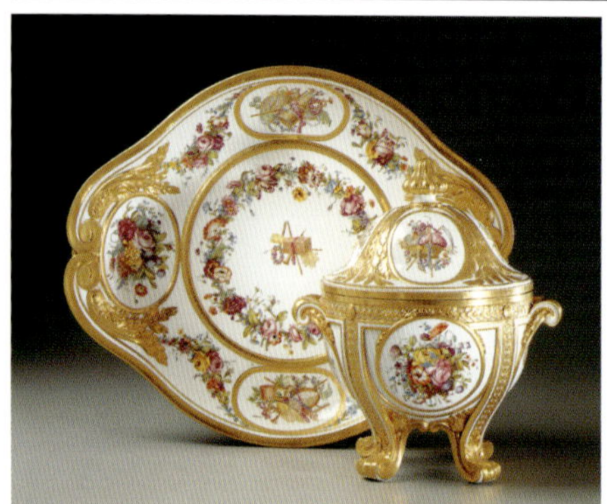

20 Tureen and Platter

(*pot à oille et son plateau*)

Sèvres, ca. 1783
Hard-paste porcelain
Henri-François Vincent, gilder
Tureen H. 13 in. (33 cm), Dia. 9⁹⁄₁₆ in. (24.3 cm)
Platter L. 21 in. (53.3 cm), W. 17½ in. (44.5 cm)
Collection of Hillwood Estate, Museum & Gardens Bequest of Marjorie Merriweather Post, 1973 (acc. nos. 24.134.3–.5)

MARKS: Ghost of crossed letters *L* surmounted by crown to indicate hard-paste porcelain; ghost of date letters *ff* for 1783; *2000* in gold for gilder Henri-François Vincent (active 1753–1806)

PROVENANCE: Duke of Montpensier (unverified); Galerie Fragonard, Paris, 1949

RELATED EXAMPLES: In 1777 Louis XVI gave Joseph II, Regent of the Holy Roman Empire (traveling in Paris incognito as Count Falkenstein) two tureens and two terrines with wheat sprigs, which are now in the collection of the Hofburg Imperial Palace, Vienna; also in 1777 the king presented two almost identical tureens to the aforementioned ones to Gustave III of Sweden, which are now in the collection of the Metropolitan Museum of Art, New York.

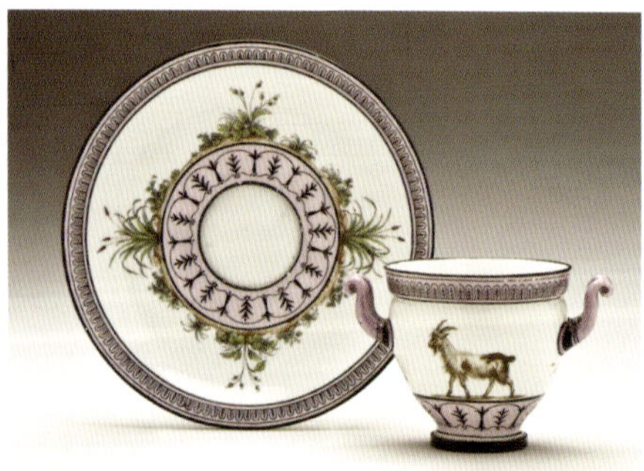

21 Cup and Saucer from the Queen's Dairy at Rambouillet

(*gobelet à anses "étrusques" et soucoupe*)

Sèvres, 1786–7
Hard-paste porcelain
Jean-Jacques Lagrenée, designer of decoration; François-Antoine Pfeiffer, painter
Cup H. 3⅛ in. (8 cm)
Saucer Dia. 6¾ in. (17.1 cm)
Private Collection

MARKS: (cup) Crossed letters *L* enclosing date letters *KK* for 1787; surmounted by a crown to indicate hard-paste porcelain; mark of painter François-Antoine Pfeiffer (active 1771–1800)

PROVENANCE: Queen Marie Antoinette's dairy at the château de Rambouillet; Piasa, Paris, 23 June 2000, lot 20

RELATED EXAMPLES: Two other examples of this type, one yellow and the other green, survive at the Musée National de Céramique, Sèvres and in the Didier Cramoisan Collection, respectively. Few other pieces of this service survive. Two milk pails were in the Baron Mayer Amschel de Rothschild Collection at Mentmore, Buckinghamshire (sold Sotheby's Parke-Bernet, 24 May 1977, lots 2079–2080); a grand *terrine base* is at the Frankfurt Museum für Kunsthandwerk; and a *gobelet cornet* and two *jattes tétons* are at the Musée National de Céramique, Sèvres.

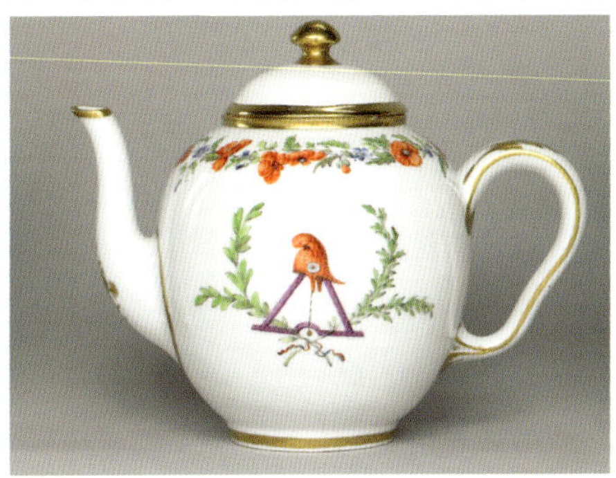

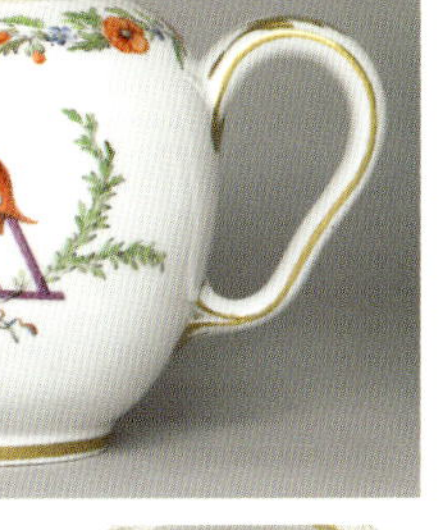

22 Revolutionary Teapot

(théière "Calabre")

Sèvres, 1795
Hard-paste porcelain
Pierre-Jean-Baptiste Vandé *fils*, painter and gilder
H. $4\frac{3}{8}$ in. (11.1 cm), W. $4\frac{1}{4}$ in. (10.8 cm)
Collection of the National Museum of American History, Smithsonian Institution, Kenneth E. Behring Center (cat. no. P779)

MARKS: Intertwined letters *RF* for République Française over the word *Sevres*; letters *V. . D.* for painter and gilder Pierre-Jean-Baptiste Vandé *fils* (active 1779–1800; 1802–24)

PROVENANCE: Bequest of Reverend Alfred Duane Pell

RELATED EXAMPLES: A similarly decorated cup and saucer set is in the collection of the State Hermitage Museum, St. Petersburg.

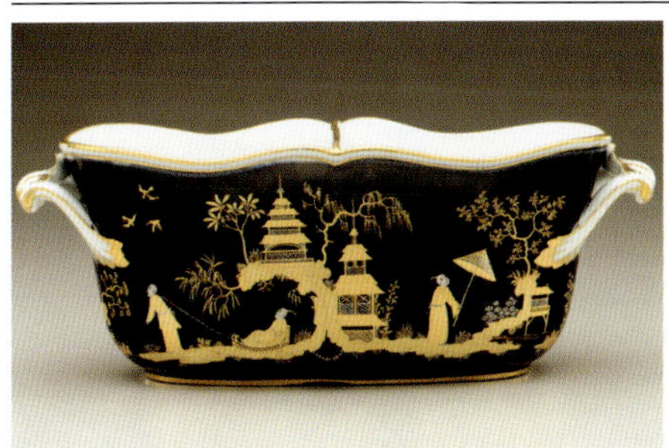

23 Chinoiserie Bottle Cooler

(seau à liqueurs)

Sèvres, 1791
Hard-paste porcelain
H. $4\frac{3}{4}$ in. (12 cm), L. $12\frac{11}{16}$ in. (32.2 cm), W. $5\frac{7}{8}$ in. (14.9 cm)
Private American Collection

MARKS: Ghost of crossed letters *L* in gold

PROVENANCE: From a service purchased from the factory by M. Milnes, an English merchant, in the course of 1792–3. Service sold at Christie's on behalf of one of Milne's descendants, E. Milnes-Gaskell, 26 June 1931; Mingledorff-Mitchell Collection

RELATED EXAMPLES: Two half wine bottle coolers with black ground and with gold and platinum chinoiserie figures are in the collection of the J. Paul Getty Museum, Los Angeles (72.DE.53.1-2); thirty-four plates decorated with a black ground and chinoiserie figures are in the collection of the Metropolitan Museum of Art, New York (62.165.1-34); a ewer and basin set with black ground and gold and platinum chinoiserie figures (ca. 1790) is in the collection of the Musée National de Céramique, Sèvres (MNC 5.291); and a dessert service with chinoiserie borders and flowers (1791–2) is in the collection of the State Hermitage Museum, St. Petersburg.

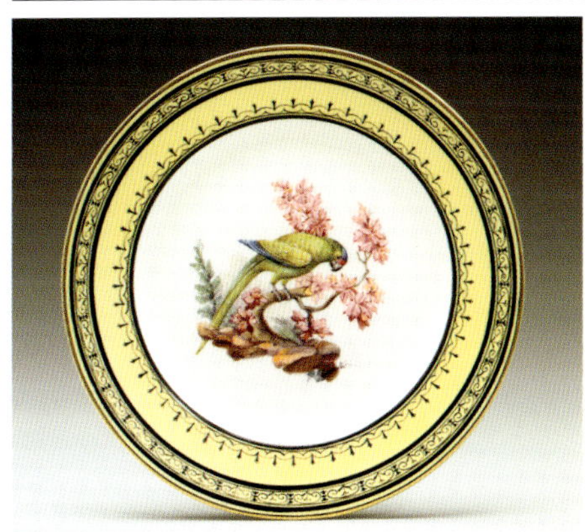

24 Plate with Birds and "Etruscan" Borders

(assiette unie)

Sèvres, 1793
Hard-paste porcelain
Edmé-François Bouillat *père* and Jean-Pierre Fumez, painters (after engravings from the comte de Buffon's *Historie naturelle des oiseaux*)
Dia. $9\frac{9}{16}$ in. (24.3 cm)
Collection of Hillwood Estate, Museum & Gardens Bequest of Marjorie Merriweather Post, 1973 (acc. no. 24.130.6)

MARKS: Inscribed on back are *Perruche à front rouge, de Brésil*; *Sevres*; *R.F.* for République Française; *y* for painter Edmé-François Bouillat *père* (active 1758–1810); and *fx* for painter Jean-Pierre Fumez (active 1777–1804)

PROVENANCE: During the French Revolution, three services incorporating components similar to the plates and square dishes at Hillwood were sold. The most complete set went to Auguste Jullien in February 1794, another was delivered to the merchant Pierre-Fédecié Empaytaz for export in December 1794, and a third went to Citoyen Speelman in October 1795. According to David Peters, this plate and the square dish belong to the Jullien service.

RELATED EXAMPLES: Five other round plates (acc. nos. 24.130.2–.5 and 24.130.7), a square dish (24.130.1) and two cups (acc. nos. 24.242–243) and saucers (24.130.8–.9) from this service are in the collection of Hillwood Estate, Museum & Gardens, Washington, D.C. Other comparable pieces can be seen in the J.P. Morgan Collection at the Wadsworth Atheneum, Hartford, CT and at the Musée des Arts Décoratifs, Paris.

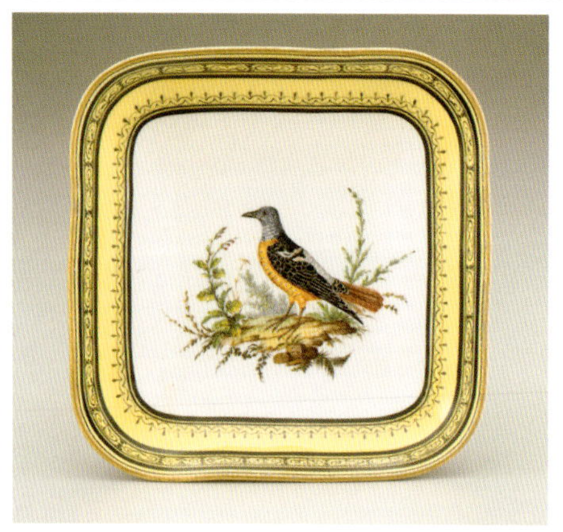

25 Square Dish with Birds and "Etruscan" Borders

(*compotier carré*)

Sèvres, 1793
Soft-paste porcelain
Étienne Evans and Madame Boitel, painters (after engravings by the comte de Buffon's *Historie naturelle des oiseaux*)
W. $8\frac{1}{8}$ in. (46 cm)
Collection of Hillwood Estate, Museum & Gardens Bequest of Marjorie Merriweather Post, 1973 (acc. no. 24.130.1)

MARKS: Inscribed on back are *Le Merle de Roche*; date letters *qq* within crossed letters *L*; sword mark for painter Étienne Evans (active 1752–1806); and *jd* for painter Madame Boitel

PROVENANCE: See cat. no. 24

RELATED EXAMPLES: See cat. no. 24

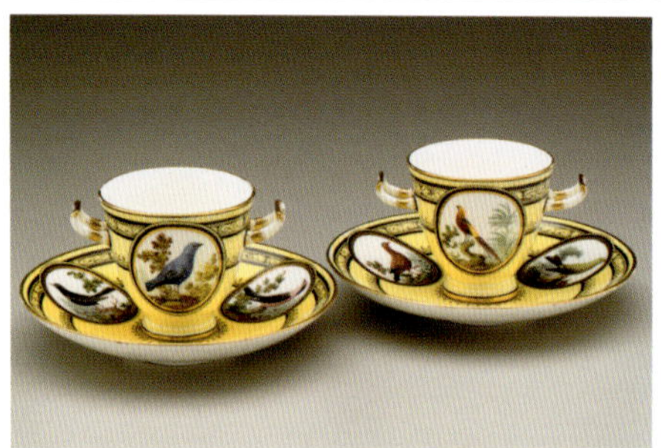

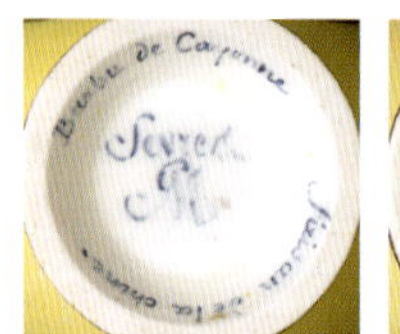

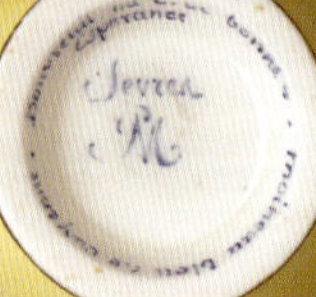

26 Two Cups and Saucers with Birds

(*gobelet "étrusque" et soucoupe*)

Sèvres, 1793–4
Soft-paste porcelain
Pierre Massy, painter
Cups H. $3\frac{1}{8}$ in. (7.9 cm)
Collection of Hillwood Estate, Museum & Gardens Museum Purchase, 2005 (acc. nos. 24.242–243)
Saucers Dia. $6\frac{15}{16}$ in. (17.6 cm)
Collection of Hillwood Estate, Museum & Gardens Bequest of Marjorie Merriweather Post, 1973 (acc. nos. 24.130.8–.9)

MARKS: (both cups) Inscribed *Sevres* in script above scrolling letter *M·* surmounted on left side with crescent shape for painter Pierre Massy (active 1779–1803); (one cup) Inscribed on bottom are *Barbu de Cayenne* and *Faisan de la Chine*; (other cup) Inscribed on bottom are *Bouvreuil [du Cap de] Bonne Espérance* and *Moineau bleu de Cayenne*

PROVENANCE: Of the yellow services mentioned above in cat. no. 24, these cups and saucers could have formed part of either the Jullien service or the Speelman service, both of which included cups and saucers. (Cups) Étude Piasa, Paris, 4 June 2004; John Whitehead Works of Art, London

RELATED EXAMPLES: See note above; also a cup and saucer set from this service is in the collection of the Musée National de Céramique, Sèvres (MNC.23.033).

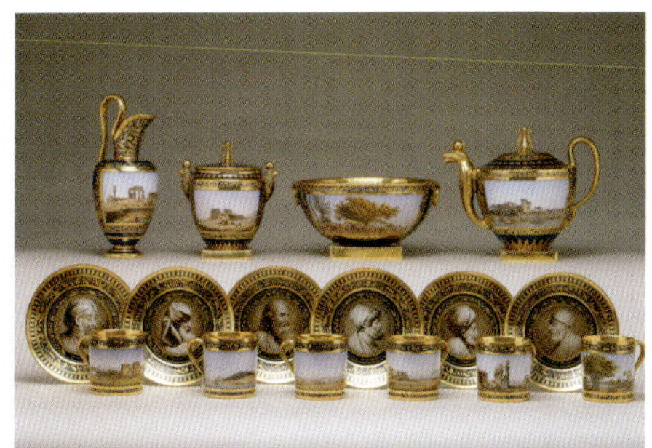

27 Selections from the *Déjeuner Égyptien* for the Duchesse de Montebello

Sèvres, 1810–12
Hard-paste porcelain
Nicolas-Antoine-Florentin Le Bel and Christophe-Ferdinand Caron, painters; Pierre-Louis Micaud *fils*, Charles-Marie Boitel, and/or Jean-Baptiste Vandé, gilders
The Twinight Collection (inv. nos. S-153.1–.6)

PROVENANCE: Gift of Napoleon to the duchesse de Montebello, 1812; acquired Wemaere-de Beaupuis, Rouen, 26 November 2006, lot 33

RELATED EXAMPLES: The Sèvres factory produced seven Egyptian-style *déjeuners*, called "Egyptian Cabarets," during the First Empire. One *beau bleu* coffee set (1809–10), owned by Napoleon who brought it with him into exile on Saint Helena, has similar portraits and Egyptian views after Vivant Denon's *Voyage dans la Basse et Haute Égypte* and is in the collection of the Musée du Louvre, Paris (OA 9493). Empress Joséphine's Egyptian Cabaret (1808), which was given to her by Napoleon as a New Year's gift, also with a *beau bleu* ground, cups in the "Etruscan" form and decorated with views of Egypt painted in sepia after Vivant Denon's *Voyage* and Egyptian hieroglyphics, is in the collection of the Musée National du Château de Malmaison (MM-83-9-1, 83-9-18, 83-9-27). Part of another Egyptian tea set (1810) that also belonged to Joséphine, with a dark blue ground, "Etruscan" cups and also featuring views of Egypt after Vivant Denon's *Voyage*, is in the collection of the Fondation Napoléon, Paris. This set is very similar to the emperor's cabaret in the Louvre.

Teapot with views of the temples on the Island of Philae and in Thebes
(inv. no. S-153.1)
H. 7⅛ in. (18 cm)

MARKS: Imperial mark *M.Imp.le Sevres* printed on back and the mark of gilder Pierre-Louis Micaud; inscribed on back *Vue des Temples de l'isle de Philae* and *Vue de Temple de Thèbes*

Milk Jug with view of a temple in Hermontis
(inv. no. S-153.2)
H. 8½ in. (21.5 cm)

MARKS: Imperial mark *M.Imp.le Sevres* printed on back and the mark of gilder Pierre-Louis Micaud; inscribed on back *Vue d'un temple d'Hermontis*

Sugar Bowl with views of Etfu
(inv. no. S-153.3)
H. 6$\frac{5}{16}$ in. (16 cm), Dia. 5$\frac{5}{16}$ in. (13.5 cm)

MARKS: Imperial mark *M.Imp.le Sevres* printed on back and the mark of gilder Pierre-Louis Micaud; inscribed on back *Vue d'Etfou du sud au nord/Vue d'Etfou du nord au sud*

Slop Bowl with a view of the garden of the Institut Français in Cairo
(inv. no. S-153.4)
H. 4 in. (10.3 cm), Dia. 8 in. (20.5 cm)

MARKS: Imperial mark *M.Imp.le Sevres* printed on back and the mark of gilder Pierre-Louis Micaud; inscribed on back *Jardin de l'Institut du Caire/Arbre auquel on fait des offrandes*

Cups and Saucers – One with a view of a desert monastery and a portrait of Koarim and the other with a view of the village of Nagadi and a portrait of Fekkah
(inv. nos. S-153.5 and S-153.6)
Cup H. 2½ in. (6.3 cm), L. 3¼ in. (8.3 cm); Saucer H. 1 in. (2.6 cm), Dia. 5¼ in. (13.3 cm)

MARKS: Imperial mark *M.Imp.le Sevres* printed on back; inscribed on back *Koarim Scherif d'Alexandrie/Couvent dans le desert* and *Fekkah Journalier Egyptien/Village de Nagadi dans le desert* respectively

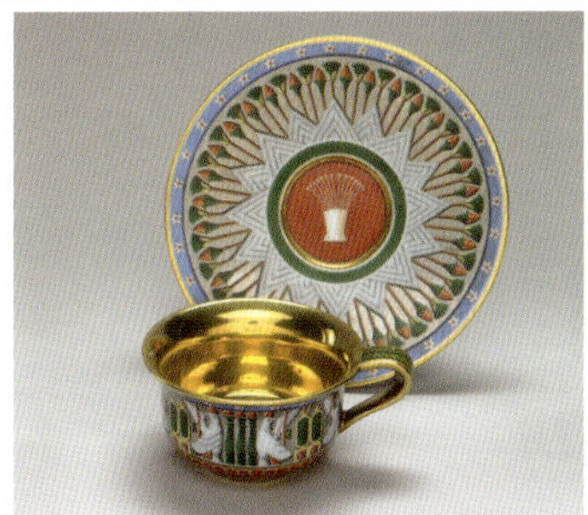

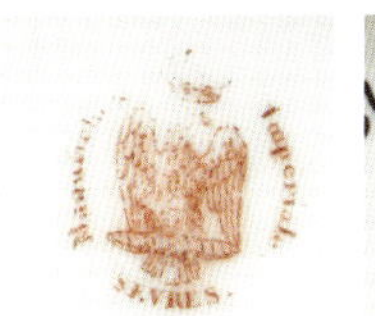

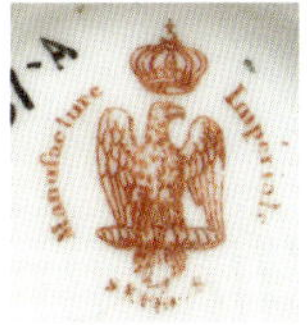

28 Egyptian Revival Cup and Saucer

(tasse à thé égyptien et soucoupe)

Sèvres, 1813–14
Hard-paste porcelain
Cup H. 1⅞ in. (4.8 cm), W. (with handle) 3⅜ in (8.6 cm)
Saucer Dia. 5$\frac{11}{16}$ in. (14.5 cm)
Collection of the National Museum of American History, Smithsonian Institution, Kenneth E. Behring Center (cat. nos. P1069a-b)

MARKS: Printed on back with *Manufacture Imperiale Sevres* around the imperial eagle

PROVENANCE: Bequest of Reverend Alfred Duane Pell

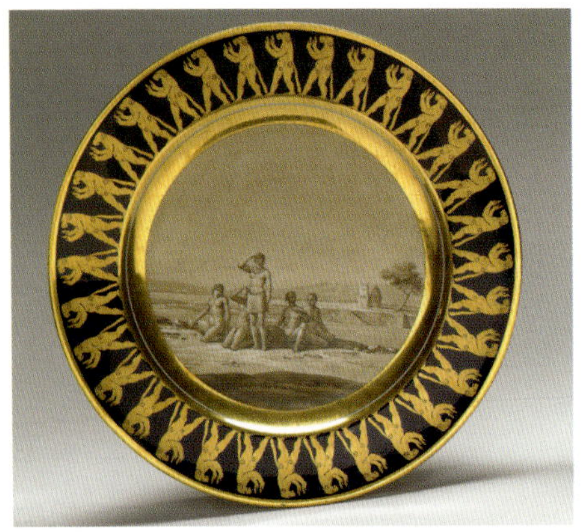

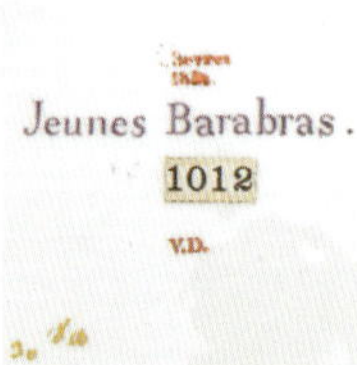

29 Plate from the *Service Égyptien*

(assiette)

Sèvres, 1804
Hard-paste porcelain
Jacques-François-Joseph Swebach, painter; Pierre-Jean-Baptiste Vandé *fils*, gilder
Dia. 9¼ in. (23.5 cm)
Collection of the National Museum of American History, Smithsonian Institution, Kenneth E. Behring Center (cat. no. P662)

MARKS: Partially stamped in red *M.Imp.le Sevres* for the First Empire (1804–14) and the date 1804; inscribed with the words *Jeunes Barabras.* in purple; stamp of the letters *V.D.* in red for gilder Pierre-Jean-Baptiste Vandé *fils* (active 1779–1824); sticker with the number *1012*

PROVENANCE: From the first Egyptian Service delivered to Tsar Alexander I in 1808; Bequest of Reverend Alfred Duane Pell

RELATED EXAMPLES: Pieces from the first Egyptian Service (1804–5), which was delivered as a diplomatic gift from Napoleon to Tsar Alexander I of Russia, are in the collection of the Museum of Ceramics and Kuskovo Estate-Museum, Moscow; pieces from a second Egyptian Service (1810–12), including parts of the centerpiece modeled after temples at Etfu and Dendera, are in the collection of the Victoria and Albert Museum, London; a plate from the second service, also decorated by Swebach, is in the collection of the Musée National du Château de Malmaison (MM 2.888); and a unique trial piece for the first service designed by Brongniart and featuring an image of the ruins at Latopolis is in the collection of the British Museum (reg. no. 1993,0610.1).

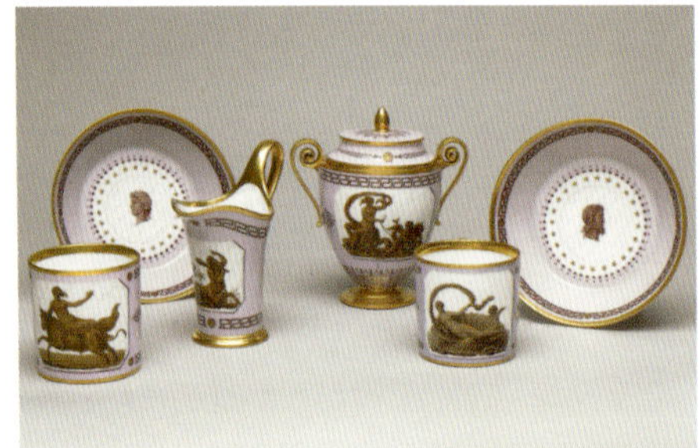

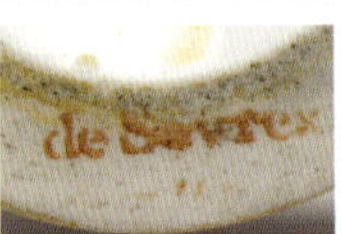

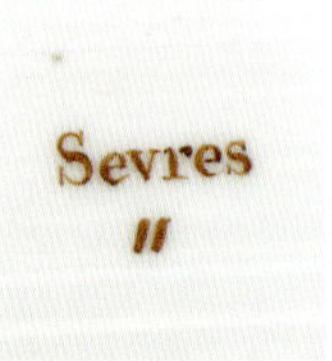

30 Partial Tea Set for Paulina Bonaparte

(cabaret à thé)

Sèvres, 1805
Hard-paste porcelain
Teapot H. 8¼ in. (21 cm), L. 4⅜ in. (11.1 cm); Milk Jug H. 8⅞ in. (22.5 cm), L. 4 in. (10.1 cm); Sugar Bowl H. 6 in. (15.2 cm), L. 3⅝ in. (9.2 cm); Cup H. 2¹⁵⁄₁₆ in. (7.5 cm), Dia. 3 in. (7.6 cm); Saucer Dia. 6 in. (15.2 cm)
Collection of the National Museum of American History, Smithsonian Institution, Kenneth E. Behring Center (cat. nos. P778A, C, D, Fa-b)

MARKS: Some partially stamped in red *M.Imp.le Sevres* for the First Empire (1804–14); others inscribed with the word *Sevres* in gold over two forward slash marks

PROVENANCE: Presented by Napoleon I in 1805 to his sister Paulina Bonaparte, who married Prince Camillo Borghese of Italy; Collection of the Borghese family until 1893; Bequest of Reverend Alfred Duane Pell

RELATED EXAMPLES: A coffee set with Egyptian iconography and similar lavender ground and gold gilding, dating from 1803, is in the collection of the Musée National du Château de Malmaison and was used by Napoleon and Joséphine. The cups in this service are of the traditional *litron* form, while the other pieces are in the more current "Etruscan" and "Paestum" forms.

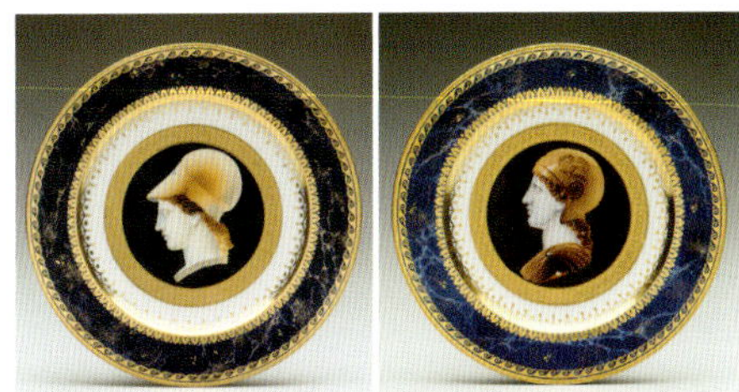

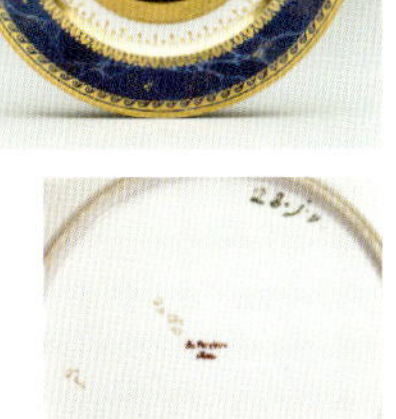

31 Two Plates from the *Service Iconographique Grec*

(*assiette plate*)

Sèvres, 1812
Hard-paste porcelain
Louis-Victor Godin *l'âiné*, painter of borders
H. 1¼ in. (3.2 cm), Dia. 9⅜ in. (23.8 cm)
Private Collection, Berlin, Germany

MARKS: (Rome) Ghost of factory mark; inscribed in green *28jv* and *15auB.T.* with *Rome* in gold; (Pallas) Ghost of factory mark and *de Sevres, 1812*; inscribed *y6yy* in gold and *no.58* with *Pallas Velletri* in gold

RELATED EXAMPLES: Twenty-two similar plates with blue lapis ground borders and portraits in imitation of cameos, either from this or the first *Service Iconographique Grec*, are in the Twinight Collection, New York (inv. nos. S-18 through S-35, S-42, S-90 through S-92); at least one plate from the second *Service Iconographique Grec* is in the collection of the Rhode Island School of Design Museum of Art, Providence (1989-010); and numerous assorted pieces from the *Service Iconographique Antique* for Cardinal Fesch are in the collection of Count Charles-André Colonna Walewski (illustrated in H. de la Verrie, 2008, p. 43) and also in the collection of the Musée National de Céramique, Sèvres.

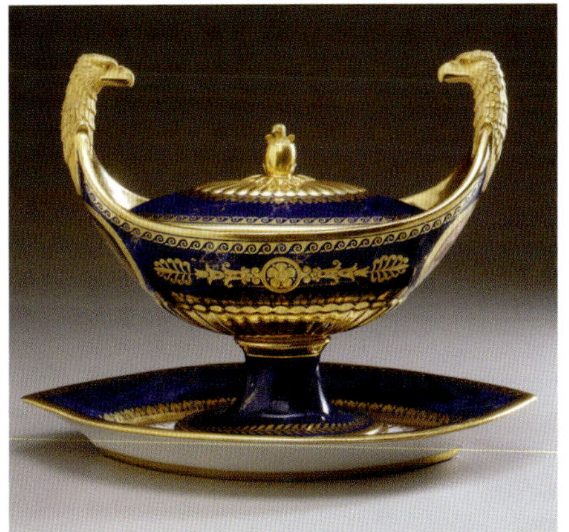

32 Sugar Bowl from the *Service Iconographique Grec*

(*sucrier à têtes d'aigles*)

Sèvres, 1817
Hard-paste porcelain
Pierre Huard, painter; Charles-Marie Boitel, gilder
H. 9⁹⁄₁₆ in. (24.3 cm), L. 12¼ in. (31.2 cm), W. 7¼ in. (18.4 cm)
The Twinight Collection (inv. no. S-17)

MARKS: Stamped *M.Imp$^{le.}$ de Sevres.* for the First Empire (1804–14)

PROVENANCE: Acquired Sotheby's London, 15 November 1996, lot 517

RELATED EXAMPLES: See note above; also a similar pair of sugar bowls dating from 1811 and that are now missing their covers are in the collection of Count Charles-André Colonna Walewski (illustrated in H. de la Verrie, 2008, p. 43).

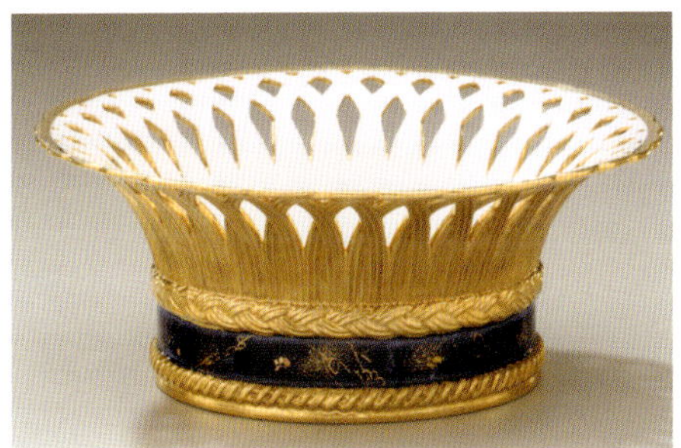

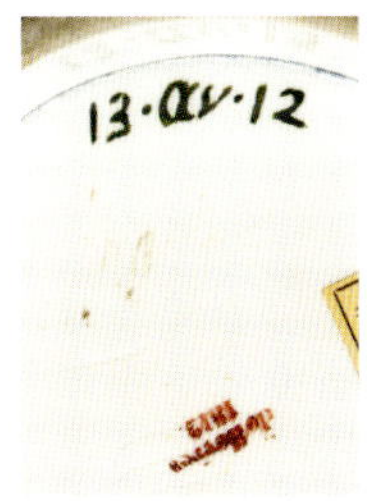

33 Basket from the *Service Iconographique Grec*

(*corbeille basse*)

Sèvres, ca. 1813
Hard-paste porcelain
H. 3 in. (7.6 cm), Dia. 7½ in. (19 cm)
Collection of Hillwood Estate, Museum & Gardens Museum Purchase, 2005 (acc. no. 24.241)

MARKS: Partially stamped *M.Imp$^{le.}$ de Sevres* in iron red and the date 1813; inscribed *13·αv·12* in green

PROVENANCE: Étude Couteau-Bergerie, Paris, 1 June 2004

RELATED EXAMPLES: Four similar baskets dating from 1811 are in the collection of Count Charles-André Colonna Walewski (illustrated in H. de la Verrie, 2008, p. 47).

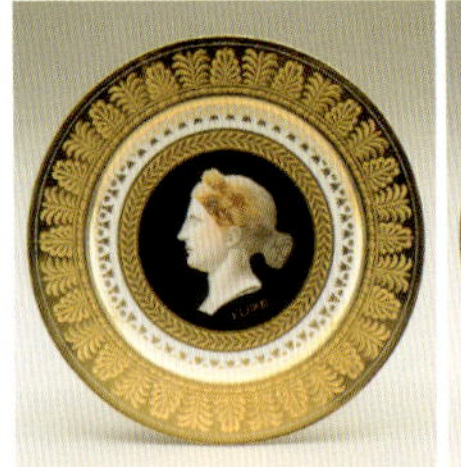
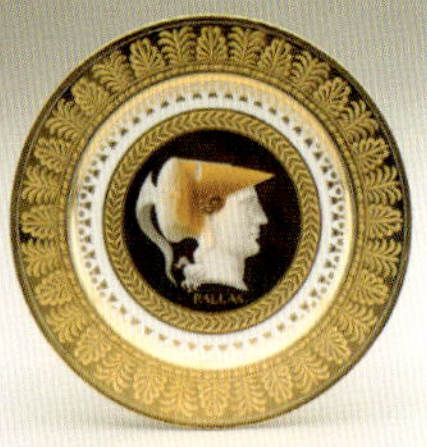
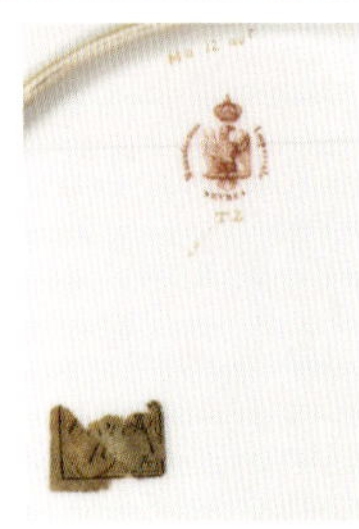
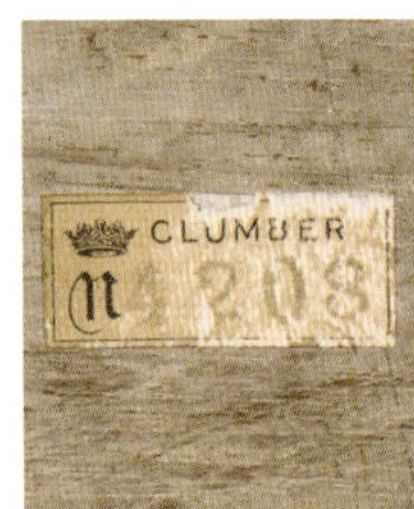

34 Two Plates from the *Service à marli d'or*

Sèvres, 1813–14
Hard-paste porcelain
H. $1\frac{1}{8}$ in. (2.9 cm), Dia. $9\frac{3}{16}$ in. (28.3 cm)
Collection of Hillwood Estate, Museum & Gardens Museum Purchase, 2005 (acc. no. 24.244 and 24.245)

MARKS: Printed mark in red of the imperial eagle surrounded by the words *Manufacture Impériale Sèvres*; with script mark *TZ* for 1813 and *MO 12 avt*

PROVENANCE: Purchased 30 September 1814 by Thomas Hope; property of Hope's granddaughter Henrietta Adela Pelham-Clinton at Clumber in Nottinghamshire until 1938; Michele Beiny, Inc., 2005

RELATED EXAMPLES: Work on *marli d'or* plates was begun in 1806 by a number of Sèvres factory painters and continued until after the restoration of the monarchy in 1814. All plates have a gold border, but the central scenes depict a variety of subjects, including historical subjects, landscapes, genre scenes, and floral motifs. Many *marli d'or* plates are in the collection of the château de Malmaison, originally from the collection of Eugène de Beauharnais, Joséphine's son who was viceroy of Italy during much of Napoleon's reign. Three *marli d'or* plates, two depicting scenes from antiquity and one with a landscape scene (1811), are in the Twinight Collection, New York (inv. nos. S-137, S-138, and S-56); and a *marli d'or* plate with a central decoration of fruits is in the collection of the Musée National de Sèvres (MNC 2.023).

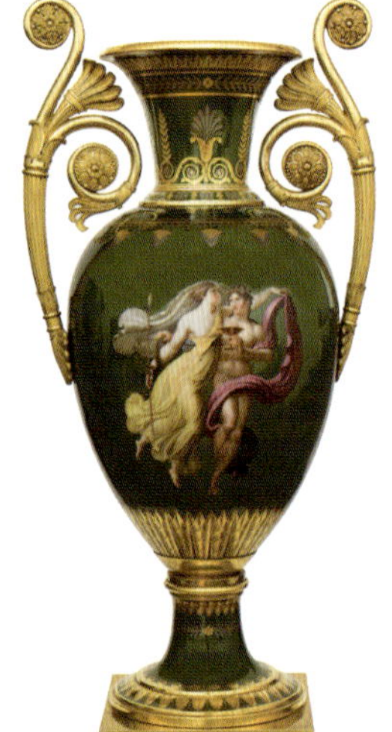

35 "Bacchus and Ariadne" Egg-Shaped Vase (one of a pair) (*vase oeuf*)

Sèvres, 1810
Hard-paste porcelain
Charles-Marie Boitel, painter and gilder; M. Godin, painter of ground color; J. Georget, painter; Mlle. Le Grand and Charles-Christian-Marie Durosey, burnishers; Pierre-Philippe Thomire, designer of bronze mounts
H. $29\frac{1}{2}$ in. (74.9 cm)
Collection of the Wadsworth Atheneum Museum of Art, Hartford, CT
Gift of Mrs. Henry B. Learned (1948.109)

MARKS: Stamped twice in red *M.Imp.*^{le} *Sevres* for the First Empire (1804–14) and the year 1809; inscribed with the words *vase oeuf 3 enT* and the numbers *35·36* in green

PROVENANCE: Delivered to Prince Louis I of Hesse-Darmstadt on 29 June 1810

RELATED EXAMPLES: The pair to this vase, with the painted decoration of "Flora and Zephyr," is in the collection at the Wadsworth Atheneum, Hartford, CT (1948.110); and two other green vases in a slightly different neoclassical style with rolled handles (dated 1811) are in the collection of the Wadsworth Atheneum (1994.40.1 and 1919.87).

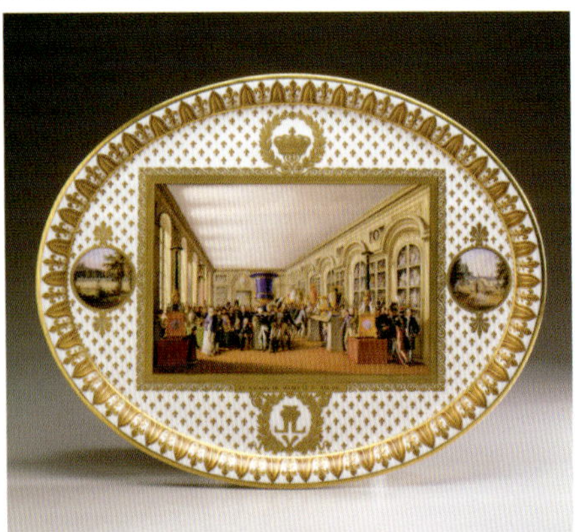

36 Tray from the *Déjeuner Service L'Art de la porcelaine (Les travaux de la manufacture de Sèvres)* (*plateau ovale 1ère grandeur*)

Sèvres, 1816
Hard-paste porcelain
Jean-Charles Develly, painter of figural decoration; Pierre Huard, painter of non-figural decoration
H. 1 in. (2.6 cm), L. $17\frac{3}{16}$ in. (43.7 cm), W. $13\frac{1}{2}$ in. (34.4 cm)
The Twinight Collection (inv. no. S-81)

MARKS: Crossed letters *L* enclosing the word *Sevres* and a fleur-de-lis for the reign of Louis XVIII (1814–24)

PROVENANCE: Presented in 1817 by King Louis XVIII to his niece, the duchesse d'Angoulême; sold Sotheby's London, 20 June 2000, lot 85

RELATED EXAMPLES: This tray is part of a tea and coffee service, a *déjeuner*, which included two "Paestum" milk jugs depicting the large kiln at the conclusion of a firing and another "Paestum" milk jug depicting the muffle kilns, one "Paestum" sugar bowl depicting the mill and a visit by students from the École des Mines, two *litron* cups, one picturing the throwers' workshop and the other the painting workshop, and two saucers, one with images of the sculptors being visited by the interested public and the other with the painting workshop being visited by laypeople. The whereabouts of these pieces are unknown.

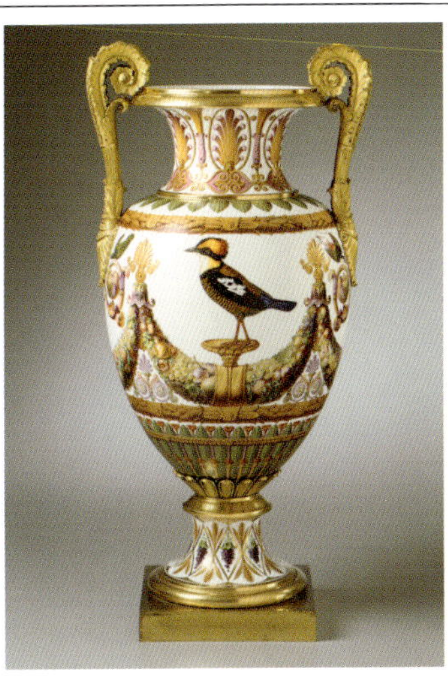

37 Vase with African Birds

(*vase floréal*)

Sèvres, 1822
Hard-paste porcelain, gilt bronze
Alexandre-Évariste Fragonard, designer; Madame Knip (née Pauline de Courcelles), painter of birds; C.-A. Didier, painter of ornaments; François-Antoine Boullemier *l'aîné*, gilder
H. 28 in. (71 cm), L. 14¼ in. (36.2 cm)
Collection of Hillwood Estate, Museum & Gardens Bequest of Marjorie Merriweather Post, 1973 (acc. no. 24-181)

MARKS: Inside neck crossed letters *L* in blue enclosing a fleur-de-lis for the reign of Louis XVIII (1814–24)

PROVENANCE: Parke-Bernet New York, 19 January 1963, lot 42 (Woronzow and Pierce liquidation sale)

RELATED EXAMPLES: Archival records at Sèvres show that three vases were made in this design, yet this is the only known example.

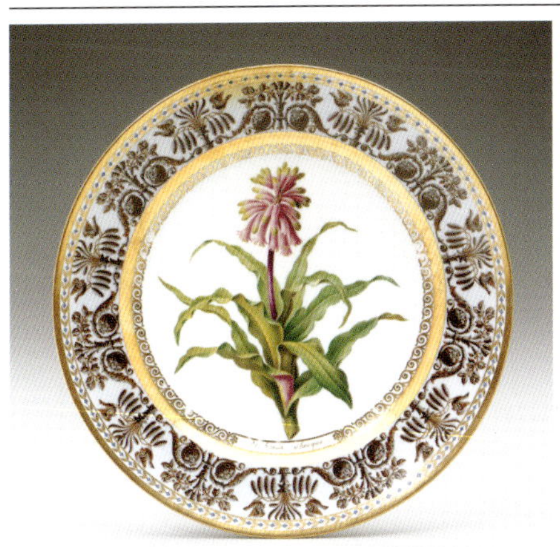

38 Plate from the *Service des liliacées*

(*assiette plate*)

Sèvres, 1821
Hard-paste porcelain
Jean-Charles-François Leloy, designer of borders (central flower designed after Pierre-Joseph Redouté's *Les Liliacées*)
H. 1¼ in. (3.4 cm), Dia. 9⅜ in. (23.8 cm)
Collection of Hillwood Estate, Museum & Gardens Museum Purchase, 2006 (acc. no. 24.246)

MARKS: Crossed letters *L* enclosing a fleur-de-lis for the reign of Louis XVIII (1814–24); date mark *21*; inscribed on front *Veltheima Glauque*

PROVENANCE: This is the only known plate to exist from the *Service des Liliacées* intended for Louis XVIII at the Palace of the Tuileries; O. Doutrebente (sold at hôtel Drouet, Paris), 2006

RELATED EXAMPLES: The Sèvres factory used Redouté's drawings to decorate a *Service des plantes et des liliacées* for Empress Joséphine (1802–5), part of which is now in the collection of the Museum of Fine Arts, Boston.

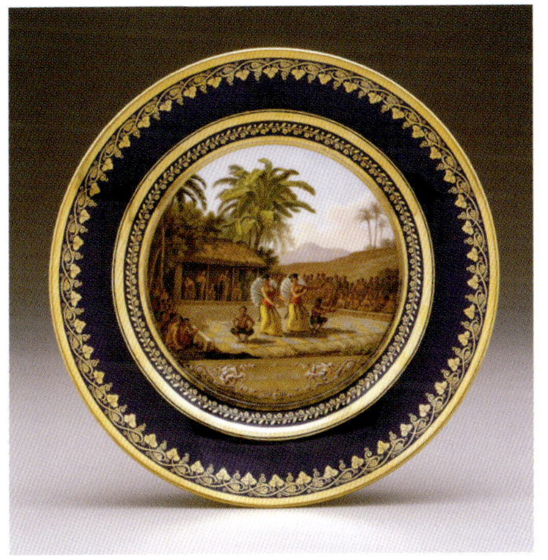

39 "Dance on Tahiti" Plate from the *Service des vues de pays hors d'Europe*

(*assiette plate*)

Sèvres, 1820
Hard-paste porcelain
Jean-Charles Develly, painter; Charles-Christian-Marie Durosey, gilder
H. 1¼ in. (3.2 cm), Dia. 9¼ in. (23.5 cm)
The Twinight Collection (inv. no. S-51)

MARKS: Crossed letters *L* enclosing the word *Sevres* with a fleur-de-lis for the reign of Louis XVIII (1814–24); date mark *21*; inscribed on front *Danse d'O Taïti*

PROVENANCE: Acquired by present owner 15 June 1998

RELATED EXAMPLES: Ten other plates from this service are in the Twinight Collection, New York (inv. nos. S-49, S-50, S-52, S-53, S-58 through S-62).

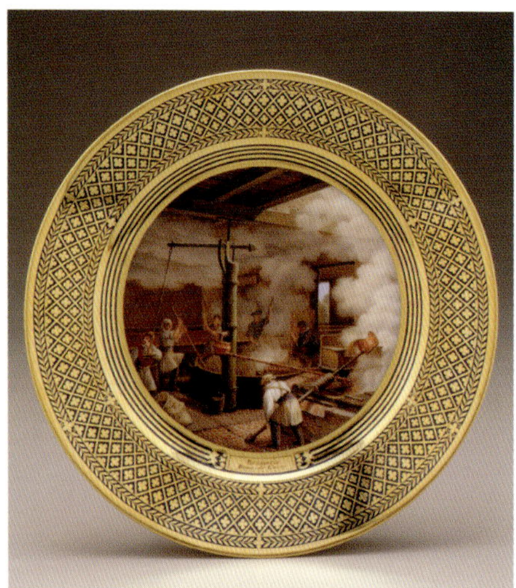

40 "Beer Brewery" Plate from the *Service des arts industriels* (*assiette plate*)

Sèvres, 1827
Hard-paste porcelain
Jean-Charles Develly, painter
H. 1⁵⁄₁₆ in. (3.3 cm), Dia. 9⁵⁄₁₆ in. (23.6 cm)
The Twinight Collection (inv. no. S-13)

MARKS: Crossed letters *L* enclosing the word *Sevres* and a fleur-de-lis and *X* for the reign of Charles X (1824–30); date mark *21*; inscribed on front *Brasserie, Banc de Cuves*

PROVENANCE: Acquired Christie's London, 3 June 1996, lot 341

RELATED EXAMPLES: This plate, depicting the fermenting vat ("Le Banc de Cuves"), is one of four relating to the brewing industry, also including the malt house ("Le Germoire"), the malt kiln ("La Touraille"), and "casking," or putting beer into barrels. Four other plates from this service are in the Twinight Collection, New York (inv. nos. S-12, S-14, S-37, and S-104); four plates from this service are in the Forsyth Wickes Collection at the Museum of Fine Arts, Boston (inv. nos. 65.1908-.1911); one plate from this service is in the collection of the Nelson-Atkins Museum of Art, Kansas City (inv. no. F83-52); one plate from this service, also featuring scenes relating to the brewing industry, is in the collection of the Cooper-Hewitt, National Design Museum, New York (inv. no. 1989.84.1); and one plate from this service is in the collection of the Rhode Island School of Design Museum of Art, Providence.

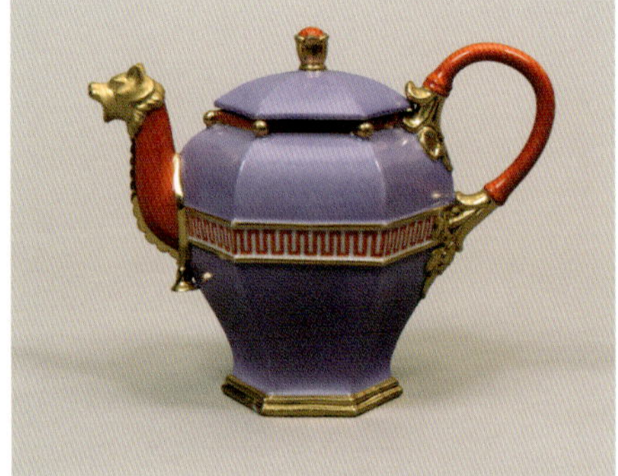

41 Chinese-style Teapot (*théière chinoise "Fragonard"*)

Sèvres, ca. 1818–21
Hard-paste porcelain
Alexandre-Évariste Fragonard, designer
H. 5⁵⁄₁₆ in. (13.5 cm), L. 6¹³⁄₁₆ in. (17.3 cm)
Private Collection

MARKS: Crossed letters *L* enclosing the word *Sevres* and a fleur-de-lis for the reign of Louis XVIII (1814–24); inscribed in gold script are *m, 11, n, 18*

RELATED EXAMPLES: A drawing of this model with a similar two-color combination signed by Fragonard and dated 1818 exists in the Sèvres factory archives (illustrated in fig. 52). This is possibly one of the first eight examples of this teapot produced in 1818, several of which sold at the Louvre exhibition of 29 December to 8 January 1819. Seventeen more examples with similar decoration were produced between 1818 and 1821.

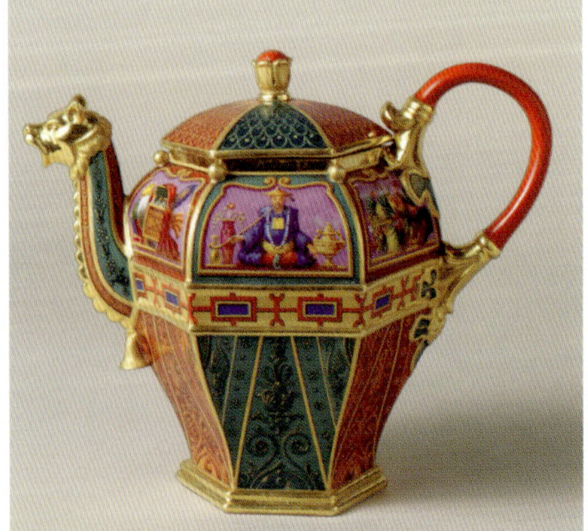

42 Chinese-style Teapot (*théière chinoise "Fragonard"*)

Sèvres, 1826–7
Hard-paste porcelain
Alexandre-Évariste Fragonard, designer; Pierre Huard, painter
H. 5⁵⁄₁₆ in. (13.5 cm), L. 6¹³⁄₁₆ in. (17.3 cm)
Collection of the Musée National de Céramique, Sèvres (MNC 24.784)

MARKS: Crossed letters *C* enclosing a fleur-de-lis for the reign of Charles X (1824–30) over *SEVRES* and the date mark *27*

PROVENANCE: This is either the example delivered to Queen Marie-Amélie in 1832 or the one the queen chose as a gift to her sister-in-law Madame Adélaïde in 1833; Museum Purchase, 1979

RELATED EXAMPLES: According to the records, two teapots with rich chinoiserie decoration were painted by Pierre Huard in 1826 and entered the sales registers in 1827, however, they remained unsold until 1832–33.

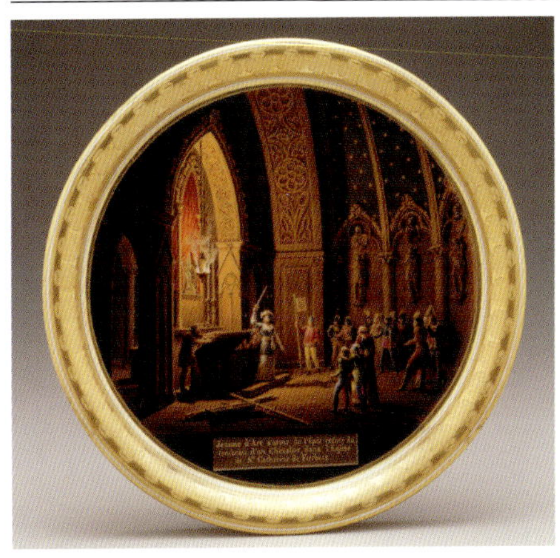

43 "Joan of Arc" Plate

Sèvres, 1818
Hard-paste porcelain
Jean-Claude Rumeau, painter; François-Antoine Boullemier *l'aîné*, gilder
H. 7/8 in. (2.2 cm), Dia. 9 5/16 in. (23.7 cm)
The Twinight Collection (inv. no. S-110)

MARKS: Crossed letters *L* enclosing the word *Sevres* and a fleur-de-lis for the reign of Louis XVIII (1814–24)

PROVENANCE: Delivered to Ernst I, Duke of Saxony-Coburg-Saalfeld, 1818; Daniela Kumpf, Munich, 2000; acquired by present owner 20 January 2005

RELATED EXAMPLES: Two other similar plates from a set of three for the Duke of Saxony-Coburg-Saalfeld are in the Twinight Collection, New York, including the plate depicting a page leading a stallion (below) and another with gazelles in a forest (inv. no. S-109).

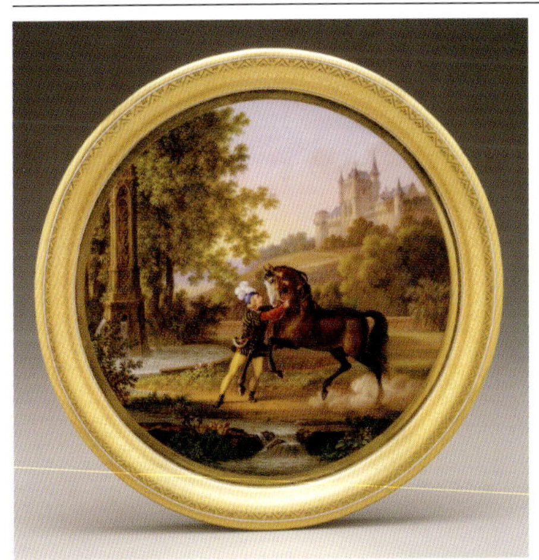

44 "Page Leading a Stallion" Plate

Sèvres, 1818
Hard-paste porcelain
Jean-Charles Develly, painter; François-Antoine Boullemier *l'aîné* or Antoine-Gabriel Boullemier *jeune*, gilder
H. 7/8 in. (2.2 cm), Dia. 9 5/16 in. (23.7 cm)
The Twinight Collection (inv. no. S-111)

MARKS: Crossed letters *L* enclosing the word *Sevres* and a fleur-de-lis for the reign of Louis XVIII (1814–24)

PROVENANCE: Delivered to Ernst I, Duke of Saxony-Coburg-Saalfeld, 1818; Daniela Kumpf, Munich, 2000; acquired by present owner 20 January 2005

RELATED EXAMPLES: Two other similar plates from a set of three for the Duke of Saxony-Coburg-Saalfeld are in the Twinight Collection, New York, including the Joan of Arc plate (above) and another with gazelles in a forest (inv. no. S-109).

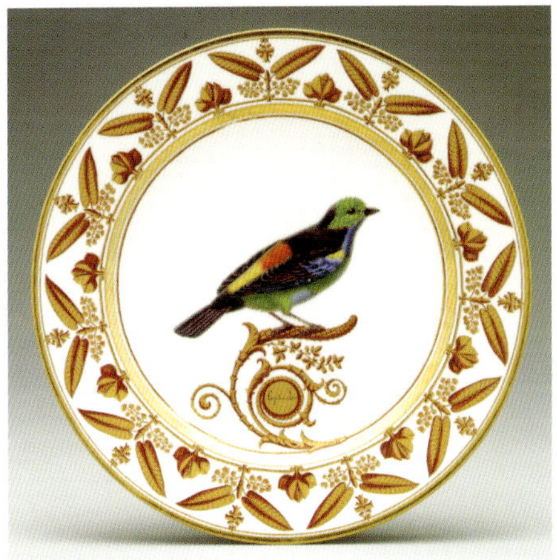

45 Plate from the South American Bird Service
(*assiette plate*)

Sèvres, 1819–21
Hard-paste porcelain
Madame Knip (née Pauline de Courcelles), painter of birds; Jean-Charles-François Leloy, designer of borders
H. 1 1/16 in. (2.8 cm), Dia. 9 1/4 in. (23.5 cm)
Collection of Hillwood Estate, Museum & Gardens Bequest of Marjorie Merriweather Post, 1973 (acc. no. 24.136.2)

MARKS: Crossed letters *L* enclosing a fleur-de-lis for the reign of Louis XVIII (1814–24); date mark *20* and *"27 janvier . T20 no. 27"* next to border in gold; inscribed on front *Euphore teïté* and signed *fme Knip*

PROVENANCE: Presented by Charles X to the duchesse d'Angoulême; sold Parke-Bernet New York, 7 March 1952, lot 55

RELATED EXAMPLES: Seven other plates (24.136.1-.8), two sugar bowls and stands (24.163.11 and .13), and a compote (24.136.16) from this service, called *Service des oiseaux d'Amérique du Sud*, are in the collection of Hillwood Estate, Museum & Gardens, Washington, D.C.; two plates from this service are in the Twinight Collection, New York (inv. nos. S-151 and S-152); another plate is in the collection of the Musée National de Céramique, Sèvres; and an ice pail from this service is in the collection of the National Museum of Wales, Cardiff.

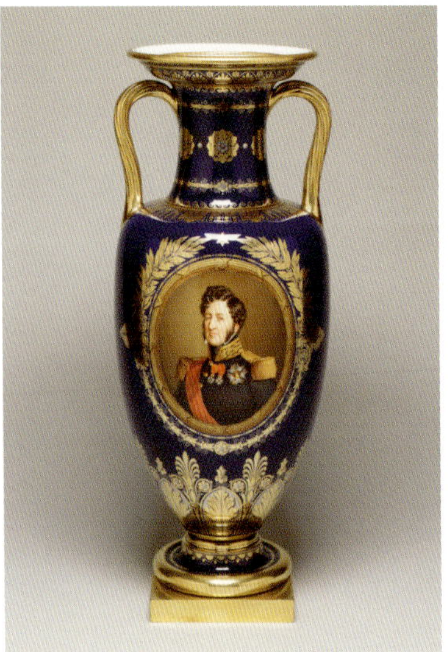

46 Vase with a Portrait of King Louis-Philippe (one of a pair)

(vase "Étrusque Caraffe")

Sèvres, 1844
Hard-paste porcelain
Nicolas-Marie Moriot, figure painter (after prints after portraits by Franz Xavier Winterhalter)
H. 17½ in. (44.4 cm)
Collection of the Walters Art Museum, Baltimore, Maryland (48.555)

MARKS: *LP* (in monogram) / *SEVRES* / *1844* on inside rim in black; signed *Moriot*

PROVENANCE: Queen Marie-Amélie (delivered to the queen on the verbal order of King Louis-Philippe, Paris, 8 January 1845; acquired by Henry Walters, Baltimore, prior to 1931

RELATED EXAMPLES: The pair to this vase, featuring a portrait of Queen Marie-Amélie, is in the collection of the Walters Art Museum, Baltimore (inv. no. 48.556); a similar pair of vases called *vases Lancel* with portraits of the Duke and Duchess of Nemours and also painted by Moriot were sold at Christie's Paris, 16 December 2003, lot 132.

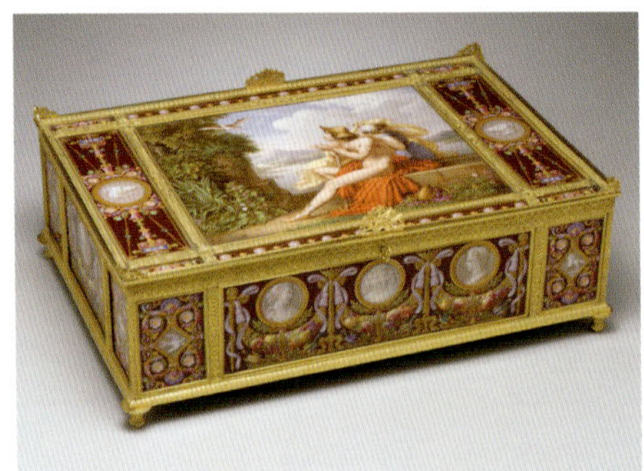

47 Letter Casket for Queen Marie-Amélie of France

(coffret épistolaire)

Sèvres, 1834
Hard-paste porcelain, gilt bronze
Jean-Charles-François Leloy, designer; Étienne-Charles Le Guay, painter of pictorial panels; Pierre Huard, painter of ornaments
H. 5 15/16 in. (15 cm), L. 17¾ in. (45 cm), W. 11 13/16 in. (30 cm)
The Twinight Collection (inv. no. S-154)

MARKS: hidden by mounts

PROVENANCE: Delivered to Marie-Amélie, Queen of the French, 2 December 1834; Collection of M. Castille, Saint-Cloud, sold, Mes. Jacques Martin & Olivier Desbenoit, Versailles, 17 March 1991, lot 185; Acquired Sotheby's New York, 10 November 2006, lot 56

RELATED EXAMPLES: Another casket, formerly the property of Queen Marie Amélie with views of the châteaux at Neuilly, St. Cloud, Eu, Fontainebleau and the château Royal (1841) is in the collection of the Fondation Napoléon, Paris.

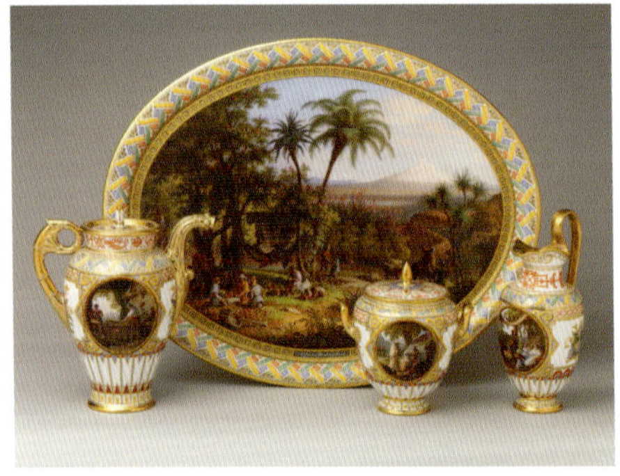

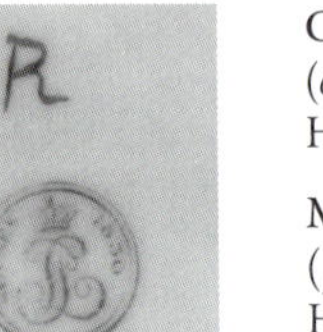

48 Partial Coffee Set

(déjeuner "Culture et récolte du cacao")

Sèvres, 1836
Hard-paste porcelain
Jean-Charles Develly, designer, painter of reserves and decorator (active 1813–47); Pierre Riton, gilder and painter of borders
Collection of the Metropolitan Museum of Art Purchase, The Charles E. Sampson Memorial Fund and Gift of Irwin Untermyer, by exchange, 1986 (1986.281.1ab–.4)

Coffee Pot
(cafetière "Campanienne")
H. 7½ in. (19.1 cm)

Milk Jug
(pot à lait ovoïde)
H. 7 7/16 in. (18.9 cm)

Sugar Bowl
(pot à sucre ovoïde)
H. 5½ in. (14 cm)

Tray
L. 17⅝ in. (44.8 cm), W. 13 11/16 in. (34.8 cm)

MARKS: All have circular stamp enclosing letters *LP* surmounted with a crown and the word *SEVRES* for the reign of Louis-Philippe (1830–48) and the date 1836; some have the letter *R* in gold (or traces of a mark) for gilder Pierre Riton (active 1821–60)

PROVENANCE: Delivered to Queen Marie-Amélie of France on 21 August 1837; Armin Allen, New York

RELATED EXAMPLES: A first identical set dated 1832 was a gift to the Spanish politician and ambassador to London and Paris, the marqués de Miraflores, in 1835, and is now in a private collection.

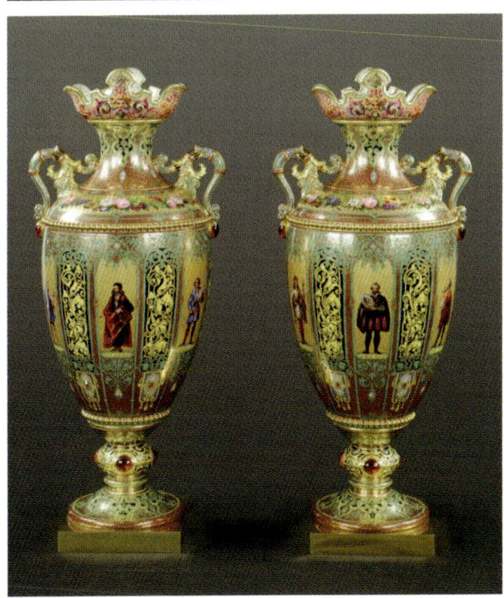

49 Pair of Renaissance Revival Vases

(*vases "Adélaïde"*)

Sèvres, 1841
Hard-paste porcelain, gilt bronze
Jean-Charles-François Leloy, designer (active 1816–44); Alexis-Étienne Julienne, painter of ornament and figures (active 1837–48); Pierre-Antoine Sinsson, painter of flowers (active 1818–48)
H. 16⅞ in. (42.9 cm)
Collection of the Wadsworth Atheneum Museum of Art, Hartford, CT
The European Decorative Arts Purchase Fund and The Douglas Tracy Smith and Dorothy Potter Smith Fund (2004.1.1 and 2004.1.2)

MARKS: Circular stamp enclosing letters *LP* surmounted with a crown and the word *SEVRES* for the reign of Louis-Philippe (1830–48) and the year 1841

PROVENANCE: Sent to Louis-Philippe in April 1843 to serve as a gift to an unidentified recipient

RELATED EXAMPLES: A pair of *vases Adélaïde* with battle scenes on blue ground in imitation of Limoges Renaissance enamels (1844) is in the collection of the Musée du Louvre, Paris; another similar pair is in the collection of the Musée Condé, Chantilly.

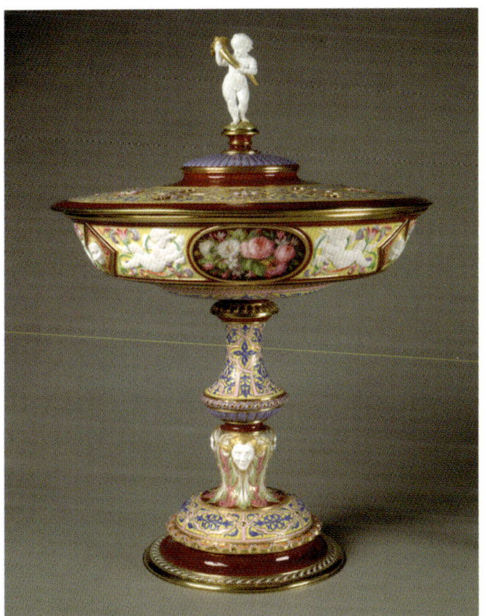

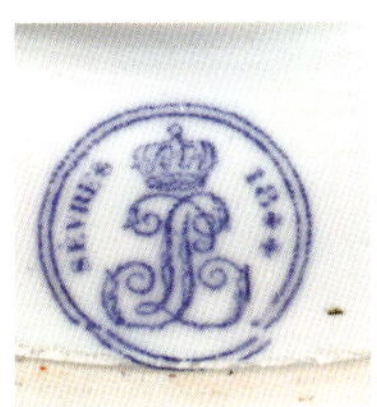

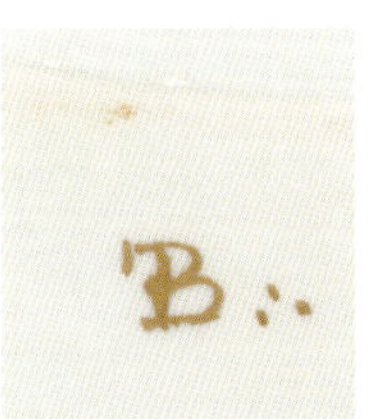

50 Covered Cup

(*coupe "Cassolette"*)

Sèvres, 1844
Hard-paste porcelain
Hyacinthe-Jean Regnier, modeler; François-Hubert Barbin, decorator; Jacques-Nicolas Sinsson, painter of flowers
H. 19¼ in. (49 cm), Dia. 14 in. (35.6 cm)
Collection of the Cleveland Museum of Art
Severance and Greta Millikin Purchase Fund (2001.121)

MARKS: Circular stamp in blue enclosing letters *LP* surmounted with a crown and the word *SEVRES* for the reign of Louis-Philippe (1830–48) and the year 1844; artist's mark of letter *B* and three dots in gold

PROVENANCE: Acquired in 1846 by Marie-Amélie, Queen of France; soon thereafter presented to an unknown person

RELATED EXAMPLES: A similar neo-Renaissance covered cup *(coupe Henri II, unie)* with grisaille enamelwork on a dark blue ground is in the collection of the Wadsworth Atheneum, Hartford, CT (2003.3.1a,b); an uncovered standing cup *(coupe "Chenavard")* with a vibrant red ground decorated in the manner of sixteenth-century Saint-Porchaire is in the collection of the Metropolitan Museum of Art, New York (2003.153).

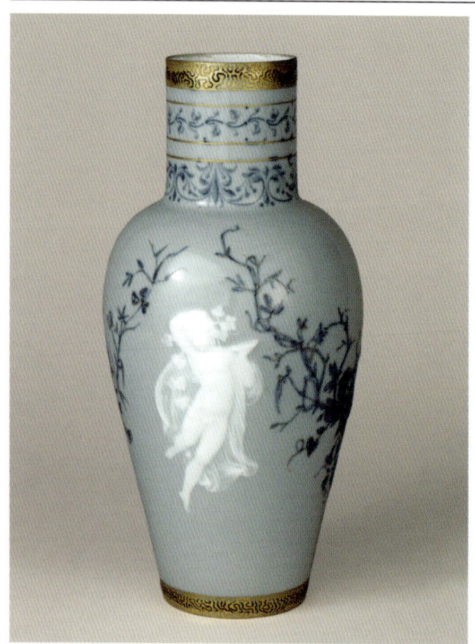

51 Vase "Ly" with Celadon Ground

Sèvres, 1850
Hard-paste porcelain *(pâte sur pâte)*
Ambroise Choiselat, designer (active 1849–56)
H. 12¼ in. (31.1 cm)
Collection of the Musée National de Céramique, Sèvres (MNC 4.178)

MARKS: Marked with *JC 50*

RELATED EXAMPLES: Another *vase Ly* with white and gold *pointillé* ground and Persian-style flowers (dated 1868) is in the collection of the Musée National de Céramique, Sèvres; a pair of *vases Ly* (dated 1851–2) with celadon ground, dark blue accents around the base and neck, and stylized flowers in white applied in *pâte sur pâte* is in the collection of the Victoria and Albert Museum, London (C.291-1921 and C.292-1921).

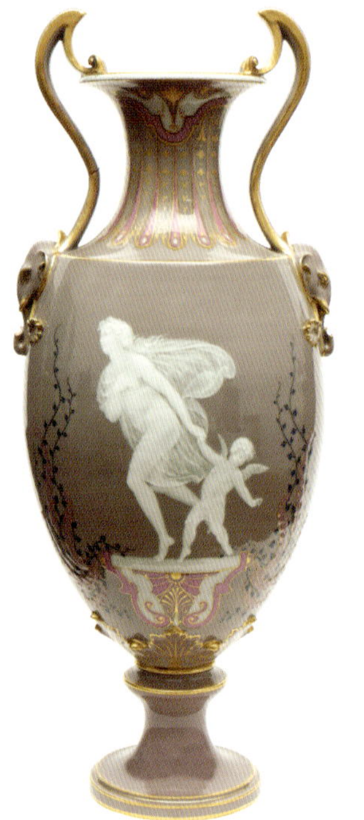

52 Vase

(vase ovoïde tronqué)

Sèvres, 1869
Hard-paste porcelain *(pâte sur pâte)*
Marc-Louis-Emmanuel Solon, decorator
H. 22 in. (55.9 cm)
Collection of the Wadsworth Atheneum Museum of Art, Hartford, CT
Bequest of Reverend Alfred Duane Pell (1925.467)

MARKS: The monogram *MLS* for artist Marc-Louis-Emmanuel Solon; stamp of an oval enclosing *S.69* in green for the year 1869; *N 69* printed and crowned in red

PROVENANCE: Collection of Reverend Alfred Duane Pell

RELATED EXAMPLES: A *vase bijou* with the same kind of changing paste, called *caméleon*, is in the collection of the Musée National de Céramique, Sèvres.

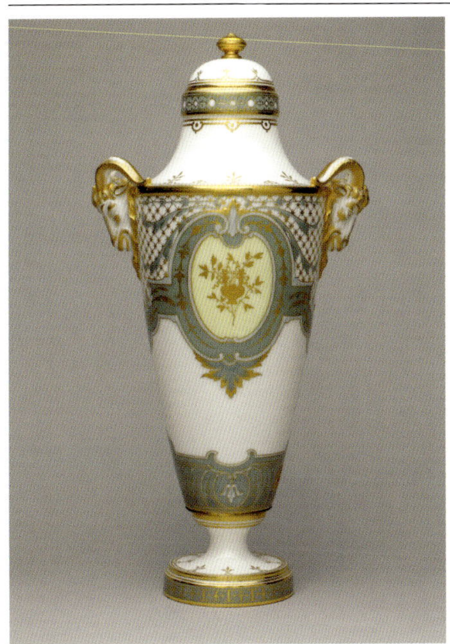

53 Vase "Boizot"

Sèvres, 1882
Hard-paste porcelain
Albert-Ernest Carrier-Belleuse, designer
H. 14¾ in. (37.5 cm); W. 7⅜ in. (18.7 cm)
Collection of the National Museum of American History, Smithsonian Institution, Kenneth E. Behring Center (cat. no. 93611a-b)

MARKS: Circular stamp in red enclosing the letters *RF* for République Française and *DECORE A SEVRES* and the date mark *82*; *S.74.* in oval stamped in green

PROVENANCE: Museum purchase from Bur Arts, Paris, about 1883

RELATED EXAMPLES: A similarly shaped *vase Boizot* with a figure of a nymph rowing a boat in *pâte sur pâte* is in the collection of the Musée National de Sèvres (MNC 26.653).

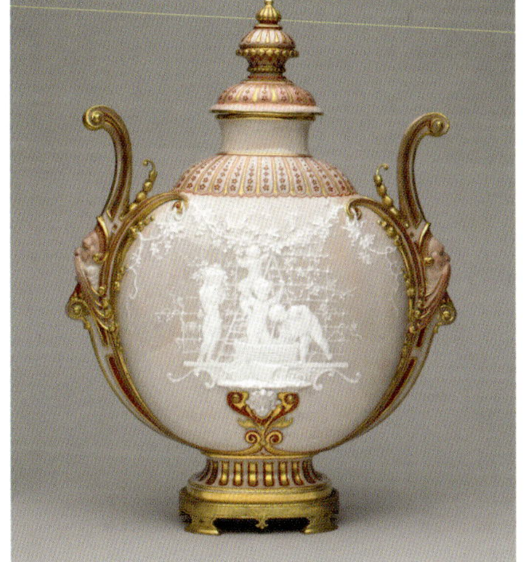

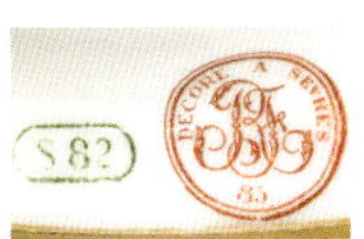

54 Pink and Gold Flask

(gourde "d'Asti")

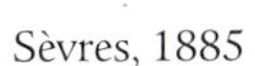

Sèvres, 1885
Hard-paste porcelain (*pâte sur pâte*)
Albert-Ernest Carrier-Belleuse, designer; Jules Archelais, decorator
H. 11⅞ in. (30.2 cm), L. 9¼ in. (23.5 cm), W. 3⅝ in. (9.2 cm)
Collection of the National Museum of American History, Smithsonian Institution, Kenneth E. Behring Center (cat. no. 93614a-b)

MARKS: Circular stamp in red enclosing intertwined letters *RF* for République Française and *DECORE A SEVRES* and the date mark *85*; *S82* stamped in oval in green; decoration signed *JA* for Jules Archelais (active 1865–1902)

RELATED EXAMPLES: A dark blue example (dated 1887), picturing a decorative paste application in the neoclassical style of a draped woman and cherubs is in the collection of the Musée National de Céramique, Sèvres (MNC 10.706); another example with a gray ground and blue and gold decoration is in the collection of the Conservatoire National des Arts et Métiers and is currently on loan to the Musée d'Orsay, Paris (CNAM 10451).

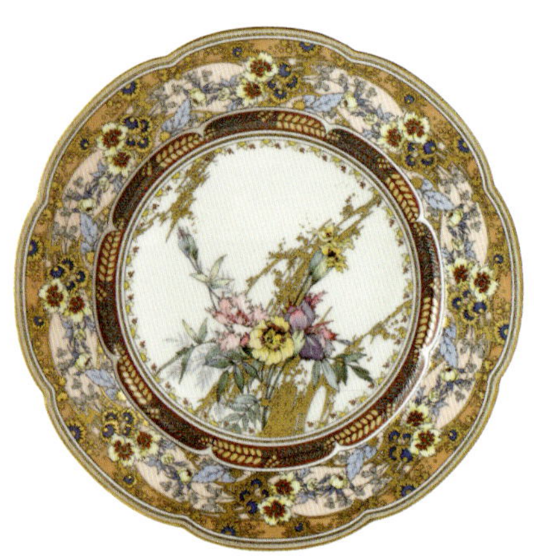

55 Plate from the *Service Lobé*

(*assiette lobée*)

Sèvres, 1888
Hard-paste porcelain
Jules-Auguste Habert-Dys, designer of decoration; Achille-Louis Bonnuit, painter (active 1858–62, 1865–93)
Dia. 10 in. (25.4 cm)
Collection of the Musée National de Céramique, Sèvres (MNC 9.148)

MARKS: Circular stamp enclosing the monogram *RFS* and the words *Décoré à Sèvres*; oval stamp enclosing *S.88* for the year 1888

RELATED EXAMPLES: This plate is part of one of the few table services produced at Sèvres at the end of the nineteenth century.

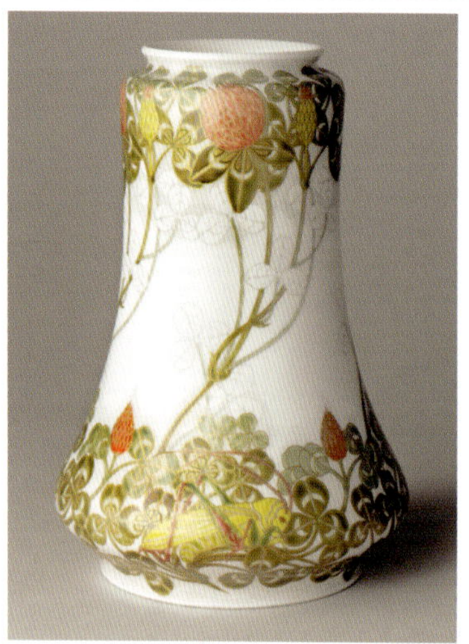

56 Vase du Bourget "B"

Sèvres, 1895–1901
Soft-paste porcelain
Alexandre Sandier, designer; Henri-Louis-Laurent Ulrich, decorator (after Geneviève Rault)
H. 7 in. (18 cm)
Collection of the Musée National de Céramique, Sèvres (MNC 16.072)

MARKS: Circular stamp enclosing the monogram *RFS/Décoré à Sèvres/1901*; triangular stamp enclosing the letter *S* and the year 1900

RELATED EXAMPLES: Sandier designed numerous forms for the factory, many of which are now in the collection of the Musée National de Céramique, Sèvres.

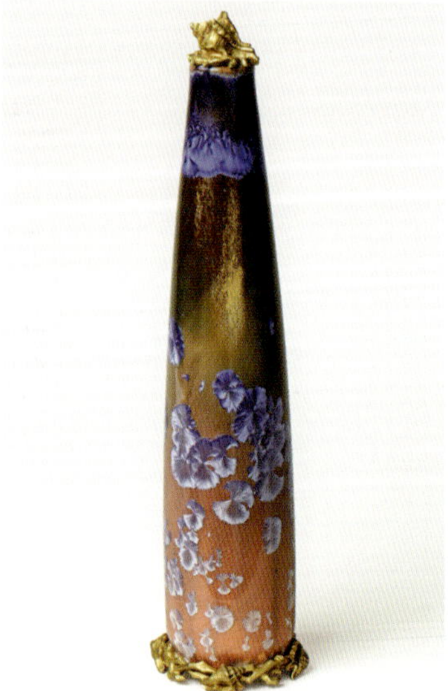

57 Vase "de Marnes"

Sèvres, 1904
Hard-paste porcelain (*pâte nouvelle*), crystallized glazes, gilt bronze
Alexandre Sandier, designer
H. 9⅘ in. (24.9 cm)
Collection of the Musée National de Céramique, Sèvres (MNC 15.519)

MARKS: Impressed triangle in black (for *pâte nouvelle*) enclosing the letter *S* over the year 1904

RELATED EXAMPLES: A *vase "de Varennes"* and a *vase "d'Igny"* with similar crystallized decorations are in the collection of the Musée National de Céramique, Sèvres.

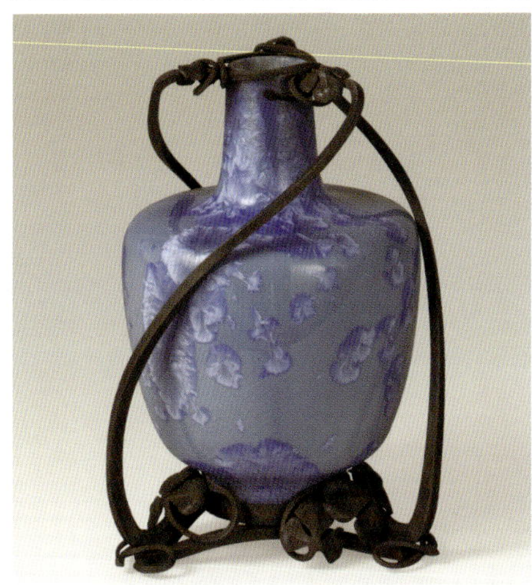

58 Vase "de Neuilly"

Sèvres, 1900
Hard-paste porcelain (*pâte nouvelle*), crystallized glazes, silver
Alexandre Sandier, designer
H. 5½ in (14 cm)
Collection of the Musée National de Céramique, Sèvres (MNC 15.529)

MARKS: Impressed triangle in black (for *pâte nouvelle*) enclosing the letter *S* over the year 1900

RELATED EXAMPLES: See cat. no. 57

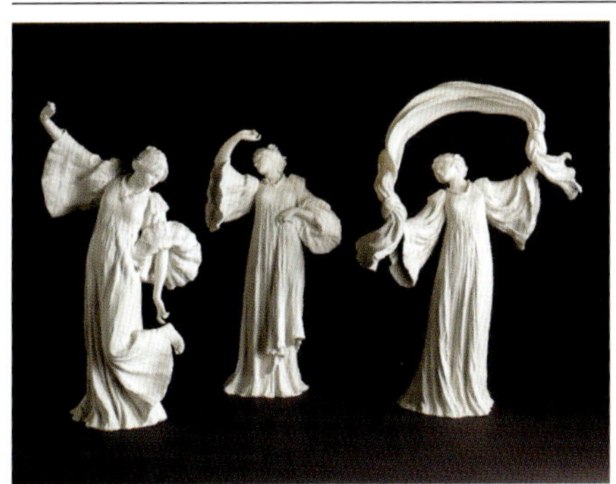

59 Dancing Figures from *Le Jeu de l'Écharpe* Centerpiece (*surtout de table*)

Sèvres, 1900 (editions of 1905 and 1914)
New hard-paste biscuit porcelain
Agathon Léonard van Weydenfeld
H. approx. 20¼ in. (51.6 cm); 18½ in. (47 cm); 17¼ in. (43.7 cm)
Collection of the Musée National de Céramique, Sèvres (MNC 16.624, MNC 17.260^{bis}, and MNC 17.262^{bis})

RELATED EXAMPLES: Figures from the scarf dance centerpiece are in the collection of the State Hermitage Museum, St. Petersburg; some figures are in the collection of the Victoria and Albert Museum, London (C.89-1971, C.89E-1971, C.89J-1971, C.89K-1971, C.89M-1971); at least six figures are in the collection the Art Institute of Chicago (1985.106a–f).

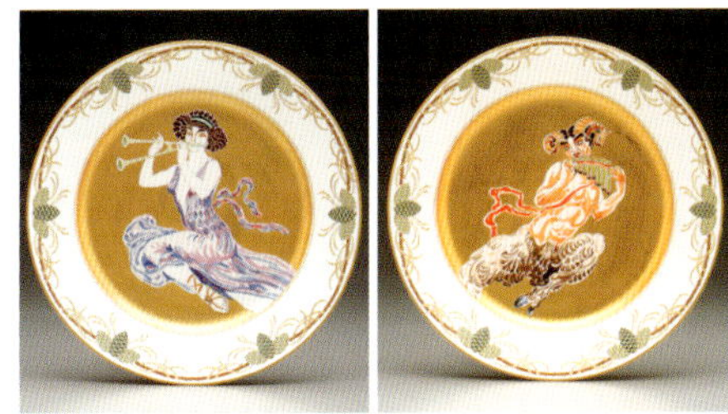

60 "Bacchante" and "Satyr" Plates

Sèvres, 1913
Hard-paste porcelain (*pâte nouvelle*)
Louis-Jules Mimard, painter; M. Maignan, designer
Dia. 9⅜ in. (23.9 cm)
Bacchante: *Collection of Hillwood Estate, Museum & Gardens Museum Purchase, 2008 (acc. no. 2008.6.1)*
Satyr: *Gift of Hillwood Museum Collectors Circle, 2008 (acc. no. 2008.6.2)*

MARKS ON BOTH PLATES: Printed factory marks in green *S85* within an oval frame; red *RF MANUFACTURE NATIONALE DÉCORÉ À SÈVRES 1913* within a heart-shaped frame for 1913; painted mark *Mimard d'après Maignan*

PROVENANCE: Private Collection, France, to 2007; Adrian Sassoon, London, 2008

RELATED EXAMPLES: This pair of plates formed part of an original set of three ("3 assiettes échantillon de la jardinière Maignan") made as trials for a new and large experimental work consisting of a big planter (*jardinière*) to be decorated with porcelain plaques of a similar subject and with the same technique. The whereabouts of the third plate are unknown.

61 Night-Light

(veilleuse "Rapin")

Sèvres, 1923
Hard-paste porcelain (*pâte nouvelle*)
Henri Rapin, designer; Jean-Baptiste Gauvenet, decorator
H. 16.9 in. (43 cm)
Collection of the Musée National de Céramique, Sèvres (MNC 25.496)

MARKS: Printed in a rectangle in black is *S/1923/DN*; marked in red with the year 1923

PROVENANCE: Transfer from the Manufacture Nationale de Sèvres to the Museum on 24 December 1986

RELATED EXAMPLES: In the 1920s, Rapin designed a series of lighting devices including a couple of sconces, a pair of vases with fruits, a luminescent fountain in collaboration with sculptor and modeler Jean-Baptiste Gauvenet, which is in the collection of Le Pavillion de Sèvres, London and an electrified lamp, which is in the collection of the Mobilier National, Paris.

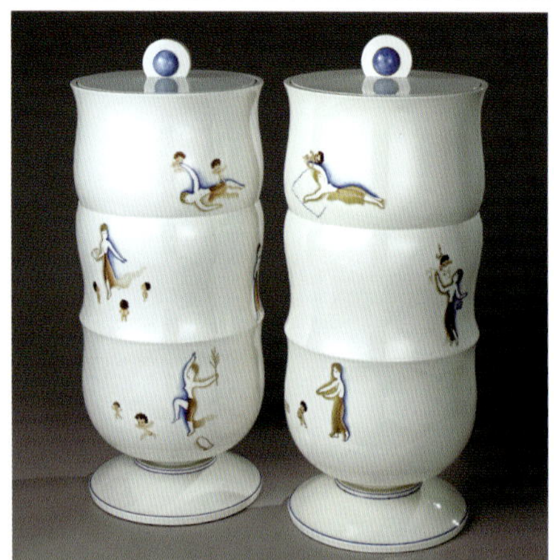

62 Pair of Vases Decorated with Stylized Figures

(vases "Prou" nº 4)

Sèvres, 1935
Hard-paste porcelain (*pâte nouvelle*)
René Prou, designer; Madame Max Vibert, decorator
H. 13⅜ in. (34 cm)
Collection of Mobilier National at Musée National de Céramique (MNC 9559.1-.2)

MARKS: Rose-shaped stamp (*à la rose*) in black with the letter *S* and *SÈVRES MANUFACTURE NATIONALE FRANCE* (fabrication mark used 1928–41) over the date letter *I* for 1935–6; inscribed in blue with *CF* (intertwined letters) *d'ap. de Me Max Vibert - nº 33–34*

RELATED EXAMPLES: A number of similarly shaped *vases Prou nº 2* (form created in 1933), with different surface decoration by artists such as Jean Serrière, Roland Goujon, and François Quelvée, are in the collection of the Mobilier National, Paris.

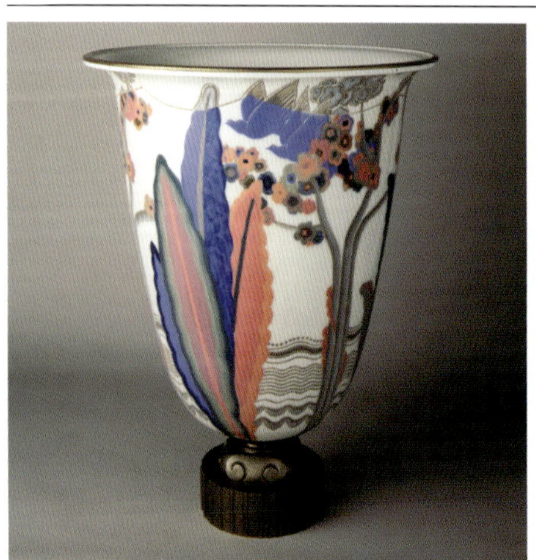

63 Vase "Ruhlmann" Nº 2

Sèvres, 1926–7
Hard-paste porcelain (*pâte nouvelle*)
Émile-Jacques Ruhlmann, designer; Anne-Marie Fontaine, decorator
H. 19½ in. (50 cm)
Collection of the Musée National de Céramique, Sèvres (MNC 17.718)

MARKS: Marked *PN* in black; inscribed with the signature of the decorator *AM FONTAINE*

RELATED EXAMPLES: Multiple vases of this form and of related forms designed by Ruhlmann with different surface decorations by various artists, such as Anne-Marie Fontaine and Irène Chambon, are in the collection of the Manufacture Nationale de Sèvres and the Mobilier National, Paris.

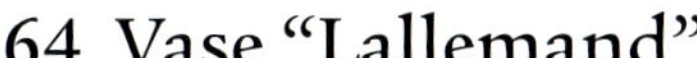

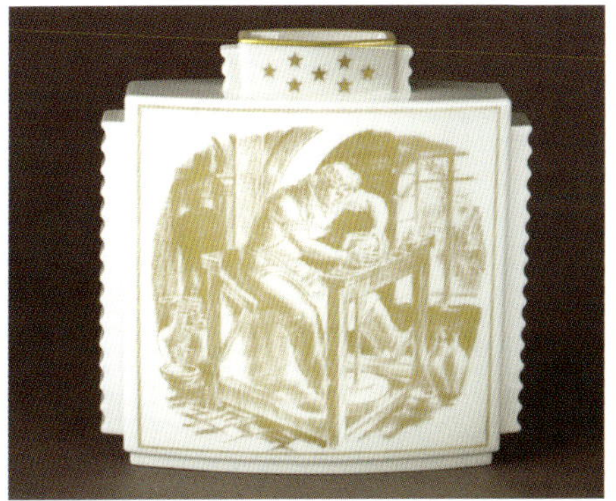

64 Vase "Lallemand"

Sèvres, 1944
Hard-paste porcelain (*pâte nouvelle*)
H. 8½ in. (21.6 cm), L. 8¾ in. (22.2 cm)
Collection of the Musée National de Céramique, Sèvres (MNC 25.573)

MARKS: Sèvres fabrication monogram in black (for *pâte nouvelle*) over the date mark *44*; circular stamp in red for the decoration (indicating low-fired decoration or *petit feu*) with the words *MANUFACTURE NATIONALE/DORÉ A SÈVRES* and the date letter *D* for 1944

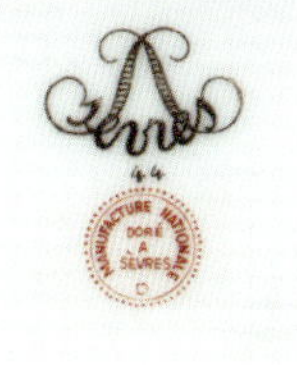

PROVENANCE: Transfer from the Manufacture Nationale de Sèvres to the Museum in 1987

RELATED EXAMPLES: Another smaller *vase Lallemand* featuring a profile portrait of the French General Philippe Pétain on one side, and his quote "Il n'y a pas de société sans amitié, sans confiance, sans dévouement" on the reverse, is in the collection of the Musée National de Céramique, Sèvres (MNC 25.571).

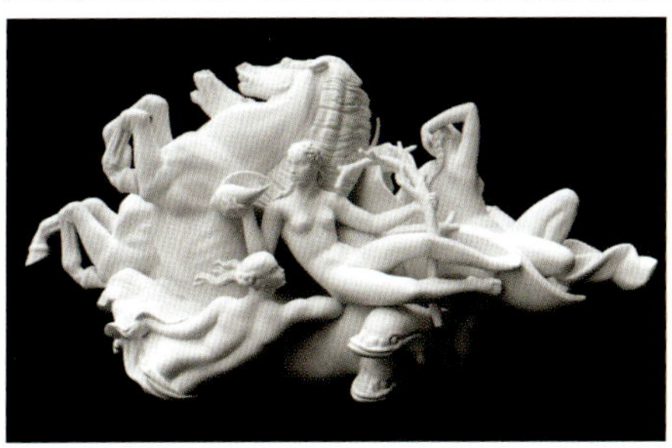

65 Central Group from the *Dauphins et Mouettes* Centerpiece

(*surtout de table*)

Sèvres, 1951–5
Biscuit porcelain
Henri-Albert Lagriffoul, sculptor
H. 14³⁄₁₆ in. (36 cm), L. 30 in. (76.2 cm)
Collection of the Manufacture Nationale de Sèvres, département des collections

66 Plate from the Wedding Service for Princess Elizabeth of England

(*assiette Uni*)

Sèvres, 1947
Hard-paste porcelain
Raymond Subes, designer
Dia. 9¾ in. (24.8 cm)
Collection of the Manufacture Nationale de Sèvres

MARKS: Rose-shaped stamp (*à la rose*) in green with the letter *S* and *SÈVRES MANUFACTURE NATIONALE FRANCE* (fabrication mark used 1928–41) and the date letter *m* for 1940; circular stamp in red for the decoration (indicating low-fired decoration or *petit feu*) with the words *MANUFACTURE NATIONALE/DORÉ A SÈVRES* and the date letter *G* for 1947; signed in gold *Décor de R. Subes*

RELATED EXAMPLES: The majority of this service is in the Queen's collection and was featured in the exhibition *A Royal Wedding: 20 November 1947*, Queen's Gallery, Buckingham Palace, 1997. Also, see cat. no. 67.

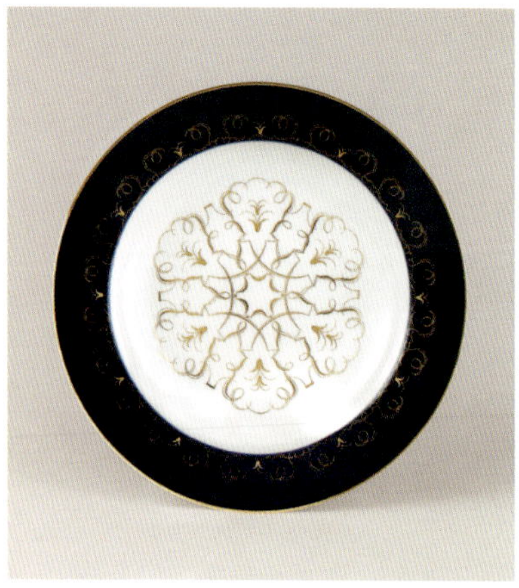

67 Plate from the Service for the French Ministry of the Post and Telecommunications

(assiette Uni)

Sèvres, 1947
Hard-paste porcelain (*pâte nouvelle*)
Raymond Subes, designer
Dia. 9⅜ in. (23.8 cm)
Collection of the Manufacture Nationale de Sèvres

MARKS: Rose shaped stamp (*à la rose*) in black (for *pâte nouvelle*) (fabrication mark used 1928–41) and the date letter *e* for 1930; circular stamp in red for the decoration with the words *MANUFACTURE NATIONALE/DORÉ A SÈVRES* and the date letter *G* for 1947

RELATED EXAMPLES: Raymond Subes decorated three similar services in the course of 1947 for official use and gifts. The first of these services was delivered to Princess Elizabeth of England in 1947 (see cat. no. 66), the second service was a gift of the French government to Eva Perón, the First Lady of Argentina, and the third service, this one, went to the French Ministry of the Post and Telecommunications.

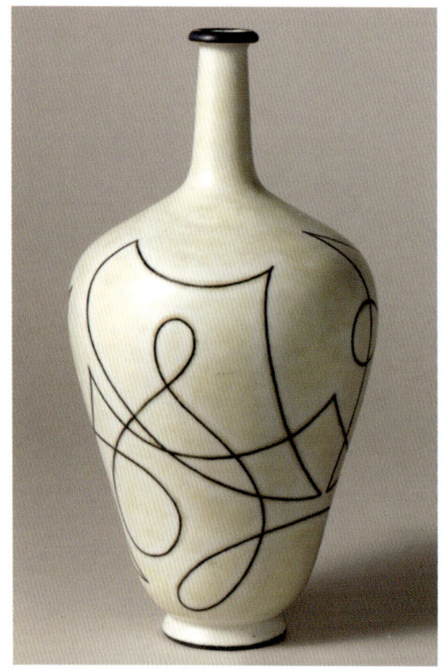

68 Vase "Métayer" 3

Sèvres, 1952–3
Hard-paste porcelain
Élaine Métayer-Trannoy, designer; René-Gabriel Marchal, decorator
H. 11 13/16 in. (30 cm)
Collection of the Musée National de Céramique, Sèvres (MNC 28.676)

MARKS: Sèvres fabrication monogram in black over the date mark *59* and the date letter *S* for 1959 indicating the year of decoration; inscribed in black with *AB d'ap. MARCHAL* and the project number 38–53

RELATED EXAMPLES: One example is in the collection of the Manufacture Nationale de Céramique, Sèvres; another is in a private collection in Paris.

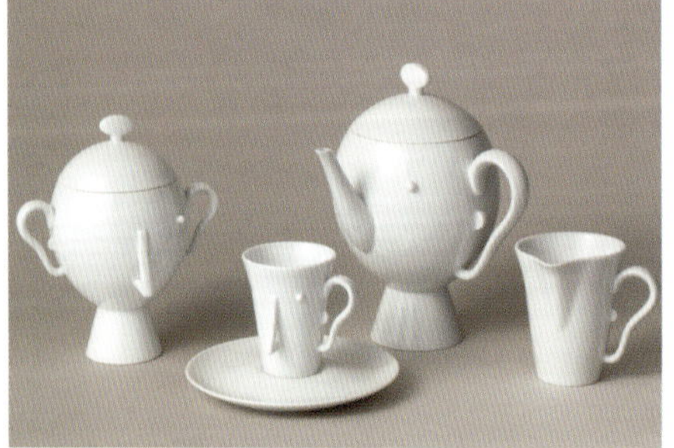

69 Coffee Service

(service à café)

Sèvres, 1959–61 (2005 edition in collaboration with Dina Vierny et Gaston galleries in Paris)
Hard-paste porcelain
Robert Couturier, sculptor
Coffee Pot H. 7⅜ in. (18.8 cm); Sugar Bowl H. 6⅛ in. (15.6 cm); Milk Jug H. 3¼ in. (8.3 cm); Cups H. 6⅛ in. (7.1 cm); Saucers Dia. 5 5/16 in. (13.5 cm)
Collection of the Manufacture Nationale de Sèvres

MARKS: Some pieces bearing the "Mathieu" fabrication monogram in green (indicating hard paste); all pieces stamped in red with *MODELE MANUFACTURE NATIONALE DE SEVRES* or *MODELE M.N.S.*; inscribed in gray with the signature of the artist *Couturier*; all pieces have a white label stating the artist's name, the title of the piece, the model number and the date *1961, édition 2005*

RELATED EXAMPLES: This set is a recent (2005) limited edition of twelve sets based on an early prototype (ca. 1961), which did not go into production at the time.

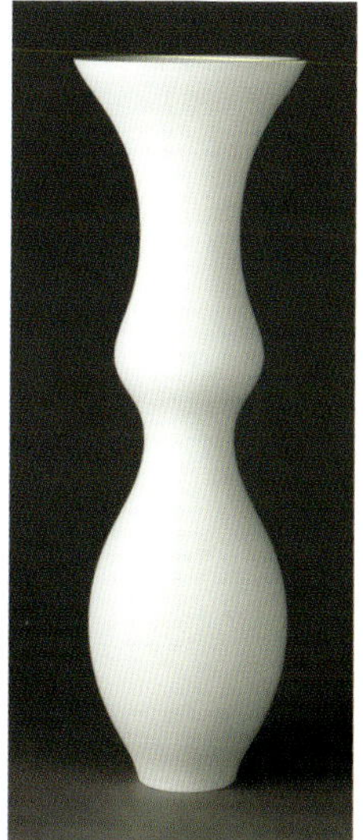

70 Vase Nº 4 from the *Amphores de rêve* Series

Sèvres, 1966
Hard-paste porcelain (*pâte nouvelle*)
Jean Arp
H. 18¾ in. (47.5 cm)
Collection of the Musée National de Céramique, Sèvres (MNC 25.355)

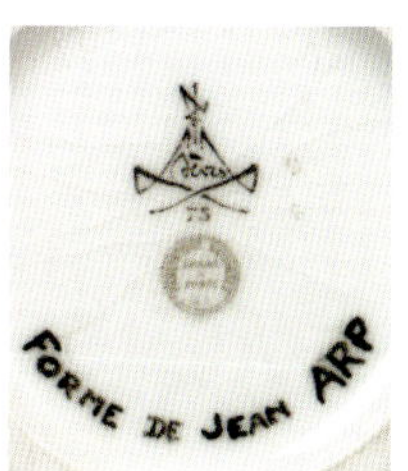

MARKS: Sèvres monogram in brown/black (for *pâte nouvelle*) (fabrication mark used from 1970) over the date mark *75*; circular stamp in gray for the decoration (indicating high-fired decoration or *grand feu*) with the words *MANUFACTURE NATIONALE/DORÉ A SÈVRES*; inscribed in black *FORME DE JEAN ARP*

RELATED EXAMPLES: This vase is from a series of six vases (in two different sizes) designed by Arp and called *Amphores de rêve*. Four of these vases went into production as limited editions of ten (of each design), with some being concluded under the supervision of Arp's widow up to 1968.

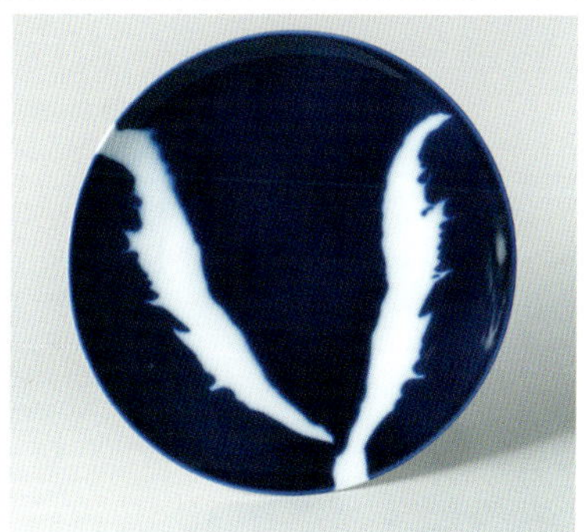

71 Plate
(*assiette à dessert "Diane"*)

Sèvres, 1972
Hard-paste porcelain (*pâte Antoine d'Albis*)
Étienne Hajdu
Dia. 8⅞ in. (22.5 cm)
Collection of the Musée National de Céramique, Sèvres (MNC 25.422)

MARKS: Sèvres monogram in blue (for *pâte Antoine d'Albis*) (fabrication mark used from 1970) over the date mark *72*; circular stamp in blue for the decoration with the words *MANUFACTURE NATIONALE/DORÉ A SÈVRES* and the date letters *AE* for 1971; inscribed in green script *17 Hajdu 70*

17 Hajdu 70

PROVENANCE: Transfer from the Manufacture Nationale de Sèvres to the Museum in 1986

RELATED EXAMPLES: Hajdu also designed a table service for the Elysée Palace under the presidency of Georges Pompidou that was delivered in 1972.

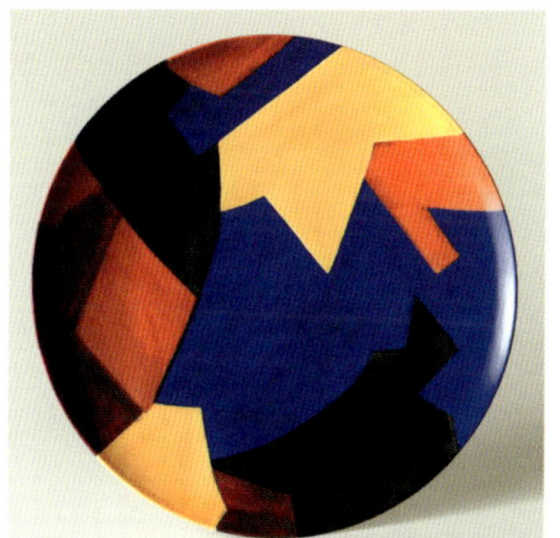

72 Plate
(*assiette plate "Diane"*)

Sèvres, 1969–72
Hard-paste porcelain
Serge Poliakoff
Dia. 10¼ in. (26 cm)
Collection of the Musée National de Céramique, Sèvres (MNC 25.458)

MARKS: Sèvres monogram in green (indicating *pâte dure*) (fabrication mark used 1942–69) over the date mark *69*; circular stamp in blue for the decoration with the words *MANUFACTURE NATIONALE/DÉCORÉ A SÈVRES* and the date letters *AF* for 1972; inscribed in grey *A.P. d'après Serge POLIAKOFF*

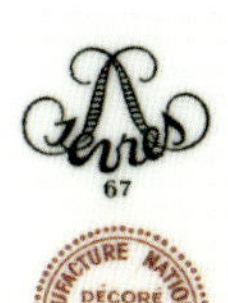

PROVENANCE: Transfer from the Manufacture Nationale de Sèvres in 1986

RELATED EXAMPLES: Produced in a limited edition of forty-eight examples.

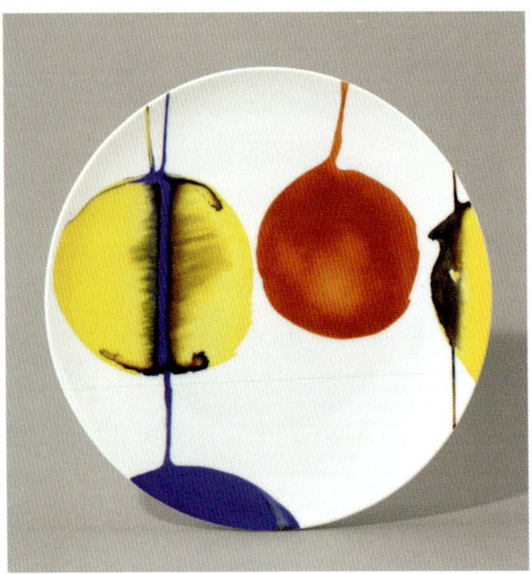

73 Plate

(assiette plate "Diane")

Sèvres, 1969–70
Hard-paste porcelain
Alexander Calder
Dia. 10¼ in. (26 cm)
Collection of the Musée National de Céramique, Sèvres (MNC 25.369)

MARKS: Sèvres monogram in blue (for *pâte Antoine d'Albis*) (mark used from 1970) over the date mark *69* and the date letters *AD* for 1970 in red; inscribed in grey *D. d'après Calder* and the project number *5.69*

RELATED EXAMPLES: Alexander Calder created four different designs of this type in 1969–73, published in forty-eight examples of each design.

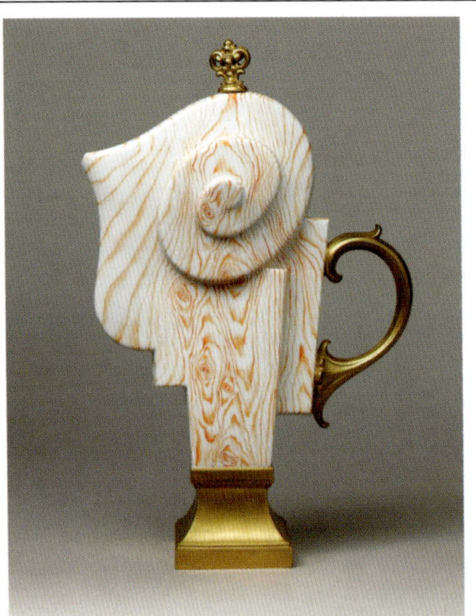

74 Teapot

(théière "Crevette")

Sèvres, 1984–5 (decorated 1991)
New soft-paste porcelain
Adrian Saxe (decorated by Gilles Bouttaz)
H. 12¾ in. (32.4 cm), L. 8¼ in. (21 cm)
Collection of the Musée National de Céramique, Sèvres (MNC 26.876)

MARKS: Sèvres monogram in blue over the date mark *91* and date letters *AY*; inscribed in blue with the letter *B* and *SAXE*

PROVENANCE: Transfer from the Manufacture Nationale de Sèvres to the Museum in 1987

RELATED EXAMPLES: Adrian Saxe created this teapot with nine different *trompe-l'oeil* surface decorations, each decoration being produced in a limited edition of twelve teapots.

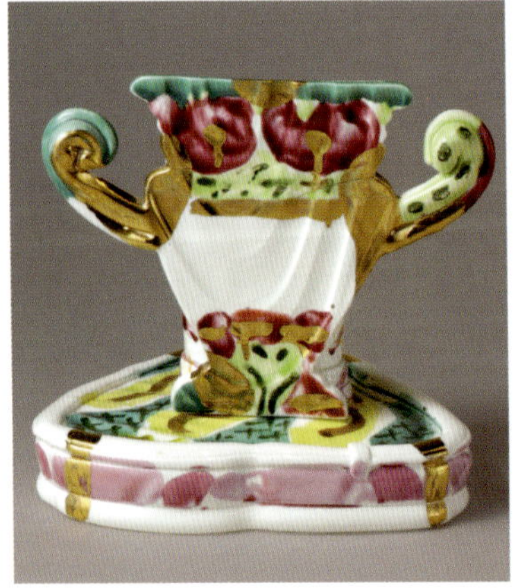

75 Vase sur console

Sèvres, ca. 1987
New soft-paste porcelain (*porcelaine de Sèvres*)
Betty Woodman
Vase H. 8³⁄₁₆ in. (20.8 cm), L. 5½ in. (14 cm); Console H. 7¹³⁄₁₆ in. (19.8 cm), W. 7¹³⁄₁₆ in. (19.8 cm)
Collection of the Musée National de Céramique, Sèvres (MNC 28.374)

MARKS: none

RELATED EXAMPLES: This vase is one of a limited edition of seven produced between 1987 and 1992. Woodman also created another vase in *pâte nouvelle* with a bracket/console, which was produced in a limited edition of fifteen. While an artist in residence at Sèvres in 1987, Woodman made a number of one-off pieces such as "Centerpiece nº 2", known as *vase sur console peint*. She also made some cups in 1988 and a series of decorated pieces in 2007.

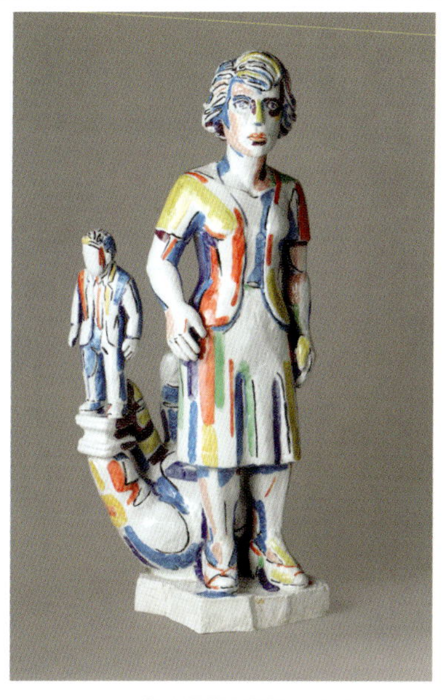

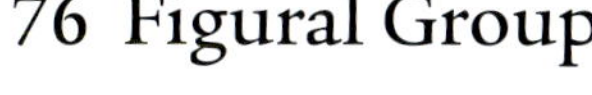

76 Figural Group

Sèvres, 1990
Soft-paste porcelain
Viola Frey
H. $12\frac{3}{4}$ in. (32.3 cm), W. 15 in. (38.1 cm)
Collection of the Musée National de Céramique, Sèvres (MNC 27.045)

MARKS: Sèvres monogram impressed; signed by the artist *V.F 90* and incised *V. FREY*

RELATED EXAMPLES: Another similar figural group is in the collection of the Musée National de Céramique, Sèvres (MNC 27.044).

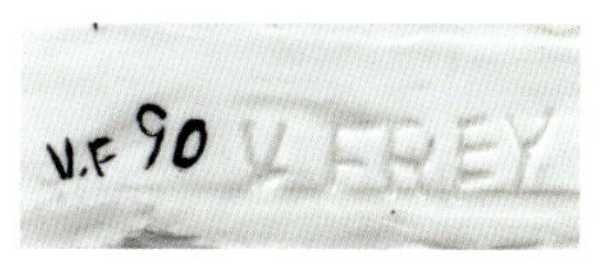

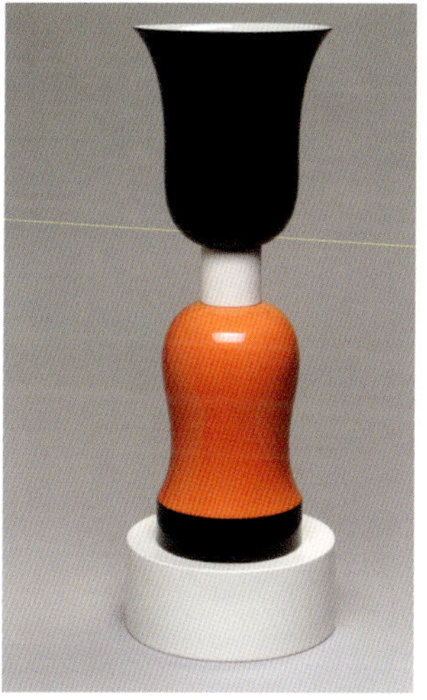

77 "Sybilla" Vase

Sèvres, 1994–5 (decorated 2006)
Enameled porcelain
Ettore Sottsass
H. $21\frac{7}{8}$ in. (55.6 cm), Dia. $8\frac{1}{16}$ in. (20.5 cm)
Collection of the Manufacture Nationale de Sèvres

MARKS: Crossed letters *L* in black with the number *2006*; the words *Manufacture nationale décoré à Sèvres* and the letters *BN*; signed in back by the artist *ETTORE SOTTSASS* over the words *MODELE M.N.S.*

RELATED EXAMPLES: This vase is from a series of fourteen vases designed by Sottsass for Sèvres between 1994 and 1996, examples of which are in the collections of the Musée National de Céramique, Sèvres and the Manufacture Nationale de Sèvres.

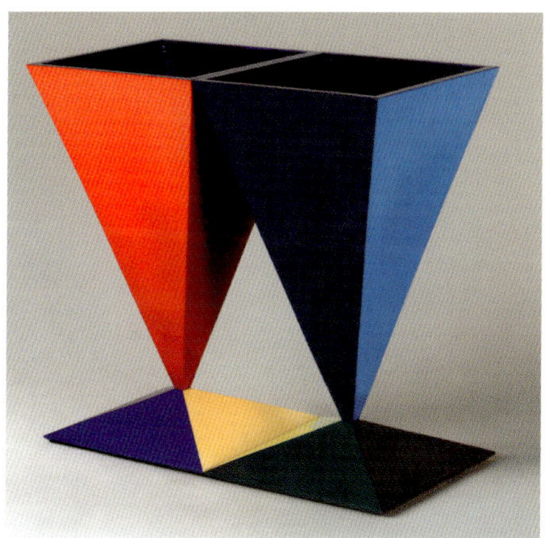

78 "Reform" Vase

Sèvres, 1995
Soft-paste porcelain
Richard Peduzzi
H. $12\frac{5}{8}$ in. (32 cm), L. $14\frac{3}{16}$ in. (36 cm)
Collection of the Musée National de Céramique, Sèvres (MNC 27.846)

MARKS: Sèvres fabrication monogram in green with a red stamp for the decoration; the date letters *BD* in red; inscribed with the signature of the artist *RICHARD PEDUZZI*

RELATED EXAMPLES: Peduzzi created additional versions of the Reform Vase, such as a green, blue, and black example, which is now in the collection of the Manufacture Nationale de Sèvres.

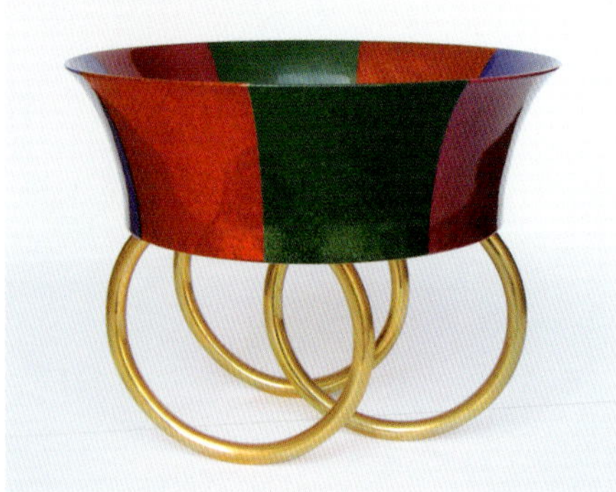

79 Coupe "Excelsior"

Sèvres, 1996–7
Soft-paste porcelain
Mathilde Bretillot
H. 7½ in. (19 cm), Dia. 9¼ in. (23.5 cm)
Collection of the Artist

MARKS: Hand-painted signature of the artist

RELATED EXAMPLES: Bretillot's *coupe Excelsior nº 2* is currently on loan to the Musée des Arts Décoratifs, Paris (inv. no. Sèvres BJ 166).

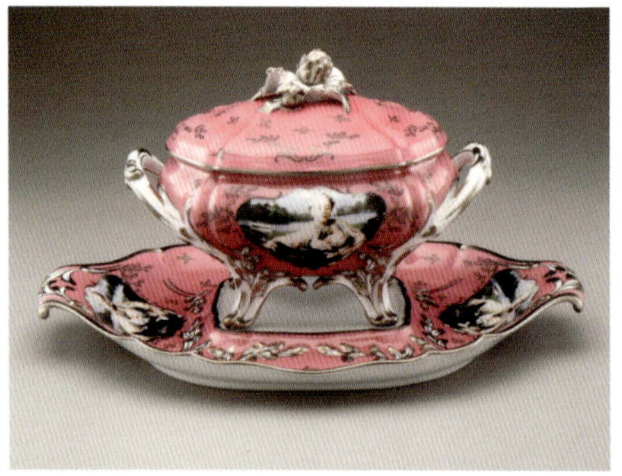

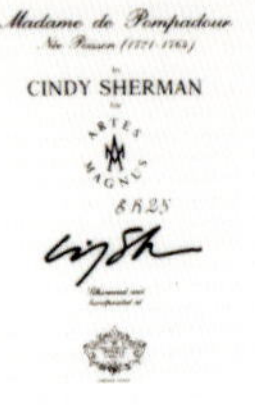

80 "Madame de Pompadour (née Poisson)" Tureen and Platter

Limoges, 1990
Porcelain
Cindy Sherman
H. 14½ in. (36.8 cm), W. 22 in. (55.9 cm)
Collection of Hillwood Estate, Museum & Gardens Museum Purchase, 2006 (acc. no. 26.283.1–.2)

MARKS: Signed and limited edition numbered by the artist and publisher

PROVENANCE: Collection of David Whitney, New York; sold Sotheby's New York, 11 November 2006, lot 260

RELATED EXAMPLES: Created by Cindy Sherman and published by Artes Magnus, this tureen and platter set was produced by the Ancienne Manufacture Royale de Limoges in four traditional eighteenth-century colors—pink, apple green, blue, and yellow—and limited to twenty-five of each color version.

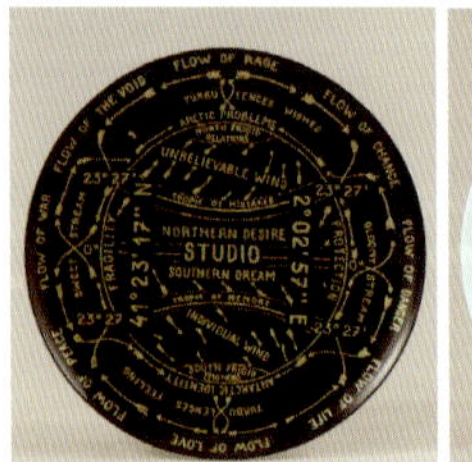

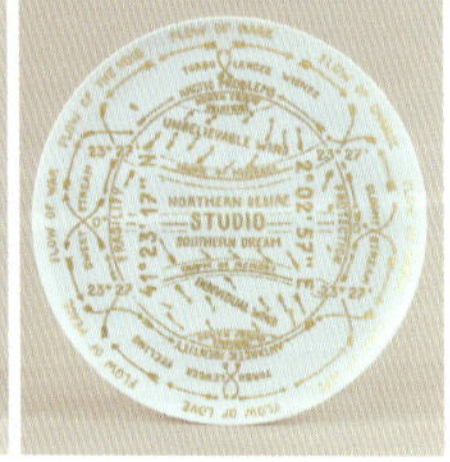

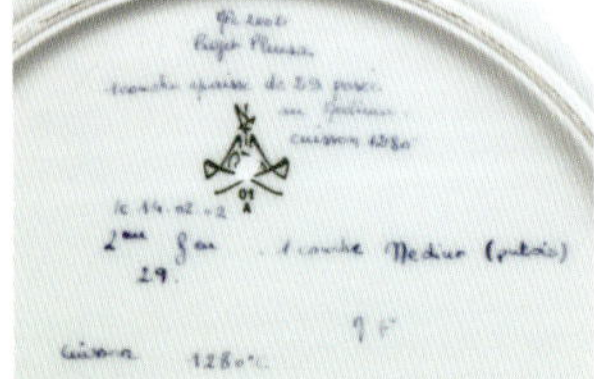

81 Plates from the Service for the Élysée Palace
(assiettes "Diane")

Sèvres, 2001–2
Hard-paste porcelain (*pâte Antoine d'Albis*)
Jaume Plensa
Dia. 11 7/16 in. (29 cm)
Collection of the Manufacture Nationale de Sèvres

MARKS: Blue plate has "Mathieu" fabrication monogram in green with *86 A. MODELE MANUFACTURE NATIONALE DE SEVRES* in blue; inscribed in blue with *essai Plensa Juin 2001 18 couches mince Essence Fontarome cuisson 1360º C Pose au minceau egalise à la mousse Sandy*; brown plate has "Mathieu" fabrication monogram in green over stamp of *01* and *A*; inscribed in blue with *MFC 2002 Projet Plensa 1 couche epaisse de 29 posée au medium cuisson 1280 le 14.02.02 2me feu 29 1 couche medium (putois) cuisson 1280º C CMF*

RELATED EXAMPLES: Plensa created various versions of this plate in different colors—with gold décor on dark brown, dark blue, medium blue, light blue, and pale yellow backgrounds.

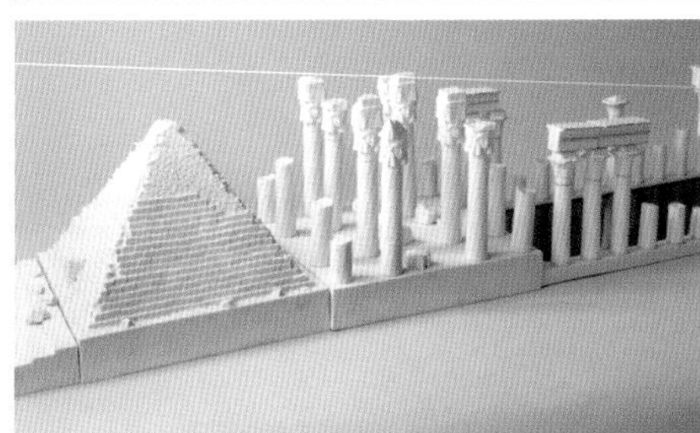

82 "Ruins of Egypt" Centerpiece

(*surtout "Ruines d'Égypte"*)

Sèvres, 1979
Hard-paste biscuit porcelain
Anne and Patrick Poirier
H. 9⅞ in. (25 cm), L. (maximum) 145¼ in. (368.9 cm)
Collection of the Musée National de Céramique, Sèvres

MARKS: One basin with the Sèvres monogram in green over the date mark *79A* and the other basin with the Sèvres monogram in green over the date mark *79*; stairs incised with *APP* with double letters *S* within an oval and *1979 DC*; pyramid incised with *APP* with double letters *S* and *Sèvres* within an oval and *1979 J-G*; colossus incised with *APP 1984* with double letters *S* within an oval and *MB*

RELATED EXAMPLES: There is another example in the collection of the Manufacture Nationale de Sèvres.

Biscuit pieces included in an Historical Table Setting

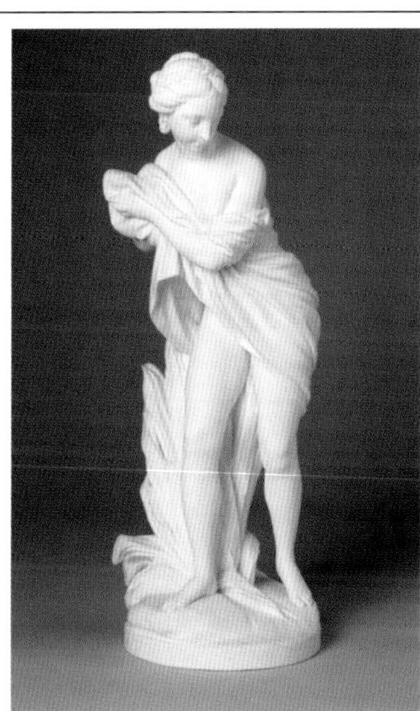

83 Biscuit Figure of a Bather

(*La Baigneuse aux roseaux*)

Sèvres, ca. 1744
Soft-paste biscuit porcelain
Model by Étienne-Maurice Falconet (ca. 1758)
H. 14 in. (35.5 cm)
Private Collection

RELATED EXAMPLES: Made in three sizes, this being of the second size, as a pendant piece to *La Baigneuse* in cat. no. 84. For a model of this group, see Émile Bourgeois, *Le Biscuit de Sèvres*, vol. II, plate 15, no. 93.

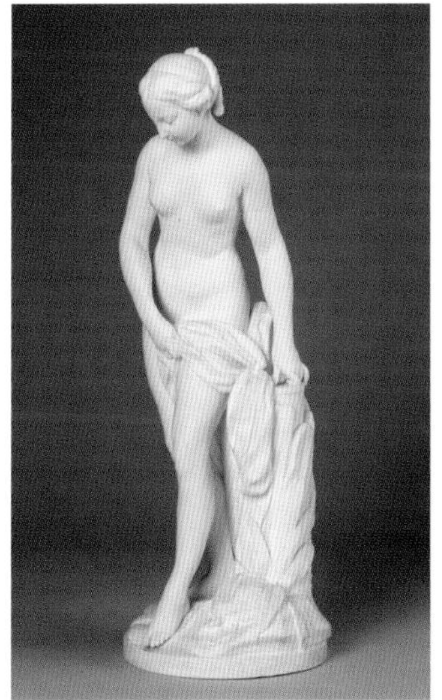

84 Biscuit Figure of a Bather

(*La Baigneuse*)

Sèvres, ca. 1770
Soft-paste biscuit porcelain
Model by Étienne-Maurice Falconet (ca. 1758)
H. 14³⁄₁₆ in. (36 cm)
Private Collection

RELATED EXAMPLES: Made in three sizes, this being of the second size, based on Falconet's life-size marble sculpture in the collection of the Musée du Louvre, Paris. For a model of this group, see Emile Bourgeois, *Le Biscuit de Sèvres*, vol. II, plate 6, no. 91.

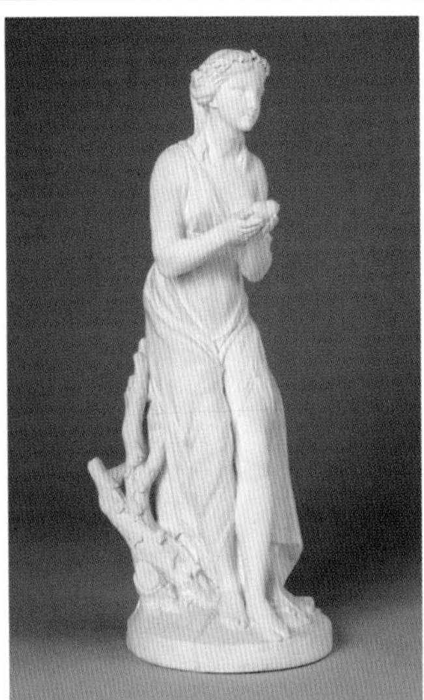

85 Biscuit Figure of *L'Amitié au Coeur* (Friendship and the Heart)

Sèvres, ca. 1766–73
Soft-paste biscuit porcelain
Model by Étienne-Maurice Falconet (1764)
H. 13⅞ in. (35.3 cm)
Private Collection

RELATED EXAMPLES: For a model of this group, see Émile Bourgeois, *Le Biscuit de Sèvres*, vol. II, plate 7, no. 16.

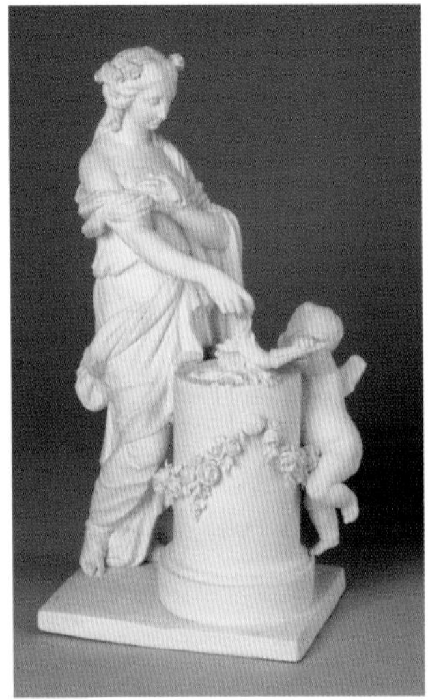

86 Biscuit Group of *L'Autel de l'Amitié* (The Altar of Friendship)

Sèvres, ca. 1772
Soft-paste biscuit porcelain
Possibly modeled by Louis-Simon Boizot
H. 14$\frac{3}{16}$ in. (36 cm)
Private Collection

MARKS: Incised with the letter *B* on the base

PROVENANCE: Sotheby's New York, 3 June 2008, lot 216.

RELATED EXAMPLES: For a model of this group, see Émile Bourgeois, *Le Biscuit de Sèvres*, vol. II, plate 43. A similar group in the collection of Mrs. Lawrence Copley Thaw, Sr. sold at Sotheby's New York, 3 October 2007, lot. 227; another example sold at Christie's London, 10 July 2007, lot 133.

Bibliography

Albainy, Tracey. "Flowers for the Empress: The Sèvres Service des plantes de la Malmaison et les liliacées." *French Porcelain Society Journal*, vol. III, 2007, pp. 191–210.

Arend, Liana Paredes. *Sèvres Porcelain at Hillwood*. Washington, D.C.: Hillwood Museum & Gardens, 1998.

Arizzoli-Clémentel, Pierre, et al. *Marie-Antoinette: Galeries nationales du Grand Palais, Paris, 15 mars–30 juin 2008*. Paris: Éditions de la Réunion des musées nationaux, 2008.

Arminjon, Catherine, and Nicole Blondel. *Objets civils domestiques: vocabulaire*. Paris: Imprimerie Nationale, 1984.

Babelon, Jean-Pierre. *Versailles et les tables royales en Europe: XVIIème – XIXème siècles*. Paris: Éditions de la Réunion des musées nationaux, 1993.

Baulez, Christian. *Versailles, deux siècles d'histoire de l'art*. Paris: Éditions Faton/Société des amis de Versailles, 2007.

Birioukova, Nina, and Natalia Kazakevitch. *Sevrskii farfor XVIII veka: Katalog kollektsii (La porcelaine de Sèvres du XVIII siècle: Catalogue de la collection)*. St. Petersburg: Izdatelstvo Gosudarstvennogo Ermitazha, 2005.

Blondel, Nicole, and Tamara Préaud. *La Manufacture nationale de Sèvres: parcours de blanc à l'or*. Charenton: Flohic Éditions, 1996.

Boone, Mary Lou. *Terre et Feu: Four Centuries of French Ceramics from the Boone Collection*. Pasadena, CA: Clark Humanities Museum, Scripps College, 1998.

Bourgeois, Émile, et al. *Les Biscuits de Sèvres: recueil des modèles de la manufacture de Sèvres au XVIIIe siècle*. Paris: Pierre Lafitte & Cie, 1914.

Clark, Garth, ed. *Ceramic Millennium: Critical Writings on Ceramic History and Art*. Halifax: Press of the Nova Scotia College of Art and Design, 2006.

Coffin, Sarah D., et al. *Rococo: The Continuing Curve, 1730–2008*. New York: Cooper-Hewitt, National Design Museum, 2008.

Corrin, Lisa G., and Joaneath Spicer, eds. *Going for Baroque: 18 Contemporary Artists Fascinated with the Baroque and Rococo*. Baltimore: The Contemporary and the Walters, 1995.

Coural, Jean. *Le Palais de l'Elysée: histoire et décor*. Paris: Délégation à l'action artistique de la ville de Paris, 1994.

Courajod, Louis, ed. *Livre-Journal de Lazare Duvaux, marchand-bijoutier ordinaire du roy (1748–58)*, 2 vols., 1st edn. 1873; Paris: F. de Nobele, 1965.

d'Albis, Antoine. "Les débuts de la peinture figurative sur porcelaine." *Salon International de la Céramique de Collection et des Arts du Feu*, 1999, pp. 62–72.

de Bellaigue, Geoffrey. *Sèvres Porcelain from the Royal Collection*. London: Queen's Gallery, 1979.

de Chavagnac, Xavier, and Gaston de Grollier. *Histoire des manufactures françaises de porcelaine*. Paris: Alphonse Picard et Fils, 1906.

de Commines, Laurent, and Eric Gizard, eds. *Un âge d'or des arts décoratifs, 1814–1848*. Paris: Éditions de la Réunion des musées nationaux, 1991.

de Humboldt, Alexandre. *Vues des Cordillères et monumens des peuples indigènes de l'Amérique*, 1st edn. 1810; Nanterre: Éditions Erasme, 1989.

de Rochebrune, Marie-Laure. "Charles Nicolas Dodin, Miniature Painter at Sèvres." *Antiques*, October 2000, pp. 524–33.

de Rochebrune, Marie-Laure. "La passion de Madame de Pompadour pour la porcelaine," in Salmon, Xavier, et al. *Madame de Pompadour et les arts*. Paris: Éditions de la Réunion des musées nationaux, 2002.

de Villechenon, Marie-Noëlle Pinot. *Sèvres: Une collection de porcelaines, 1740–1992*. Paris: Éditions de la Réunion des musées nationaux, 1993.

Dauterman, Carl Christian. "Sèvres Figure Painting in the Anne Thompson Dodge Collection." *The Burlington Magazine*, November 1976, pp. 753–62.

Dauterman, Carl Christian. *The Wrightsman Collection, Vol. IV: Porcelain*. New York: The Metropolitan Museum of Art, 1970.

Dawson, Aileen. *French Porcelain: A Catalogue of the British Museum Collection*. London: British Museum Press, 1994.

Dawson, Aileen. "Some Thoughts on the Clientele of the Vincennes/Sèvres Factory in the Eighteenth Century." *French Porcelain Society Journal*, vol. III, 2007, pp. 36–44.

Ducamp, Emmanuel, ed. *Pavlovsk: The Palace and the Park, The Collection*, vols. 1–2. Paris: Alain de Gourcuff Éditeur, 1993.

Ennès, Pierre. "Four Plates from the Sèvres Service des Arts Industriels." *Journal of the Museum of Fine Arts Boston*, 1990, pp. 89–106.

Ennès, Pierre. "The Visit of the comte and comtesse du Nord to the Sèvres Manufactory." *Apollo*, March 1989, pp. 150–6 and 220–2.

Ennès, Pierre. *Un défi au goût: 50 ans de création à la manufacture royale de Sèvres (1740–1793)*. Paris: Éditions de la Réunion des musées nationaux, 1997.

Eriksen, Svend. *Davids Samling, fransk porcelæn (The David Collection, French Porcelain)*. København (Copenhagen): Davids Samling, 1980.

Erisken, Svend. *Sèvres Porcelain: The James A. de Rothschild Collection at Waddesdon Manor*. Fribourg, Switzerland: Office du Livre, 1968.

Eriksen, Svend, and Geoffrey de Bellaigue. *Sèvres Porcelain: Vincennes and Sèvres 1740–1800*. London: Faber and Faber, 1987.

Faÿ-Hallé, Antoinette. *Cinquante ans de céramique française, 1955–2005: une collection nationale*. Paris: Éditions de la Réunion des musées nationaux, 2005.

Faÿ-Hallé, Antoinette. *De l'immense au minuscule: la virtuosité en céramique*. Paris: Éditions de la Réunion des musées nationaux, 2005.

Gascar, Pierre. *Humboldt l'explorateur*. Paris: Éditions Gallimard, 1985.

Glueck, Grace. "Betty Woodman, Turning the Humble Vase into High Art." *New York Times*, April 28, 2006.

Grandjean, Serge, and Marcelle Brunet. *Les grands services de Sèvres: Exposition 25 mai – 29 julliet*. Paris: Éditions de la Réunion des musées nationaux, 1951.

Hargrove, June. *The Life and Work of Albert Carrier-Belleuse*. New York and London: Garland Publishing, 1977.

Kazakevitch, Nathalie. "Porcelaine de Sèvres: le service égyptien en Russie." *Sèvres, Revue de la Société des Amis du Musée National de Céramique*, no. 4, 1995, pp. 24–9.

Krog, Ole Villumsen. "Service Diplomatique." *Connaissance des Arts*, November 1993, pp. 152–61.

Lambán, Javier, et al. *Sèvres, 1740–2006*. Zaragoza, Spain: Diputación de Zaragoza, 2006.

Laurin, Isabelle. "L'Art déco à Sèvres: retour à une porcelaine tendre siliceuse." *Sèvres, Revue de la Société des Amis du Musée National de Céramique*, November 2005, pp. 83–92.

Laurin, Isabelle. "Les artistes russes à Sèvres au temps des avant-gardes." *L'Estampille/L'Objet d'Art*, January 2008, pp. 60–7.

Laurin, Isabelle. "Sèvres au féminin." *L'Estampille/L'Objet d'Art*, February 2005, pp. 52–9.

Lechevallier-Chevignard, Georges. *La Manufacture de porcelaine de Sèvres*. Paris: Renouard, 1908.

Le Taillandier, C. "Une bouillotte en porcelaine bordelaise." *Sèvres, Revue de la Société des Amis du Musée National de Céramique*, no. 17, 2008, pp. 49–65.

Louvre des antiquaires. *Sèvres: de 1850 à nos jours: exposition du 4 février au 10 avril 1983*. Paris: Le Louvre, 1983.

Manufacture nationale de Sèvres. *Années 50: l'effet céramique*. Paris: Éditions courtes et longues, 2006.

Manufacture nationale de Sèvres. *Créations diverses à Sèvres depuis 1965*. Paris: Bernard Chauveau, 2003.

Manufacture nationale de Sèvres. *Sèvres: tradition et innovation de Bachelier à Jim Dine*, 1999.

"Mélanges en souvenir d'Elisalex d'Albis." *Sèvres, Revue de la Société des Amis du Musée National de Céramique*, 1999.

Midant, Jean Paul. *Sèvres: la manufacture au XXème siècle*. Paris: Michel Aveline Éditeur, 1992.

Milam, Jennifer. "Matronage and the Direction of Sisterhood: Portraits of Madame Adélaïde," in Hyde,

Melissa and Jennifer Milam. *Women, Art and the Politics of Identity in Eighteenth-Century Europe*. Burlington, VT: Ashgate, 2003.

Munger, Jeffrey. "A Bouillotte in the Museum of Fine Arts, Boston." *Mélanges en souvenir d'Elisalex d'Albis* (Paris, 1999), pp. 103–9.

Musée céramique de Sèvres. *Catalogue de l'Exposition d'Oeuvres de Céramistes Modernes, 1890–1930*. Organisée sous les auspices du Syndicat d'Initiative de Paris et de la Société des amis de Sèvres, 27 mai - 17 juillet 1931. Paris: Lapina imp., 1931.

Musée national de céramique. *Sèvres Musée national de céramique: nouvelles acquisitions (1979–1989)*. Paris: Éditions de la Réunion des musées nationaux, 1989.

Odom, Anne, and Liana Paredes Arend. *A Taste for Splendor: Russian Imperial and European Treasures from the Hillwood Museum*. Alexandria, VA: Art Services International, 1998.

Ostergard, Derek E., ed. *The Sèvres Porcelain Manufactory: Alexandre Brongniart and the Triumph of Art and Industry, 1800–1847*. New Haven and London: Yale University Press, 1997.

Peters, David. *Sèvres Plates and Services of the Eighteenth Century*, 7 vols., Little Berkhamsted: privately printed, 2005.

Préaud, Tamara. "Brongniart and the Imperial Iconography at the Manufacture de Sèvres," in Nouvel, Odile and Anne Dion-Tenenbaum. *Symbols of Power: Napoleon and the Art of the Empire Style, 1800–1815*. New York: Harry N. Abrams and Paris: Les Arts Décoratifs, 2007.

Préaud, Tamara, and Serge Gauthier. *Ceramics of the 20th Century*. New York: Rizzoli International Publications, Inc., 1982.

Préaud, Tamara, and Antoine d'Albis. *La Porcelaine de Vincennes*. Paris: Éditions Adam Biro, 1991.

Préaud, Tamara. *Sèvres Porcelain*. Washington, D.C.: Smithsonian Institution Press, 1980.

Roth, Linda H., and Clare Le Corbeiller. *French Eighteenth-Century Porcelain at the Wadsworth Atheneum*. Hartford, CT: Trustees of the Wadsworth Atheneum, 2000.

Roth, Linda H. "Mixing Metaphors: The Renaissance Revival at Sèvres." *French Porcelain Society Journal*, 2006, pp. 211–26.

Roth, Linda H. "Neoclassical Variations at Sèvres: Early Nineteenth-Century Vases in the Wadsworth Atheneum." An illustrated lecture presented to the French Porcelain Society, St. Stephen's Club, London, 16 June 1995. *French Porcelain Society Journal*, vol. XII, 1995, pp. 1–19.

Sadde, Guilhem. "Jean-Claude Duplessis: la liberté de style rocaille." *L'Estampille/L'Objet d'Art*, June 2004, pp. 42–51.

Salmon, Xavier, et al. *Madame de Pompadour et les arts*. Paris: Éditions de la Réunion des musées nationaux, 2002.

Sassoon, Adrian. *Vincennes and Sèvres Porcelain: Catalogue of the Collections*. Malibu, CA: The J. Paul Getty Museum, 1991.

Savill, Rosalind. *The Wallace Collection: Catalogue of Sèvres Porcelain*, 3 vols. London: Trustees of the Wallace Collection, 1988.

Schama, Simon. *Citizens: A Chronicle of the French Revolution*. New York: Knopf, 1989.

Sottsass, Ettore. *Sèvres, les temps d'un voyage*. Paris: La Garenne-Colombes, Bernard Chauveau Éditeur, 2006.

Schwartz, Selma. "The Sèvres Porcelain Service for Marie-Antoinette's Dairy at Rambouillet: An Exercise in Archaeological Neo-Classicism." An illustrated lecture presented to the French Porcelain Society, St. Stephen's Club, London, 12 June 1992. *French Porcelain Society Journal*, vol. IX, 1992, pp. 1–35.

Touzenis, Georges. *Créations diverses à Sèvres depuis 1765*, 2 vols. Paris: Couleurs Contemporaines, Bernard Chauveau Éditeur, 2002.

Truman, Charles. "Emperor, King and Duke." *The Connoisseur*, November 1979, pp. 148–55.

Verrie, Hervé de la. *Le Service "Iconographique Antique" du Cardinal Fesch*. Éditions de la Réunion des musées nationaux, 2008.

Verlet, Pierre, and Marcelle Brunet. *Sèvres (Les marques de Sèvres)*. Paris: G. Le Prat, 1953.

"Vincennes 1753: Le premier fond vert?" *Connaissance des Arts*, July–August 1988, pp. 81–7.

Wittwer, Samuel, ed. *Refinement and Elegance: Early Nineteenth-Century Royal Porcelain from the Twinight Collection, New York*. Munich: Hirmer Verlag, 2007.

Zénon, Sophie. *La Terre transfigurée: 250 ans de porcelaine à Sèvres*. Paris: Éditions Paradox, 2006.

Index

Information about the Sèvres Factory and Museum

Manufacture Nationale de Sèvres
Place de la Manufacture
92310 Sèvres
T: +33 (01) 46 29 22 00
F: +33 (01) 46 29 22 08
www.manufacturedesevres.fr

Galleries:
At the Musée National de Céramique
Place de la Manufacture
92310 Sèvres
T: +33 (01) 46 29 22 10
At the Palais Royal
4, Place André Malraux
75001 Paris
T: +33 (01) 47 03 40 20

Musée National de Céramique, Sèvres
Place de la Manufacture
92310 Sèvres
T: +33 (01) 41 14 04 20
F: +33 (01) 45 34 67 88
www.musee-ceramique-sevres.fr

Photographic Credits

Private Collection; Photography by Richard P. Goodbody
Frontispiece, pp. 21, 26–27, 48, 54, 139, 142, 144

The Twinight Collection
Table of contents page, pp. 60, 66–67, 70, 76–77, 82–83, 86, 94, 136–37, 147, 149–54

Réunion des Musées Nationaux/Art Resource, NY; Musée National de Céramique, Sèvres, France; Photography by Martine-Beck Coppola
Front cover; pp. 9, 85, 95, 100, 102, 104–106, 109, 113–15, 121, 123–28, 130–31, 152, 156, 158–65, 167

Hillwood Estate, Museum & Gardens; Photography by Ed Owen
Front cover; pp. 10, 13, 16, 23–25, 34, 38–43, 55, 71–72, 78–81, 88, 107, 138–39, 143–46, 149–51, 153, 159, 166

Réunion des Musées Nationaux/Art Resource, NY; Musée National de Céramique, Sèvres, France
pp. 14, 111, 160

Mathilde Bretillot
pp. 15, 132, 166

Manufacture Nationale de Sèvres, Collections/Archives
pp. 17, 22, 61–62, 84, 89, 103–04, 108, 110, 112, 115–19, 121, 123, 161

Private Collection; Photography by Baxter Buck
pp. 18–19, 34, 50–51, 138, 142, 167–68

Photos © The Walters Art Museum, Baltimore
pp. 28–29, 47, 87, 140–41, 154

Private American Collection; Photography by Ed Owen
Back cover; pp. 30, 31–33, 35, 36–37, 44–46, 56–57, 140, 141, 143, 145

Photographs from Christie's New York
pp. 52–53, 142

National Museum of American History, Smithsonian Institution, Kenneth E. Behring Center
pp. 58, 64–65, 73, 99, 145, 147–48, 157

Private Collection, Berlin, Germany; Photography by Ed Owen
pp. 68–69, 149

Wadsworth Atheneum Museum of Art, Hartford, CT
pp. 74–75, 91–93, 96, 150, 155–56

Private Collection; Photography by William H. Bengtson
pp. 84, 152

Images © The Metropolitan Museum of Art
pp. 88–89, 154

The Cleveland Museum of Art
pp. 90, 155

Library of Congress, General Collections
p. 97

Réunion des Musées Nationaux/Art Resource, NY; Musée National de Céramique, Sèvres, France; Photography by Christian Jean
pp. 122, 164

Manufacture Nationale de Sèvres, Collections/Archives; Plate 13 from *Créations diverses à Sèvres depuis 1965* (Paris: B. Chauveau, 2003) from the Hillwood Estate, Museum & Gardens Library
p. 122

Photograph by G. Lloyd C. Solly II (GLCS II Studios)
p. 129

Manufacture Nationale de Sèvres, Collections; Photography by Martine Beck-Coppola
pp. 118–19, 120, 133–35, 161–62, 165–66